Discourses

19.95

DISCOURSES

Meher Baba

Sheriar Press

1987

Seventh revised edition 1987.

Cover photograph of Meher Baba, Meherabad, 1927.
Copyright © Lawrence Reiter.

Frontispiece photograph of Meher Baba, Ahmednagar, 1945.
Copyright © Lawrence Reiter.

Photograph retouching by Chris Riger.

Printed in the U.S.A. by Sheriar Press, Inc.

Library of Congress Cataloging in Publication Data:
Meher Baba, 1894-1969.
Discourses.

Bibliography: p.
Includes index.
1. Spiritual life. I. Title.
BP610.M43127 1987 299'.93 86-15489
ISBN 0-913078-57-3
ISBN 0-913078-58-1 (pbk.)

Contents

Foreword

The editors of this seventh edition felt that it would be useful to present a brief publishing history of the *Discourses* and to comment on the reasons why a new, revised edition was desirable at this time.

Publishing History of the Discourses

From time to time and over a period of years, Meher Baba dictated discourses and messages on His alphabet board to various individuals and groups. When the *Meher Baba Journal* first appeared in November 1938, it was arranged that a discourse or message by Meher Baba would be included in each issue. Dr. Chakradhar D. Deshmukh, a member of the Meher Editorial Committee, had the primary responsibility of editing and preparing the dictated material for inclusion in the *Journal*, though several other individuals also participated in this task. At the end of each year, the monthly articles by Meher Baba were compiled into one volume. In this way the first four volumes of the *Discourses* appeared in book form. After the *Journal* ceased production in October 1942, a subsequent volume of additional discourses was brought out, thus completing the first five-volume edition of the *Discourses*, which were printed for private distribution in India between 1939 and 1943.

As each volume of the five-volume set went out of print, it was reprinted, with only minor corrections. These reprints constituted the second through fifth "editions" of the *Discourses*, which were also issued in India, between 1941 and 1954.

Over the years, readers made inquiries about various points in the *Discourses* and asked Meher Baba and His close disciples for clarifications. The problems of misinterpretations and the possible need for revisions were addressed by Mani (Manija S. Irani), Meher Baba's sister, in a letter that appeared in *The Awakener* (vol. 3, no. 1, 1955): "There are those who believe that literally every word in the original Discourses is Baba's and are reluctant to accept any revised version; but actually, though Baba dictated for hours on the board, Professor Deshmukh embellished and worked up the points. Though Deshmukh has undoubtedly done brilliant work in many places, we feel there are many places where simplification of sentence structure or correction of grammar would enhance the beauty and simplicity which are the essence of Baba's teachings. . . . Now we find there are places in the original Discourses where Deshmukh obviously misinterpreted the point, with the result that there are several important errors. . . ." This quotation is given here, not to disparage Dr. Deshmukh or in any way minimize his and the other editors' monumental work, but to indicate that the original edition of the *Discourses* did contain some stylistic problems and points that needed rectification.

In 1948 Meher Baba authorized Charles B. Purdom to edit and condense the *Discourses* into one volume for publication in the West. Meher Baba chose the title Himself for this version, *God to Man and Man to God: the Discourses of Meher Baba.* It was first published in England in 1955.

With the publication of Meher Baba's book *God Speaks* in 1955, certain points and terms had been refined and redefined. In 1967 the sixth edition of the *Discourses*, in three volumes, was published by Sufism Reoriented, San Francisco, California, U.S.A. With Meher Baba's approval, the editors, Ivy Oneita Duce and Don E. Stevens, made some revisions based on *God Speaks* and other subsequent explanations He had given on various points. The three-volume edition also simplified some of the sentence structure and presented the chapters in a more logical arrangement. There have been three reprints, with minor corrections, of the sixth edition.

The Seventh Edition

When the sixth edition was almost out of print, the Avatar Meher Baba Perpetual Public Charitable Trust made plans to have the *Discourses* republished. At first it was planned to simply reprint the text as it appeared in the sixth edition; thus the initial emphasis was on completing the supplementary material to be added: a new introduction, a glossary, and an index. But it soon became clear that some textual changes would have to be made. In the years since the 1967 edition, additional inquiries had accumulated, and some points needed further clarification. As translations were being prepared for French, German, Italian, and Spanish editions, linguistic as well as textual questions came up. It also became apparent that stylistic changes had to be made. The individual discourses, it must be remembered, appeared over a period of years, mostly as journal articles—which inadvertently resulted in inconsistencies in spelling, capitalization, use of italics, punctuation, and so forth.

Once the decision was made that a revised edition was needed, it was decided that the text should be gone over as carefully as possible. As mentioned earlier, Meher Baba's explanations had become more detailed and profound over the years, as He expanded and further elucidated many points. For instance, terms that had been used in their broadest sense were redefined to become more specific—often coming to mean only one aspect of a larger concept they had earlier encompassed. Meher Baba unfolded the divine theme, in *God Speaks* and through discussions with His close disciples, to an audience now ready to understand and accept ideas and concepts of greater profundity.

In answer to questions about the Circles of the Perfect Masters and the Avatar, Meher Baba expanded the explanations He had given in "The Circle" discourse; and in 1955 this clarification appeared as an article entitled "The Circles" in *The Awakener* (vol. 3, no. 1). The importance of this discourse, and its relative inaccessibility to most readers, convinced the editors to include it as the only new textual material added to this edition—under the title "The Circles of the Avatar." This addition necessitated a minor rearrangement of chapters.

Also, after due consideration, it was decided to publish the seventh edition of the *Discourses* in a one-volume format.

Because people are often wary of any change in a work such as the *Discourses*, which is much studied and often reread, the editors thought it best to allay any fears of massive revisions by specifying just how the editing was approached and what types of changes have been made. The following criteria and guidelines were used: make as few changes as possible; make textual changes only when points conflicted with *God Speaks* or later explanations; change obsolete or archaic words and rephrase awkward sentence structure only when the reader might be misled or confused; and correct stylistic inconsistencies.

The stylistic changes fall into the following broad categories: (1) regularizing spelling, hyphenation, grammar, and punctuation, using authoritative style manuals and dictionaries—especially the latest editions of *The Chicago Manual of Style* and *Webster's New Collegiate Dictionary,* which were the main sources consulted to achieve editorial uniformity in usage, style, and form; (2) arriving at a pattern for capitalizing spiritual terms and applying it consistently, except for rare cases of emphasis; (3) adjusting the spelling and form of non-English terms and names to *God Speaks* usage or other reference sources if appropriate; (4) eliminating most italics, except for their standard use for occasional emphasis and for the first occurrence of non-English words.

Readers sensitive to current trends in English usage will certainly notice the frequent occurrence of masculine forms and pronouns to denote both men and women—for example, man, mankind, the Master/he, a person/him, the aspirant/his, and so forth. Although some adjustments have been made, retention of these forms was based on the editorial policy to make a minimum of changes in the text; and changing these forms throughout would have entailed considerable rewriting. The consistent use of masculine forms was not intended to exclude women or imply a male bias in Meher Baba's teachings; they simply reflect the writing style of the period in which the *Discourses* first appeared.

One final, minor but amusing point. The word *surrenderance* is used throughout the text as a variant of surrender, but it does not appear in any major dictionary. The question of course arose whether it should be retained or not, as it did not "officially" exist. An inquiry to Merriam-Webster Inc. produced a delightful reply: Although there was lack of evidence that *surrenderance* had ever been used anywhere else, it need not be regarded as a nonword and should be judged on its own merits. Since Meher Baba had actually spelled out this word on His alphabet board, it was felt that *surrenderance* certainly merited retention.

The editors have taken great care to see that the *meaning* behind the words of Meher Baba in the text remained unchanged when making any revisions. All the efforts of the editors are offered to Meher Baba in surrenderance to His will and pleasure, and it is hoped that Meher Baba Himself will help each reader *understand* the meaning He wished to convey through His *Discourses*.

The Editors

Meherazad, India Eruch B. Jessawala, J. Flagg Kris, Bal Natu
1986

Introduction to the Seventh Edition

Merwan Sheriar Irani was born in Poona,* India, on 25 February 1894. His parents, Sheriar and Shirin, were Zoroastrians of Persian descent. His father, Sheriar, was a genuine seeker of God. Merwan attended St. Vincent High School; he was a lively and happy boy who excelled in both studies and sports, and was not overly interested in spirituality. However, a school friend once gave Merwan a booklet on the life of Buddha; and years later when He reminisced about this incident, He remarked: "I opened the book to the place that told about the second coming of the Buddha as Maitreya, the Lord of Mercy. And I realized all of a sudden, 'I am that, actually'—and I felt it deep within me. Then I totally forgot about it, and years passed by."

One day in May 1913, while studying at Deccan College in Poona, He cycled past the venerable Muslim woman Hazrat Babajan, one of the five Perfect Masters of the time. She beckoned Him to her and kissed Him on the forehead, subsequently revealing to Him His true state as the *Avatar*, the total manifestation of God in human form.

At first Merwan was dazed; but gradually over a period of months the focus of His consciousness returned sufficiently to His surroundings to lead Him to the Perfect Master Sai Baba of Shirdi—who in turn guided Him to another of the Perfect Masters, Upasni Maharaj, a Hindu, in Sakori. (Sai Baba did not disclose his religion. The two

*Now officially spelled Pune. Sassoon Hospital, in which Merwan was born, was maintained at the time by a well-known, philanthropic Jewish family.

remaining Perfect Masters of the period were the Muslim Tajuddin Baba and the Hindu Narayan Maharaj.) For seven years Upasni Maharaj integrated Merwan's God-consciousness with consciousness of the gross world, establishing Him in His role as the Avatar of the Age. This Avataric mission started its outward expression in 1921 with the gathering together of His first disciples, who gave Him the name *Meher Baba*, which means "Compassionate Father."

After months of intensive work with these disciples and travel in India (including present-day Pakistan) and Iran, Meher Baba and His followers took up residence in 1923 in a vacant World War I military camp near Ahmednagar, India. This became known as Meherabad. Here He instituted a number of projects, such as a free hospital and dispensary, shelters for the poor and the mad, and a free school for boys of all religions where spiritual training was stressed. In the school no caste lines were observed, as the high and the low mingled in common fellowship forged by love of the Master. To all, Meher Baba offered regular instruction in moral discipline, spiritual understanding, selfless service, and above all, love of God.

All these activities moved at high speed despite Meher Baba's silence, which He commenced with little advance warning on 10 July 1925. When asked previous to the start of His silence how He would continue to give discourses and teachings to His followers, He countered, "I come not to teach but to awaken." In later years, during one of His visits to the West, His comments were equally profound and thought-provoking: "Things that are real are given and received in silence"; and again, "If my silence cannot be heard, of what avail words?" After also giving up writing in 1927 (except for His signature), He communicated by pointing to letters on an alphabet board; but this too was given up in 1954. Subsequently He conversed through His own unique system of hand gestures. However, His *Discourses* and His book *God Speaks* were dictated before giving up the alphabet board.

During the early 1930s Meher Baba's travels began to reach into Europe and then on to America. Contacting hundreds on both continents, His name rapidly became known to those deeply and sincerely interested in the spiritual life. Only some of these were permitted to come later to India in small groups. Their visits ranged generally from weeks to years; but just before World War II, all but a handful were asked to return to the West.

Meher Baba visited the West again in 1952, 1956 and 1958; Australia was also visited during the last two tours. After this He did not travel outside of India, and He allowed Westerners to visit Him in India only on rare occasions. One of these rare occasions was the great East-West Gathering of November 1962. At His invitation, thousands of His devotees from all over the world converged on Poona. For almost a week Meher Baba gave unstintingly of Himself. The activities were as varied as the assemblage: brief discourses, group meetings, personal interviews, songs and prayers in praise of God, an open day of public *darshan* attended by multitudes surging from the city to pay homage to the Master and receive His blessings. The world's literature contains many references to the need for transfusions between East and West. Here was a rich confluence in which mutual respect, affection, and unity in praise of the Beloved Avatar bridged vast differences in culture and tradition.

Persistent throughout decades of Meher Baba's Avataric activities was His seeking out and contacting God-intoxicated souls, or *masts* (pronounced "musts"). Through Dr. William Donkin's book *The Wayfarers,* * Meher Baba has described most clearly the states of *masti* (divine intoxication). The *masts* are those who have lost contact with the external world through intense absorption in their love of God, rather than through breakdown and insanity. Especially in the 1940s, Meher Baba contacted hundreds of these God-intoxicated souls throughout the subcontinent of India, often tending personally to their daily needs, giving each what only He knew they needed in their journey to God.

Meher Baba also personally served the poor, the mentally ill, and physically handicapped, and showed a special concern for those stricken by leprosy. With infinite care and love He washed their feet, bowed His forehead to the often twisted stumps on which they hobbled, and sent them on their way with small gifts and renewed hope. "They are like beautiful birds in ugly cages," He conveyed on one such occasion. "Of all the tasks I have to perform, this touches me most deeply."

While traveling widely and contacting many thousands of people, Meher Baba continued to emphasize that He had not come to teach or lay down new precepts. He stressed repeatedly that the Truth had been revealed by the great Ones of the past, and that the present task

*William Donkin, *The Wayfarers* (Ahmednagar, India: Meher Publications, 1948; 2nd edition, San Francisco: Sufism Reoriented, 1969).

for humanity is to realize the Truth embodied in their teachings. Meher Baba's Avataric work is therefore the awakening of humanity to that realization through His age-old message of Love. His life is a gauge "against which man can measure what he is and what he may become."

In essence, however, one does not know how Meher Baba achieved, and continues to elicit, unexpected responses from those drawn to Him. All that the individual senses is a powerful force sweeping through the snarls of life, energizing and freeing the inner being in a manner that is intuitively trusted. One of the great wonders of contact with Meher Baba is *acceptance*. Charles Purdom in his book *The God-Man** notes that, "He invites people to look at themselves, to accept their egoistic selves not as good or bad, clever or stupid, successful or unsuccessful, but as illusions of their true selves, and to cease to identify themselves with the illusion."

The history of man's search for his soul has produced few works that lay out in minute detail the techniques for the soul's discovery. Meher Baba's *Discourses* are a major contribution to that small body of literature. In this work, given to His close disciples during the 1930s and early 1940s, He describes the means for incorporating daily life into one's spiritual ongoing. He also outlines the structure of creation and clarifies the relationship of the aspirant to the Avatar and the Master. In His later classic work, *God Speaks*, Meher Baba describes in detail the states of God, His will to know His divinity consciously, and the consequent role of creation. The *Discourses*, on the other hand, are practical guides to daily life for those slowly finding their way back to Oneness after having developed consciousness through the deeps of evolution.

The *Discourses* not only provide descriptions of the spiritual path and its disciplines but also shed powerful light on the goal for the wayfarer who aspires to attain it. The reader will discover that they in no way provide a cut-and-dried formula for spiritual development. Rather, they are a reminder of the continuous need for love of God and surrender to Him. Love for God is the guiding force along the path, and it is love for and surrender to God that eventually attains the goal by the grace of a Perfect Master. Such a Master is the knowing guide who has already traversed the path and experienced the Truth, and who

*C. B. Purdom, *The God-Man* (London: Allen & Unwin, 1964; 2nd edition, Crescent Beach, S.C.: Sheriar Press, 1971).

provides the infinite patience, the security, and the steady pace that can lead the disciple to the goal.

As described in detail in the discourse "The Avatar," it is the periodic manifestation of God as the Avatar—the God-Man, the Messiah, the Buddha, the Christ, the Rasool—that brings about the spiritual rebirth of humanity; for it is the Avatar who releases a spiritual dispensation that assumes unlimited dimensions. Independent of the grace of the Perfect Master, the grace of the Avatar flows to all alike at every step toward the Truth, provided there is intense love and longing for God. It is not just during the period of His physical presence that the guidance and the grace of the Avatar are available. He is not only for contemporary humanity during His advent but for posterity as well. His grace and His guidance toward the Truth are constantly accessible and available to one and all. In all instances, to attain the goal and make the final leap from the realms of duality to the abiding experience of the oneness of Reality, it is necessary to have the grace of a living Perfect Master or of the Avatar—who is THE ETERNAL LIVING PERFECT MASTER.*

Meher Baba's silence of forty-four years remained unbroken when He passed away on 31 January 1969. His last years were marked by great physical suffering due to two severe auto accidents. The first occurred near Prague, Oklahoma, while traveling across the United States in 1952; the second occurred in India, near Satara, in late 1956. In both accidents Meher Baba sustained serious injuries that made walking—even standing—extremely painful and difficult thereafter. Such physical pain is an outward manifestation of the intense inner suffering the Avatar takes on for the sake of humanity each time He comes in our midst.

His final years were largely spent in close seclusion and in intense and exhausting preoccupation with His universal work. In mid-1968 Meher Baba announced that His work had been completed to His one-hundred-percent satisfaction. The same period also witnessed the explosive growth in the numbers of those who look to Him for the key to meaning in life. At His passing, thousands came for a last glimpse and to pay homage to the well-loved form as it lay for seven days in the Tomb at Meherabad, before His interment there. More thousands from all over the world attended the April to June, 1969 Darshan

*This revealing discussion of the unique availability of the Avatar at all times is from one of Meher Baba's *mandali* (close disciples).—D.E.S.

Program in Poona, which He had arranged months before His passing; and they deeply felt His love and presence in their hearts.

Today, Meher Baba's love spreads out in ever-widening circles, drawing people from all corners of the world, from all walks of life, and from all religions to search for Truth under His loving guidance. Although hundreds of Meher Baba groups function throughout the world, in the West He personally established two major centers: Meher Spiritual Center in Myrtle Beach, South Carolina, U.S.A.; and Avatar's Abode in Woombye, Queensland, Australia. Each year hundreds of seekers visit these centers, and thousands more make pilgrimages to Avatar Meher Baba's Tomb-Shrine as well as the long-time residence of His later years at Meherazad, also near Ahmednagar, India.

Don E. Stevens

The Seven Realities

Existence, Love, Sacrifice, Renunciation, Knowledge, Control, and Surrender

I give no importance to creed, dogma, caste, or the performance of religious ceremonies and rites but to the *understanding* of the following seven Realities:

1. The only **Real Existence** is that of the one and only God, who is the Self in every finite self.

2. The only **Real Love** is the love for this Infinity (God), which arouses an intense longing to see, know, and become one with its Truth (God).

3. The only **Real Sacrifice** is that in which, in pursuance of this love, all things—body, mind, position, welfare, and even life itself—are sacrificed.

4. The only **Real Renunciation** is that which abandons, even in the midst of worldly duties, all selfish thoughts and desires.

5. The only **Real Knowledge** is the knowledge that God is the inner dweller in good people and in so-called bad, in saint and in so-called sinner. This knowledge requires you to help all equally as circumstances demand without expectation of reward; when compelled to take part in a dispute, to act without the slightest trace of enmity or hatred; to try to make others happy with brotherly or sisterly feeling for each one; and to harm no one in thought, word, or deed—not even those who harm you.

6. The only **Real Control** is the discipline of the senses to abstain from indulgence in low desires, which alone ensures absolute purity of character.

7. The only **Real Surrender** is that in which poise is undisturbed by any adverse circumstance; and the individual, amidst every kind of hardship, is resigned with perfect calm to the will of God.

The New Humanity

As in all great critical periods of human history, humanity is now going through the agonizing travail of spiritual rebirth. Great forces of destruction are afoot and seem to be dominant at the moment, but constructive and creative forces that will redeem humanity are also being released through several channels. Although the working of these forces of light is chiefly silent, they are eventually bound to bring about those transformations that will make the further spiritual advance of humanity safe and steady. It is all a part of the divine plan, which is to give to the hungry and weary world a fresh dispensation of the eternal and only Truth.

Divine plan

At present the urgent problem facing humanity is to devise ways and means of eliminating competition, conflict, and rivalry in all the subtle and gross forms that they assume in the various spheres of life. Military wars are, of course, the most obvious sources of chaos and destruction. However, wars in themselves do not constitute the central problem for humanity but are rather the external symptoms of something graver at their root. Wars and the suffering they bring cannot be completely avoided by mere propaganda against war; if they are to disappear from human history, it will be necessary to tackle their root cause. Even when military wars are not being waged, individuals or groups of individuals are constantly engaged in economic or some other subtle form of

War a symptom of graver causes

warfare. Military wars, with all the cruelty they involve, arise only when these underlying causes are aggravated.

Egoism and selfishness

The cause of the chaos that precipitates itself in wars is that most persons are in the grip of egoism and selfish considerations, and they express their egoism and self-interest individually as well as collectively. This is the life of illusory values in which man is caught. To face the truth is to realize that life is one, in and through its manifold manifestations. To have this understanding is to forget the limiting self in the realization of the unity of life.

Wars unnecessary and unreasonable

With the dawn of true understanding, the problem of wars would immediately disappear. Wars have to be so clearly seen as both unnecessary and unreasonable that the immediate problem would not be how to stop wars but to wage them spiritually against the attitude of mind responsible for such a cruel and painful state of things. In the light of the truth of the unity of all life, cooperative and harmonious action becomes natural and inevitable. Hence, the chief task before those who are deeply concerned with the rebuilding of humanity is to do their utmost to dispel the spiritual ignorance that envelops humanity.

Self must be eliminated in all spheres of life

Wars do not arise merely to secure material adjustment. They are often the product of uncritical identification with narrow interests, which through association come to be included in that part of the world regarded as "mine." Material adjustment is only part of the wider problem of establishing spiritual adjustment. Spiritual adjustment requires the elimination of self, not only from the material aspects of life, but also from those spheres that affect the intellectual, emotional, and cultural life of man.

Material adjustment requires spiritual understanding

To understand the problem of humanity as merely a problem of bread is to reduce humanity to the level of animality. But even when man sets himself the limited task of securing purely material adjustment, he can only succeed in this attempt if he has spiritual understanding. Economic adjustment is impossible unless people realize that there can be no planned and cooperative action in economic matters until self-interest gives way to self-giving love. Otherwise, with the best of equipment and efficiency in the material spheres, humanity cannot avoid conflict and insufficiency.

The *New Humanity* that emerges from the travail of the present struggle and suffering will not ignore science or its practical attainments. It is a mistake to look upon science as antispiritual. Science is a help or hindrance to spirituality according to the use to which it is put. Just as true art expresses spirituality, science, when properly handled, can be the expression and fulfillment of the spirit. Scientific truths concerning the physical body and its life in the gross world can become mediums for the soul to know itself; but to serve this purpose they must be properly fitted into larger spiritual understanding. This includes a steady perception of true and lasting values. In the absence of such spiritual understanding, scientific truths and attainments are liable to be used for mutual destruction and for a life that will tend to strengthen the chains that bind the spirit. All-sided progress of humanity can be assured only if science and religion proceed hand in hand.

Rightful place of science

The coming civilization of the New Humanity shall be ensouled not by dry intellectual doctrines but by living spiritual experience. Spiritual experience has a hold on the deeper truths that are inaccessible to mere intellect; it cannot be born of unaided intellect. Spiritual truth can often be stated and expressed through the intellect, and the intellect surely is of some help for the communication of spiritual experience. But by itself, the intellect is insufficient to enable man to have spiritual experience or to communicate it to others. If two persons have had headaches, they can cooperatively examine their experience of headaches and make it explicit to themselves through the work of the intellect. If a person has never experienced a headache, no amount of intellectual explanation will suffice for making him understand what a headache is. Intellectual explanation can never be a substitute for spiritual experience; it can at best prepare the ground for it.

Need for spiritual experience

Spiritual experience involves more than can be grasped by mere intellect. This is often emphasized by calling it a mystical experience. Mysticism is often regarded as something anti-intellectual, obscure and confused, or impractical and unconnected with experience. In fact, true mysticism is none of these. There is nothing irrational in

Nature and place of spiritual experience

true mysticism when it is, as it should be, a vision of Reality. It is a form of perception that is absolutely unclouded, and it is so practical that it can be lived every moment of life and expressed in everyday duties. Its connection with experience is so deep that, in one sense, it is the final understanding of all experience.

When spiritual experience is described as mystical, one should not assume that it is something supernatural or entirely beyond the grasp of human consciousness. All that is meant is that it is not accessible to the limited human intellect until the intellect transcends its limits and is illumined by direct realization of the Infinite. Jesus Christ pointed out the way to spiritual experience when He said, "Leave all and follow me." This means that man must leave limitations and establish himself in the infinite life of God. A real spiritual experience involves not only realization of the nature of the soul while traversing the higher planes of consciousness but also a right attitude toward worldly duties. If it loses its connection with the different phases of life, what we have is a neurotic reaction that is far from being a spiritual experience.

Spiritual experience not found in escape

The spiritual experience that is to enliven and energize the New Humanity cannot be a reaction to the stern and uncompromising demands made by the realities of life. Those without the capacity for adjustment to the flow of life have a tendency to recoil from the realities of life and to seek shelter and protection in a self-created fortress of illusions. Such a reaction is an attempt to perpetuate one's separate existence by protecting it from the demands made by life. It can only give a pseudo solution to the problems of life by providing a false sense of security and self-completeness. It is not even an advance toward the real and lasting solution; on the contrary, it is a sidetrack from the true spiritual path. Man will be dislodged again and again from his illusory shelters by fresh and irresistible waves of life, and will invite upon himself fresh forms of suffering by seeking to protect his separative existence through escape.

Just as a person may seek to hold on to his separative experience through escape, he may also seek to hold on to it through uncritical identification with forms, ceremonies and rituals, or with traditions and conventions. Forms, ceremonies and rituals, traditions and conventions, are in most cases fetters to the release of infinite life. If they were pliant mediums for the expression of unlimited life, they would be an asset rather than a handicap for securing the fulfillment of divine life on earth. But they mostly have a tendency to gather prestige and claims in their own right, independently of the life they might express. When this happens, any attachment to them must eventually lead to a drastic curtailment and restriction of life.

New Humanity will not be attached to external forms

The New Humanity will be freed from a life of limitations, allowing unhampered scope for the creative life of the spirit; and it will break the attachment to external forms and learn to subordinate them to the claims of the spirit. The limited life of illusions and false values will then be replaced by unlimited life in the Truth; and the limitations, through which the separative self lives, will wither away at the touch of true understanding.

Just as a person may seek to hold on to his separative existence through escape or identification with external forms, he may seek to hold on to it through identification with some narrow class, creed, sect, or religion, or with the divisions based upon sex. Here the individual may seem to have lost his separative existence through identification with a larger whole. But, in fact, he is often *expressing* his separative existence through such an identification, which enables him to delight in his feeling of being separate from others who belong to another class, nationality, creed, sect, religion, or sex.

Identification with narrow group is a form of limited self

Separative existence derives its being and strength from identifying itself with one of the opposites and contrasting itself with the others. An individual may seek to protect his separate existence through identification with one ideology rather than another or with his conception of good as contrasted with his idea of evil. What results from identification with narrow groups or limited ideals is not a real merging of the separative self but only a semblance of it. A real merging of the limited self in the ocean of universal life involves complete surrender of separative existence in all its forms.

Limited self lives through opposites

The large mass of humanity is caught up in the clutches of separative and assertive tendencies. For one who is overpowered by the spectacle of these fetters of humanity, there is bound to be nothing but unrelieved despair about its future. One must look deeper into the realities of the day if one is to get a correct perspective on the present distress of humanity. The real possibilities of the New Humanity are hidden to those who look only at the surface of the world situation, but they exist and only need the spark of spiritual understanding to come into full play and effect. The forces of lust, hate, and greed produce incalculable suffering and chaos. However, the one redeeming feature about human nature is that even in the midst of disruptive forces there invariably exists some form of love.

Hope for the future

Even wars require cooperative functioning, but the scope of this cooperative functioning is artificially restricted by identification with a limited group or ideal. Wars often are carried on by a form of love, though it is a love that has not been understood properly. In order that love should come into its own, it must be untrammeled and unlimited. Love does exist in all phases of human life; but it is latent or is limited and poisoned by personal ambition, racial pride, narrow loyalties and rivalries, and attachment to sex, nationality, sect, caste, or religion. If there is to be a resurrection of humanity, the heart of man will have to be unlocked so that a new love is born into it—a love that knows no corruption and is entirely free from individual or collective greed.

Love must be free from limitations

The New Humanity will come into existence through a release of love in measureless abundance, and this release of love can come through the spiritual awakening brought about by the Perfect Masters.* Love cannot be born of mere determination; through the exercise of will one can at best be dutiful. Through struggle and effort, one may succeed in assuring that one's external action is in conformity with one's concept of what is right; but such action is spiritually barren because it lacks the inward beauty of spontaneous love.

Love essentially self-communicative

Love has to spring spontaneously from within; it is in no way amenable to any form of inner or outer force. Love and coercion can

*See Glossary.

never go together; but while love cannot be forced upon anyone, it can be awakened through love itself. Love is essentially self-communicative; those who do not have it catch it from those who have it. Those who receive love from others cannot be its recipients without giving a response that, in itself, is the nature of love. True love is unconquerable and irresistible. It goes on gathering power and spreading itself until eventually it transforms everyone it touches. Humanity will attain a new mode of being and life through the free and unhampered interplay of pure love from heart to heart.

Redemption of humanity through divine love

When it is recognized that there are no claims greater than the claims of the universal Divine Life—which, without exception, includes everyone and everything—love will not only establish peace, harmony, and happiness in social, national, and international spheres but it will shine in its own purity and beauty. Divine love is unassailable to the onslaughts of duality and is an expression of divinity itself. It is through divine love that the New Humanity will tune in to the divine plan. Divine love will not only introduce imperishable sweetness and infinite bliss into personal life but it will also make possible an era of New Humanity. Through divine love the New Humanity will learn the art of cooperative and harmonious life. It will free itself from the tyranny of dead forms and release the creative life of spiritual wisdom; it will shed all illusions and get established in the Truth; it will enjoy peace and abiding happiness; it will be initiated in the life of Eternity.

Selfishness

Selfishness comes into existence owing to the tendency of desires to find fulfillment in action and experience. It is born of fundamental ignorance about one's own true nature. Human consciousness is clouded by the accumulation of various types of impressions deposited by the long course of the evolution of consciousness. These impressions express themselves as desires, and the range of the operation of consciousness is strictly limited by these desires. The *sanskaras*, or impressions, form an enclosure around the possible field of consciousness. The circle of sanskaras constitutes that limited area in which alone the individual consciousness can be focused.

Analysis of selfishness

With some of the desires action is merely latent, but others can actually translate themselves into action. The capacity of a desire to find expression in conduct depends upon the intensity and the amount of sanskaras connected with it. To use a geometric metaphor, we might say that when a desire passes into action, it traverses a distance that is equal to the radius of a circle describing the boundary of the sanskaras connected with it. When a desire gathers sufficient strength, it projects itself into action in order to get fulfilled.

The range of selfishness is equal to the range of desires. Owing to the hindrance of multifarious desires, it becomes impossible for the soul to find free and full expression of its true being; and life becomes self-centered and narrow. The entire life of the personal ego is continually in the grip of wanting, that is, an attempt to seek fulfillment of desires through things that change and vanish. But there can be no real fulfillment through transient things. The satisfaction derived from the fleeting things of life is not lasting, and the wants of man remain unfulfilled. There is thus a general sense of dissatisfaction accompanied by all kinds of worries.

Wanting ends in dissatisfaction

The chief forms in which the frustrated ego finds expression are lust, greed, and anger. Lust is very much like greed in many respects; but it differs in the manner of its fulfillment, which is directly related to the gross sphere. Lust finds its expression through the medium of the physical body and is concerned with the flesh. It is a form of entanglement with the *gross* sphere.* Greed is a state of restlessness of the heart, and it consists mainly of craving for power and possessions. Possessions and power are sought for the fulfillment of desires. Man is only partially satisfied in his attempt to have the fulfillment of his desires, and this partial satisfaction fans and increases the flame of craving instead of extinguishing it. Thus greed always finds an endless field of conquest and leaves the individual endlessly dissatisfied. The chief expressions of greed are related to the emotional part of man. It is a form of entanglement with the *subtle* sphere.

Lust, greed, anger

Anger is the fume of an irritated mind. It is caused by the thwarting of desires. It feeds the limited ego and is used for domination and aggression. It aims at removing the obstacles existing in the fulfillment of desires. The frenzy of anger nourishes egoism and conceit, and it is the greatest benefactor of the limited ego. Mind is the seat of anger, and its expressions are mostly through the activities of the mind. Anger is a form of entanglement with the *mental* sphere. Lust, greed, and anger respectively have body, heart, and mind as their vehicles of expression.

Man experiences disappointment through lust, greed, and anger; and the frustrated ego, in its turn, seeks further gratification through lust, greed, and anger. Consciousness is thus caught up in a vicious circle of endless disappointment. Disappointment comes into existence when either lust, greed, or anger is thwarted in its

Vicious circle

*See Glossary under the terms *gross, subtle,* and *mental.*

expression. It is thus a general reaction of gross, subtle, and mental entanglements. It is a depression caused by the nonfulfillment of lust, greed, and anger, which together are coextensive with selfishness. Selfishness, which is the common basis of these three ingredient vices, is thus the ultimate cause of disappointment and worries. It defeats itself. It seeks fulfillment through desires but succeeds only in arriving at unending dissatisfaction.

Selfishness inevitably leads to dissatisfaction and disappointment because desires are endless. The problem of happiness is therefore the problem of dropping one's desires. Desires, however, cannot be effectively overcome through mechanical repression. They can be annihilated only through Knowledge. If you dive deep in the realm of thoughts and think seriously for just a few minutes, you will realize the emptiness of desires. Think of what you have enjoyed all these years and what you have suffered. All that you have enjoyed through life is today nil. All that you have suffered through life is also nothing in the present. All was illusory.

Road to happiness

It is your right to be happy, and yet you create your own unhappiness by wanting things. Wanting is the source of perpetual restlessness. If you do not get the thing you want, you are disappointed. And if you get it, you want more and more of it and become unhappy. Say "I do not want anything" and be happy. The continuous realization of the futility of wants will eventually lead you to Knowledge. This Self-knowledge will give you the freedom from wants that leads to the road to abiding happiness.

Wants should be carefully distinguished from needs. Pride and anger, greed and lust, are all different from needs. You might think, "I need all that I want," but this is a mistake. If you are thirsty in a desert, what you need is good water, not lemonade. As long as one has a body there will be some needs, and it is necessary to meet those needs. But wants are an outcome of infatuated imagination. They must be scrupulously killed if there is to be any happiness. As the very being of selfishness consists of desires, renunciation of wants becomes a process of death. Dying in the ordinary sense means parting with the physical body, but dying in the real sense means renunciation of low desires. The priests prepare people for false death by painting gloomy pictures of hell and heaven; but their death is

Renunciation of wants

illusory, as life is one unbroken continuity. The real death consists of the cessation of desires, and it comes by gradual stages.

The dawn of love facilitates the death of selfishness. Being is dying by loving. If you cannot love one another, how can you love even those who torture you? The limits of selfishness are created by ignorance. When a person realizes that he can have more glorious satisfaction by widening the sphere of his interests and activities, he is heading toward the life of service. At this stage he entertains many good desires. He wants to make others happy by relieving distress and helping them. And though even in such good desires there is often an indirect and latent reference to the self, narrow selfishness has no grip over good deeds. Even good desires may, in a sense, be said to be a form of enlightened and extended selfishness; for, like bad desires, they too move within the domain of duality. But as the person entertains good desires his selfishness embraces a larger conception that eventually brings about its own extinction. Instead of merely trying to be illustrious, arresting, and possessive, he learns to be useful to others.

Love and service

The desires that enter into the constitution of the personal ego are either good or bad. Bad desires are ordinarily referred to as forms of selfishness, and good desires are referred to as forms of selflessness. However, there is no hard-and-fast line dividing selfishness from selflessness. Both move in the domain of duality; and from the ultimate point of view that transcends the opposites of good and bad, the distinction between selfishness and selflessness is chiefly one of range. Selfishness and selflessness are two phases of the life of the personal ego, and these two phases are continuous with each other.

Arising of selfishness

Selfishness arises when all the desires are centered around the narrow individuality. Selflessness arises when this crude organization of desires suffers disintegration and there is a general dispersing of desires, with the result that they cover a much wider sphere. Selfishness is the narrowing down of interests to a limited field; selflessness is the extension of interests over a wide field. To put it paradoxically, selfishness is a restricted form of selflessness, and selflessness is the drawing out of selfishness into a wide sphere of activity.

Selfishness must be transmuted into selflessness before the

domain of duality is completely transcended. Persistent and continuous performance of good deeds wears out selfishness. Selfishness extended and expressed in the form of good deeds becomes the instrument of its own destruction. The good is the main link between selfishness thriving and dying. Selfishness, which in the beginning is the father of evil tendencies, becomes through good deeds the hero of its own defeat. When the evil tendencies are completely replaced by good tendencies, selfishness is transformed into selflessness, that is, individual selfishness loses itself in universal interest. Though this selfless and good life is also bound by the opposites, goodness is a necessary step toward freedom from the opposites. Goodness is the means by which the soul annihilates its own ignorance.

Transformation of selfishness into selflessness

From the good, the soul passes on to God. Selflessness is merged into universal Selfhood—which is beyond good and bad, virtue and vice, and all the other dual aspects of *Maya* (Illusion, or Ignorance). The height of selflessness is the beginning of the feeling of oneness with all. In the state of Liberation there is neither selfishness nor selflessness in the ordinary sense, but both of these are taken up and merged into the feeling of *Selfness* for all. Realization of the unity of all is accompanied by peace and unfathomable bliss. It does not in any way lead either to spiritual stagnation or to the obliteration of relative values. Selfness for all brings about undisturbed harmony without loss of discrimination, and unshakable peace without indifference to the surroundings. This Selfness for all is not an outcome of merely subjective synthesis. It is a result of an actual attainment of union with the ultimate Reality, which includes all.

Universal Selfhood

Open your heart by weeding out all desires and by harboring only one longing—the longing for union with the ultimate Reality. The ultimate Reality is not to be sought in the changing things of the external environment but in one's own being. Every time your soul intends to enter your human heart, it finds the door locked and the inside too full of desires. Do not keep the doors of your hearts closed. Everywhere there is the source of abiding bliss, and yet all are miserable because of desires born of ignorance. The goal of lasting happiness shines forth fully only when

Union with ultimate Reality

the limited ego, with all its desires, finds its complete and final extinction.

Renunciation of desires does not mean asceticism or a merely negative attitude to life. Any such negation of life would make man inhuman. Divinity is not devoid of humanity. Spirituality must make man more human. It is a positive attitude of releasing all that is good, noble, and beautiful in man. It also contributes to all that is gracious and lovely in the environment. Spirituality does not require the external renunciation of worldly activities or the avoiding of duties and responsibilities. It only requires that, while performing the worldly activities or discharging the responsibilities arising from the specific place and position of the individual, the inner spirit should remain free from the burden of desires.

Spirituality a positive attitude toward life

Perfection consists in remaining free from the entanglements of duality. Such freedom from entanglements is the most essential requirement of unhindered creativity. But this freedom cannot be attained by running away from life for fear of entanglement. This would mean denial of life. Perfection does not consist in shrinking from the dual expressions of nature. The attempt to escape from entanglement implies fear of life. Spirituality consists in meeting life adequately and fully without being overpowered by the opposites. It must assert its dominion over all illusions—however attractive or powerful. Without avoiding contact with the different forms of life, a Perfect One functions with complete detachment in the midst of intense activity.

God and the Individual

God is infinite. He is beyond the opposites of good and bad, right and wrong, virtue and vice, birth and death, pleasure and suffering. Such dual aspects do not belong to God. If you take God as one separate entity, He becomes one term in relational existence. Just as good is the counterpart of bad, God becomes the counterpart of not-God; and the Infinite comes to be looked upon as the opposite of the finite. When you talk of the Infinite and the finite, you are referring to them as two; and the Infinite has already become the second part of the duality. But the Infinite belongs to the nondual order of being. If the Infinite is looked upon as the counterpart of the finite, it is strictly speaking no longer infinite but a species of the finite; for it stands outside the finite as its opposite and is thus limited. Since the Infinite cannot be the second part of the finite, the apparent existence of the finite is false. The Infinite alone exists. God cannot be brought down to the domain of duality. There is only one being in reality and it is the universal Soul. The existence of the finite or the limited is only apparent or imaginary.

God is the only Reality

You are infinite. You are really everywhere. But you think that you are the body, and therefore consider yourself limited. If you think you are the body, which is sitting, you do not know your true nature. If you were to look within and experience your own soul in its true nature, you would realize that you are infinite and beyond all creation. However, you identify yourself

Apparent existence of the finite

with the body. This false identification is due to ignorance, which makes itself effective through the medium of the mind. An ordinary person thinks that he is the physical body. A spiritually advanced individual thinks that he is the subtle body. The saint thinks that he is the mind. But in none of them is the soul having direct Self-knowledge. It is not a case of pure thinking unmixed with illusion.

The soul as Soul is infinite—aloof from mind or body—yet owing to ignorance, the soul comes under the sway of the mind and becomes a "thinker," sometimes identifying itself with the body and sometimes with the mind. From the limited point of view of a person who has not gone beyond the domain of Maya, there are numberless individuals. It seems that there are as many individuals as there are minds and bodies. In fact, there is only one universal Soul, but the individual thinks that he is different from other individuals. The one and the same Soul is ultimately behind the minds of seemingly different individuals, and through them it has the multifarious experiences of duality. The One *in* the many comes to experience itself as one *of* the many. This is due to imagination or false thinking.

Cause of false thinking

Thinking becomes false because of the interference of sanskaras accumulated during the process of the evolution of consciousness. The function of consciousness is perverted by the operation of sanskaras, which manifest themselves as desires. Through many lives, consciousness is continually being burdened by the aftereffects of experience. The perception of the soul is limited by these aftereffects. The thinking of the soul cannot break through the hedge created by sanskaras, and consciousness becomes a helpless captive of illusions projected by its own false thinking. This falsification of thought is present not only in cases where consciousness is partly developed but also in man, where it is fully developed.

Scope of full consciousness

The progressive evolution of consciousness from the stone stage culminates in man. The history of evolution is the history of a gradual development of consciousness. The fruit of evolution is full consciousness, which is characteristic of man. But even this full consciousness is like a mirror covered by dust. Owing to the operation of sanskaras, it does not yield clear and true knowledge of the nature of the soul. Though fully developed, it yields not truth but imaginative construction, since its free functioning is hindered by the weight of the sanskaras. Moreover, it cannot extend beyond the cage created by its desires and therefore is limited in its scope.

The boundary in which consciousness can move is prescribed by the sanskaras, and the functioning of consciousness is also determined by the desires. As desires aim at self-satisfaction, the whole consciousness becomes self-centered and individualized. The individualization of consciousness may in a sense be said to be the effect of the vortex of desires. The soul gets enmeshed in the desires and cannot step out of the circumscribed individuality constituted by these desires. It imagines these barriers and becomes self-hypnotized. It looks upon itself as being limited and separate from other individuals. It gets entangled in individualistic existence and imagines a world of manifold separateness composed of many individuals with their respective minds and bodies.

Individualization of consciousness

When the rays of the sun are made to pass through a prism, they get dispersed and become separate because of the refraction. If each of these rays had consciousness, it would consider itself as being separate from the other rays, forgetting entirely that at the source and on the other side of the prism it had no separate existence. In the same way, the one Being descends into the domain of Maya and assumes a multiplicity that does not in fact exist. The separateness of individuals does not exist in reality but only in imagination. The one universal Soul imagines separateness in itself, and out of this division there arises the thought of "I" and "mine" as opposed to "you" and "yours." Although the soul is in reality an undivided and absolute unity, it appears as being manifold and divided owing to the working of its own imagination. Imagination is not a reality. Even in its highest flight, it is a departure from truth. It is anything but the truth. The experience the soul gathers in terms of the individualized ego is all imagination. It is a misapprehension of the soul. Out of the imagination of the universal Soul are born many individuals. This is Maya, or Ignorance.

Separateness exists only in imagination

Side by side with the birth of the separate and limited individuality, there also comes into existence the objective universe. As the limited individuality has separate existence not in fact but only in imagination, the objective universe also has no independent and

Objective universe

separate reality. It is the one universal Self appearing in the second role of manifestation through these attributes. When the soul descends into the domain of Maya, it takes upon itself the limitations of manifold existence. This self-limitation of the soul might be looked upon as its self-sacrifice on the altar of consciousness. Although it eternally remains the same infinite Absolute, it suffers a kind of *timeless* contraction through its apparent descent into the world of time, variety, and evolution. What really evolves, however, is not the soul itself but only the consciousness—which, because of its limitations, gives rise to the limited individuality.

Triple entanglement and duality

The history of the limited individuality is a history of the development of a triple entanglement with mind, energy, and matter (body). Duality prevails in all these domains; and the soul gets entangled therein, although it is in essence beyond duality. Duality implies the existence of opposites limiting and balancing each other through mutual tension. Good and bad, virtue and vice, are examples of such opposites. The ignorant soul enmeshed in duality is in the clutches of both good and bad. The duality of good and bad arises due to Ignorance; but once entangled with it, the soul comes under its sway.

During the evolution of the triple entanglement with matter (body), energy, and mind, the ignorant soul is continually in the grip of wanting. It wants the good and bad of the gross world; it wants the good and bad of the subtle world; and it wants the good and bad of the mental world. And owing to this distinction of good and bad, wanting itself becomes good and bad. Wanting thus comes to be inevitably limited by the perpetual tension of the opposites. This gives rise to unending oscillation from one state to another without arriving at the unlimited state, which can only be discovered in the unchanging, eternal aspect of life. The Infinite is to be sought beyond the domain of duality. This becomes possible only when consciousness can emerge from the limited individuality by breaking through the barriers of sanskaras.

We have seen that the possible field of consciousness is limited by the sanskaras. This limitation creates a division of the human psyche into two parts. One part falls within the range of consciousness, and the other part falls beyond it. The unconscious part, in its full extent, is identical with the power that is behind matter. It is referred to as God by the orthodox religions. The ultimate Reality, which is symbolically represented through such concepts, can be known fully only by bringing the unconscious into consciousness. An extension of consciousness consists in being conscious of that which was formerly a part of the unconscious. The progressive conquest of the unconscious by the conscious culminates in *consummate* consciousness, which is unlimited in scope and unhindered in function. Between this highest state of consciousness and the limited—though full—consciousness of average humanity, there are about forty-nine degrees of illumined consciousness. They mark the important stages of growing Illumination.

Chasm between consciousness and unconsciousness

The gulf between the clouded consciousness of average humanity and the fully illumined consciousness of a Perfect Master is created by sanskaras that give rise to egoism. These can be removed through perfect character, devotion, and selfless service; but the best results in this direction are attained through the help of a Perfect Master. Spiritual advancement consists not in the further *development* of consciousness (for it is already fully developed in man), but in the *emancipation* of consciousness from the bondage of sanskaras. Although, in essence, consciousness is the same in all the different states of existence, it can never be consummate unless it can reflect the knowledge of Infinity without the least shadow of ignorance, and also cover the whole extent of creation illumining the different spheres of existence.

Spiritual advancement

Every time you go to sleep you are unconsciously united with the infinite Reality. This unification involves the extension of unconsciousness over consciousness. It thus bridges over the chasm between the unconscious and the conscious. But being unconscious of this union, you do not consciously derive any benefit from it. This is the reason why, when you wake up again from deep sleep, you become aware of the selfsame, humdrum individual; and you begin to act and experience exactly as you acted and experienced before going to sleep. If your union with the supreme Reality had been a conscious union, you would have awakened into a completely new and infinitely rich life.

Deep sleep

A Perfect Master is consciously united with the infinite Reality. In his case the chasm between consciousness and unconsciousness is bridged, not by the extension of the unconscious over the conscious (as with the person who enjoys deep sleep) but by the extension of consciousness over unconsciousness. The waxing and waning of consciousness is applicable only to the limited individual. In the case of the Perfect Master, the conquest of the unconscious by the conscious is final and permanent; and therefore his state of Self-knowledge is continuous and unbroken, and remains the same at all times without any diminution. From this you can see that the Perfect Master never sleeps in the ordinary sense of the word. When he rests his body he experiences no gap in his consciousness.

Conscious union with infinite Reality

In the state of Perfection, full consciousness becomes consummate by the disappearance of all obstacles to Illumination. The conquest of the unconscious by the conscious is complete, and the person continuously dwells in the full blaze of Illumination or as one with Illumination. He becomes Illumination itself.

State of Perfection

As long as a person remains under the sway of duality and looks upon manifold experience as being true and final, he has not traversed the domain of Ignorance. In the state of final understanding, a person realizes that the Infinite, which is one without a second, is the only Reality. The Infinite pervades and includes all existence, leaving nothing as its rival. A person who has such realization has attained the highest state of consciousness. In this state the full consciousness, which is the fruit of evolution, is retained; but the limitations of sanskaras and desires are completely transcended. The limited individuality, which is the creation of Ignorance, is transformed into the divine Individuality, which is unlimited. The illimitable consciousness of the universal Soul becomes individualized in this focus without giving rise to any form of illusion. The person is free from all self-centered desires, and he becomes the medium of the spontaneous flow of the supreme and universal will, which expresses divinity.

Individuality becomes limitless by the disappearance of Ignorance. As it is unimpaired by the separateness of Maya and unentangled in its duality, it enjoys the state of Liberation in which there is objectless awareness, pure being, and unclouded joy. Such a person has no longer any of the illusions that perplex and bewilder man. In one sense he is dead. The personal ego, which is the source of the sense of separateness, has been forever annihilated. But in another sense, he is alive forevermore with unconquerable love and eternal bliss. He has infinite power and wisdom, and the whole universe is to him a field for his spiritual work of perfecting mankind.

The Beginning and the End of Creation

As long as the human mind does not directly experience ultimate Reality as it is, the mind is baffled in every attempt to explain the origin and purpose of creation. The ancient past seems to be shrouded in inscrutable mystery, and the future seems to be a completely sealed book. The human mind can at best make brilliant conjectures about the past and the future of the universe because it is bound by the spell of Maya. It can neither arrive at final knowledge of these points, nor can it remain content with ignorance about them. "Whence?" and "Whither?" are the two everlasting and poignant queries that make the human mind divinely restless.

Whence and whither?

The human mind cannot reconcile itself to infinite regress in its search for the origin of the world, nor can it reconcile itself to endless change without a goal. Evolution is unintelligible if it has no initial cause, and it is deprived of all direction and meaning if it all does not lead to a terminus. The very questions "Whence?" and "Whither?" presuppose the beginning and the end of this evolving creation. The beginning of evolution is the beginning of time, and the end of evolution is the end of time. Evolution has both beginning and end because time has both beginning and end.

Beginning and end

Between the beginning and the end of this changing world there are many cycles; but there is, in and through these cycles, a continuity of cosmic evolution. The real termination of the evolutionary process is called *Mahapralaya,* or the great annihilation of the world, when the world becomes what it was in the beginning, namely *Nothing.* The Mahapralaya of the world may be compared with the sleep of a person. Just as the varied world of experience completely disappears for the individual who is in deep sleep, the entire objective cosmos, which is the creation of Maya, vanishes into nothingness at the time of Mahapralaya. It is as if the universe had never existed at all.

Mahapralaya

Even during the evolutionary period the universe is in itself nothing but imagination. There is in fact only one indivisible and eternal Reality, and it has neither beginning nor end. It is beyond time. From the point of view of this timeless Reality, the whole time process is purely imaginary. And the billions of years that have passed and the billions of years that are to pass do not have even the value of a second. It is as if they had not existed at all.

Reality is timeless and absolute

So the manifold and evolving universe cannot be said to be a real outcome of this one Reality. If it were an outcome of this one Reality, Reality would be either a relative term or a composite being, which it is not. The one Reality is absolute.

The one Reality includes in itself *all* existence. It is Everything, but it has Nothing as its shadow. The idea of all-inclusive existence implies that it leaves nothing outside its being. When you analyze the idea of being, you arrive by implication at the idea of that which does not exist. This idea of nonexistence, or Nothing, helps you to define clearly your notion of being. The complementary aspect of Being is thus Nonbeing or Nothing. But Nothing cannot be looked upon as having its own separate and independent existence. It is nothing in itself. Nor can it, in itself, be a cause of anything. The manifold and evolving universe cannot be the outcome of Nothing taken by itself, and you have seen that it also cannot be the outcome of the one Reality. How then does the manifold and evolving universe arise?

Reality and Nothing

The manifold evolving universe arises from the mixing of the one Reality and Nothing. It springs out of Nothing when this Nothing is taken against the background of the one Reality. But this should not be taken to mean that the universe is partly the outcome of the one Reality, or that it has an element of Reality.

Reality and the universe

It is an outcome of Nothing and is nothing. It only *seems* to have existence. Its apparent existence is due to the one Reality, which is, as it were, behind the Nothing. When Nothing is added to the one Reality, the result is the manifold and evolving universe.

The one Reality, which is infinite and absolute, does not thereby suffer any modification. It is absolute and is as such entirely unaffected by any addition or subtraction. The one Reality remains what it was, complete and absolute in itself and unconcerned and unconnected with the panorama of creation that springs out of Nothing. This Nothing might be compared to the value of zero in mathematics. In itself it has no positive value, but when it is added to another number it gives rise to the many. In the same way the manifold and evolving universe springs out of Nothing when it is combined with the one Reality.

The whole evolutionary process is within the domain of imagination. When in imagination the one ocean of Reality gets apparently disturbed, there arises the manifold world of separate centers of consciousness. This involves the basic division

Imagined division between self and environment

of life into the *self* and the *not-self,* or the "I" and its environment. Owing to the falseness and the incompleteness of this limited self (which is only an imagined part of a really indivisible totality), consciousness cannot remain content with eternal identification with it. Thus consciousness is trapped in ceaseless restlessness, forcing it to attempt identification with the not-self. That portion of the not-self, or the environment, with which consciousness succeeds in identifying itself gets affiliated with the self in the form of "mine." And that portion of the not-self with which it does not succeed in identifying itself becomes the irreducible environment that inevitably creates a limit and an opposition to the self.

Thus consciousness arrives not at the *termination* of its limiting duality but at its *transformation.* As long as consciousness is subject to the working of vitiating imagination, it cannot successfully put an end to this duality. All the varied attempts it makes for the assimilation of the not-self (or the environment) result merely in the replacement of the initial duality by other innumerable novel forms of the *same* duality. The acceptance and the rejection of certain portions of the environment express themselves respectively as "wanting" and "not-wanting," thus giving rise to the opposites of pleasure and pain, good and bad, and so forth. But neither acceptance nor rejection can lead to freedom from duality, and consciousness therefore finds itself engaged in ceaseless oscillation from one opposite to the other. The entire process of the evolution of the individual is characterized by this oscillation between the opposites.

The evolution of the limited individual is completely determined by the sanskaras accumulated by him through ages; and though it is all part of imagination, the determinism is thorough and automatic.

Thorough determinism of sanskaras

Every action and experience, howsoever ephemeral, leaves behind it an impression in the mental body. This impression is an *objective* modification of the mental body; and as the mental body remains the same, the impressions accumulated by the individual are capable of persisting through several lives. When the sanskaras thus accumulated begin to express themselves (instead of merely lying latent in the mental body), they are experienced as desires, that is, they are apprehended as being *subjective.* The objective and the subjective are the two aspects of sanskaras: the former is a passive state of latency, and the latter is an active state of manifestation.

Through the active phase, the accumulated sanskaras determine each experience and action of the limited self. Just as several feet of film have to pass in a cinema to show a brief action on the screen, many sanskaras are often involved in determining a single action of the limited self. Through such expression and fulfillment in experience, the sanskaras get spent up. The weak sanskaras are spent up mentally; the stronger ones are spent up subtly in the form of desires and imaginative experience; and those sanskaras that are powerful are spent up physically by expressing themselves through bodily action.

Though this spending up of sanskaras is going on continually, it does not end in freedom from sanskaras because new sanskaras are inevitably being created—not only through fresh actions, but even through the very process of spending up. So the load of sanskaras goes on increasing, and the individual finds himself helpless before the problem of throwing off the burden.

The sanskaras deposited by specific actions and experiences

render the mind susceptible to similar actions and experiences. But after a certain point is reached, this tendency is checked and counteracted by a natural reaction consisting in a complete changeover to its direct opposite, making room for the operation of opposite sanskaras.

Balancing through opposites

Very often the two opposites form parts of one and the same chain of imagination. For example, a person might first experience that he is a famous writer—with wealth, fame, family, and all the agreeable things of life—and later in the same life, might experience that he has lost his wealth, fame, family, and all the agreeable things of life. Sometimes it seems that a chain of imagination does not contain both the opposites in the same lifetime. For instance, a man might experience throughout his life that he is a powerful king always victorious in battles. In this case he has to balance this experience by the experience of defeats or the like in the next life, taking one more life to complete his chain of imagination. The purely psychological compulsion of the sanskaras is thus subject to the deeper need of the soul to know its Self.

Suppose a person has killed someone in this life. This deposits in his mental body the sanskaras of killing. If consciousness were to be solely and simply determined by this initial tendency created by these sanskaras, he would go on killing others again and again ad infinitum, each time gathering further momentum from subsequent acts of the same kind. There would be no escape from this recurring determinism, were it not for the fact that the logic of experience provides a necessary check to it. The person soon realizes the incompleteness of the experience of one opposite, and he unconsciously seeks to restore the lost balance by going over to the other opposite.

Example of killing

Thus the individual who has had the experience of killing will develop the psychological need and susceptibility for getting killed. In killing another person he has appreciated only one portion of the total situation in which he is a party, namely, the part of killing. The complementary half of the total situation (that is, the role of being killed) remains for him ununderstood and foreign, though it nevertheless has introduced itself into his experience. There thus arises the need to complete the experience by attracting to oneself the opposite of what one has personally gone through, and consciousness has a tendency to fulfill this new and pressing need. A person who has killed will soon develop a tendency to get himself killed in order to cover the entire situation by personal experience.

The question that crops up here is, Who would arise to kill him in the next life? It may be the same person who was killed in the previous life, or it may be some other person with similar sanskaras. As a result of action and interaction between individuals, there come into existence sanskaric links or ties; and when the individual takes a new physical body, it may be among those who have previous sanskaric ties or among those who have similar sanskaras. But the adjustment of life is such as to make possible the free play of evolving duality.

Through opposites to beyond opposites

Like the shuttle of the weaver's loom, the human mind moves within two extremes, developing the warp and the woof of the cloth of life. The development of spiritual life is best represented not as a straight line but as a zigzag course. Take the function of the two banks of a river. If there were no banks, the waters of the river would disperse, making it impossible for the river to reach its destination. In the same way, the life-force would dissipate itself in endless and innumerable ways, were it not confined between the two poles of the opposites.

These banks of the river of life are best looked upon not as two parallel lines but as two converging lines that meet at the point of Liberation. The amount of oscillation becomes less and less as the individual approaches the goal, and completely subsides when he realizes it. It is like the movement of the doll that has its center of gravity at the base, with the result that it has a gradual tendency to become steady in the sitting posture. If shaken, it continues to swing from side to side for some time; but each movement covers a shorter span, and in the end the doll becomes stationary. In the case of cosmic evolution, such subsiding of alternation between the opposites means Mahapralaya; and in the spiritual evolution of the individual, it means Liberation.

The step from duality to nonduality is not merely a matter of difference in the state of consciousness. As the two are qualitatively different, the difference between them is infinite. The former is a not-God state and the latter is the God state. This infinite difference constitutes the abyss between the sixth plane of consciousness and the seventh. The lower six planes of involution of consciousness* are also separated from each other by a kind of a valley or distance. But though the difference between them is great, it is not infinite because all are equally subject to the bipolarity of limited experience, consisting in the alternation between the opposites.

Planes of involution of consciousness

The difference between the first plane and the second, the second and the third, and so on up to the sixth plane, is great but not infinite. It follows that, strictly speaking, none of the six planes of duality can be said to be really nearer to the seventh plane than any others. The difference between any of the six planes and the seventh plane is infinite, just as the difference between the sixth and the seventh planes is infinite. The progress through the six planes is progress in imagination; but the realization of the seventh plane is the *cessation* of imagination and, therefore, the awakening of the individual into Truth-consciousness.

The illusory progress through the six planes cannot, however, be altogether avoided. Imagination has to be completely exhausted before a person can realize the Truth. When a disciple has a Perfect Master, he has to traverse all the six planes. The Master may take his disciple through the inner planes either with open eyes or under a veil. If the disciple is taken under cover and is not conscious of the planes he is crossing, desires persist until the seventh plane; but if he is taken with open eyes and is conscious of the planes he is crossing, no desires are left on and after the fifth plane. If the Master comes for work, he often chooses to take his disciples under cover; for they are likely to be more actively useful for the Master's work when taken blindfolded than when taken with open eyes.

Progress through inner planes

The crossing of the planes is characterized throughout by the unwinding of sanskaras. This process of unwinding should be carefully distinguished from that of spending up. In the process of spending up, the sanskaras become dynamic and release themselves into action or experience. This does not lead to final emancipation from sanskaras, as the never-ceasing fresh accumulation of sanskaras more than replaces those that are spent up; and the spending up itself is

*See Glossary.

responsible for further sanskaras. In the process of unwinding, however, the sanskaras get weakened and annihilated by the flame of longing for the Infinite.

Longing for the Infinite may be the cause of much spiritual suffering. There is no comparison between the acuteness of ordinary suffering and the poignancy of the spiritual suffering a person has to go through while crossing the planes. The former is the effect of sanskaras, and the latter is the effect of their unwinding. When physical suffering reaches its climax, a person becomes unconscious and so gets relief from it; but there is no such automatic relief for spiritual suffering. Spiritual suffering, however, does not become boring because there is also intermingled with it a kind of pleasure.

Peace of Realization

The longing for the Infinite gets accentuated and acute until it arrives at its climax, and then gradually begins to cool down. While cooling down, consciousness does not altogether give up the longing for the Infinite but continues to stick to its aim of realizing the Infinite. This state of cooled but latent longing is preliminary to realization of the Infinite. Longing is at this stage the instrument of annihilating all other desires and is itself ready to be quenched by the unfathomable stillness of the Infinite. Before the longing for the Infinite is fulfilled through the realization of the Infinite, consciousness has to pass from the sixth to the seventh plane. It has to pass from duality to nonduality. Instead of wandering in imagination, it has to arrive at the end of imagination.

The Master understands the one Reality as being the only Reality and the Nothing as being merely its shadow. For him, time is swallowed up in eternity. As he has realized the timeless aspect of Reality, he is beyond time and holds within his being both the beginning and the end of time. He remains unmoved by the temporal process consisting of the action and interaction of the many. The ordinary person knows neither the beginning nor the end of creation. Thus he is overpowered by the march of events, which loom large because of the lack of proper perspective as he is caught up in time. He looks upon everything in terms of possible fulfillment or nonfulfillment of his sanskaras. He is, therefore, profoundly disturbed by the happenings of this world. The whole objective universe appears to him as an unwelcome limitation that has to be overcome or tolerated.

The Master, on the other hand, is free from duality and the

sanskaras characteristic of duality. He is free from all limitation. The storm and stress of the universe do not affect his being. All the bustle of the world, with its constructive and destructive processes, can have no special importance for him. He has entered into the sanctuary of Truth, which is the abode of that eternal significance which is only partially and faintly reflected in the fleeting values of ever-changing creation. He comprehends within his being all existence, and looks upon the entire play of manifestation as merely a game.

The Formation and Function of Sanskaras

There are two aspects of human experience—the subjective and objective. On the one hand there are mental processes that constitute essential ingredients of human experience, and on the other hand there are things and objects to which they refer. The mental processes are partly dependent upon the immediately given objective situation, and partly dependent upon the functioning of accumulated sanskaras, or impressions, of previous experiences. The human mind thus finds itself between a sea of past sanskaras on the one side and the whole extensive objective world on the other.

Analysis of human experience

Human actions are based upon the operation of the impressions stored in the mind through previous experiences. Every thought, emotion, and act is grounded in groups of impressions that, when considered objectively, are seen to be modifications of the mind. These impressions are deposits of previous experiences and become the most important factors in determining the course of present and future experience. The mind is constantly creating and gathering such impressions in the course of its experience.

Sanskaras originate in experience

When occupied with the physical objects of this world (such as the body, nature, and other things), the mind is, so to say, externalized and creates gross impressions. When it is busy with its own subjective mental processes, which are the expressions of already existing sanskaras, it creates subtle and mental impressions. The question whether sanskaras come first or experience comes first is like the question whether the hen or the egg comes first. Both are conditions of each other and develop side by side. The problem of understanding the significance of human experience, therefore, turns around the problem of understanding the formation and function of sanskaras.

The sanskaras are of two types—natural and nonnatural—according to the manner in which they come into existence. The sanskaras the soul gathers during the period of organic evolution are natural. These sanskaras come into existence as the soul successively takes up and abandons the various subhuman forms, thus gradually passing from the apparently inanimate states (such as stone or metal) to the human state, where there is full development of consciousness. All the sanskaras that cluster around the soul *before* it attains the human form are the product of natural evolution and are referred to as natural sanskaras. They should be carefully distinguished from the sanskaras cultivated by the soul *after* the attainment of the human form.

Natural and nonnatural sanskaras

The sanskaras that get attached to the soul during the human stage are cultivated under the moral freedom of consciousness with its accompanying responsibility of choice between good and bad, virtue and vice. They are referred to as nonnatural sanskaras. Though these posthuman sanskaras are directly dependent upon the natural, they are created under fundamentally different conditions of life and are, in their origin, comparatively more recent than the natural sanskaras. This difference in the length of the formative periods and in the conditions of formation is responsible for the difference in the degree of firmness of attachment of the natural and nonnatural sanskaras to the soul. The nonnatural sanskaras are not as difficult to eradicate as the natural, which have an ancient heritage and are therefore more firmly rooted. The obliteration of the natural sanskaras is practically impossible unless the neophyte is the recipient of the grace and the intervention of a *Sadguru,* or Perfect Master.

The nonnatural sanskaras are dependent upon the natural, and the natural sanskaras are a result of evolution. The next important question is, Why should manifested life in different stages of evolution emerge out of the absolute Reality, which is infinite? The need for manifested life arises out of the impetus in the Absolute to become conscious of itself. The progressive manifestation of life through evolution is ultimately brought about by the *will-to-be-conscious,* which is inherent in the Infinite. In order to understand creation in terms of thought, it is necessary to posit this will-to-be-conscious in the Absolute in a latent state prior to the act of manifestation.

Manifested life arises out of will-to-be-conscious in Absolute

Although for the purposes of an intellectual explanation of creation the impetus in the Absolute has to be regarded as a will-to-be-conscious, to describe it as a sort of inherent desire is to falsify its true nature. It is better described as a *lahar,* or an impulse, which is so inexplicable, spontaneous, and sudden that to call it this or that is to have its reality undone. As all intellectual categories necessarily turn out to be inadequate for grasping the mystery of creation, the nearest approach to understanding its nature is not through intellectual concept but through analogy.

Lahar within Absolute compared to a wave on the ocean

Just as a wave going across the surface of a still ocean calls forth into being a wild stir of innumerable bubbles, the lahar creates myriads of individual souls out of the indivisible infinity of the Oversoul. But the all-abounding Absolute remains the substratum of all the individual souls. The individual souls are the creations of a sudden and spontaneous impulse and have, therefore, hardly any anticipation of their destined continuity of existence throughout the cyclic period until the final subsiding of the initial stir. Within the undifferentiated being of the Absolute is born the mysterious point (the *Om* Point) through which comes forth the variegated manyness of creation. And the vasty deep, which a fraction of a second before was icy-still, is astir with the life of innumerable frothy selves who secure their separateness in definite size and shape through self-limitation within the foamy surface of the ocean.

All this is merely an analogy. It would be a mistake to imagine that some real change takes place in the Absolute when the lahar of the latent will-to-be-conscious makes itself effective by bringing into existence the world of manifestation. There can be no act of involution or evolution within the

Absolute unchanged by bhas of manifestation

being of the Absolute; and nothing real can be born from the Absolute, as any real change is necessarily a negation of the Absolute. The change implied in the creation of the manifested world is not an ontological change—that is, not a change in the being of the absolute Reality. It is only an apparent change.

In one sense the act of manifestation must be regarded as a sort of *expansion* of the illimitable being of the Absolute, as through that act the Infinite, which is without consciousness, seeks to attain its own consciousness. As this expansion of Reality is effected through its self-limitation in various forms of life, the act of manifestation might with equal aptness be called the process of timeless *contraction.* Whether the act of manifestation is looked upon as a sort of expansion of Reality or as its timeless contraction, it is preceded by an initial urge or movement, which might (in terms of thought) be regarded as an inherent and latent desire to be conscious.

The manifoldness of creation and the separateness of the individual souls exist only in imagination. The very existence of creation or of the world of manifestation is grounded in *bhas,* or illusion; so that in spite of the manifestation of numberless individual souls, the Oversoul remains the same without suffering any real expansion or contraction, increment or decrement. Although the Oversoul undergoes no modification due to the bhas, or illusion, of individuation, there comes into existence its apparent differentiation into many individual souls.

Most original bhas

The most original bhas, or illusion, into which the Oversoul was allured synchronizes with the first impression. It therefore marks the beginning of the formation of sanskaras. The formation of sanskaras starts in the most finite center, which becomes the first focus for the manifestation of the individuality of the soul. In the gross sphere a focus of this manifestation is represented by the tri-dimensional and inert stone, which has the most rudimentary and partial consciousness. This vague and undeveloped state of consciousness is hardly sufficient to illumine its own shape and form, and is hopelessly inadequate to fulfill the purpose of creation, which was to enable the Oversoul to know itself.

Whatever little capacity for illumination consciousness has in the stone phase is ultimately derived from the Oversoul and not from the body of the stone. But consciousness is unable to enlarge its scope independently of the body of the stone, because the Oversoul first gets identified with consciousness and then through it with the stone form. Since all further development of consciousness is arrested by the body of the stone and its langour, evolution of the higher forms, or vehicles, of manifestation becomes indispensable. The development of consciousness has to proceed side by side with the evolution of the body by which it is conditioned. Therefore the will-to-be-conscious, which is inherent in the vastness of the Oversoul, seeks by divine determination a progressive evolution of the vehicles of expression.

Thus the Oversoul forges for itself a new vehicle of expression in the metal form, in which consciousness becomes slightly more intensified. Even at this stage it is very rudimentary; and so it has to get transferred to still higher forms of vegetation and trees, in which there is an appreciable advance in the development of consciousness through the maintenance of the vital processes of growth, decay, and reproduction. Emergence of a still more developed form of consciousness becomes possible when the Oversoul seeks manifestation through the instinctive life of insects, birds, and animals, which are fully aware of their bodies and their respective surroundings, and develop a sense of self-protection and aim at establishing mastery over their environment.

Progressive evolution of consciousness and forms

In the higher animals, intellect or reasoning also appears to a certain extent; but its working is strictly limited by the play of their instincts, like the instinct of self-protection and the instinct for the care and preservation of the young. So even in animals consciousness has not had its full development, with the result that it is unable to serve the initial purpose of the Oversoul to have Self-illumination.

The Oversoul finally takes the human form, in which consciousness attains its fullest development with complete awareness of the self and the environment. At this stage the capacity of reasoning has the widest range of activity and is unlimited in its scope. But as the Oversoul gets identified through its consciousness with the gross body, consciousness does not serve the purpose of illuminating the nature of the Oversoul. However, as consciousness has its fullest development in the human form, there is in it a latent potentiality for Self-realization. And the will-to-be-conscious with which evolution

Human consciousness

started becomes fructified in the Sadguru, or Man-God, who is the fairest flower of humanity.

Winding of sanskaras

The Oversoul cannot attain Self-knowledge through the ordinary consciousness of humanity because it is enveloped in a multitude of sanskaras, or impressions. As consciousness passes from the apparently inanimate state of stone or metal, then to the vegetative life of the trees, then onward to the instinctive states of insects, birds, and animals, and finally to the full consciousness of the human state, it is continually creating new sanskaras and becoming enveloped in them. These natural sanskaras are increased even after attaining the human state by the further creation of nonnatural sanskaras through manifold experiences and multitudinous activities.

Thus the acquisition of sanskaras is unceasingly going on during the process of evolution as well as during the later period of human activities. This acquisition of sanskaras may be likened to the winding up of a piece of string around a stick—the string representing the sanskaras and the stick representing the mind of the individual soul. The winding up starts from the beginning of creation and persists through all the evolutionary stages and the human form; and the wound string represents all the sanskaras, natural as well as nonnatural.

Examples of potency of impressions

The fresh sanskaras that are constantly being created in human life are due to the multifarious objects and ideas with which consciousness finds itself confronted. These sanskaras bring about important transformations in the various states of consciousness. Impressions created by beautiful objects have the potency of arousing in consciousness the innate capacity for appreciating and enjoying beauty. When one hears a good piece of music or sees a beautiful landscape, the impressions caught from these objects gives one a feeling of exaltation. In the same way, when one contacts the personality of a thinker, one may become interested in new avenues of thought and inspired with an enthusiasm utterly foreign to one's consciousness formerly. Not only impressions of objects or persons but also impressions of ideas and superstitions have great efficacy in determining the conditions of consciousness.

The power of impressions of superstitions might be illustrated by means of a ghost story. Of the different realms of human thought there are perhaps none as abounding in superstitions as those connected with ghosts, who according to popular belief are supposed to harass and torture their victims in curious ways. Once upon a time, during the Mogul rule in India, a highly educated man who was very skeptical of the stories about ghosts made up his mind to verify them from personal experience. He had been warned against visiting a certain graveyard on the night of *amavasya* (the darkest night of the month); for it was reported to be the habitation of a very dreadful ghost who unfailingly made its appearance whenever an iron nail was hammered into the ground within the limits of the graveyard.

Impressions of superstitions

With a hammer in one hand and a nail in the other, he walked straight into the graveyard on the night of amavasya and chose a spot bare of grass in order to drive in the nail. The ground was dark, and his loosely hanging cloak was equally dark. When he sat on the ground and tried to hammer in the nail, an end of his cloak lay between the nail and the ground and was pinned down. He finished hammering and felt that he was successful with the experiment without encountering the ghost. But as he tried to rise to leave the spot, he felt a strong pull toward the ground; and he became panic-stricken. Owing to the operation of previous impressions, he could not think of anything except the ghost who, he thought, had caught him at last. The shock of the thought was so great that the poor man died of heart failure. This story illustrates the tremendous power that sometimes resides in the impressions created by superstition.

The power and effect of impressions can hardly be overestimated. An impression is solidified might, and its inertness makes it immobile and durable. It can become so engraved upon the mind of a person that despite his sincere desire and effort to eradicate it, it takes its own time and has a way of working itself into action directly or indirectly. The mind contains many heterogenous sanskaras; and while seeking expression in consciousness, they often clash with each other. The clash of sanskaras is experienced in consciousness as mental conflict. Experience is bound to be chaotic and enigmatic, full of oscillations, confusion, and complex tangles until consciousness is freed from all sanskar-

Experience becomes harmonious when freed from sanskaras

as, good and bad. Experience can become truly harmonious and integral only when consciousness is emancipated from the impressions.

Types of sanskaras and states of consciousness

Sanskaras can be classified according to essential differences in the nature of the spheres to which they refer. Referring to these different spheres of existence, they are found to be of three kinds: (1) Gross sanskaras, which enable the soul to experience the gross world through the gross medium and compel it to identify itself with the gross body. (2) Subtle sanskaras, which enable the soul to experience the subtle world through the subtle medium and compel the soul to identify itself with the subtle body. (3) Mental sanskaras, which enable the soul to experience the mental world through the mental medium and compel it to identify itself with the mental body. The differences between the states of the individual souls are entirely due to the differences existing in the kinds of sanskaras with which their consciousness is loaded. Thus gross-conscious souls experience only the gross world; subtle-conscious souls experience only the subtle world; and mental-conscious souls experience only the mental world. The qualitative diversity in the experience of these three types of souls is due to the difference in the nature of their sanskaras.

Self-conscious souls free from sanskaras

The Self-conscious souls are radically different from all other souls because they experience the Oversoul through the medium of the Self; whereas the other souls experience only their bodies and the corresponding worlds. This radical difference between the consciousness of Self-conscious souls and other souls is due to the fact that whereas the consciousness of most souls is conditioned by some kinds of sanskaras, the consciousness of Self-conscious souls is completely free from all sanskaras. It is only when consciousness is unobscured and unconditioned by any sanskaras that the initial will-to-be-conscious arrives at its final and real fruition, and the infinity and the indivisible unity of the Absolute is consciously realized. The problem of deconditioning the mind through the removal of sanskaras is therefore extremely important.

The Removal of Sanskaras

Part I
The Cessation, the Wearing Out, and the Unwinding of Sanskaras

Sanskaras prevent Self-illumination

Human beings do not have Self-illumination because their consciousness is shrouded in sanskaras, or the accumulated imprints of past experience. In the human form the will-to-be-conscious with which evolution started has succeeded in creating consciousness. However, unconsciousness does not arrive at the knowledge of the Oversoul because the individual soul is impelled to use it for experiencing sanskaras instead of utilizing it for experiencing the soul's own true nature as the Oversoul. The experiencing of sanskaras keeps it confined to the illusion of being a finite body trying to adjust itself in the world of things and persons.

Problem of securing release from sanskaras

Individual souls are like drops in the ocean. Just as each drop in the ocean is fundamentally identical with the ocean, the soul—which is individualized due to bhas, or illusion—is still the Oversoul and does not really become separate from the Oversoul. Yet the envelope of sanskaras, by which consciousness is covered, prevents the drop-soul from having Self-illumination and keeps it within the domain of duality. In order for the soul to consciously realize its identity with the Oversoul, it is necessary that consciousness should be retained and that sanskaras should be entirely removed. The sanskaras, which are contributory to the evolution of consciousness, themselves become impediments to its efficacy in illuminating the nature of the Oversoul. Henceforth the problem with which the will-to-be-conscious is confronted is not that of evolving consciousness but that of releasing it from sanskaras.

The release from sanskaras takes place in the following five ways:

Five ways of securing release from sanskaras

1. *The cessation of creating new sanskaras.*

This consists in putting an end to the ever-renewing activity of creating fresh sanskaras. If the formation of sanskaras is compared to the winding of a string around a stick, this step amounts to the cessation of the further winding of the string.

2. *The wearing out of old sanskaras.*

If sanskaras are withheld from expressing themselves in action and experience, they are gradually worn out. In the analogy of the string, this process is comparable to the wearing out of the string at the place where it is.

3. *The unwinding of past sanskaras.*

This process consists in annulling past sanskaras by mentally reversing the process that leads to their formation. Continuing our analogy, it is like unwinding the string.

4. *The dispersion and exhaustion of some sanskaras.*

If the mental energy that is locked up in sanskaras is sublimated and diverted into other channels, they are dispersed and exhausted and tend to disappear.

5. *The wiping out of sanskaras.*

This consists in completely annihilating the sanskaras. In the analogy of the string, this is comparable to cutting the string with a pair of scissors. The final wiping out of sanskaras can be effected only by the grace of a Perfect Master.

It should be carefully noted that many of the concrete methods of undoing sanskaras are found to be effective in more than one way, and the five ways mentioned above are not meant to classify these methods into sharply distinguished types. They represent rather the different principles characterizing the spiritual processes that take place while sanskaras are being removed. For the sake of convenience, this Part will deal only with those methods that preeminently illustrate the first three principles (namely, the cessation of creating fresh sanskaras and the wearing out and the unwinding of past sanskaras). The methods that predominantly illustrate the last two principles (the dispersion and exhaustion through sublimation of sanskaras, and the wiping out of sanskaras) will be explained in Parts II and III.

If the mind is to be freed from the bondage of ever-accumulating sanskaras, it is necessary that there should be an end to the creation of new sanskaras. Fresh multiplication of sanskaras can be stopped through renunciation. Renunciation may be external or internal. External, or physical, renunciation consists in giving up everything to which the mind is attached—home, parents, marriage, children, friends, wealth, comforts, and gross enjoyments. Internal, or mental, renunciation consists in giving up all cravings, particularly the craving for sensual objects.

Renunciation

Though external renunciation in itself is not necessarily accompanied by internal renunciation, it often paves a way for internal renunciation. Spiritual freedom consists in internal renunciation and not in external renunciation, but external renunciation is a great aid in achieving internal renunciation. The person who renounces his possessions disconnects himself from everything that he had or has. This means that the things he renounces are no longer a source of fresh sanskaras. He thus takes an important step toward emancipating himself from his sanskaras by putting an end to the process of forming new sanskaras. This is not all that is achieved through external renunciation. With the renouncing of everything, he also renounces his past bindings. The old sanskaras connected with his possessions get detached from his mind; and since they are withheld from expressing themselves, they get worn out.

For most persons, external renunciation creates a favorable atmosphere for the wearing out of sanskaras. An individual who possesses wealth and power is exposed to a life of indulgence and extravagance. His circumstances are more favorable for temptations. Man is mostly what he becomes by being chopped, chiseled, and shaped by the sculptor of environment. Whether or not he can surmount his surroundings depends upon his strength of character. If he is strong, he remains free in his thought and action, even in the midst of action and reaction with his environment. If he is weak, he succumbs to its influence. Even if he is strong, he is likely to be swept off his feet by a powerful wave of the collective mode of life and thought. It is difficult to withstand the onslaught of a current of ideas and avoid falling prey to circumstances. If he resists the circumstances, he is likely to be carried away by some wild wave of collective passion and get caught up in modes of thought that he is unable to renounce. Though it is difficult to resist and overcome these influences and surroundings, it is easier to escape from them. Many persons would live a chaste and straightforward life if they were not surrounded by luxuries and temptations. The renunciation of all superfluous things helps the wearing out of sanskaras and is therefore contributory to the life of freedom.

The two important forms of external renunciation that have special spiritual value are solitude and fasting. Withdrawal of oneself from the storm and stress of the multifarious worldly activities and occasional retirement into solitude are valuable for wearing out the sanskaras connected with the gregarious instinct. But this is not to be looked upon as a goal in itself.

Solitude and fasting

Like solitude, fasting also has great spiritual value. Eating is satisfaction; fasting is denial. Fasting is physical when food is not taken, in spite of the craving for the enjoyment of eating; it is mental when food is taken not for its delights and attachments but merely for the survival of the body. External fasting consists in avoiding direct contact with food in order to achieve mental fasting.

Food is a direct necessity of life, and its continued denial is bound to be disastrous to health. Therefore, external fasting should be periodical and only for a short time. It has to be continued till there is complete victory over the craving for food. By bringing into action the vital forces to withstand the craving for food, it is possible to free the mind from attachment to food. External fasting has no spiritual value when it is undertaken with the motive of securing the health of the body or for the sake of self-demonstration. It should not be used as an instrument for self-assertion. In the same way, it should not be carried to the extreme—until the body is reduced to its limits. Self-mortification through prolonged fasting does not necessarily promote freedom from the craving for food. On the contrary, it is likely to invite a subsequent reaction toward a life of extravagant indulgence in food. If, however, external fasting is undertaken in moderation and for spiritual purposes, it facilitates the achievement of internal fasting. When external and internal fasting are wholehearted and faithful, they bring about the unwinding of the sanskaras connected with the craving for food.

The unwinding of many other sanskaras can be brought about through penance. This consists in augmenting and expressing the feeling of remorse an individual feels after realizing that he has done some wrongful act. Repentance consists in mentally reviving the wrongs with severe self-condemnation. It is facilitated by availing oneself of the different circumstances and situations that stir up penance, or by remaining vulnerable during periods of emotional outbursts, or by deliberate efforts to recall the past incidents with a remorseful heart and acute disapproval. Such penance unwinds the sanskaras that are responsible for the action. Self-condemnation accompanied by deep feeling can negate the sanskaras of anger, greed, and lust. Suppose a person has done irreparable wrong to someone through uncontrolled greed, anger, or lust. Sometime or other he is bound to have the reaction of self-killing remorse and experience the pricks of conscience. If at this time he vividly realizes the evil for which he was responsible, the intensity of emotional awareness by which it is accompanied consumes the tendencies for which he stands self-condemned.

Penance

Self-condemnation sometimes expresses itself through different forms of self-mortification. Some aspirants even inflict wounds on their body when they are in a mood of penitence, but such drastic expression of remorse must be discouraged as a general usage. Some Hindu aspirants try to cultivate humility by making it a rule to fall at the feet of everyone whom they meet. To those of strong will and stable character, penance can bring the desired good effect through self-humiliation, which unwinds and eradicates the different sanskaras connected with good and bad actions. Others who might be feeble in their willpower also derive benefit from penance if they are under sympathetic and loving direction. When penance is carefully nourished and practiced, it inevitably results in the mental revocation of undesirable modes of thought and conduct, and makes one amenable to a life of purity and service.

It should, however, be carefully noted that there is always the danger in penance that the mind might dwell too long upon the wrongs done and thus develop the morbid habit of wailing and weeping over petty things. Such sentimental extravagance is often an indiscriminate waste of energy and is in no way helpful in the wearing out or the unwinding of sanskaras. Penance should not be like the everyday repentance that follows everyday weaknesses. It should not become a tedious and sterile habit of immoderate and gloomy pondering over one's own failings. Sincere penance does not consist in perpetuating grief for the wrongs but in resolving to avoid in the future those deeds that call forth remorse. If it leads to lack of self-respect or self-confidence, it has not served its true purpose, which is merely to render impossible the repetition of certain types of action.

Denying desires their fulfillment

The wearing out and the unwinding of sanskaras can also be effected by denying to desires their expression and fulfillment. People differ in their capacity and aptitude for rejecting desires. Those in whom desires arise with great impulsive velocity are unable to curb them at their source, but they can refrain from seeking their fulfillment through action. Even if someone has no control over the surging of desires, he can prevent them from being translated into action. Rejection of desires by controlling actions avoids the possibility of sowing seeds of future desires.

On the other hand, if a person translates his desires into action, he may spend up and exhaust some impressions. But he is creating fresh impressions during the very process of fulfilling the desires and is thus sowing seeds for future desires, which in their turn are bound to demand their own satisfaction. The process of spending up or exhausting impressions through expression and fulfillment does not in itself contribute toward securing release from sanskaras.

When desires arise and their release into action is barred, there is plenty of opportunity for spontaneous cogitation about these desires. This cogitation results in the wearing out of the corresponding sanskaras. It should be noted, however, that such spontaneous cogitation does not bring about the desired result if it takes the form of mental indulgence in the desires. When there is a deliberate and wanton attempt to welcome and harbor the desires in the mind, such cogitation will not only have no spiritual value but may itself be responsible for creating subtle sanskaras. Cogitation should not be accompanied by any conscious sanction for the desires that arise in consciousness, and there should not be any effort to perpetuate the memory of these desires. When desires are denied their expression and fulfillment in action and are allowed to pass through the intensity of the fire of a cogitative consciousness that does not sanction them, the seeds of these desires are consumed. The rejection of desires and the inhibition of physical response effect, in time, an automatic and natural negation of the past sanskaras.

Rejection of desires is a preparation for desirelessness, or the state of nonwanting, which alone can bring about true freedom. Wanting is necessarily binding, whether it is fulfilled or not. When it is fulfilled, it leads to further wanting and thus perpetuates the bondage of the spirit. When it is unfulfilled, it leads to disappointment and suffering, which—through their sanskaras—fetter the freedom of the spirit in their own way.

Desirelessness

There is no end to wanting because the external and internal stimuli of the mind are constantly alluring it into a state of wanting or disliking (which is another form of wanting) something. The external stimuli are the sensations of sight, hearing, smell, taste, and touch. The internal stimuli are those that arise in the mind of man from the memories of the present life and the totality of sanskaras gathered by consciousness during the evolutionary period and during human lives. When the mind is trained to remain unmoved and balanced in the presence of all external and internal stimuli, it arrives at the state of nonwanting. And by not wanting anything (except the absolute Reality, which is beyond the opposites of stimuli) it is possible to unwind the sanskaras of wanting.

Wanting is a state of disturbed equilibrium of mind, and nonwanting is a state of stable poise. The poise of nonwanting can only be maintained by an unceasing disentanglement from all stimuli—whether pleasant or painful, agreeable or disagreeable. In order to remain unmoved by the joys and sorrows of this world, the mind must be completely detached from the external and internal stimuli. Though the mind is constantly fortifying itself through its own constructive suggestions, there is always the chance of these outposts of defense being washed away by some sudden and unexpected wave arising in the ocean of the natural and mental environment. When this happens you may, for a time, feel completely lost; but the attitude of nonattachment can keep you safe.

Poise of nonwanting and principle of neti neti

This attitude consists in the application of the principle of *neti*

neti (not-this, not-this). It implies constant effort to maintain a watchful detachment in relation to the alluring opposites of limited experience. It is not possible to deny only the disagreeable stimuli and remain inwardly attached to the agreeable stimuli. If the mind is to remain unmoved by the onslaughts of the opposites, it cannot continue to be attached to the expressions of agreeable stimuli and be influenced by them. The equipoise consists in meeting both alternatives with complete detachment.

The "yes, yes" meaning of the positive sanskaras can only be annulled through the negative assertion of "no, no." This negative element is necessarily present in all aspects of asceticism, as expressed through renunciation, solitude, fasting, penance, withholding desires from fulfillment, and nonwanting. The happy blending of all these methods and attitudes creates a healthy form of asceticism in which there is no toil or exertion. But to ensure all this, the negative element in them must come naturally without giving rise to any perversions or further limitations.

Negative element in all aspects of asceticism

Trying to coerce the mind to a life of asceticism is of no use. Any forcible adjustment of life on ascetic lines is likely to stunt the growth of some good qualities. When the healthy qualities of human nature are allowed to develop naturally and slowly, they unfold the knowledge of relative values and thereby pave the way for a spontaneous life of asceticism. Whereas any attempt to force or hasten the mind toward an ascetic life is likely to invite reaction.

The process of being freed from some attachments is often accompanied by the process of forming some other new attachments. The grossest form of attachment is that which is directed toward the world of objects; but when the mind is being detached from the world of objects, it has a tendency to arrive at some finer attachments of a subjective kind. After the mind has succeeded in cultivating a certain degree of detachment, it might easily develop that subtle form of egotism which expresses itself through aloofness and a superior air. Detachment should not be allowed to form any nucleus upon which the ego could fasten itself; and at the same time, it should not be an expression of one's inability to cope with the storm and stress of worldly life.

The things that limit pure and infinite being should be given up through an attitude of immense strength, which is born of purity and enlightenment, and not from a sense of helplessness in the face of strife and struggle. Further, true detachment does not consist in clinging to the mere formula of *neti neti,* which sometimes becomes an obsession of the mind without any deep-felt longing for enlightenment. Such interest in a mere formula of negation often exists side by side with an inward dwelling on the temptations. Detachment can be integral and wholehearted only when it becomes an inseparable part of one's nature.

Negative sanskaras must also disappear before enlightenment

The negative assertion of "no, no" is the only way of unwinding the positive sanskaras gathered through evolution and human lives. Although this process does destroy the positive sanskaras, it results in the formation of the *negative* sanskaras, which in their own way condition the mind and create a new problem. The assertion of "no, no" has to be sufficiently powerful to effect the eradication of all the physical, subtle, and mental sanskaras; but after it has served its purpose, it has to be ultimately abandoned. The finality of spiritual experience does not consist of bare negation. To bring it under a negative formula is to limit it by means of an intellectual concept. The negative formula has to be used by the mind to decondition itself, but it must be renounced before the ultimate goal of life can be attained.

Thought has to be made use of in order to overcome the limitations set up by its own movement; but when this is done, it has itself to be given up. This amounts to the process of going beyond the mind, and this becomes possible through nonidentification with the mind or its desires. To look objectively upon the body, as well as all thoughts and lower impulses, is to get established in blissful detachment and to negate all sanskaras. This means freeing the soul from its self-imposed illusions—like "I am the body," "I am the mind," or "I am desire"—and gaining ground toward the enlightened stage of "I am God" (*"Anal Haqq,"* or *"Aham Brahmasmi"*).

The Removal of Sanskaras

Part II
The Dispersion and
Exhaustion of Sanskaras

Negation of sanskaras attained through control

At the end of Part I, the methods of removing sanskaras are explained that depend chiefly on the principle of negating the positive sanskaras, which also veil the Truth from consciousness and prevent Self-illumination—for which the whole creation came into being. All these methods of negating the positive sanskaras are ultimately based upon the control of the body and mind. Control of the habitual tendencies of the mind is much more difficult than control of physical actions. The fleeting and evasive thoughts and desires of the mind can be curbed only with great patience and persistent practice. But the restraint of mental processes and reactions is necessary to check the formation of new sanskaras and to wear out or unwind the old sanskaras of which they are expressions. Though control might be difficult at the beginning, through sincere effort it gradually becomes natural and easy to achieve.

Control is deliberate and involves effort as long as the mind is trying to decondition itself through the removal of sanskaras. But after the mind is released from the sanskaras, control becomes spontaneous because the mind is then functioning in freedom and understanding. Such control is born of strength of character and health of mind, and it invariably brings with it freedom from fear and immense peace and calmness. The mind, which appears feeble when it is wanton and uncontrolled in its functioning, becomes a source of great strength when it is controlled. Control is indispensable for the conservation of mental energy and the economical use of thought force for creative purposes.

However, if control is purely mechanical and aimless, it defeats its own purpose, which is to make possible the free and unconditioned functioning of the mind. Control that has true spiritual value does not consist in the mechanical repression of thoughts and desires, but is the natural restraint exercised by perception of positive values discovered during the process of experience. True control is therefore not merely negative. When some positive values come within the focus of consciousness, their claims for being expressed in life generate mental responses that ultimately remove all the tendencies obstructing a free and full expression of those values. Thus the tendencies for lust, greed, and anger are removed through an appreciative recognition of the value of a life of purity, generosity, and kindness.

True control a creative readjustment in light of true values

The mind, becoming accustomed to certain habits of thought and response, does not find it easy to adjust itself to these new claims of its own perceptions, owing to the inertia caused by impressions of previous modes of thought and conduct. This process of readjustment in the light of true values takes the form of what we call controlling the mind. This control is not a mechanical or forcible twisting of the mind. It is an effort of the mind to overcome its own inertia. It is fundamentally creative and not negative in its purpose, for it is an attempt of the mind to arrive at self-adjustment in order to release the expression of the true values of life.

Creative control becomes possible because the source of light is within everyone; and though Self-illumination is prevented by the veil of sanskaras, it is not all darkness even within the boundaries of ordinary human consciousness. The ray of light consists of a sense for true values and guides man onward with varying degrees of clarity according to the thickness of the veil of sanskaras. The process of the negation of sanskaras is at the same time the process of understanding

Dispersion and exhaustion of sanskaras

true values. Spiritual progress is thus characterized by the dual aspect of renouncing the false values of sanskaras in favor of the true values of understanding. The process of replacing lower values by higher values is the process of sublimation, which consists in diverting the mental energy locked up in the old sanskaras toward creative and spiritual ends. When this energy locked up in the sanskaras is thus diverted, they get dispersed and exhausted.

Process of sublimation sustained by unfailing interest

The method of sublimation is the most natural and effective method of breaking through the grooves of old sanskaras, and has the special advantage of having an unfailing interest for the aspirant at all stages. The method of mere negation without any substitution is sometimes likely to be boring and may seem to lead to vacuity. But the method of sublimation consists in replacing lower values with higher ones and is therefore full of absorbing interest at every stage, bringing an ever-increasing sense of fulfillment. Mental energy can be sublimated into spiritual channels through (1) meditation, (2) selfless service for humanity, and (3) devotion.

Meditation: its nature and purpose

Meditation is deep and constant concentration upon an ideal object. In such concentration upon an ideal object, the person is conscious only of the object of meditation, completely forgetting the mind as well as the body. Thus no new sanskaras are formed and old ones are dispersed and exhausted through the mental activity of dwelling on the object of concentration. Finally, when the sanskaras completely disappear, the soul as individualized is dissolved in the intensity of concentration and is merged in the ideal object.

Forms of meditation

There are many forms of meditation according to the aptitude of different persons. The imaginative genius of persons who have to labor hard is often dried up due to overwork. For such persons the form of meditation most suitable consists in disconnecting oneself from one's thoughts, and then looking upon these thoughts and the body *objectively*. After the aspirant is successful in regarding his thoughts and his body with complete objectivity, he tries to identify himself with the cosmic Being through constructive suggestions—such as "I am the Infinite," "I am in everything," "I am in all."

Those who have vivid and lively imaginations can try intensive concentration on some point, but fixing the mind on some point should be avoided by those who have no liking for it. Ordinarily, the energy of the mind is scattered, through its diverse thoughts. Meditation on a point is very salutary for the mind to gather itself and settle down, but it is a mechanical process and therefore lacks creative and blissful experiences. However, in the initial stages, this form of meditation might be used as a preparation for other more successful forms of meditation.

The more successful and deeper forms of meditation are preceded by deliberate and constructive thinking about God, the Beloved. Meditation on God is spiritually most fruitful. God can become the object of meditation either in His *impersonal* aspect or in His *personal* aspect. Meditation on the impersonal aspect of God is suitable only for those who have a special aptitude for it. It consists in focusing all thoughts on the abstract and unmanifest existence of God. On the other hand, meditation on the personal aspect of God consists in centering all thoughts upon the form and attributes of God.

Meditation on personal and impersonal aspects of God

After intensive meditation the mind might want to settle down, not on the object of meditation, but on the steadiness of the expansive peace experienced during meditation. Such moments are the natural result of the fatigue of the faculty of imagination, and they should be effortlessly encouraged. Meditation should be spontaneous and not forced. In the moments of the surging up of divine impulses, imagination should be let loose and allowed to soar. The flight of imagination should be controlled only by the set purpose of becoming one with the Infinite. It should not be influenced by the currents of the diverse feelings of lust, greed, or anger.

Success in concentration comes only gradually, and the novice is likely to be disheartened because he does not get satisfactory results in the beginning. Often the disappointment that he experiences is in itself a serious obstruction to beginning the meditation of the day and to persist in it. Other obstacles like idleness and ill health also may be difficult to overcome, but they can be gotten over by having fixed and regular hours for meditation and steady practice. During early morning or at sunset the quiet condition of nature is

Obstacles in meditation

particularly helpful for meditation, but it may also be undertaken at any other suitable time.

Importance of solitude for meditation

Solitude is one of the essential conditions for attaining success in meditation. In the world of thought there is a constant intermingling of thought forms and colors. Some mighty ideas tend to strengthen the mind by facilitating integration; whereas some frivolous thoughts are dissipating. The mind is either attracted or repelled by these diverse thoughts in the mental environment. It is advisable to avoid the influence of these variegated thoughts in order to get established in one's own ideal thoughts. For this purpose solitude has immense possibilities. Solitude means economy of mental energy and increased power of concentration. Having nothing extraneous to attract or repel the mind, you are drawn inward and learn the art of opening yourself to the higher currents, which have the potency of giving you strength, bliss, and peaceful expansiveness.

Selfless service

While meditation on the personal and impersonal aspects of God requires withdrawal of consciousness into the sanctuary of one's own heart, concentration on the universal aspect of God is best achieved through selfless service for humanity. When a person is completely absorbed in the service of humanity, he is completely oblivious of his own body or mind or their functions, as in meditation; and therefore new sanskaras are not formed. Further, the old sanskaras that bind the mind are shattered and dispersed. Since the individual is now centering his attention and interest not upon his own good but upon the good of others, the nucleus of the ego is deprived of its nourishing energy. Selfless service is therefore one of the best methods of diverting and sublimating the energy locked up in the binding sanskaras.

Implications of selfless service

Selfless service is accomplished when there is not the slightest thought of reward or result, and when there is complete disregard of one's own comfort or convenience or the possibility of being misunderstood. When you are wholly occupied with the welfare of others, you can hardly think of yourself. You are not concerned with your comfort and convenience or your health and happiness. On the contrary you are willing to sacrifice everything for their well-being. Their comfort is your convenience, their health is your delight, and their happiness is your joy. You find your life in losing it in theirs. You live in their hearts, and your heart becomes their shelter. When there is true union of hearts, you completely identify yourself with the other person. Your act of help or word of comfort supplies to others whatever might be lacking in them; and through their thoughts of gratitude and goodwill, you actually receive more than you give.

Thus, through living for others, your own life finds its amplification and expansion. The person who leads a life of selfless service is therefore hardly conscious of serving. He does not make those whom he serves feel that they are in any way under obligation to him. On the contrary, he himself feels obliged for being given a chance of making them happy. Neither for show nor for name and fame does he serve them. Selfless service is completely achieved only when an individual derives the same happiness in serving others as in being served himself. The ideal of selfless service frees him from the sanskaras of craving for power and possession, of self-pity and jealousy, of evil deeds actuated through selfishness.

Freedom and fulfillment through service

Selfless service and meditation are both spontaneous when they are inspired by love. Love is therefore rightly regarded as being the most important avenue leading to the realization of the Highest. In love the soul is completely absorbed in the Beloved and is therefore detached from the actions of the body or mind. This puts an end to the formation of new sanskaras and also results in the undoing of old sanskaras by giving to life an entirely new direction. Nowhere does self-forgetfulness come so naturally and completely as in the intensity of love. Hence it has been given the foremost place among the methods that secure release of consciousness from the bondage of sanskaras.

Love

Love comprehends in itself the different advantages belonging to other paths leading to emancipation, and is in itself the most distinguished and effective path. It is at once characterized by self-sacrifice and happiness. Its uniqueness lies in the fact that it is accompanied by an exclusive and wholehearted

Purifying efficacy of love

offering to the Beloved without admitting the claims of any other object. Thus there is no room for the diversion of mental energy, and concentration is complete. In love the physical, vital, and mental energies of man are all gathered up and made available for the cause of the Beloved, with the result that this love becomes a dynamic power. The tension of true love is so great that any foreign feeling that might intervene is at once thrown out. The expulsive and purifying efficacy of love is unparalleled.

Love is present throughout creation

There is nothing unnatural or artificial about love. It exists from the very beginning of evolution. At the inorganic stage it is crudely expressed in the form of cohesion or attraction. It is the natural affinity that keeps things together and draws them to each other. The gravitational pull exercised by the heavenly bodies upon each other is an expression of this type of love. At the organic stage love becomes self-illumined and self-appreciative, and plays an important part from the lowest forms like the amoeba to the most evolved form of human beings. When love is self-illumined, its value is intensified by its conscious sacrifice.

Love expressed through conscious sacrifice

The sacrifice of love is so complete and ungrudging that it has all to give and nothing to expect. The more it gives the more it wants to give, and the less it is aware of having given. The stream of true love is ever increasing and never failing. Its simple expression is its simple giving over. The complexities of the Beloved are a concern of its best attention and care. Endlessly and remorselessly it seeks to please the Beloved in a thousand ways. It does not hesitate to welcome suffering in order to satisfy but one wish of the Beloved or to relieve the Beloved of the slightest pain of neglect or indifference. The lover would gladly pine and perish for the sake of the Beloved. Careworn and tormented, love waits not to attend to the very body that houses and nourishes it. It brooks no compromise, and the Beloved is the concern of the lover's lifetime. The tabernacle of love bursts under unmanageable restlessness and gives birth to streams of love and supreme sweetness, until the lover breaks through his limitations and loses himself in the being of the Beloved.

When love is deep and intense, it is called *bhakti,* or devotion. In its initial stages devotion is expressed through symbol worship, supplication before the deities, reverence and allegiance to the revealed scriptures, or the pursuit of the Highest through abstract thinking. In its more advanced stages devotion expresses itself as interest in human welfare and the service of humanity, love and reverence for saints, and allegiance and obedience to a spiritual Master. These stages have their relative values and relative results. Love for a living Perfect Master is a unique stage of devotion, for it eventually gets transformed into *para-bhakti,* or divine love.

Different stages of devotion

Para-bhakti

Para-bhakti is not merely intensified bhakti. It begins where bhakti ends. At the stage of para-bhakti, devotion is not only single-minded but is accompanied by extreme restlessness of the heart and a ceaseless longing to unite with the Beloved. This is followed by lack of interest in one's own body and its care, isolation from one's own surroundings, and utter disregard for appearances or criticism—while the divine impulses of attraction to the Beloved become more frequent than ever. This highest phase of love is most fruitful because it has as its object the One who is love incarnate and who can, as the supreme Beloved, respond to the lover most completely. The purity, sweetness, and efficacy of the love that the lover receives from the Master contributes to the insuperable spiritual value of this highest phase of love.

The Removal of Sanskaras

Part III
The Wiping Out Of Sanskaras

Love for the Sadguru, or Perfect Master, is particularly important because it invites contact with the Sadguru. Through such contact the aspirant receives from the Master impressions that have the special potency of undoing other past impressions, thus completely transforming the tenor of his life. The recipient of the impressions may entirely give up old habits of life and ways of thought. Such contact changes and elevates the tone of the most depraved life. A person might have been leading a life of reckless dissipation without ever thinking of anything other than the fulfillment of mundane desires. He might have been caught up in the thirst for possession and power, with no ideal other than that of acquiring and hoarding money and making merry.

Impressions from Sadguru transform life

However, even such a person, who cannot by any stretch of imagination think of freedom from earthly fetters, may find that the sanskaras he receives from his contact with the Sadguru are potent enough to drop forever a curtain on his old manner of thought and existence, and to open for him entirely new vistas of a higher and freer life. The impressions received from the Master might be equally beneficial to an intellectual and cultured person whose vision is nevertheless circumscribed, whose imagination can at best appreciate the beauty of art and literature, and whose altruism cannot go beyond the limits of his neighborhood or the boundaries of his country. Such a person would, on receiving impressions from a Master, be lifted to still higher modes of life.

The Sadguru can raise the aspirant from the ordinary intellectual level of consciousness to the level of consciousness where there is inspiration and intuition, and then onward to the level of insight and illumination that culminates in his merging into the Infinite. This rising of the aspirant corresponds to his progress from the mundane sphere to the subtle sphere, from the subtle sphere to the mental sphere, and finally from the mental sphere to the state of Freedom. The last step implies complete wiping out of all sanskaras — natural or nonnatural, positive or negative. To take the analogy of the string wound around a stick, this process of the wiping out of sanskaras consists in cutting the string with a pair of scissors. The erasing of all sanskaras, which is implied in the final release of consciousness from all illusion and bondage, can never be achieved except through the grace of a Sadguru.

Wiping out all sanskaras through intervention of Sadguru

But such active intervention by the Sadguru presupposes an unrestrained relationship between the aspirant and the Master, which can be established only when the aspirant succeeds in complete self-surrender to him. Self-surrender implies obedience to all the orders of the Master. When all your desires and actions are guided by him and are the result of your obeying his orders, he becomes directly responsible for them. Thus, when self-surrender is thorough, the responsibility for your release from sanskaras is devolved upon the Master; and under this new condition the Master annihilates all your sanskaras in no time.

Need for complete self-surrender

Obedience to the Master as implied in full self-surrender is of two kinds: intellectual and literal. Of these two types of obedience, intellectual obedience comes first and is a preliminary to literal obedience, which is more fruitful. When you are intellectually convinced about the greatness and Perfection of the Master, you have love and respect for him but are unable to follow his orders literally. Reason being the basis of your conviction, you find it difficult to divorce it from

Intellectual obedience

your understanding of the Master and his orders. As the two are inextricably intertwined with each other, your reasoned faith holds you within the limits of intellectual obedience. This phase of the pupil is left undisturbed by the Master, and all the "pills" of obedience offered by him are intellectualized in order to suit the pupil's taste and caliber.

Through intellectual obedience to the Master, you can annihilate all your sanskaras, provided you are sincere in your logical interpretation of his orders and in their execution. But the result comes much quicker if your obedience is literal. Literal obedience is the effect of the rocklike faith and deep love that the Master inspires in the pupil through his human appeal. The overflowing radiance of the Master's halo and the effulgence of his purity and compassion are mainly responsible for creating in the pupil an unswerving faith, which prepares him to follow the Master's orders implicitly—irrespective of their satisfying his critical spirit.

Literal obedience

Such literal obedience is not even bound by the requirement that the real significance of the orders should be within the intellectual comprehension of the pupil, and it is the best type of obedience to which you can aspire. Through such implicit and unquestioning obedience, all the crooked knots of your desires and sanskaras are set straight. It is also through such obedience that a deep link is created between the Master and the pupil, with the result that there is an unhindered and perennial flow of spiritual wisdom and power into the pupil. At this stage the pupil becomes the spiritual son or daughter of the Master, and in due time he or she is freed from all individualistic and sanskaric ties. Then such a rare one also becomes a Master.

The Sadguru, or Perfect Master, has a position and power that is unique. There are many souls in the world who are more or less advanced on the spiritual path, but there are few who have crossed all six stages of the internal spheres of consciousness and become one with the infinite source of existence, knowledge, and bliss. The Sadguru has not only experienced the different planes of consciousness, but he actually permeates the very being of all souls because of his having become one with the Infinite. He is the pivot of universal activity.

Role of Sadguru

In a sense, to him are due all your thoughts and actions, your joys and sorrows, your frets and fumes, your strengths and weaknesses, your possessions and surrenderance, and your love and longing. He not only pervades all existence but is consciously conversant with the cosmic law of cause and effect and the complex working of the sanskaras of individual souls. The causes of individual happiness or misery, vices or virtues, are as much known to him as the causes of cosmic changes and upheavals. Every being is an open book for the infinite searchlight of his omnipresent consciousness. Because of his union with the Infinite, the Master is endowed with unlimited power; and in the twinkling of an eye he can annihilate all the sanskaras of the soul and liberate it from all entanglements and bondage.

Good and Evil

The human mind is not only going through experiences but is constantly evaluating them. Some experiences are regarded as agreeable and some disagreeable; some experiences are found to bring happiness and some suffering; some experiences are perceived as being pleasant and some unpleasant. Some experiences are apprehended as restricting the life of man and some as leading it toward fullness and freedom. And some experiences are looked upon as being good and some bad. These are the opposites created by human imagination when it is meeting life with a particular point of view.

Evaluation of experience through opposites

Man's conception of what is acceptable or unacceptable goes on evolving and changing according to the nature of desires that happen to be dominant at any particular moment. But as long as there is any kind of desire in his mind, he is impelled to appraise his experience in relation to that desire and divide it into two parts: the one contributing toward its fulfillment and therefore acceptable, and the other tending to prevent its fulfillment and therefore unacceptable. Instead of meeting life and all that it brings without expectation, entanglement, or shirking, the mind creates a standard whereby it divides life into opposites—one of which is regarded as acceptable and the other as not acceptable.

Acceptable and unacceptable

Of the opposites created by the human mind, the division between good and bad is spiritually most significant. It is based upon man's desire to be free from the limitation of all desires. Those experiences and actions that increase the fetters of desire are bad, and those experiences and actions that tend to emancipate the mind from limiting desires are good. Since good experiences and actions also exist in relation to desire, they also bind in the same way as do bad experiences and actions. All binding can truly disappear only when all desires disappear. Therefore, true freedom comes when good and bad balance each other and become so merged into each other that they leave no room for any choice by the limited self of desire.

Even good is relative to desire

Although in humans consciousness is fully developed, one finds in it a preponderance of bad elements; since at the subhuman stages of evolution, consciousness has been chiefly operating under limiting tendencies like lust, greed, and anger. The experiences and actions created and sustained by such egocentric tendencies have left their imprints on the developing mind, and the mind has stored these imprints in the same manner as film records the movement of actors. It is therefore easy to be bad and difficult to be good. Animal life, from which human consciousness emerges, is mostly determined by animal lust, animal greed, and animal anger—though some animals do at times develop the good qualities of self-sacrifice, love, and patience. If all the accumulated animal sanskaras had been bad and none good, the appearance of good tendencies in human consciousness would have been impossible.

Man starts with animal sanskaras

Though some animal sanskaras are good, most are bad; so, at the start, human consciousness finds itself subject to a propelling force that is mostly bad. Right from the beginning of human evolution, the problem of emancipation consists in cultivating and developing good sanskaras so that they may overlap and annul the accumulated bad sanskaras. The cultivation of good sanskaras is achieved by fostering experiences and actions opposite to those that predominate in animal life. The opposite of lust is love, the opposite of greed is generosity, and the opposite of anger is tolerance or patience. By trying to dwell in love, generosity, and tolerance, man can erase the tendencies of lust, greed, and anger.

Need for cultivating good sanskaras

The general process of freeing oneself from the limitation of sanskaras has therefore to be accompanied by the process of renouncing the bad for the good. But whether a person happens to be good or bad at any given time is dependent upon the inexorable operation of his sanskaras. From this point of view the sinner and the saint are both what they are according to the laws operative in the universe. They have both the same beginning and the same end.

Sinner and saint

The sinner need not have the stigma of eternal degradation, and the saint need not have pride in his moral attainments. No one, however saintly he may be, has attained the heights of moral virtues except after a life of moral failings; and no one is so bad as to be unable to improve and become good. Everyone, no matter how depraved, can gradually become better and better until he becomes the best example for all mankind. There is always hope for everyone; no one is utterly lost, and none need despair. It remains true, however, that the way to divinity lies through the renunciation of evil in favor of good.

The gradual unfoldment of good brings in its train love, generosity, and peace. The good sanskaras deposited by the manifestations of these qualities overlap and balance the opposite bad sanskaras of lust, greed, and anger. When there is an exact balancing and overlapping of good and bad sanskaras, there is at once a termination of both types and the precipitation of consciousness from a state of bondage to a state of Freedom. The credit and debit sides must be exactly equal to each other if the account is to be closed. But usually either the debit side is greater or the credit side is greater, and the account is kept running.

Limited self lives in good sanskaras as well as bad

It is important to note that the account is kept running not only by an excess of the debit side, but also by an excess of the credit side. It can be closed only when the two sides balance each other. In the field of sanskaras such balance is a rare happening because at any particular time, either the good or bad sanskaras are predominant. Just as the account can be kept running by an excess on either the debit or credit side, the life of the limited self is prolonged and sustained through the excess of either bad or good sanskaras. The limited self can linger through good as well as bad sanskaras. What is required for its final extinction is an exact balancing and overlapping of the bad and good sanskaras.

The problem of the exact balancing and overlapping of the good and bad sanskaras is not a mathematical problem of matching equal amounts. If it were purely a question of equal quantities it could be solved solely through the persistent accumulation of the good sanskaras. If there is a cessation or slowing down of the accumulation of bad sanskaras and if, side by side, there is an unceasing accumulation of good sanskaras at a greater rate, sooner or later the good would be a quantitative match for the accumulated bad; and they would effect the necessary balancing. For emancipation of consciousness, the good and bad sanskaras have not only to balance each other in strength, but there has to be a point to point overlapping of the one opposite by the other. So, in a sense, the problem before each center of consciousness is a specific problem relating to the qualitative variety of the nature of accumulated sanskaras.

Balancing and overlapping good and bad sanskaras

If the accumulation of good sanskaras proceeds irrespective of the specific constitution of the existing ones, there is a possibility of accumulating in some directions an excess of good sanskaras, side by side with the existence of the bad of a different type. For example, through self-mortification and severe types of asceticism, some forms of attachment might be annulled; but other forms of attachment may remain untouched by these practices and may continue to exist. The aspirant is not only likely to ignore the forms of attachment that have remained untouched, but he may even carry on further his practices of self-mortification and asceticism by the propelling force of the sanskaras created by these very practices. In such cases an excess of good sanskaras is being created without termination of the limited ego. Even if the other forms of attachment remaining untouched are subsequently undone, the ego can get transferred to these new good sanskaras and continue to live through them.

Transference of ego to good sanskaras

Emancipation is not a matter of mere accumulation of virtue; it requires intelligent adjustment of sanskaras. Each center of consciousness is unconsciously gravitating toward the final emancipation of Truth-realization, and there is a natural tendency of the mind to invite to itself just that opposite which would meet the spiritual requirements of the situation. But

Need for adjustment of sanskaras

it is not a mechanical and automatic process that can be left to itself, independent of intelligent and right effort on the part of the aspirant. More often than not, the aspirant finds it impossible to strike upon the really needful unless he has the good fortune to have the unfailing help of a Perfect Master, who alone has a direct and unerring insight into exactly what is necessary in a specific case.

Prison of the good

It has been seen that good sanskaras can be the medium for the lingering life of the limited self. When a person looks upon himself as being good and not bad, he is engaged in self-affirmation through identification with this conviction, which is a continuation of separative existence in a new form. In some cases this new house the ego constructs for itself is more difficult to dismantle, because self-identification with the good is often more complete than self-identification with the bad. Identification with the bad is easier to deal with because, as soon as the bad is perceived as being bad, its grip on consciousness becomes less firm. The loosening of the grip of the good presents a more difficult problem, since the good carries a semblance of self-justification through favorable contrast with the bad. However, in the course of time the aspirant gets tired of his new prison-house, and after this perception he surrenders his separative existence by transcending the duality of good and bad.

Good compared with evil

The ego exchanges the abode of identification with evil for the abode of identification with good because the latter gives it a greater sense of expansion. Sooner or later the aspirant perceives the new house to be no less of a limitation. Then he finds that the process of breaking through it is less difficult than the process of breaking through the former abode of identification with evil. The difficulty concerning the abode of evil is not so much in perceiving that it is a limitation but in actually dismantling it after arriving at such a perception. The difficulty concerning the abode of good is not so much in dismantling it as in perceiving that it is, in fact, a limitation. This difference arises because the animal sanskaras are more firmly rooted owing to their ancient origin and long-term accumulation. It is important to note that the good binds as much as the evil, though the binding of the good can be more easily undone *after* it is perceived as being a limitation.

The ego lives either through bad sanskaras or through good

sanskaras, or through a mixture of good and bad sanskaras. Therefore the emancipation of consciousness from all sanskaras can come either through the good sanskaras balancing and overlapping the bad; or through some good sanskaras balancing and overlapping the bad, and some bad sanskaras balancing and overlapping the good. If a dish is dirty you may cleanse it by covering it with soap and washing it with water. This is like good sanskaras overlapping the bad. Now if the dish is full of grease, one way of getting rid of the grease is to cover it with ashes and then wash it with water. Ashes are one of the most greaseless things in the world and, in a sense, the opposite of grease; so that when ashes are applied to the dish soiled with grease, it is easy to cleanse it. This is like bad sanskaras overlapping good sanskaras.

Analogies for overlapping sanskaras

When there is exact balancing and overlapping of good and bad sanskaras, they both disappear; with the result that what remains is a clean slate of mind on which nothing is written and which therefore reflects the Truth as it is without perversion. Nothing is ever written on the soul. The sanskaras are deposited on the mind and not on the soul. The soul always remains untarnished, but it is only when the mind is a clean mirror that it can reflect the Truth. When the impressions of good and bad both disappear, the mind sees the Soul. This is Illumination.

Realization free from sanskaras and beyond good and bad

The mind seeing the Soul, however, is not the same as the Soul knowing itself, for the Soul is not the mind but God, who is beyond the mind. Therefore, even after the mind has seen the Soul, it has to be merged in the Soul if the Soul is to know itself as Truth. This is Realization. In this state the mind itself with all its good and bad sanskaras has disappeared. It is a state beyond mind, and therefore it is also beyond the distinction of good and bad. From the point of view of this state there is only one indivisible existence—characterized by infinite love, peace, bliss, and knowledge. The perpetual strife between good and evil has disappeared because there is neither good nor evil, only the one inclusive and undivided life of God.

Violence and Nonviolence

Going beyond words

Man has a tendency to cling to catchwords and to allow his actions to be determined by them almost mechanically without bringing his actions into direct relation with the living perception that these words embody. Words have their own place and use in life; but if action is to be intelligent, it is imperative that the meaning these words are intended to convey should be carefully analyzed and fixed. Among the words that need such exploration, few are as important as "violence" and "nonviolence." They have a direct bearing upon the ideologies that shape not only particular actions but also the entire tenor of life.

Spiritual understanding goes beyond formulations

Spiritual life is a matter of perception and not of mechanical conformity to rules, even when these rules are meant to stand for the highest values. It implies an understanding that goes beyond all words or formulations. All words and formulations have a tendency to limit the Truth. Therefore, those who seek to bring out the spirit underlying these formulations often have to launch upon a searching analysis of the formulated principles and to supplement this analysis by constantly retaining touch with concrete examples taken from life. This is particularly true of those guiding principles formulated through the opposite concepts of violence and nonviolence.

The words "violence" and "nonviolence" are, in ordinary references, applicable to such diverse situations in practical life that no exposition of the issues involved can be complete unless it takes note of

Representative situations

these diverse situations and uses them as a starting point. However, for the purpose of exposition, it is not necessary to exhaust numerically all the possible diversities that would be covered by these words. It is enough to consider some of the most representative situations. The representative situations mentioned below have been selected because of their capacity to shed abundant light on the fundamental values that center around the concepts of violence and nonviolence.

Case of drowning man

Situation No. 1. Suppose a man who does not know how to swim has fallen into a lake and is drowning, and that there is another person nearby who is good at swimming and wants to save him. The drowning man has a tendency to grasp desperately at the person who comes to his aid; and the hold is often so restricting that it may not only make it impossible to save the drowning man but may even cause the drowning of the one who came to help. The one who wishes to save the drowning man may therefore have to strike him unconscious before he can help him. Striking the drowning man under such circumstances cannot be looked upon either as violence or nonviolence.

Case of surgery

Situation No. 2. Suppose a person is suffering from some disease that can only be cured through an operation. Thus in order to cure this suffering patient as well as to protect others from catching this infection, a surgeon may have to remove the infected part. This cutting of the body with a knife also cannot be looked upon either as violence or nonviolence.

Case of aggressive nation

Situation No. 3. Suppose an aggressive nation invades a weaker nation for selfish purposes; and another nation, inspired solely by the noble desire of saving the weak nation, resists this aggressive invasion by armed force. Fighting in defense of the weak nation cannot be looked upon as either violence or nonviolence, but can be called nonviolent violence.

Case of mad dog

Situation No. 4. Suppose a mad dog has run amuck and is likely to bite some schoolchildren, and the teachers in the school destroy the mad dog in order to protect the children. This destruction of the mad dog does imply violence, but there is no hatred in it.

Situation No. 5. Suppose a physically strong man is insulted and spat upon by an arrogant man who is nevertheless weak. And suppose that the strong man who has the power to crush the arrogant man not only desists from hurting him, but calmly explains to him the gospel of love. This action implies nonviolence, but it is the nonviolence of the strong.

Case of nonviolence of the strong

The first three situations mentioned above clearly bring out that the question whether a situation implies violence or nonviolence cannot be decided except by entering into many subtle and delicate considerations regarding the diverse details of the situation and the motive that prompts action. The last two situations show that even where violence or nonviolence is implied, certain other factors give meaning beyond the ordinary sense attached to these words "violence" and "nonviolence."

Need for delicate considerations

A detailed analysis of situation no. 1 shows that though it involves the use of force without prior consent of the victim, the motive was to save the drowning man. The application of force without the consent of the man on whom it is used may be termed a case of violence. But force is used for the good of the drowning man and not with any desire to inflict injury or harm on him; and in that sense it may be said that it is not a case of violence. In these special senses the situation can be said to involve violence and nonviolence respectively; but in the ordinary sense of the words, it cannot be looked upon as a case of either violence or nonviolence.

Comments on case of drowning man

Situation no. 2 is slightly different. Here also there is application of force (even to cutting the body), which is for the good of the patient. But in most cases the patient gives his prior consent to the operation. Further, the operation is intended not only to protect the patient himself from the further ravages of the disease but is also intended to protect others from the spread of infection. The application of force here springs out of the motive of doing unmixed good, both to the patient as well as many others who might come into contact with him. Since no harm is intended, the application of force does not amount to violence in the ordinary sense. Nor can it be adequately looked upon as nonviolence, since it is a clear

Comments on case of surgery

case of cutting a part of a living body.

Situation no. 3 is also very interesting and instructive. Here the fighting involves offering resistance to aggression, with no selfish motive or personal interest but solely with a purpose of defending the weaker nation. This may inflict much injury and even destruction upon the aggressor nation, and the use of force is not only without its prior consent but against its deliberate and conscious will. Even in this situation we do not have a clear case of violence. In spite of the injury and harm involved, the application of force is not only for the good of the weaker nation, which is the victim, but in a very important sense it is also for the good of the aggressor nation itself. Because through the resistance encountered to its aggression, it is gradually cured of its spiritual weakness or disease of having a tendency to invade and exploit weaker nations. This violence is really not violent, and so it is called nonviolent violence.

Comments on case of aggressor nation

The case of fighting with an aggressor nation is very similar to the case of surgery on an infected part of the body. In the case of fighting with the aggressor nation, the good of the weaker nation appears to be the primary result and the good of the aggressor nation (against which force is exercised) appears to be a secondary result. In the case of the operation, the good of the patient (on whom force is exerted) appears to be the primary result and the good of others appears to be a secondary result. But this is only a minor difference in benefit; and when the two situations are carefully analyzed and compared, it is found that both promote equally the good of the target of force as well as many others involved in the situation.

Comparison between aggressor nation and surgery

Defending the weak is an important form of selfless service, and it is a part of *karma-yoga*, or the yoga of action. Use of force, when necessary for this purpose, is completely justified as an indispensable instrument for securing the desired objective. But any fighting undertaken to defend the weak must be without any selfish motives or hatred if it is to have unalloyed spiritual importance. It resembles, for example, a case of a man who defends a woman being attacked by another man for vile purposes —thus saving the woman's honor and life, and punishing the attacker

Defending weak a form of selfless service

and making him repent.

Situation no. 4 is definitely a case of violence. However, it is justified because there is no hatred in it and because it is intended to promote the greater good of the children who might be attacked by the mad dog. The case of the strong man who gives a sermon instead of seeking revenge (situation no. 5) implies nonviolence, but it is not a case of inaction. It implies neither passivity nor weakness but strength and true creative action of an impersonal nature. It is nonviolence of the strong.

Comments on cases of mad dog and non-violence of the strong

The detailed analysis and comparison of the above diverse situations bring out the fact that questions concerning violence and nonviolence—their justification or otherwise, and the ascertainment of their true value or lack of value—cannot be decided by any formal enunciation of a universal rule. They involve many delicate spiritual issues and implications. A right understanding of the status of violence and nonviolence in the scheme of spiritual values requires a true perception of the meaning of the purpose of existence. Action, therefore, should not be governed by means of any slogans (however high-sounding) based upon incomplete and insufficient ideas of mere violence or mere nonviolence. It should be a spontaneous outcome of divine love, which is above duality, and of spiritual understanding, which is above rules.

Spiritual understanding above rules and requires divine love

Violence and Nonviolence Further Explained

Nonviolence

I

Nonviolence Pure and Simple
(based on divine love)

Here one sees all as one's own Self and is beyond both friendship and enmity. Never under any circumstances does a single thought of violence enter one's mind.

II

Nonviolence of the Brave
(based on unlimited pure love)

This applies to those who, although not one with all through actual Realization, consider no one as their enemy. They try to win over even the aggressor through love and give up their lives if attacked, not through fear but through love.

Violence

III

Nonviolent Violence
(based on unlimited love)

Violence done solely to defend the weak, where there is no question of self-defense or of self-motivation, is nonviolent violence.

IV
Selfless Violence
(based on limited human love)

Here violence is done in self-defense when one is attacked treacherously and with no other selfish motive. For example, when one's mother's honor is on the point of being violated by a lustful man, one defends one's mother. Also when a nation's honor is at stake and it is being attacked by enemies, the nation's selfless effort at defending itself is selfless violence.

V
Nonviolence of the Coward
(based on unlimited weakness of character and mind)

Those who do not resist aggression because of fear, and for no other reason, belong to this class.

VI
Selfish Violence
(based on hatred and lust)

When violence is done for selfish motives by an individual or nation for power, selfish gains, and so forth, it is called selfish violence.

Nonviolence pure and simple means love infinite. It is the goal of life. When this state of pure divine love is reached, the aspirant is at one with God. To reach this goal there must be intense longing, and the aspirant who has this longing to realize the supreme state has to begin by practicing what is termed nonviolence of the brave. This applies to those who, though not one with all through actual Realization, consider no one as their enemy. They try to win over even the aggressor through love and give up their lives if attacked, not through fear but through love.

As pointed out, nonviolence of the brave is practicable for those individuals who have an intense longing to attain the supreme state. This longing is not to be found in the masses. If, therefore, it is intended to lead the masses to pure nonviolence, it is necessary first to prepare them for the nonviolence of the brave. To achieve this aim in a practical way it is necessary to make them follow, in the beginning, the principle of nonviolent violence—that is, violence done solely to defend the weak without any selfish motive whatever.

In times of actual war when the masses are taken by surprise, they are not in the mood even to listen to advice about having intense longing to attain the supreme goal of life. The only practical way to lead them finally toward the goal is to begin by inculcating in them the principle of nonviolent violence and then gradually introducing the nonviolence of the brave. A premature attempt to introduce nonviolence of the brave among the unprepared masses in actual wartime would not only fail but incur a serious danger of bringing in the fatal nonviolence of the coward, that is, the masses would not resist the aggression simply because of fear and for no other reason.

The masses may also be educated and led to the nonviolence of the brave by making them follow the principles of selfless violence instead of those of nonviolent violence. Selfless violence is violence done in self-defense when attacked treacherously. No other selfish motive should be allowed to justify the violence. Thus, for example, when one's mother's honor is on the point of being violated by a lustful man and one defends her by resorting to violence, one is said to have followed the principles of selfless violence. Similarly, when the honor of a nation is at stake and it is being attacked by enemies, the nation's selfless effort in defending itself is selfless violence. A tinge of selfishness being present (as the mother is one's own mother), the love expressed here is limited human love.

Nonviolence of the coward is, as pointed out, fatal. So also is selfish violence, that is, violence for selfish motives by individuals or nations to gain power or for other selfish ends.

It will therefore be seen that while nonviolence pure and simple is the goal of life, this goal has to be attained by individual seekers of God by following nonviolence of the brave. The masses who have not the requisite intense longing for being one with Him have to be led gradually toward this goal by the principles of nonviolent violence or those of selfless violence, according to the circumstances. In conclusion, it must be very clearly understood that nonviolent violence and selfless violence are merely means of attaining the goal of life—namely, pure and simple nonviolence, or love infinite. The means must not be confused or otherwise mixed up with the goal itself.

The motive and the result are always judged by general acceptance as to whether they are good or bad. For example, nonviolence of the brave and nonviolence of the coward are both nonviolence. But from the viewpoint of the motive force behind it, nonviolence of the brave is born of *love* and nonviolence of the coward is born of *fear,* which is the opposite of love. While as nonviolence they are not opposites, their motives are infinitely opposed to each other. The motive behind nonviolence of the brave is losing one's life to gain infinite love; but the motive behind nonviolence of the coward is to save one's own life, which gains infinite contempt. Nonviolence of the coward we put therefore under the heading of "nonlove," while we put nonviolence of the brave under the heading of "love."

Nonviolent violence is not placed under the heading of love, but under the heading of "duty"—duty done selflessly to others according to karma-yoga—which eventually is linked up with unlimited love, but motivated by human love.

The difference between the two opposite forces cannot be obliterated, but the transformation of one force to another can happen when expressed rightly through the right channels. Food given wrongly becomes poison, while poison (like strychnine) given in small quantities as a tonic becomes food for the nerves. Although food in substance does not become poison and vice versa, the action and the result due to the use can become transformed.

Action and Inaction

All action except that which is intelligently designed to attain God-realization creates a binding for consciousness. It is not only an expression of accumulated ignorance but a further addition to that accumulated ignorance.

Forms and ceremonies are sidetracks on path

Religious forms and ceremonies, as well as rituals and injunctions of different creeds and spiritual institutions, have a tendency to encourage the spirit of love and worship. As such they are helpful to a limited extent in wearing out the ego-shell in which human consciousness is caught. But if they are unintelligently and mechanically followed, the inner spirit of love and worship gets dried up. Then they only result in hardening the ego-shell rather than wearing it out.

Therefore, rituals and ceremonies cannot carry man very far on the spiritual path; and if they are unintelligently followed, they create as much binding as any other unintelligent action. Deprived of all inner life and meaning, they might be said to be even more dangerous than other forms of unintelligent action because man pursues them with the belief that they are helpful for God-realization; whereas in fact they are far from being helpful. Owing to this element of self-delusion, lifeless forms and ceremonies become sidetracks on the path. Often, through mere force of habit, man becomes so attached to these external forms that he cannot be disillusioned about their imaginary value except through intense suffering.

In many ways inaction is preferable to unintelligent action, for it has at least the merit of not creating further sanskaras and complications. Even good and righteous action creates sanskaras and means one more addition to the complications created by past actions and experiences. All life is an effort to attain freedom from self-created entanglement. It is a desperate struggle to undo what has been done in ignorance, to throw away the accumulated burden of the past, to find rescue from the debris left by a series of temporary achievements and failures. Life seeks to unwind the limiting sanskaras of the past and to obtain release from the mazes of its own making, so that its further creations may spring directly from the heart of eternity and bear the stamp of unhampered freedom and intrinsic richness of being that knows no limitation.

Life seeks freedom from self-created entanglement

Action that helps in attaining God is truly intelligent and spiritually fruitful because it brings release from bondage. It is second only to that action that springs spontaneously from the state of God-realization itself. All other forms of action (however good or bad and however effective or ineffective from a worldly point of view) contribute toward bondage and are inferior to inaction. Inaction is less helpful than intelligent action; but it is better than unintelligent action, for it amounts to the nondoing of that which would have created a binding. The movement from unintelligent action to intelligent action (that is, from binding karma to non-binding karma) is often through inaction. This is characteristic of the stage where unintelligent action has stopped because of critical doubt, but intelligent action has not yet begun because no adequate momentum has arisen. This special type of inaction, which plays its part in progress on the path, should in no way be confused with ordinary inaction, which springs from inertia or fear of life.

Inaction often necessary stage

Perfection

In order to have a comprehensive idea of what is implied in perfection, it is necessary to classify it into two categories. There is spiritual Perfection, which consists in the inner Realization of a transcendent state of consciousness beyond duality. There is also perfection as expressed and seen in the domain of duality. All related existence, which is a part of the manifold world of manifestation, admits of degrees. And when one is concerned with perfection as seen in this manifested world, one finds that like other things subject to duality it also admits of degrees. Bad and good, weakness and strength, vice and virtue, are all opposites within duality. In fact, all these aspects are expressions of the one Reality in different degrees.

Two types of perfection

Thus, evil is not utterly evil but goodness in its lowest degree; weakness is not mere incapacity but strength in its lowest degree; and vice is not pure vice but virtue at its lowest. In other words, evil is the minimum of good; weakness is the minimum of strength; and vice is the minimum of virtue. All the aspects of duality have a minimum and a maximum and all intervening degrees; perfection is no exception to this. The whole range of humanity is included within the two extremes of perfection and imperfection; and both perfection and imperfection are essentially matters of comparison, contrast, and relative existence. Perfection in the domain of duality is only *relative* perfection. It is only when one

Only relative perfection in duality

compares it with imperfection that it appears to one as perfection.

When perfection is concerned with duality, it consists in the *excellence* of some attribute or capacity. In this context perfection in one aspect does not necessarily include perfection in other aspects. For example, someone who is perfect in science may not be perfect in singing, or someone who is perfect in singing may not be perfect in science. There is a sense in which excellence can be exhibited even in crimes. When a murder is committed in such a manner that not a single clue is left for tracing the murderer, it is called a perfect crime. Even in crimes or sins, then, there is a sort of perfection. But this type of perfection, which consists in the excellence of a quality or capacity, should be carefully distinguished from *spiritual* Perfection, which is not in the domain of duality.

Spiritual Perfection distinguished from excellence

The different types of excellence that are characteristic of duality are all within the scope of the intellect. For such excellence can be easily envisaged by the extension (in imagination) of something good that is found in the limited experience of everyday life. The Perfection that belongs to the spiritually realized souls is not in the domain of duality, and as such is entirely beyond the scope of the intellect. It has no parallel in the domain of duality. When a person becomes spiritually perfect, he knows that nothing exists but God, and that what seems to exist in the domain of duality and is capable of being grasped by the intellect is only illusion. For the spiritually perfect, God is the only Reality. Science, art, music, weakness, strength, good, and evil are all nothing to him but dreams. His perfection consists in the knowledge of one indivisible Existence.

When a spiritually perfect being wants to use all his knowledge and powers, it is always for the spiritual upliftment of other souls. His knowledge of others is not based upon their expressed thoughts: thought comes first, and its expression in words follows later. As he directly knows the minds of all, he is not dependent upon the expression of thought. For him words are unnecessary. If he wants to know something before it is manifested, he can do so; but he does so only when it is necessary for spiritual reasons. In the same way, if he wants to show excellence in any other matter, he can show it without any difficulty. All sorts of

All forms of excellence in spiritual Perfection

excellence are latent in spiritual Perfection.

Krishna, as the Avatar, was not only spiritually perfect but Perfection personified. He was also perfect in everything. If He had wanted to, He could have shown Himself as a perfect drunkard, a perfect sinner, a perfect rogue, or a perfect murderer; but that would have shocked the world. Though possessed of perfection in every respect, it was not necessary for Him to exhibit it in fulfilling His mission.

The spiritually perfect can exhibit supreme excellence in any mode of life that they may be required to adopt for the spiritual upliftment of other souls, but they do not do so merely to show themselves as perfect. This excellence is used by them only when there is a spiritual need for it, not merely to satisfy the curiosity of others. When they use such excellence, they do so with utter detachment. Just as a person who wears gloves may touch the dirt of the world without getting soiled, a spiritually perfect being can be engaged in universal activity without being bound by it.

Perfection must be all-sided

Spiritual Perfection is the full development of all the aspects of personality, so Perfection must be all-sided. Perfection in one aspect is not Perfection. It is only a lopsided growth of a faculty or capacity, resulting in inflexibility or the incapacity to adjust oneself to the ever-changing and multitudinous vicissitudes of life. Such a person cannot maintain a moving equilibrium of mind while keeping pace with the swift changes of life. If he is in an environment that by its nature gives scope for the faculty he has developed, he is temporarily happy and enjoys a sense of being in harmony with the world. But if he finds himself in a hostile environment where his faculty is unsuitable, he has a sense of failure and his poise is disturbed. Therefore Perfection implies perfection in every respect.

Perfection includes opposites

If you try to grasp the nature of Perfection by means of a set standard (implying an opposite), you are bound to limit it and thus fail to understand its real significance. Perfection includes the opposites and transcends them; therefore a Perfect One is not bound by any rule or limited ideal. He is beyond good and bad; but his law for those who are good provides good rewards, and for those who are bad it responds in their own coin.

Krishna proved to Arjuna, who was His devotee, that His apparent bringing about of the physical and mental annihilation of the vicious Kauravas was for their spiritual salvation. Perfection might manifest itself through killing or saving according to the spiritual demands of the situation.

The heart of a Perfect One is at once as soft as butter and as hard as steel. Perfection is not limited in its expression to any *one* of the opposites and does not exclude the possibility of finding expression through the opposite. It can express itself through either of the opposites according to the logic implied in the situation. That is why Perfection transcends the opposites and is capable of giving a rational response to all the possible situations in life. It ensures perfect adaptability without surrendering the standpoint of Truth and secures an unshakable peace and sense of harmony in the midst of diverse situations—which must be baffling to those who have not achieved all-sided development.

Full development of human rationality

Human activities are limited by the opposites, and Perfection is beyond them. It should not be imagined, however, that Perfection has no human element about it. When human beings are unhappy, they laugh to make themselves and others happy. But even a Perfect One, who is eternally happy, is not without a sense of humor. In other words, Perfection does not consist in being inhuman but superhuman; it is the full development of that rationality which is implicit in humanity.

Perfection is man becoming God or God becoming man

Perfection does not belong to God as God, nor does it belong to man as man. Perfection is attained when man becomes God or when God becomes man. The finite being who is conscious of his being finite is obviously short of Perfection; but when he is conscious of being one with the Infinite, he is perfect. That is what happens when man gives up the illusion of being finite and attains Godhood by realizing his divinity. If by the Infinite one means that which is opposed to the finite or is separate from the finite and necessarily other than the finite, this Infinite is already limited by its being unable to assert itself in and through the finite. In other words, Perfection cannot belong to such an Infinite. The Infinite, therefore, has to discover its unlimited life in and through the finite without getting limited by this process.

God's Perfection is revealed only when He manifests Himself as man. The conscious descent of God into the limited form of man is the *Avatar*. This again is a case of Perfection. Thus we have Perfection when the finite transcends its limits and realizes its infinity or when the Infinite gives up its supposed aloofness and becomes man. In both cases the finite and the Infinite do not stand outside each other. When there is a happy and a conscious blending of the finite and the Infinite, we have Perfection. Then we have the Infinite revealing itself through the finite without getting limited thereby and the finite transcending its sense of limitation in the full knowledge of its really being the revelation of the Infinite.

The Life of the Spirit

In true karma-yoga, or the life of perfect action, there is proper adjustment between the material and the spiritual aspects of life. In this type of life, consciousness is not fettered by mundane and material things, but at the same time it is not allowed to run away from everyday existence. The mind is not allowed to be immersed in the material life of gnawing wants, nor is it allowed to be merged in spiritual bliss. It is used to face and tackle the problems of life from the point of view of spiritual understanding.

True karma-yoga

Proper adjustment between the material and the spiritual aspects of life is not secured by giving equal importance to them. It is not secured by taking something from the material and something from the spiritual and then striking a balance between the two. The spirit must and ever will have an inviolable primacy over matter; however, the primacy is not expressed by avoiding or rejecting matter but rather by using it as an adequate vehicle for the expressions of the spirit. In intelligent adjustment matter has to play the role of a pliable instrument for the self-manifestation of the spirit and must not in any way become obtrusive in its own right. Just as a musical instrument is valuable only if it gives expression to the song of a musician and

Matter as pliable instrument for expression of spirit

becomes a hindrance if it does not yield complete subservience, matter is valuable if it gives free and adequate expression to the creative flow of life and becomes an obstacle if it interferes with it.

Owing to the multifarious cravings of the mind, matter has a tendency to assume importance for itself. For the drunkard wine is everything; for the greedy the hoarding of money is all-important; and for the flirt the chase of sensations is the supreme end of life. These are examples of how, through diverse cravings of the mind, matter becomes unduly obtrusive and perverts the expressions of the spirit. The way to restore the dignity of the spirit is not to reject matter but to use it for the claims of the spirit.

Spirituality requires subordination of matter, not rejection

This is possible only when the spirit is free from all cravings and is fully conscious of its own true status. When this is achieved, an individual may have material goods but is not caught up in them. When necessary he may use them as means for the life of the spirit, but he is not allured by them nor does he become restless for them. He realizes that in themselves they do not constitute the real significance of life. He dwells in the material and social environment without any hankering for them and, being unattached, is able to convert them into spiritual life.

When once true adjustment between spirit and matter is secured, there is no phase of life that cannot be utilized for the expression of divinity. No longer is there any need to run away from everyday life and its tangles. The freedom of the spirit that is sought by avoiding contact with the world and retiring to a cave or to the mountains is a negative freedom. When such retirement is temporary and is meant to digest worldly experiences and develop detachment, it has its own advantages. It gives breathing time in the race of life. But when such retirement is grounded in fear of the world or lack of confidence in the spirit, it is far from helpful in the attainment of real freedom. Real freedom is essentially positive and must express itself through unhampered dominion of the spirit over matter. This is the true life of the spirit.

Freedom of spirit expressed through dominion over matter

The life of the spirit is the expression of Infinity and, as such, knows no artificial limits. True spirituality is not to be mistaken for an exclusive enthusiasm for some fad. It is not concerned with any "ism."

Spirituality covers the whole of life

When people seek spirituality apart from life, as if it had nothing to do with the material world, their search is futile. All creeds and cults have a tendency to emphasize some fragmentary aspect of life, but true spirituality is total in its outlook. The essence of spirituality does not consist in a specialized or narrow interest in some imagined part of life but in a certain enlightened attitude to all the various situations that obtain in life. It covers and includes the whole of life. All the material things of this world can be made subservient to the divine game; and when they are thus subordinated, they become auxiliary to the self-affirmation of the spirit.

The value of material things depends upon the part they play in the life of the spirit. In themselves they are neither good nor bad. They become good or bad according to whether they help or hinder the manifestation of divinity through them.

Body not necessarily hindrance to spiritual life

Take, for example, the place of the physical body in the life of the spirit. It is a mistake to set up an antithesis between "flesh" and "spirit." Such contrast almost inevitably ends in an unqualified condemnation of the body. The body obstructs spiritual fulfillment only if it is pampered as having claims in its own right. Its proper function is rightly understood as ancillary to spiritual purposes.

The rider needs a horse if he is to fight a battle, though the horse can become an impediment if it refuses to be completely submissive to his will. In the same way, the spirit needs to be clothed in matter if it is to come into full possession of its own possibilities, although the body can at times become a hindrance if it refuses to be compliant with the requirements of the spirit. If the body yields to the claims of the spirit as it should, it is instrumental in bringing down the kingdom of heaven on earth. It becomes a vehicle for the release of divine life; and when it subserves this purpose, it might aptly be called the temple of God on earth.

Since the physical body and other material things can be used for the life of the spirit, true spirituality does not take any hostile attitude toward them but seeks expression in and through them. Thus a perfected person does not look down upon things of beauty or works of art, attainments of science or achievements of politics. Things of beauty can be degraded by being made objects of craving or jealous and exclusive possessiveness; works of art can often be used to augment and exploit egoism and other human frailties. The attainments of science can be used for mutual destruction, as in modern wars; political enthusiasm without spiritual insight can perpetuate social and international chaos. But all these can also be rightly handled and spiritualized. Things of beauty can become the source of purity, happiness, and inspiration; works of art can ennoble and raise the consciousness of people. The attainments of science can redeem humanity from unnecessary suffering and handicaps; political action can be instrumental in establishing a real brotherhood of humanity. The life of the spirit does not consist in turning away from worldly spheres of existence but in reclaiming them for the divine purpose—which is to bring love, peace, happiness, beauty, and spiritual Perfection within the reach of everyone.

Science, art, politics can serve spiritual ends

However, those who would live the life of the spirit must remain detached in the midst of worldly things without becoming cold or indifferent to them. Detachment should not be misunderstood as lack of appreciation. It is not only compatible with the true evaluation of things but is its very condition. Craving creates delusion and prevents right perception. It nourishes obsessions and sustains the feeling of dependence upon external objects. Detachment promotes right understanding and facilitates perception of the true worth of things without making consciousness dependent upon external objects.

Detachment does not mean indifference

To see things as they are is to grasp their real significance as parts of the manifestation of the One Life, and to see through the veil of their apparent multiplicity is to be free from the insistent obsession for anything in its imagined isolation and exclusiveness. The life of the spirit is to be found in comprehensiveness that is free from clinging and in appreciation that is free from entanglement. It is a life of positive freedom in which the spirit infuses itself into matter and shines through it without submitting to any curtailment of its own claims.

The things and the happenings of this earthly existence are looked upon as extraneous only until they are engulfed in the advancing tide of comprehensive spirituality. When once they find their right place in the scheme of life, each of them is seen to participate in the symphony of creation. Then spirituality does not require a separate or exclusive expression; it does not become degraded by being concerned with the ordinary physical, intellectual, and emotional needs of people. The life of the spirit is a unified and integral existence that does not admit of exclusive or unrelated compartments.

True spirituality is comprehensive

The life of the spirit is an unceasing manifestation of divine love and spiritual understanding, and both these aspects of divinity are unrestricted in their universality and unchallengeable in their inclusiveness. Thus divine love does not require any special type of context for making itself felt. It need not await some rare moments for its expression, nor is it on the lookout for somber situations that savor of special sanctity. It discovers its expression in every incident and situation that might be passed over by an unenlightened person as too insignificant to deserve attention.

Divine love a creative and dynamic response to environment

Ordinary human love is released only under suitable conditions. It is a response to certain types of situations and is relative to them. But divine love, which springs from the source within, is independent of stimuli. It is released, therefore, even in circumstances that would be looked upon as unfavorable by those who have tasted only human love. If there is lack of happiness or beauty or goodness in those by whom a Perfect Master is surrounded, these very things become for him the opportunity to shower his divine love on them and to redeem them from the state of material or spiritual poverty. His everyday responses to his worldly environment become expressions of dynamic and creative divinity, which spreads itself and spiritualizes everything he puts his mind to.

Spiritual understanding, which is the complementary aspect of the life of the spirit, must be distinguished from worldly wisdom, which is the quintessence of the conventions of the world. Spiritual wisdom does not consist in the unquestioning acceptance of the ways of the world. The ways of the world are almost always the collective effect of the actions of materially inclined people. Worldly people consider

Spiritual understanding not born of blind imitation

something to be right and make it right for persons of similar inclination. Therefore the blind following of conventions does not necessarily secure wise action. The life of the spirit cannot be a life of uncritical imitation; it must have its basis in the true understanding of values.

Selfless Service

The *karma-yogi* avoids the chaotic activity of selfish desires as well as the apparent inaction of total nonwanting. He leads a life of selfless service, in which there is not the slightest alloy of any personal motive and which furthers the release of divinity in all phases of life. It is very important that service, even when it is utterly selfless, be guided by spiritual understanding; for selfless service, when unintelligently handled, often creates chaos and complications. Many good persons are ceaselessly active in public causes through social institutions. But what does that activity lead to? For every problem it solves, it often creates ten other problems owing to the unforeseen and uncontrollable side results of such activity. Worldly people try to counteract evil through opposition, but in doing so they often unconsciously become authors of other evils.

Karma-yogi avoids chaotic activity as well as inaction

Suppose a group of ants has climbed onto the body of an individual, and one of them bites him. He might instinctively want to punish the ant by killing it; but if he were to strike it with his hands he might, in so doing, kill many other ants that were in no way involved in the biting. In trying to secure justice against one ant, he is thus inevitably drawn into an activity that means injustice to many other ants. The person who is drawn into the vortex of public life through a generous

Unintelligent service creates chaos and complications

impulse, without having mastered the art of pure service, finds himself in a similar situation. He may be selfless, but his actions create chaos instead of harmony because he has not learned how to render real and effective service without creating complications. If action is to be a pure blessing for the universe, it must be born of consummate understanding of life. Those who come into contact with me should develop true understanding of life and cultivate that type of service which creates no complications.

Selfless service based upon understanding

When service is rendered in a selfless spirit, it always benefits the karma-yogi, although he himself does not do it for the sake of any reward or result. There is no doubt that even when he renders selfless service unintelligently he derives some spiritual benefit thereby; but in doing so he cannot avoid causing much unnecessary suffering to others. However, when he renders selfless service with spiritual understanding, it not only confers spiritual benefit upon himself but also promotes the material and spiritual well-being of others involved. Selfless service must be based upon understanding if it is to be an unmixed boon for *all* concerned.

Apparent service may really be disservice

That which is looked upon as service by ordinary persons might, under special circumstances, be considered as disservice by a Perfect Master; for he has an unerring knowledge of the situation and a deeper grasp of its spiritual demands. Hence, though it is normally an undeniable act of service to give food to those who are needy, there may be some qualifying circumstances, which in a particular situation require that the needy person should not be given food for his own good. The tendency to beg for food as charity creates undesirable sanskaras; and in feeding a person who comes to you with this tendency, you may help him to increase the burden of such sanskaras. So, though you may appear to do him good by offering food, you may in reality be successful only in binding him further. Though it may not have been your motive to crush him under your obligations, you may in actuality be doing nothing else when you are charitable, not through understanding but through habit.

What applies to the above instance of giving food also applies to the dispensation of many other things—tangible and intangible. And though from the narrower point of view a thing may definitely seem to be nothing but service for the recipient, it may, from the higher point of view, be a definite act of disservice to him. Just as what is nourishing to the healthy may be poison to the sick, what is good for people generally may be evil for some particular person. Hence intelligent charity requires profound understanding of the spiritual needs of the situation.

All this should only make people more careful and discriminating in their service. It need not discourage their spirit of selfless service. It is true that only a Perfect Master can be unerring in gauging the spiritual demands of any situation; but it would be a pity if those who cannot be so sure about their judgment withheld their spontaneous urge for selfless service lest they might unwittingly render a disservice. Even when a person renders selfless service unintelligently, he always derives spiritual benefit through it.

Even unintelligent service confers spiritual benefit

In fact, from the spiritual point of view, the real danger in service lies more in the possibility of your rendering it from a false motive than in making a mistake about the spiritual demands of the situation. If you render service in order to oblige a person and if you feel proud of doing it, you are not only doing spiritual harm to the recipient of your service but also to yourself. If, while serving, you take delight in it and develop pride in doing a good thing, you are getting attached to your act and thereby binding yourself. Just as one may get bound by an iron or a golden chain, so also a person can get spiritually bound by his attachment to evil or good deeds. Hence the way to remain free from karma is to remain completely detached in service.

Service rendered with utter detachment

The consciousness that "I am obliging someone" is the first to occur during the process of serving; but it can be annulled by the contrary thought, "I am obliged by being given this opportunity of serving." This latter thought facilitates the attitude of detachment and secures freedom from the bondage of good actions. Service based upon comprehensive understanding is not only selfless and adjusted to the spiritual demands of the recipient but is rendered with complete detachment. Such service takes the aspirant to the goal most rapidly.

The value of service depends upon the kind of good secured through it. Ministering to the bodily needs of others is service; cultivation of the intellect of others is service; feeding the hearts of people is service; satisfying the aesthetic requirements of society is service. All these forms of service are not of the same value, even if they are all accompanied by a spirit of selflessness. The kind of well-being that is sought through service will depend upon the vision of the person, and one who has the clearest perception of the final good will be in a position to render the most important and valuable type of service. Those who have not found the supreme Truth are incapable of this highest type of service. Their service cannot have the same value for creation as the service of a person who has arrived at finality in spiritual understanding. In a sense, true service begins after Realization.

True service begins after Realization

Nevertheless, the spirit of service that is invariably present in aspirants and good persons can be harnessed and creatively utilized for spiritual purposes if it is allied with the work of a Master. The Master serves the whole universe out of the finality of his infinite consciousness, and those who serve the Master and obey him also have their share in his universal work. Their service has the advantage of his wisdom and insight. Willing participation in the work of the Master not only raises the value of service but creates the best opportunities for spiritual enlightenment. Service originating in the instructions of the Master is second in importance only to the service rendered by the Master himself.

Serving Master facilitates enlightenment

For most persons the idea of service is inextricably bound with securing certain definite results in the objective world. For them service consists in the removal of human suffering or illiteracy or other difficulties and handicaps that thwart the flourishing of individual or social life. This is the type of service rendered by aspirants, politicians, social reformers, and other good people. Though this type of service is of immense spiritual importance, it is in its very nature unending. In spite of what any individual might attain in these fields, there always remains much that is to be achieved. Therefore, as long as the idea of service is thus tied to the idea of results, it is inevitably fraught with a sense of incompleteness. There can be no realization of Infinity through the pursuit of a never-ending series of consequences. Those who aim at

Service free from attachment to results

sure and definite results through a life of service have an eternal burden on their minds.

On the other hand, service that comes after realization of the Truth is a spontaneous expression of spiritual understanding of the true nature of the Self. And though it also brings about important results in the objective world, it is in no way complicated by any longing for them. The sun shines because it is its nature to do so and not because it wants to achieve something through shining. In the same way, the God-realized person also lives a life of self-offering because of the basic structure of the divine life that is at the heart of Reality and not because he longs to achieve anything. His life is not a reaching out toward something with the hope of some kind of attainment. He does not seek enrichment through attainments but is already established in the fullness of the realization of the Infinite. The overflow of his being is a blessing to life in other forms and actually brings about their upliftment from the material as well as the spiritual point of view. As his own happiness is grounded in the realization of the Divinity within him, it does not suffer any diminution due to the imperfection or suffering of life in other forms; and his consciousness is not tinged by the ache of something unrealized.

Service after Realization

There is thus a vast gulf between service before the realization of the Truth and service after realizing it. The life of the Man-God is a life of service; it is a perpetual offering to other forms of his own Self. This service, which is characteristic of the life of a God-realized person, is fundamentally different from service found in the lives of those who have not realized the Truth.

The Avenues to Understanding

The different avenues that lead to spiritual understanding can be understood best through an initial distinction between spirit and matter. In order to understand matter we have material means, and in order to understand the spirit we have spiritual means. Matter is understood through the mind or the intellect working upon data given through the different senses, but spirit can be understood only through the spirit itself. This highest form of understanding, in which the spirit enjoys Self-knowledge without using any instrument or medium, is very rare and most difficult to attain. The best approach for the understanding of the spirit is through the heart and not through the mind.

Spirit not understood through mind

The mind is accustomed to work upon material things, and its driving power for this intellectual understanding of material objects is derived from lusts and cravings. When mind is turned toward spiritual problems, it tackles them along lines it is accustomed to; and in so doing, mind uses concepts it has invented for the intellectual understanding of material things. However, this approach to understanding spiritual problems is doomed to fail, because all concepts that the intellect evolves for knowledge of material things are inadequate for understanding the spirit. It is like trying to see through the ears or hear with the eyes. If the mind tries to understand the spirit independently

Concepts of mind toward matter inadequate for spirit

of the heart, it is bound to use analogues from the material world; and this inevitably leads to the spirit being looked upon as an object of the mind, which it is not.

As contrasted with the method of the mind—which has its foundation in sensations and proceeds through inference and proofs to conclusions—there is the more direct method of the heart. The heart intuitively grasps the values that are progressively realized in the life of an individual as he goes through the diverse experiences of the world, and as his attention is centered on arriving at spiritual understanding. In the life of most persons the mind and the heart are at loggerheads, and the conflict between the two creates confusion.

Conflict between mind and heart

The heart, which in its own way feels the unity of life, wants to fulfill itself through a life of love, sacrifice, and service. It is keen about giving instead of taking. It derives its driving power from the inmost spiritual urge, expressing itself through the immediate intuitions of the inner life. It does not care about the proofs or intellectual corroborations that the mind seeks while dealing with material objects. In its objective handling of the material world, mind is saturated with experiences of multiplicity and separateness and therefore feeds the egocentric tendencies that divide humanity and make it selfish and possessive. But the heart, feeling in its inner experiences the glow of love, has glimpses of the unity of the spirit and thus seeks expression through self-giving tendencies that unite humanity and make it selfless and generous. Therefore, there is necessarily a conflict between the inner voice and the deliverances of the intellect, which are based upon the apparent and superficial aspects of life.

When the mind encroaches upon the province of the heart, it does so by requiring assurance or conviction as a precedent condition that must be fulfilled before there is a release of love. But love is nothing if it is not spontaneous. It cannot be a conclusion of reasoning. It is not a fruit of the spirit of bargaining. If you want to be certain about the object of love before giving your love, it is only a form of calculating selfishness. Many persons, for example, want to be convinced of my divinity in order to be able to love me. That is to say, they want me to give them objective proofs of my spiritual status by performing miracles. Conviction of this type is

Mind craves assurance or conviction

often a hindrance rather than a help in releasing the highest form of love—which is utterly indifferent to what it might receive from the object of love.

When the mind seeks conviction or corroboration (through objective proofs and miracles as an aid to spiritual understanding), it is encroaching upon the sphere that properly belongs to the heart. Conviction and corroboration become important when a person desires guarantees for securing certain definite and tangible results in the objective world. Even if we suppose that a person is intellectually convinced of the existence of God by means of miracles or some such objective data, this will not necessarily release his heart. The allegiance he might perhaps give to God as a result of such cold revelation will be either through fear or through a sense of duty. Love in which there is no sense of restraint cannot be born of a conviction that is based upon things accessible to the mind. And where there is no love, there is no bliss or beauty of being. In fact, God's nature as the Ocean of Love cannot be grasped by the mind. God has to be known through love and not through an intellectual search for miracles.

Intellectual conviction hinders spontaneous love

That is the reason why I do not perform miracles for those who are closest and dearest to me. I would rather have no following than use miracles for convincing others of my divinity. It is true that, while loving me, people often do have spiritual experiences that were hitherto unknown to them; and these experiences help them in the further opening of their hearts. But they are not meant to feed the mental craving for intellectual conviction, and they should not be regarded as the goal.

When a person has his eye on the results of actions instead of being concerned solely with their intrinsic worth, he is trying to tackle spiritual problems through the mind alone and, in doing so, is interfering with the proper functioning of the heart. Mind wants to have all kinds of things and therefore seeks objective proofs, convictions, and assurances. This demand of the mind fetters the spontaneous outflow of love, which at once depends upon and furthers true spirituality. You cannot love through the intellect. What you may get through the mind is a *theory* of love, but not love itself. The kind of knowledge that certain types of yogis have

Spirit glimpsed only through heart

attained through their minds is merely intellectual and dry. It cannot give them the spiritual bliss that characterizes the life of love.

Love and happiness are the only important things in life, and they are both absent in the dry and factual knowledge accessible to the intellect. Spirituality does not consist in intellectual knowledge of true values but in their realization. It is this knowledge of inner realization that is worthy of being called spiritual understanding, and this is far more dependent upon the heart than on the mind. Knowledge of the intellect alone is on the same footing as mere information, and being superficial, it moves on the surface of life. It gives the shadow and not the substance of reality. The hidden depths of the ocean of life can be gauged only by sounding the heart.

Freedom from wants possible only in supramental existence

The intellect of most persons is harnessed by innumerable wants. From the spiritual point of view, such a life is the lowest type of human existence. The highest type of human existence is free from all wants and is characterized by sufficiency or contentment. Everyone is seeking happiness, but few have it; for lasting happiness dawns only when there is complete freedom from wants. This highest state of nonwanting may outwardly seem to imply inaction and to be easy to attain. However, if anyone tries to sit quietly without inwardly wanting anything and with full consciousness (that is, without going to sleep), he will realize that such a state of nonwanting is very difficult to attain and that it can be sustained only through tremendous spiritual activity. In fact, complete nonwanting is unattainable as long as life is mind-ridden. It is possible only in supramental existence. One has to go beyond the mind to experience the spiritual bliss of desirelessness.

Conditions for harmony between mind and heart

Between the two extremes of a life harassed by wants and a life completely free from wants, it is possible to arrive at a mode of practical life in which there is harmony between the mind and the heart. When there is such harmony, the mind does not dictate the ends of life but only helps to realize those ends that are given by the heart. It does not lay down any conditions to be fulfilled before an utterance of the heart is adopted for translation into practical life. In other words, the mind surrenders its role of judge—which it is accustomed to play in its intellectual queries concerning the nature of the universe—and accepts unquestioningly the dictates of the heart.

The mind is the treasure-house of learning, but the heart is the treasure-house of spiritual wisdom. The so-called conflict between religion and science arises only when there is no appreciation of the relative importance of these two types of knowledge. It is futile to try to glean knowledge of true values by exercise of the mind alone. Mind cannot tell you which things are worth having; it can only tell you how to achieve the ends accepted from intellectual sources. In most persons the mind accepts ends from the promptings of wants, but this means denial of the life of the spirit. Only when the mind accepts its ends and values from the deepest promptings of the heart does it contribute to the life of the spirit. Thus mind has to work in cooperation with the heart. Factual knowledge has to be subordinated to intuitive perceptions, and the heart has to be allowed full freedom in determining the ends of life without any interference from the mind. The mind has a place in practical life, but its role begins after the heart has had its say.

Heart must be free to determine ends of life

Spiritual understanding is born of harmony between mind and heart. This harmony of mind and heart does not require the mixing up of their functions. It does not imply cross-functioning but cooperative functioning. Their functions are neither identical nor coordinate. Mind and heart must of course be balanced, but this balance cannot be secured by pitting the mind against the heart or by pitting the heart against the mind. It can be attained not through mechanical tension but through intelligent adjustment. Mind and heart may be said to be balanced when they serve their proper purpose and when they perform their respective functions without erring this way or that. It is only when they are so balanced that there can be true harmony between them. Such harmony of mind and heart is the most important condition of the integral, undivided life of spiritual understanding.

Harmony of mind and heart implies cooperative functioning

The Problem of Sex

Element of sex

Sex is decidedly one of the most important problems with which the human mind is confronted in the domain of duality. It is one of the givens in the makeup of human nature that one has to deal with. Like everything else in human life, sex comes to be judged through the opposites, which are the necessary creations of the limited mind. Just as the mind tries to fit life into a scheme of alternatives—such as joy or pain, good or bad, solitude or company, attraction or repulsion—in relation to sex it tends to think of indulgence and repression as alternatives from which there is no escape.

It seems as if the mind must accept the one alternative or the other. Yet it cannot wholeheartedly accept either. When it tries repression, it is dissatisfied with its lot and longingly thinks of indulgence. When it tries indulgence, it becomes conscious of its bondage to the senses and seeks freedom by going back to mechanical repression. The mind remains dissatisfied with *both* alternatives, and there thus arises one of the most vital and complicated problems of human life.

Opposites of indulgence and repression

In order to solve the problem of sex, the mind must first understand that both alternatives are equally the creation of imagination working under the deluding influence of craving. Craving is implicitly present in the repression of sex as well as in its gratification. Both result in the vitiation of consciousness through lust or the desire for sensations. The mind is therefore inevitably restless in either alternative. Just as when there are clouds in the sky, there is gloom and lack of sunshine, whether it rains or not; so when the human mind is shrouded by craving there is a diminution of being and lack of true happiness, whether this craving is gratified or not.

The mind when restless with desire creates an illusory idea of happiness in the gratification of desire and then, knowing that the soul remains dissatisfied even after gratification of desire, seeks freedom through repression. Thus searching for happiness and freedom, the mind gets caught up in the opposites of indulgence and repression, which it finds equally disappointing. Since it does not try to go *beyond* these opposites, its movement is always from one opposite to the other and consequently from one disappointment to another.

False promises of opposites

Thus, craving falsifies the operation of imagination and presents the mind with the option between the alternatives of indulgence and repression, which prove to be equally deceptive in their promise of happiness. However, in spite of alternate and repeated disappointment in indulgence as well as in repression, the mind usually does not renounce the cause of unhappiness, which is craving. Hence, while experiencing disappointment in repression, it is easily susceptible to the false promise of gratification; and while experiencing disappointment in gratification, it is easily susceptible to the false promise of purely mechanical repression.

Renunciation of craving through awakening

This is like moving within a cage. The gateway to the spiritual path of internal and spontaneous renunciation of craving remains closed for those who have not the good fortune to be awakened by a Perfect Master. True awakening is the entering into the path of wisdom—which, in course of time, surely leads to the freedom and abiding happiness of life eternal. Internal and spontaneous renunciation of craving is as different from mechanical repression as it is from indulgence. Mind turns to the mechanical repression of craving because of disappointment, but it turns to internal and spontaneous renunciation of craving because of disillusionment or awakening.

The need for indulgence or mechanical repression arises only when the nature of craving is not clearly grasped. When aspirants become fully awake to the inevitable bondage and suffering entailed by craving, they begin voluntarily to disburden themselves of craving through intelligent understanding. The question of indulgence or repression arises only when there is craving. The need for both vanishes with the complete disappearance of craving. When the mind is free from craving, the mind can no longer be moved by the false promises of indulgence or mechanical repression.

Understanding craving

However, it should be borne in mind that the life of freedom is nearer to the life of restraint than to the life of indulgence (though in quality it is essentially different from both). Hence for aspirants, a life of strict celibacy is preferable to married life, if restraint comes to them easily without undue sense of self-repression. Such restraint is difficult for most persons and sometimes impossible, and for them married life is decidedly more helpful than a life of celibacy. For ordinary persons, married life is undoubtedly advisable unless they have a special aptitude for celibacy.

Restraint nearer to freedom than indulgence

Just as the life of celibacy requires and calls forth the development of many virtues, married life in turn also nourishes the growth of many spiritual qualities of utmost importance. The value of celibacy lies in the habit of restraint and the sense of detachment and independence it gives. But as long as the mind is not altogether free from craving, there is no true freedom. In the same way, the value of marriage lies in the lessons of mutual adjustment and the sense of unity with the other. True union or dissolution of duality is possible, however, only through divine love, which can never dawn as long as there is the slightest shadow of lust or craving in the mind. Only by treading the path of inner and spontaneous renunciation of craving is it possible to attain true freedom and unity.

Possibilities of celibacy or marriage

For those who are celibate as well as for married persons, the path of inner life is the same. When aspirants are drawn by the Truth, they long for nothing else; and as the Truth increasingly comes within their ken, they gradually disburden themselves of craving. Whether in celibacy or in marriage, they are no longer swayed by the deceptive promises of indulgence or mechanical repression, and they practice internal and

Path of perfection open through celibacy or marriage

spontaneous renunciation of craving until they are freed from the deceptive opposites. The path of perfection is open to aspirants whether in celibacy or in marriage; and whether they begin from celibacy or from marriage will depend upon their sanskaras and karmic ties of the past. They cheerfully accept the conditions that their past lives have determined for them and utilize these conditions for spiritual advancement in the light of the ideal they have come to perceive.

Necessity of clear choice

Aspirants must choose one of the two courses that are open to them. They must take to a life of celibacy or to a married life and must avoid at all costs a cheap compromise between the two. Promiscuity in sexual gratification is bound to land the aspirants in the most pitiful and dangerous chaos of ungovernable lust. As such diffused and undirected lust veils the higher values, it perpetuates entanglement and creates in the spiritual path insuperable difficulties to the internal and spontaneous renunciation of craving. Sex in marriage is entirely different from sex outside marriage. In marriage the sanskaras of lust are much lighter and are capable of being removed more easily. When a sexual relationship is accompanied by a sense of responsibility, love, and spiritual idealism, conditions for the sublimation of sex are much more favorable than when it is cheap and promiscuous.

Dangers of promiscuity

In promiscuity the temptation to explore the possibilities of mere sexual contact is formidable. It is only by the maximum restriction of the scope of mere sex that aspirants can arrive at any real understanding of the values attainable through the gradual transformation of sex into love. If the mind tries to understand sex through increasing the scope of sex, there is no end to the delusions to which it is prey—for there is no end to the enlarging of its scope. In promiscuity the suggestions of lust are necessarily the first to present themselves to the mind, and the individuals are doomed to react to people within the limitation of this initial perversion and thus close the door to deeper experiences.

Truth cannot be grasped by skipping over the surface of life and multiplying superficial contacts. It requires the preparedness of mind, which can center its capacities upon selected experiences and free itself from its limiting features. This process of discrimination between the higher and the lower, and the transcendence of the lower in favor of the higher, is made possible through wholehearted concentration and a real and earnest interest in life. Such wholehearted concentration and real interest is necessarily precluded when the mind becomes a slave to the habit of running at a tangent and wandering between many possible objects of similar experience.

Infinity attainable through marriage

In married life the range of experience to be had in the company of the partner is so wide that the suggestions of lust are not necessarily the first to present themselves to the mind. There is therefore a real opportunity for the aspirants to recognize and annul the limiting factors in experience. By the gradual elimination of lust and the progression through a series of increasingly richer experiences of love and sacrifice, they can finally arrive at Infinity.

The Sanctification of Married Life

Most persons enter into married life as a matter of course, but marriage will become a help or a hindrance according to the manner in which it is handled. There is no doubt that some immense spiritual possibilities are accessible through married life, but all this depends upon having the right attitude. From the spiritual point of view, married life will be a success only if it is thoroughly determined by the vision of Truth. It cannot offer much if it is based upon nothing more than the limited motives of mere sex, or if it is inspired by considerations that usually prevail in a business partnership. It has to be undertaken as a real spiritual enterprise that is intended to discover what life can be at its best. When the two partners launch together upon the spiritual adventure of exploring the higher possibilities of the spirit, they cannot at the outset limit their experiment by any nice calculations concerning the nature and amount of individual gain.

Married life a spiritual enterprise

Married life almost always makes many demands upon both partners for mutual adjustment and understanding, and creates many problems that were not originally expected. Though this might in a sense be true of life in general, it is particularly true of married life. In married life two souls get linked in many ways, with the result that they are called upon to tackle the whole complex problem of personality rather

Married life utterly different from promiscuity

than any simple problem created by some isolated desire. This is precisely why married life is utterly different from promiscuous sexual relations. Promiscuous sex attempts to separate the problem of sex from other needs of the developing personality and seeks to solve it in isolation from them. Although this kind of solution might seem to be easy, it turns out to be very superficial and has the further disadvantage of sidetracking aspirants from attempting the real solution.

The relative values of the various sides of the limited personality can best be appreciated when they become intertwined and appear in varied settings and perspectives. It is difficult to discriminate between them if they appear fitfully in a disconnected series. In married life there is ample room for varied experience, with the result that the different tendencies latent in the mind begin to organize around the crystallized scheme of married life. This organization of varied purposes not only provides an unlimited field for discrimination between the higher and lower values but also creates between them a necessary tension, which requires and calls forth effective and intelligent sublimation.

Married life calls forth sublimation

In one sense married life may be looked upon as the intensification of most human problems. As such it becomes the rallying ground for the forces of bondage as well as for the forces of freedom, the factors of ignorance as well as the factors of light. As the married life of ordinary persons is determined by mixed motives and considerations, it inevitably invites an uncompromising opposition between the higher and the lower self. Such opposition is necessary for the wearing out of the lower self and the dawning of the true divine Self.

Conditions of marriage precipitate changes in inner life

Married life develops so many points of contact between two souls that severance of all connection would mean the unsettlement and disarrangement of practically the whole tenor of life. Since this difficulty of breaking away from one another invites and precipitates inner readjustment, marriage is really a disguised opportunity for the souls to establish a real and lasting understanding that can cope with the most complex and delicate situations.

The spiritual value of married life is directly related to the nature of the preponderant factors that determine its daily course. If it is based upon shallow considerations, it can deteriorate into a partnership in selfishness aimed against the rest of the world. If it is inspired by lofty idealism, it can rise to a fellowship that not only requires and calls forth increasingly greater sacrifices for each other but actually becomes a medium through which the two souls can offer their united love and service to the whole family of humanity. When married life is thus brought into direct line with the divine plan for the evolution of the individuals, it becomes a pure blessing for the children who are the fruit of the marriage. For they have the advantage of absorbing a spiritual atmosphere from the very beginning of their earthly career.

Married life must be in line with divine plan

Though the children are thus the beneficiaries of the married life of the parents, the married life of the parents is in its turn enriched by the presence of the children. Children give to parents an opportunity for expressing and developing a real and spontaneous love in which sacrifice becomes easy and delightful. And the part played by children in the life of parents is of tremendous importance for the spiritual advancement of the parents themselves. It therefore follows that when children make their appearance in married life, they ought to be wholeheartedly welcomed by the parents.

Married life enriched by children

In view of the claims that children have on married lives, birth control deserves careful attention and critical examination. The question must not be considered from the point of view of any one special or limited interest but from the standpoint of the ultimate well-being of the individuals and society. The right opinion in this respect, as in all respects, must above everything be based upon spiritual considerations. The attitude that most persons have toward birth control is oscillating and confused because it contains an admixture of good and bad elements. While birth control is right in its aim of securing the regulation of population, it is disastrously unfortunate in the choice of its means.

Birth control

There can be no doubt that the regulation of childbearing is often desirable for personal and social reasons. Uncontrolled breeding intensifies the struggle for existence and may bring about a social order where ruthless competition becomes inevitable. Apart from creating a responsibility for parents, which they may be unable to adequately discharge, it becomes an indirect and contributory cause of crime, war, and poverty. Though humane and rational considerations demand and justify all serious attempts to regulate the birth of children, the use of physical means for securing this purpose remains fundamentally indefensible and unjustifiable.

The purely physical means generally advocated by the supporters of birth control are most objectionable from the spiritual point of view. Although the physical means of birth control are advocated on humanitarian grounds, they are almost always used by the generality of people to serve their own selfish ends and to avoid the responsibility of bearing and bringing up children. Since the physical consequences of yielding to lust can be so successfully avoided through the use of these means, those who have not begun to awaken to the higher values have no incentive to moderation in the gratification of passion. They thus become victims of excessive indulgence and bring about their own physical, moral, and spiritual ruin by neglecting mental control and becoming slaves to animal passion.

Physical means remove incentive for mental control

The easy use of physical means obscures the spiritual side of the question and is far from contributory to the awakening of individuals to their real dignity and freedom as spiritual beings. Thoughtless and uncontrolled indulgence must inevitably lead to reaction and spiritual bondage. For spiritual aspirants in particular, but also for all human beings (because they are all potentially spiritual aspirants), it is extremely inadvisable to rely upon physical means for the regulation of childbearing. For such regulation the individuals must rely upon nothing but mental control.

Mental control indispensable for rising from passion to peace

Mental control secures the humanitarian purposes that inspire birth control but keeps clear of the spiritual disasters entailed by the use of physical means. Mental control is not only useful for regulating the number of children but is also indispensable for restoring to humanity its divine dignity and spiritual well-being. Only through the wise exercise of mental control is it possible for humanity to rise from passion to peace, from bondage to freedom, and from animality to purity. In the minds of thoughtful persons the much ignored spiritual side of this question must assume the importance it deserves.

Since the woman has to undertake the trouble and the responsibility of bearing and rearing children, she may seem to be affected more seriously by any possible failure in mental control than the man. In fact, it does not mean any real unfairness to the woman. While it is true that the woman has to undertake the trouble and the responsibility of bearing and rearing children, she also has the compensating joy of feeding and cuddling them. Thus the joy of motherhood is much greater than the joy of fatherhood. Further, the man must also face and shoulder the economic and educational responsibilities for the children. In a properly adjusted marriage there need not be any injustice in the distribution of parental responsibility to be shared between the man and the woman. If both are truly conscious of their mutual responsibility, inconsiderateness will give way to an active and cooperative endeavor to attain full mental control. In the event there is any failure in mental control, they will cheerfully and willingly discharge the joint responsibility of parenthood.

Joint responsibility of parenthood

For those who are not prepared to undertake the responsibility of children, there is only one course left to them. They must remain celibate and practice strict mental control; though such mental control is extremely difficult to attain, it is not impossible. From the purely spiritual point of view, strict celibacy is best; but since it is so difficult, few can practice it. For those who cannot practice it, the next best course is to marry rather than fall prey to promiscuity. Within married life one can learn to control animal passion. It is bound to be a gradual process; and in cases of failure in practicing control, the couple must allow nature to take its own course rather than interfere with it through artificial means. They must cheerfully welcome the consequences and be prepared to shoulder the responsibility of bringing up the children.

Children must be welcome

From the spiritual point of view, birth control must essentially be effected through mental control and nothing else. Physical means are under no circumstances advisable even when the partners seek to use them merely as a provisional and secondary aid, without intending to ignore the ideal of developing mental control. While using physical means they can never arrive at real mental control, though they might truly want it in earnest. On the

Physical means become addictive

contrary, they become addicted to the use of physical means and even begin to justify them.

To explain still more clearly, what happens in the use of physical means is that, while the individuals think they are using them merely as a preliminary step before mental control is fully developed, they actually get addicted to their use and become slaves to the habit. Though they may remain for some time under the delusion that they are trying to develop mental control (side by side with the use of physical means), they are actually losing it gradually. In short, mental power is necessarily undermined by reliance on physical means. Thus the use of physical means is detrimental to the development of self-control and is positively disastrous for spiritual advancement. It is therefore entirely inadvisable even for the best of motives.

Spiritual advancement through married life

In the beginning of married life the partners are drawn to each other by lust as well as love; but with conscious and deliberate cooperation they can gradually lessen the element of lust and increase the element of love. Through this process of sublimation, lust ultimately gives way to deep love. By the mutual sharing of joys and sorrows the partners march on from one spiritual triumph to another — from deep love to ever deeper love — till the possessive and jealous love of the initial period is entirely replaced by a self-giving and expansive love. In fact, through the intelligent handling of marriage they may traverse so much of the spiritual path that it needs only a touch by a Perfect Master to raise them into the sanctuary of Eternal Life.

Love

Life and love are inseparable from each other. Where there is life, there is love. Even the most rudimentary consciousness is always trying to burst out of its limitations and experience some kind of unity with other forms. Though each form is separate from other forms, in reality they are all forms of the same unity of life. The latent sense for this hidden inner reality indirectly makes itself felt even in the world of illusion through the attraction that one form has for another form.

Love pervades universe

The law of gravitation, which all the planets and the stars are subject to, is in its own way a dim reflection of the love that pervades every part of the universe. Even the forces of repulsion are in truth expressions of love, since things are repelled from each other because they are more powerfully attracted to some other things. Repulsion is a negative consequence of positive attraction. The forces of cohesion and affinity, which prevail in the very constitution of matter, are positive expressions of love. A striking example of love at this level is found in the attraction the magnet exercises for iron. All these forms of love are of the lowest type, since they are necessarily conditioned by the rudimentary consciousness in which they appear.

Love in inanimate nature

In the animal world love becomes more explicit in the form of conscious impulses that are directed toward different objects in the surroundings. This love is instinctive, and it takes the form of gratifying different desires through the appropriation of suitable objects. When a tiger seeks to devour a deer, it is in a very real sense in love with the deer. Sexual attraction is another form of love at this level. All the expressions of love at this stage have one thing in common, namely, they all seek to satisfy some bodily impulse or desire through the object of love.

Love in animal world

Human love is much higher than all these lower forms of love because human beings have fully developed consciousness. Though human love is continuous with the lower subhuman forms of love, in one way it is different from them. For henceforth its operations have to be carried on side by side with a new factor, which is reason. Sometimes human love manifests itself as a force that is divorced from reason and runs parallel to it. Sometimes it manifests itself as a force that gets mixed up with reason and comes into conflict with it. Finally, it expresses itself as a constituent of the harmonized whole where love and reason have been balanced and fused into an integral unity.

Human love has to adjust to reason

Thus human love can enter into three types of combination with reason. In the first type, the sphere of thought and the sphere of love are kept as separate as possible; that is, the sphere of love is practically inaccessible to the operation of reason, and love is allowed little or no access to the sphere of thought. Complete separation between these two aspects of the spirit is of course never possible. But when there is an alternate functioning of love and reason (oscillating in their predominance), we have love that is unillumined by reason or reason unenlivened by love.

Three combinations of love and reason

In the second type, love and reason are both simultaneously operative, but they do not work in harmony with each other. Though this conflict creates confusion, it is a necessary phase in the evolution of the higher state where there is a real synthesis of love and reason. In the third type of love, this synthesis between love and reason is an accomplished fact—with the result that both love and reason are so completely transformed that they precipitate the emergence of a new level of consciousness that, compared to the normal human consciousness, is best described as *superconsciousness*.

Human love makes its appearance in the matrix of ego-consciousness, which has countless desires. Love is colored by these factors in many ways. Just as we get an ever-changing variety of designs in a kaleidoscope by the various combinations of simpler elements, we find an almost limitless qualitative variety in the range of love owing to novel combinations of factors. And just as there are infinite shades of color in different flowers, there are diverse, delicate differences in human love.

Qualitative variety in love

Human love is encircled by a number of obstructive factors, such as infatuation, lust, greed, anger, and jealousy. In one sense, even these obstructive factors are either forms of lower love or the inevitable side results of these lower forms of love. Infatuation, lust, and greed might be looked upon as perverted and lower forms of love. In infatuation a person is enamored of a sensual object; in lust he develops a craving for sensations in relation to it; and in greed he desires to possess it. Of these three forms of lower love, greed has a tendency to extend from the original object to the means of obtaining it. Thus a person becomes greedy for money or power or fame, which can be instruments for possessing the different objects that are craved. Anger and jealousy come into existence when these lower forms of love are thwarted or threatened to be thwarted.

Lower forms of love

These lower forms of love obstruct the release of pure love. The stream of love can never become clear and steady until it is disentangled from these limiting and perverting forms of lower love. The lower forms are the enemy of the higher. If consciousness is caught in the rhythm of the lower, it cannot emancipate itself from the self-created ruts, finding it difficult to get out of them and advance further. Thus the lower forms of love continue to interfere with the development of the higher form and have to be given up in order to allow for the untrammeled appearance of the higher form of love.

Lower forms of love enemy of the higher

The emergence of higher love from the shell of lower love is helped by the constant exercise of discrimination. Therefore, love has to be carefully distinguished from the obstructive factors of infatuation, lust, greed, and anger. In infatuation, the person is a passive

Love and infatuation

victim of the spell of conceived attraction for the object. In love there is an active appreciation of the intrinsic worth of the object of love.

Love and lust

Love is also different from lust. In lust there is reliance upon a sensual object and consequent spiritual subordination of oneself to it, whereas love puts one into direct and coordinate relation with the reality behind the form. Therefore lust is experienced as being heavy, and love is experienced as being light. In lust there is a narrowing down of life, and in love there is an expansion of being. To have loved someone is like adding another life to your own. Your life is, as it were, multiplied, and you virtually live in two centers. If you love the whole world, you vicariously live in the whole world; but in lust there is an ebbing down of life and a general sense of hopeless dependence upon a form regarded as another. Thus, in lust there is the accentuation of separateness and suffering, while in love there is the feeling of unity and joy. Lust is dissipation; love is restoration. Lust is a craving of the senses; love is the expression of the spirit. Lust seeks fulfillment, but love experiences fulfillment. In lust there is excitement, and in love there is tranquility.

Love and greed

Love is equally different from greed. Greed is possessiveness in all its gross and subtle forms. It seeks to appropriate persons and gross objects, as well as such abstract and intangible things as fame and power. In love, the annexation of another person to one's individual life is out of the question, and there is a free and creative outpouring that enlivens and replenishes the being of the beloved independently of any expectations for the self. We have the paradox that greed, which seeks the appropriation of another object, in fact leads to the opposite result of bringing the self under the tutelage of the object. Whereas love, which aims at giving away the self to the object, in fact leads to a spiritual incorporation of the beloved in the very being of the lover. In greed the self tries to possess the object, but is itself possessed by the object. In love the self offers itself to the beloved without any reservations, but in that very act it finds that it has included the beloved in its own being.

Infatuation, lust, and greed constitute a spiritual malady, which is often rendered more virulent by the aggravating symptoms of anger and jealousy. Pure love, in sharp contradistinction, is the bloom of spiritual Perfection. Human love is so tethered by these limiting conditions that the spontaneous appearance of pure love from within becomes impossible. So when such pure love arises in the aspirant, it is always a gift. Pure love arises in the heart of the aspirant in response to the descent of grace from a Perfect Master. When pure love is first received as a gift of the Master, it becomes lodged in the consciousness of the aspirant like a seed in favorable soil; and in the course of time the seed develops into a plant and then into a full-grown tree.

Pure love awakened through grace

The descent of the grace of the Master is conditioned, however, by the preliminary spiritual preparation of the aspirant. This preliminary preparation for grace is never complete until the aspirant has built into his spiritual makeup some divine attributes. For example, when a person avoids backbiting and thinks more of the good points in others than of their bad points, and when he can practice supreme tolerance and desires good for others even at cost to himself—he is ready to receive the grace of the Master. One of the greatest obstacles hindering this spiritual preparation of the aspirant is *worry*. When, with supreme effort, this obstacle of worry is overcome, a way is paved for the cultivation of the divine attributes that constitute the spiritual preparation of the disciple. As soon as the disciple is ready, the grace of the Master descends; for the Master, who is the ocean of divine love, is always on the lookout for the soul in whom his grace will fructify.

Spiritual preparation for grace

The kind of love that is awakened by the grace of the Master is a rare privilege. The mother who is willing to sacrifice all and to die for her child, and the martyr who is prepared to give up his very life for his country are indeed supremely noble; but they have not necessarily tasted this pure love born through the grace of the Master. Even the great yogis who sit in caves and on mountain tops and are completely absorbed in deep *samadhi* (meditative trance) do not necessarily have this precious love.

Pure love very rare

Pure love awakened through the grace of the Master is more valuable than any other stimulus that may be utilized by the aspirant. Such love not only combines in itself the merits of all the disciplines but excels them all in its efficacy to lead the aspirant to the goal. When this love is born, the aspirant has only one desire—and that is to be united with the divine Beloved. Such withdrawal of consciousness from all other desires leads to infinite purity; therefore nothing purifies the aspirant more completely than this love. The aspirant is always willing to offer everything for the divine Beloved, and no sacrifice is too difficult for him. All his thoughts are turned away from the self and come to be exclusively centered on the divine Beloved. Through the intensity of this ever-growing love, he eventually breaks through the shackles of the self and becomes united with the Beloved. This is the consummation of love. When love has thus found its fruition, it has become *divine.*

Pure love excels all disciplines

Divine love is qualitatively different from human love. Human love is for the *many* in the One, and divine love is for the *One* in the many. Human love leads to innumerable complications and tangles, but divine love leads to integration and freedom. In divine love the personal and the impersonal aspects are equally balanced; in human love the two aspects are in alternating ascendency. When the personal note is predominant in human love, it leads to utter blindness to the intrinsic worth of other forms. When, as in a sense of duty, love is predominantly impersonal, it often makes one cold, rigid, and mechanical. A sense of duty comes to the individual as an external constraint on behavior, but in divine love there is unrestrained freedom and unbounded spontaneity. Human love in its personal and impersonal aspects is limited; divine love with its fusion of the personal and the impersonal aspects is infinite in being and expression.

Divine love and human love

Even the highest type of human love is subject to the limitations of the individual nature, which persists till the seventh plane of involution of consciousness. Divine love arises after the disappearance of the individual mind and is free from the trammels of the individual nature. In human love the duality of the lover and the beloved persists, but in divine love the lover and the Beloved become one. At this stage the aspirant has stepped out of the domain of duality and becomes one with God; for Divine Love *is* God. When the lover and the Beloved are one, that is the end and the beginning.

In divine love the lover becomes one with Beloved

It is for love that the whole universe sprang into existence, and it is for the sake of love that it is kept going. God descends into the realm of Illusion because the apparent duality of the Beloved and the lover is eventually contributory to His conscious enjoyment of His own divinity. The development of love is conditioned and sustained by the tension of duality. God has to suffer apparent differentiation into a multiplicity of souls in order to carry on the game of love. They are His own forms, and in relation to them He at once assumes the roles of the divine Lover and the divine Beloved. As the Beloved, He is the real and the ultimate object of their appreciation. As the divine Lover, He is their real and ultimate savior, drawing them back to Himself. Thus, though the whole world of duality is only an illusion, that illusion has come into being for a significant purpose.

Universe sprang into existence for love

Love is the reflection of God's unity in the world of duality. It constitutes the entire significance of creation. If love were excluded from life, all the souls in the world would assume complete externality to each other; and the only possible relations and contacts in such a loveless world would be superficial and mechanical. It is because of love that the contacts and relations between individual souls become significant. It is love that gives meaning and value to all the happenings in the world of duality. But while love gives meaning to the world of duality, it is at the same time a standing challenge to duality. As love gathers strength, it generates creative restlessness and becomes the main driving power of that spiritual dynamic which ultimately succeeds in restoring to consciousness the original unity of Being.

Dynamics of love

The Infinity of the Truth

Source of error in spiritual valuation

Most persons are under the impression that anything that can claim to have spiritual importance must necessarily be very great from the worldly point of view. Thus, to be considered spiritual, an act must have far-reaching effects or must substantially affect an extensive area of life. They are constantly judging the worth of an action by the magnitude of its consequences. Man is ordinarily so immersed in the objects of the gross world that the dimensions, magnitudes, and quantities of the gross world unconsciously creep into his estimate of spiritual worth and pervert his evaluation.

Mathematical infinity

All this confusion is due to the fact that man's mind is often dominated by mathematical ideas, even when it is concerned with estimates of a spiritual nature. But that which is spiritually great is different in kind from that which is mathematically great. The mathematical idea of infinity is constructed by imagining the collection of an infinite number of units, each of which has a fixed and identical value or importance. Actually such mathematical infinity is unreachable even in imagination, because for any imaginable number we can conceive a number that would be still greater. Each unit is false if it is taken to have separate and exclusive existence or importance. The mathematical idea of infinity thus turns out to be a product of an imagination activated by false assumptions.

Spiritual infinity is not a result of imaginative additions of the false. It is Reality itself, which is perceived when false imagination is at rest. The infinity of the Truth cannot suffer any increase through additions, nor can it suffer any decrease through subtractions. In fact, nothing *can* be added to it and nothing *can* be taken away from it, because it is all-inclusive and leaves no room for any other, small or great. It is immeasurable, indivisible, and integral.

Spiritual infinity

The infinity of the Truth remains unaffected by any changes in the universe. All that happens in the universe is phenomenal and as such amounts to zero from the viewpoint of the Truth. An earthquake, for example, is regarded as an appalling and disastrous calamity by the worldly-minded because of the immense destruction of life and property it brings. However, even a calamity like this cannot in any way touch the infinite Truth, which is at the heart of Reality. In fact, the spiritual infinity of the Truth does not suffer any limitation even if the entire universe is dissolved. Therefore it is futile to measure it in terms of what is great according to the standards of the world.

The illusion that most aspirants find difficult to shake is the belief that infinite Truth is an object that has to be attained in some distant future, and that all life is just a means for this attainment. If Truth were to be confined only to the future and not to the past or the present, it would not be infinite. It would at once become limited as an event that has its origin in time. All that life is and has, is at once deprived of intrinsic significance if it comes to be regarded as merely instrumental to some far-off event. This is definitely a false point of view.

Truth not goal only for future

Life is not meant to be rich in spiritual significance at some distant date, but it can be so at every moment if the mind is disburdened of illusions. Only through a clear and tranquil mind is the true nature of spiritual infinity grasped — not as something that is yet to be but that already has been, is, and ever will be eternal Self-fulfillment. When every moment is rich with eternal significance, there is neither the lingering clinging to the dead past nor a longing expectation for the future but an integral living in the eternal Now. Only through such living can the spiritual infinity of the Truth be realized in life.

Eternal Now

It is not right to deprive the present of all importance by subordi-

Fullness of being

nating it to an end in the future. For this means the imaginary accumulation of all importance in the imagined future rather than the perception and realization of the true importance of everything that exists in the eternal Now. There cannot be an ebb and flow in eternity, no meaningless intervals between intermittent harvests, but a fullness of being that cannot suffer impoverishment for a single instant. When life seems to be idle or empty, it is not due to any curtailment of the infinity of the Truth but to one's own lack of capacity to enter into its full possession.

Great and grand things

Just as it is not right to save up all spiritual importance for some anticipated future, it is equally not right to arrogate it exclusively to things that create much ado. The great and grand things of life are not the only ones surcharged with spiritual meaning. A thing need not be unusual or particularly striking in order to be spiritually significant. The unusual and the striking exist relative to the usual and the habitual, and they are not in themselves necessarily representative of absolute spiritual beauty.

Thus it is not necessary for an individual to give huge sums of money for a cause in order to be spiritually great. A poor person may be unable to do this and yet be none the less spiritual if he gives what he can. It is not the amount that endows the gift with spiritual meaning; it is the spirit in which it is given. In fact, a large donation may often be accompanied with pride or some selfish motive, and then it loses its spiritual value. Even a small gift, given with humility and utterly unselfish love, is endowed with much greater spiritual value.

Spiritual infinity comprises greatest and smallest

Spiritual life is not a matter of quantity but of inherent quality of living. Spiritual infinity includes in its scope all phases of life. It comprises acts that are great as well as acts that are small. Being greater than the greatest, spiritual infinity is also smaller than the smallest; and it can equally express itself through happenings irrespective of whether they are outwardly small or great. Thus a smile or a look stands on the same level as offering one's life for a cause, when the smile or the look springs from Truth-consciousness. There are no gradations in spiritual importance when all life is lived in the shadow of Eternity. If life were to consist only of big things and if all the little things were to be omitted from its scope, it would not only be finite but would be extremely poor. The infinite Truth, which is latent in everything, can reveal itself only when life is seen and accepted in its totality.

Limitation comes into existence owing to ego-centered desires and self-will. Possessiveness in all its forms leads to a life of limitation. For example, if one covets the love of someone but instead of winning the love of that person loses it to another, there ensues a narrowing down and strangling of the free life of the spirit—and one has an acute consciousness of limitation. This is the origin of the pain of suffocating jealousy. But if one looks at the situation with a heart purged of longing, the love that is received by the other will be seen in its natural beauty. In the clarity of perception that comes through nonpossessiveness, one will not only taste the freedom of nonduality but also its joy. When someone else receives that love, it is like oneself receiving it — since no longer does one insist upon the claims of a single form, having identified oneself with life in all its forms.

Freedom and joy of nonduality

In nonduality there is freedom from limitation, as well as the knowledge and appreciation of things as they are. In nonduality alone is there the realization of the true spiritual infinity that secures abiding and unfading bliss. The limitation of jealousy is like all other limitations, such as anger, hate, and cravings: they are all of one's own creation. All finitehood and limitations are subjective and self-created. With the surrenderance of self-will and ego-centered imagination, there arises a true perception of the infinite worth of that which IS.

Realizing spiritual infinity through nonduality

When the infinity of the Truth is adequately grasped from the point of view of nonduality, this understanding also becomes fruitful for the adequate solution of social problems based on duality as an irreducible fact. Mere manipulation of numbers, however clever, can neither yield the right adjustment between the individual and society, nor can it yield true harmony between various groups that come to exist within the society.

Social problems

If social claims of a general nature are determined by the considerations of a small minority, the interests of the vast majority remain unreconciled; and the majority remains inevitably in rivalry and opposition to the minority. On the other hand, in democratic countries the claims of a general nature are determined by consideration of the majority viewpoint rather than by the minority. This point of view, however, is still within the domain of duality, where the many exist; and therefore the problem of minorities remains unsolved. Since their interests remain unreconciled, the minority remains inevitably in rivalry and opposition to the majority.

Minority and majority

As long as a social problem is dominated by the idea of numbers and multiplicity, there is no lasting solution for it. The lasting solution can come only when it is illuminated by the truth of the indivisible totality and intrinsic unity of all. The One in all cannot be contacted through the multiplication of the many but only by shedding the false idea of the many. Any number, however great, is bound to be finite. Spiritual infinity is not a number, however great; it is the sole Reality without rival.

Indivisible totality

Where there are many, there is necessarily comparison between them. There is a smaller and a greater, a hierarchy of claims, privileges, and rights; and all valuation gets twisted by the recognition of gradations of different types. From the spiritual point of view all these are forms of false consciousness, because the same Truth vibrates in everyone. The unity that is experienced in Realization, however, is necessarily different from the principle of equality.

World of the many

In duality, one person may be equal to any other single person in respect to claims, rights, and worth, but can never be equal within duality to two or more persons. On the other hand, the spiritual infinity of the Truth has room for the paradox that one individual can be regarded as the totality itself. Therefore one person is not only capable of being looked upon as equal in importance to two or more persons but even as equal to all. In spiritual infinity all comparison is out of place. There is no smaller or greater, or hierarchy of claims, privileges, and rights; and valuation remains unclouded because of the unmarred perception of the One in each and all. Since everyone in creation is not only in spiritual infinity but *is* that indivisible spiritual infinity, then everyone is first in importance and no one is second.

The One in each and all

Civilization based on infinity of Truth

In social life the recognition of the spiritual infinity of the Truth will mean a challenge to individualism as well as to collectivism. It initiates a new way of thinking in terms of an indivisible totality, and it discards all the relative values of comparison in favor of the recognition of the intrinsic worth of everything. In a civilization based upon a true idea of the spiritual infinity of the Truth, there will therefore be no problems of majority and minority, of rivalry and competition, and of those comparisons and laborious assessments that so often become a shelter for pride and separative ego. Life then will be infinitely simple and integral, because the illusions that create rifts and complexities will all have disappeared.

The Search for God

Most persons do not even suspect the real existence of God, and naturally they are not very keen about God. There are others who, through the influence of tradition, belong to some faith or another and acquire the belief in the existence of God from their surroundings. Their faith is just strong enough to keep them bound to certain rituals, ceremonies, or beliefs; and it rarely possesses that vitality which is necessary to bring about a radical change in one's entire attitude toward life. There are still others who are philosophically minded and have an inclination to believe in the existence of God, either because of their own speculations or because of the assertions of others. For them, God is at best an hypothesis or an intellectual idea. Such lukewarm belief in itself can never be sufficient incentive for launching upon a serious search for God. Such persons do not know of God from personal knowledge, and for them God is not an object of intense desire or endeavor.

Grades of belief in God

A true aspirant is not content with knowledge of spiritual realities based on hearsay, nor is he satisfied with pure inferential knowledge. For him the spiritual realities are not the object of idle thinking, and the acceptance or rejection of these realities is fraught with momentous implications for his inner life. Hence he naturally insists upon direct knowledge about them. This may be illustrated from an occurrence in the life of a great sage. One day he was discussing spiritual topics with

True aspirant seeks direct knowledge of spiritual realities

a friend who was quite advanced upon the path. While they were engaged in this discussion their attention was diverted to a dead body that was being carried past them. "This is the end of the body but not of the soul," the friend remarked. "Have you *seen* the soul?" asked the sage. "No," the friend answered. And the sage remained skeptical about the soul, for he insisted upon *personal* knowledge.

Although the aspirant cannot be content with secondhand knowledge or mere guesses, he does not close his mind to the possibility that there could be spiritual realities that have not come within his experience. In other words, he is conscious of the limitations of his own individual experience and refrains from making it the measure of all possibilities. He has an open mind toward all things that are beyond the scope of his experience. While he does not accept them on hearsay, he also does not rush to deny them. The limitation of experience often tends to restrict the scope of imagination; and thus a person comes to believe that there are no realities other than those which may have come within the ken of his past experience. But usually some incidents or happenings in his own life will cause him to break out of his dogmatic enclosure and become really open-minded.

Aspirant has open mind

This stage of transition may also be illustrated by a story from the life of the same sage, who happened to be a prince. Some days after the incident mentioned above, as he was riding on horseback, he came upon a pedestrian advancing toward him. Since the way of the horse was blocked by the presence of the pedestrian, the sage arrogantly ordered the man out of the way. The pedestrian refused, so the sage dismounted and the following conversation was held: "Who are you?" asked the pedestrian. "I am the prince," answered the sage. "But I do not *know* you to be the prince," said the pedestrian and continued, "I shall accept you as a prince only when I know you to be a prince and not otherwise." This encounter awakened the sage to the fact that God *may* exist even though he did not know Him from personal experience, just as he was actually a prince although the pedestrian did not know it from his own personal experience. Now that his mind was open to the possible existence of God, he set himself to the task of deciding that question in earnest.

Illustrative story

God either exists or does not exist. If He exists, the search for Him is amply justified. And if He does not exist, there is nothing to lose by seeking Him. However, man does not usually turn to a real search for God as a matter of voluntary and joyous enterprise. He has to be driven to this search by disillusionment with those worldly things that allure him and from which he cannot deflect his mind. The ordinary person is completely engrossed in his activities in the gross world. He lives through its manifold experiences of joys and sorrows without even suspecting the existence of the deeper Reality. He tries as best he can to have pleasures of the senses and to avoid different kinds of suffering.

Ordinary person indifferent to existence of God

"Eat, drink, and be merry" is the ordinary individual's philosophy. But in spite of his unceasing search for pleasure, he cannot altogether avoid suffering; and even when he succeeds in having pleasures of the senses, he is often satiated by them. While he thus goes through the daily round of varied experiences, there often arises some occasion when he begins to ask himself, "What is the point of all this?" Such a thought may arise from some untoward happening for which the person is not mentally prepared. It may be the frustration of some confident expectation, or it may be an important change in his situation demanding radical readjustment and the giving up of established ways of thought and conduct. Usually such an occasion arises from the frustration of some deep craving. If a deep craving happens to meet an impasse so that there is not the slightest chance of it ever being fulfilled, the psyche receives such a shock that it can no longer accept the type of life that may have been accepted hitherto without question.

Occasions that provoke thought

Under such circumstances a person may be driven to utter desperation. And if the tremendous power generated by this disturbance of the psyche remains uncontrolled and undirected, it may even lead to serious mental derangement or attempts to commit suicide. Such a catastrophe overcomes those in whom desperateness is allied with thoughtlessness, for they allow impulse to have free and full sway. The unharnessed power of desperateness can only work destruction. The desperateness of a thoughtful person under similar circumstances is altogether different in results because the energy it releases is intelli-

Unharnessed power of desperateness is destructive

gently harnessed and directed toward a purpose. In the moment of such *divine* desperateness, a person makes the important decision to discover and realize the aim of life. There thus comes into existence a true search for lasting values. Henceforth the burning query that refuses to be silenced is, "What does it all lead to?"

When the mental energy of an individual is thus centered upon discovering the goal of life, he uses the power of desperateness creatively. He can no longer be content with the fleeting things of this life, and he is thoroughly skeptical about the ordinary values he had so far accepted without doubt. His only desire is to find the Truth at any cost, and he does not rest satisfied with anything short of the Truth. Divine desperateness is the beginning of spiritual awakening because it gives rise to the aspiration for God-realization. In the moment of divine desperateness, when everything seems to give way, the person decides to take any risk to ascertain what of significance to his life lies *behind* the veil.

Divine desperateness the beginning of spiritual awakening

All the usual solaces have failed him, but at the same time his inner voice refuses to reconcile itself completely with the position that life is devoid of all meaning. If he does not posit some hidden reality he has not hitherto known, then there is nothing at all worth living for. For him there are only two alternatives: either there is a hidden spiritual Reality, which prophets have described as God, or everything is meaningless. The second alternative is utterly unacceptable to the whole of man's personality, so he must try the first alternative. Thus the individual turns to God when he is at bay in worldly affairs.

God or nothing

Now since there is no direct access to this hidden reality that he posits, he inspects his usual experiences for possible avenues leading to a significant *beyond*. Thus he goes back to his usual experiences with the purpose of gathering some light on the path. This involves looking at everything from a new angle and entails a reinterpretation of each experience. He now not only has experience but tries to fathom its spiritual significance. He is not merely concerned with what it *is* but with what it *means* in the march toward this hidden goal of existence.

Reevaluation of experiences in light of posited Reality

All this careful reevaluation of experience results in his gaining an insight that could not come to him before he began his new search. Reevaluation of an experience amounts to a new bit of wisdom, and each addition to spiritual wisdom necessarily brings about a modification of one's general attitude toward life. So the purely intellectual search for God—or the hidden spiritual Reality—has its reverberations in the practical life of a person. His life now becomes a real experiment with perceived spiritual values.

The more he carries on this intelligent and purposive experimentation with his own life, the deeper becomes his comprehension of the true meaning of life. Until finally he discovers that as he is undergoing a complete transformation of his being, he is arriving at a true perception of the real significance of life as it is. With a clear and tranquil vision of the real nature and worth of life he realizes that God, whom he has been so desperately seeking, is no stranger nor hidden and foreign entity. He is Reality itself and not a hypothesis. He is Reality seen with undimmed vision—that very Reality of which he is a part and in which he has had his entire being and with which he is in fact identical.

Finding God is coming to one's Self

Thus, though he begins by seeking something utterly new, he really arrives at a new understanding of something ancient. The spiritual journey does not consist in arriving at a new destination where a person gains what he did not have or becomes what he was not. It consists in the dissipation of his ignorance concerning himself and life, and the gradual growth of that understanding which begins with spiritual awakening. The finding of God is a coming to one's own Self.

The Stages of the Path

All persons have to pass through the state of bondage, but this period of bondage is not to be looked upon as a meaningless episode in the evolution of life. One has to experience being caged if one is to appreciate freedom. If in the entire span of its life a fish has not come out of the water even once, it has no chance of appreciating the value of water. From its birth till its death it has lived only in water, and it is not in a position to understand what water really means to its being. But if it is taken out of water even for a moment, it longs for water and becomes qualified by that experience to appreciate the importance of water. In the same way, if life were constantly free and manifested no bondage, man would miss the real significance of freedom. To experience spiritual bondage and know intense desire to be free from it are both a preparation for the full enjoyment of the freedom that is to come.

Bondage adds to value of freedom

As the fish that is taken out of the water longs to go back in the water, the aspirant who has perceived the goal longs to be united with God. In fact, the longing to go back to the source is present in *each* being from the very time that it is separated from the source by the veil of ignorance; but the being is unconscious of the longing till it, as an aspirant, enters the spiritual path. One can in a sense become accustomed to ignorance, just as a person in a train may get accustomed to the

Path begins with longing for deeper reality

darkness of a tunnel when the train has been passing through it for some time. Even then there is a definite discomfort and a vague and undefinable sense of restlessness owing to the feeling that *something* is missing. This something is apprehended from the very beginning as being of tremendous significance. In the stages of dense ignorance, this something is often inadvertently identified with the variegated things of this mundane world.

When one's experience of this world is sufficiently mature, however, the repeated disillusionments in life set one on the right track to discover what is missing. From that moment the individual seeks a reality that is deeper than changing forms. This moment might aptly be described as the first initiation of the aspirant. From the moment of initiation into the path, the longing to unite with the source from which he has been separated becomes articulate and intense. Just as the person in the tunnel longs for light all the more intensely after he sees a streak of light coming from the other end, the person who has had a glimpse of the goal longs to hasten toward it with all the speed he can command.

On the spiritual path there are six stations, the seventh station being the terminus, or the goal. Each intermediate station is, in its own way, a kind of imaginative anticipation of the goal. The veil that separates man from God consists of false imagination, and this veil has many folds. Before entering the path the person is shrouded in this veil of manifold imagination, with the result that he cannot even entertain the thought of being other than a separate, enclosed, finite individual. The ego-consciousness has crystallized out of the working of the manifold false imagination; and the conscious longing for union with God is the first shaking of the entire structure of the ego, which has been built during the period of the false working of imagination.

Veil of manifold imagination

Traversing the spiritual path consists in undoing the results of the false working of imagination, or dropping several folds of the veil, which has created a sense of unassailable separateness and irredeemable isolation. Thus far, the person had clung firmly to the idea of his separate existence and secured it behind the formidable walls of thick ignorance, but from now on he enters into some kind of communication with the larger Reality. The more he communes with Reality, the thinner becomes the veil of ignorance. With the gradual wearing out of separateness and egoism, he gains an increasing sense of merging in the larger Reality.

The building up of a sense of separateness is a result of flights of imagination. Therefore the breaking through of the self-created sense of separateness and being united with Reality is secured through reversing the false working of imagination. The act of getting rid of imagination altogether may be compared with the act of awakening from deep sleep. The different stages in the process of ridding oneself of false imagination might be compared with the dreams that often serve as a bridge between deep sleep and full wakefulness. The process of getting rid of the manifold working of false imagination is gradual and has seven stages.

Gradual reversing of false working of imagination

The shedding of one fold of the veil of imagination is decidedly an advance toward Light and Truth, but it does not amount to becoming one with Reality. It merely means renouncing the more false imagination in favor of the less false imagination. There are different degrees of falseness of imagination corresponding to the degrees of the sense of separateness constituted by ego-consciousness. Each stage in the process of ridding oneself of false imagination is a definite wearing out of the ego. But all intermediate stages on the path, until final realization of the Goal, consist in leaving one flight of imagination for another. They do not amount to cessation of imagination.

These flights of imagination do not bring about any real change in the true being of the Self as it is. What changes is not the Self but its idea of what it is. Suppose in a daydream or fantasy you imagine yourself to be in China while your body is actually in India. When the fantasy comes to an end, you realize that your body is actually not in China but in India. From the subjective point of view, this is like returning from China to India. In the same way, gradual nonidentification with the body and progressive identification with the Oversoul is comparable to the actual traversing of the path, though in fact the different intermediate stages on the path are all equally creations of the play of imagination.

Intermediate stages on path are creations of imagination

The six ascending stages are thus all within the domain of imagination. However at each stage, breaking down the sense of separateness and discovering a merging in the larger Reality are both so strong and clear that the person often has a pseudo sense of Realization. Just as when a person climbing a mountain comes upon a deep valley and is so fascinated by the sight of it that he forgets the real goal and believes for a time that he has arrived at his goal, the aspirant also mistakes the intermediate stages for the goal itself. But a person who is really in earnest about climbing the mountain realizes after a while that the valley has to be crossed, and the aspirant also realizes sooner or later that the intermediate stage has to be transcended. The pseudo sense of Realization that comes at the intermediate stages is like an individual dreaming that he has awakened from sleep although he is actually still asleep. After becoming awake he realizes that his first feeling of awakening was really a dream.

Pseudo sense of Realization

Each definite stage of advancement represents a state of consciousness, and advancement from one state of consciousness to another proceeds side by side with crossing the inner planes. Thus six intermediate planes and their states of consciousness have to be experienced before reaching the seventh plane, which is the end of the journey and where there is final realization of the God state. A plane is comparable to a railway *station* where a train halts for some time, and the state of consciousness is comparable to the *movements* of the passenger after getting down at the station.

Planes and states

After entering a new plane of consciousness, a person usually takes some time before he can freely function on that plane. As there is a radical change in the total conditions of mental life, the person experiences a sort of paralysis of mental activity known as *samadhi*. When the pilgrim enters a new plane, he merges into the plane before he can experience the state characteristic of that plane. Just as a pilgrim who is tired by the strain of a journey sometimes goes to sleep, consciousness—which has made the effort of ascending to a new plane—goes through a period of lowered mental activity comparable to sleep. However, samadhi is fundamentally different from sleep. A person is totally unconscious in sleep; whereas in samadhi he is conscious of bliss or light or power, although he is unconscious of his body and surroundings. After a period of comparative stillness, the

Nature of samadhi

mind begins to function on the new plane and experiences a state of consciousness that is utterly different from the state it has left behind.

When the aspirant enters a new plane, he is merged into it; and along with the slowing down of mental activity, he experiences a substantial diminution in the ego-life. This curtailment of the ego-life is different from the final annihilation of the ego, which takes place at the seventh plane. But like the final annihilation at the seventh plane, the different stages of the curtailment of the ego at the intermediate six planes deserve special mention owing to their relative importance. In the Sufi spiritual tradition, the final annihilation of the ego is described as *Fana-Fillah*. And the earlier samadhi of the six planes of duality have also been recognized as kinds of *fana*, since they also involve a *partial* annihilation of the ego.

Each stage on path a curtailment of ego-life

Through all these fanas of ascending order there is a continuity of progression toward the final Fana-Fillah, and each has some special characteristic. When the pilgrim arrives at the first plane, he experiences his first fana, or minor annihilation of the ego. The pilgrim is temporarily lost to his limited individuality and experiences bliss. Many pilgrims thus merged think they have realized God and hence get stuck in the first plane. If the pilgrim keeps himself free from self-delusion or comes to realize that his attainment is really a transitional phase in his journey, he advances further on the spiritual path and arrives at the second plane.

First three fanas

The merging into the second plane is called *fana-e-batili*, or the annihilation of the false. The pilgrim is now absorbed in bliss and infinite light. Some think that they have attained the goal and get stranded in the second plane, but others who keep themselves free from self-delusion march onward and enter the third plane. The merging into the third plane is called *fana-e-zahiri*, or the annihilation of the apparent. Here the pilgrim loses all consciousness of his body and his world for days and experiences infinite power. Since he has no consciousness of the world, he has no occasion for the expression of this power. This is *videh samadhi*, or the state of divine coma. Consciousness is now completely withdrawn from the entire world.

If the pilgrim advances still further, he arrives at the fourth plane. The merging into the fourth plane is called *fana-e-malakuti*, or the annihilation leading toward freedom. The pilgrim experiences a peculiar state of consciousness at the fourth plane, since he now not only *feels* infinite power but also has plenty of occasion for the *expression* of that power. Further, he not only has occasion for the use of his powers but has a definite inclination to express them. If he falls prey to this temptation, he goes on expressing these powers and gets caught up in the alluring possibilities of the fourth plane. For this reason the fourth plane is one of the most difficult and dangerous to cross. The pilgrim is never spiritually safe, and his reversion is always possible until he has successfully crossed the fourth plane and arrived at the fifth.

Dangers of fourth plane

The merging into the fifth plane is called *fana-e-jabruti*, or the annihilation of all desires. Here the incessant activity of the lower intellect comes to a standstill. The pilgrim does not think in the ordinary way, and yet he is indirectly a source of many inspiring thoughts. He sees, but not with the physical eyes. Mind speaks with mind, and there is neither worry nor doubt. He is now spiritually safe and beyond the possibility of a downfall; and yet many a pilgrim on this exalted plane finds it difficult to resist the delusion that he has attained Godhood. In his self-delusion he thinks and says, "I am God," and believes himself to have arrived at the end of the spiritual path.

Fanas of fifth and sixth planes

But if he moves on, he perceives his mistake and advances to the sixth plane. The merging into the sixth plane is called *fana-e-mahabubi*, or the annihilation of the self (lover) in the Beloved. Now the pilgrim sees God as directly and as clearly as an ordinary person sees the different things of this world. This continual perception and enjoyment of God does not suffer a break even for an instant. Yet the wayfarer does not become one with God, the Infinite.

If the pilgrim ascends to the seventh plane, he experiences the last merging, which is called *Fana-Fillah*, or the final annihilation of the self in God. Through this merging the pilgrim loses his separate existence and becomes permanently united with God. He is now one with God and experiences himself as being none other than God. This seventh-plane Fana-Fillah is the terminus of the spiritual path, the goal of all

Fana-Fillah, or Nirvikalpa, the state of conscious Godhood

search and endeavor. It is the *Nirvikalpa* state, which is characteristic of *conscious* Godhood. It is the only real awakening. The pilgrim has now reached the opposite shore of the vast ocean of imagination, and he realizes that this last Truth is the only Truth and that all the other stages on the path are entirely illusory. He has arrived at the final destination.

Arriving at Self-Knowledge

When the time is ripe, the advancement of a person toward Self-knowledge comes about as naturally as the physical body of a child grows into full-fledged form. The growth of the physical body is worked out by the operation of natural laws, and the progress of the aspirant toward Self-knowledge is worked out by the operation of spiritual laws pertaining to the transformation and emancipation of consciousness. The physical body of a child grows very gradually and almost imperceptibly, and the same is true of the spiritual progress of a person once he has entered the path. The child does not know how its physical body grows; in the same way, the aspirant also is often oblivious of the law by which he makes headway toward the destination of his spiritual progress.

Progress toward Self-knowledge gradual and imperceptible

The aspirant is generally conscious of the manner in which he has been responding to the diverse situations in life but rarely conscious of the manner in which he makes progress toward Self-knowledge. Without consciously knowing it, the aspirant is gradually arriving at Self-knowledge by traversing the inner path—through his joys and sorrows, his happiness and suffering, his successes and failures, his efforts and rest, and through his moments of clear perception and harmonized will as well as the moments of confusion and conflict. These are the manifestations of the diverse sanskaras that he has brought from the past; and the aspirant forges his way toward Self-knowledge through the tangles of these sanskaras like the traveler threading his way through a wild and thick forest.

Human consciousness might be compared to a flashlight that reveals the existence and the nature of things. The province illuminated by this flashlight is defined by the medium through which it works, just as a person confined to a boat can wander anywhere on the surface of the water but can have no access to remote places on land or in the air. The actual working of the flashlight of consciousness is determined by the accumulated sanskaras, just as the course of the rivulets flowing down a mountain is determined by the channels created by the natural contours of the mountain.

Scope of consciousness and its working

In the case of an average person, the sphere of life and the stage of action are restricted to the gross world because in him the flashlight of consciousness falls on the physical body and works through it. Being restricted to the medium of the gross body, he can be conscious of anything within the gross world but is unable to establish contact with subtle or mental realities. The gross sphere thus constitutes the arena of the average individual, and all his activities and thoughts have a tendency to be directed toward the gross objects that are accessible to him. During this time he remains unconscious of the subtle and the mental spheres of existence, since the flashlight of his consciousness cannot be focused through the medium of the subtle or the mental body.

Average person only conscious of gross world

At this stage the soul is conscious of the gross world but is completely ignorant of its own true nature. It identifies itself with the gross body on which the flashlight of consciousness falls, and this naturally becomes the base for all the activities within its range. The soul does not directly know itself through itself but by means of the physical body. And since all the knowledge it can gather through the physical body points to the physical body itself as the center of activities, it knows itself as being the physical body—which in fact is only its instrument. The soul therefore imagines itself to be man or woman, young or old, and takes upon itself the changes and limitations of the body.

Identification with physical body

After several rounds of lives in the setting given by the gross world, the impressions connected with the gross world become weak through the long duration of the experience of opposites, like great happiness and intense suffering. The weakening of the impressions is the beginning of spiritual awakening, which consists in the gradual withdrawal of the flashlight of consciousness from the allurements of the gross world. When this happens the gross impressions become subtle, facilitating and inducing the soul's transference of the base of conscious functioning from the gross body to the subtle body.

Identification with subtle body

Now the flashlight of consciousness falls on the subtle body and works through it as its medium, no longer working through the gross body. Therefore the whole gross world drops from the consciousness of the soul, and it becomes conscious only of the subtle world. The subtle sphere of existence now constitutes the context of its life; and the soul now considers itself to be the subtle body, which becomes and is seen to be the center of all its activities. Even when the soul has thus become subtle-conscious, it remains ignorant of its own true nature, since it cannot know itself directly through itself but only by means of the subtle body.

However, the change of the stage of action from the gross to the subtle sphere of existence is of considerable significance. In the subtle sphere the conventional standards of the gross world are replaced by new standards that are nearer the Truth, and a new mode of life is rendered possible by the dawning of new powers and a release of spiritual energy. Life in the subtle world is only a passing phase in the spiritual journey and is far from being the goal; but out of millions of gross-conscious souls, only a rare one is capable of becoming subtle-conscious.

Impressions connected with the subtle world get worn out in turn through, for instance, some forms of penance or yoga. This facilitates and brings about a further withdrawal of consciousness inwardly, whereby the flashlight of consciousness comes to be focused on the mental body and begins to function through it. The severance of conscious connection with the subtle and gross bodies means that the gross and subtle spheres of existence become completely excluded from the scope of consciousness. The soul is now conscious of the mental world, which affords

Identification with mental body

deeper possibilities for spiritual understanding and a clearer perception of the ultimate Truth.

In this new setting of the mental sphere, the soul enjoys continuous inspiration, deep insight, and unfailing intuition; and it is in direct contact with spiritual Reality. Although it is in direct contact with God, the soul does not see itself as God, since it cannot know itself directly through itself but only through the medium of the individual mind. It knows itself by means of the individual mind and considers itself to be the individual mind, for it sees the individual mind as being the base and the center of all its activities.

Although the soul is now much closer to God than in the gross or subtle spheres, it is still enclosed in the world of shadow; and it continues to feel separate from God owing to the veil created by the impressions connected with the mental sphere. The flashlight of consciousness is functioning through the limitation of the individual mind and does not therefore yield the knowledge of the soul as it is, in itself. Though the soul has not yet realized itself as being God, its life in the mental sphere of existence constitutes a tremendous advance beyond the stage of the subtle sphere. Out of millions of subtle-conscious souls, only a rare one can establish conscious contact with the mental sphere of existence.

It is possible for an aspirant to rise to the mental sphere of existence through his own unaided efforts, but dropping the mental body amounts to the surrenderance of individual existence. This last and all-important step cannot be taken except through the help of a Perfect Master, who is himself God-realized. Out of millions of souls who are conscious of the mental sphere, only a rare one can withdraw the flashlight of consciousness from the individual mind. Such withdrawal implies the complete vanishing of the last traces of the impressions connected with the mental life of the soul. When the flashlight of consciousness is no longer centered upon any of the three bodies, it serves the purpose of reflecting the true nature of the soul.

Need for a Master

The soul now has direct knowledge of itself without being dependent upon any medium, seeing itself not as some finite body but as infinite God and knowing itself to be the only Reality. In this major crisis in the life of the soul, there is a complete severance of connections with all three bodies. Since consciousness of the different

Direct Self-knowledge

spheres of existence is directly dependent upon the corresponding bodies, the soul is now entirely oblivious of the whole universe. The flashlight of consciousness is no longer focused upon anything foreign or external but is turned upon the soul itself. The soul is now truly Self-conscious and has arrived at Self-knowledge.

The process of arriving at Self-knowledge throughout the three spheres of existence is attended by the acquisition of *false* self-knowledge consisting in identification with the gross or the subtle or the mental body, according to the stage of the process. This is due to the initial purpose of creation, which is to make the soul Self-conscious. The soul cannot have true Self-knowledge except at the end of the spiritual journey, and all the intermediate forms of false self-knowledge are, as it were, temporary substitutes for true Self-knowledge. They are mistakes necessary in the attempt to arrive at true Self-knowledge.

False self-knowledge a temporary substitute

Since the flashlight of consciousness is turned throughout the journey toward the objects of the environment and not upon the soul itself, the soul has a tendency to become so engrossed in these objects that it is almost completely oblivious of its own existence and nature. This danger of utter and unrelieved self-forgetfulness is counterbalanced by the self-affirmation of the soul by means of the three bodies, which happen to be used as the focal points of the flashlight of consciousness. Thus the soul knows itself as its own bodies and knows other souls as their bodies, thereby sustaining a world of duality where there is sex, competition, aggression, jealousy, mutual fear, and self-centered exclusive ambition. Hence self-knowledge of the soul by means of any external sign is a source of untold confusion, complication, and entanglement.

This form of ignorance may be illustrated by means of the famous pumpkin story referred to by the Persian poet Jami in one of his couplets. Once upon a time there was an absentminded man who had no equal in forgetting things, even his own identity. He had an intelligent and trusted friend who wanted to help him to remember himself. This friend attached a pumpkin to his neck and said, "Now listen, old man, one day you might completely lose yourself and not know who you are. Therefore, as a sign, I tie this pumpkin around your neck so that every morning when you wake up you will see the

Pumpkin story

pumpkin and know it is you who are there."

Every day the absentminded man saw the pumpkin upon waking in the morning and said to himself, "I am not lost!" After some time, when he had become used to self-identification through the pumpkin, the friend asked a stranger to remain with the absentminded man, take the pumpkin from his neck during his sleep, and tie it around his own neck. The stranger did this; and when the absentminded man woke up in the morning, he did not see the pumpkin around his neck. So he said to himself, "I am lost!" Then he saw the pumpkin on the other man's neck and said to him, "You are me! But then who am I?"

This pumpkin story offers an analogy to the different forms of false self-knowledge growing from identification with one of the bodies. To know oneself as the body is like knowing oneself by means of the pumpkin. The disturbance caused by ceasing to identify with the gross, subtle, or mental body is comparable to the confusion of the absentminded man when he could no longer see the pumpkin around his own neck. The beginnings of a dissolution of the sense of duality are equivalent to the man's identification of himself as the stranger who wore his pumpkin. Further, if the absentminded man in the story were to learn to know himself through himself independently of any external sign, his self-knowledge would be comparable to the true Self-knowledge of the soul—which, after ceasing to identify with the three bodies, knows itself to be none other than infinite God. Arriving at such Self-knowledge is the very goal of creation.

Analogy made explicit

God-Realization

To arrive at true Self-knowledge is to arrive at God-realization. God-realization is a unique state of consciousness. It is different from all the other states of consciousness because all the other states of consciousness are experienced through the medium of the individual mind. Whereas the state of God-consciousness is in no way dependent upon the individual mind or any other medium. A medium is necessary for knowing something other than one's own Self. For knowing one's own Self no medium is necessary.

To realize the Self is to realize God

In fact, the association of consciousness with the mind is definitely a hindrance rather than a help for the attainment of Realization. The individual mind is the seat of the ego, or the consciousness of being isolated. It creates the limited individuality, which at once feeds on and is fed by the illusions of duality, time, and change. So, in order to know the Self as it is, consciousness has to be completely freed from the limitation of the individual mind. In other words, the individual mind has to disappear, but consciousness has to be retained.

Throughout the past life history of the soul, its consciousness has grown with the individual mind; and all the workings of consciousness have proceeded against the background of the individual mind. Consciousness has therefore come to be firmly embedded in the individual mind and cannot be extricated from this setting into which it has been woven. The result is that if the

Consciousness and mind intertwined

mind is stilled, consciousness also disappears. The intertwining of the individual mind and consciousness is amply illustrated by the tendency to become unconscious when there is any effort to stop mental activity through meditation.

Explanation of sleep

The everyday phenomenon of going to sleep is not essentially different from the lull experienced during meditation, but it is slightly different in its origin. Since the individual mind is continuously confronted by the world of duality, it is involved in ceaseless conflict; and when it is wearied by its unrelieved struggle, it wants to lose its identity as a separate entity and go back to the Infinite. It then recedes from the world of its own creation and experiences a lull, and this lull is also invariably accompanied by the cessation of consciousness.

Resuming wakefulness

The quiescence of mental activity in sleep entails the complete submerging of consciousness; but this cessation of mental life and conscious functioning is only temporary because the impressions stored in the mind goad it to renewed activity. After a while the stimuli of the impressions result in stirring the mind and reviving the conscious functioning that is performed through its medium. So the period of sleep is followed by a period of wakefulness; and the period of wakefulness is followed by a period of sleep, according to the law of alternating activity and rest. As long as the latent impressions in the mind are not completely undone, however, there is no final annihilation of the individual mind or emancipation of consciousness. In sleep the mind temporarily forgets its identity, but it does not finally lose its individual existence. When the person awakens, he finds himself subject to his old limitations. There is a resurrection of consciousness, but it is still mind-ridden.

Obstacle of ego

The limited mind is the soil in which the ego is securely rooted, and this ego perpetuates ignorance through the many illusions in which it is caught. The ego prevents manifestation of infinite knowledge, which is already latent in the soul; it is the most formidable obstacle to the attainment of God. A Persian poem says truly, "It is extremely difficult to pierce through the veil of ignorance, for there is a rock on the fire." Just as a flame cannot rise very high if a rock is placed upon it, a desire to know one's own true nature cannot lead to the Truth as long as the burden of the ego is placed on consciousness.

Success in finding one's Self is rendered impossible by the continuation of the ego, which persists throughout the journey of the soul. In old age, an aching tooth can give untold trouble because it is not easily uprooted, although loose within its socket. In the same way the ego, which might become feeble through love or penance, is yet difficult to eradicate. It persists till the very end. Though it becomes looser as the soul advances on the path, it remains till the last stage, which is the seventh plane of involution of consciousness.

Difficulty of overcoming ego

The ego is the center of all human activity. The attempts of the ego to secure its own extinction might be compared to the attempt of a person to stand on his own shoulders. Just as the eye cannot see itself, the ego is unable to end its own existence. All that it does to bring about self-annihilation only goes to add to its own existence. It flourishes on the very efforts directed against itself. Thus it is unable to vanish altogether through its own desperate activity, although it succeeds in transforming its own nature. The disappearance of the ego is conditioned by the melting away of the limited mind, which is its seat.

Parallel between sleep and God-realization

The problem of God-realization is the problem of emancipating consciousness from the limitations of the mind. When the individual mind is dissolved, the whole universe relative to the mind vanishes into nothingness; and consciousness is no longer tied to anything. Consciousness is now unlimited and unclouded by anything and serves the purpose of illumining the state of infinite Reality. While immersed in the bliss of Realization, the soul is completely oblivious of sights or sounds or objects in the universe. In this respect it is like sound sleep, but there is an infinite difference that distinguishes God-realization from sound sleep.

During sleep the illusion of the universe vanishes, since all consciousness is in abeyance; but there is no conscious experience of God, since this requires the complete dissolution of the ego and the turning of full consciousness toward the ultimate Reality. Occasionally, when the continuity of deep sleep is interrupted for brief intervals, one may have the experience of retaining consciousness without being conscious of anything in particular. There is consciousness, but this consciousness is not of the universe. It is consciousness of *nothing*.

Such experiences parallel those of God-realization, in which consciousness is completely freed from the illusion of the universe and manifests the infinite knowledge that was hitherto hidden by the ego.

Difference between sleep and God-realization

In sleep, the individual mind continues to exist, although it has forgotten everything including itself; and the latent impressions in the mind create a veil between the submerged consciousness and infinite Reality. Thus during sleep, consciousness is submerged in the shell of the individual mind; but it has not yet been able to escape from that shell. Though the soul has forgotten its separateness from God and has actually attained unity with Him, it is unconscious of this unity. In God-realization, however, the mind does not merely forget itself but has (with all its impressions) actually lost its identity. The consciousness, which was hitherto associated with the individual mind, is now freed and untrammeled and brought into direct contact and unity with the ultimate Reality. Since there is now no veil between consciousness and the ultimate Reality, consciousness is fused with the Absolute and eternally abides in it as an inseparable aspect, promoting an unending state of infinite knowledge and unlimited bliss.

God-realization a personal attainment

The manifestation of infinite knowledge and unlimited bliss in consciousness is, however, strictly confined to the soul that has attained God-realization. The infinite Reality in the God-realized soul has explicit knowledge of its own infinity. Such explicit knowledge is not experienced by the unrealized soul, which is still subject to the illusion of the universe. Thus if God-realization were not a personal attainment of the soul, the entire universe would come to an end as soon as any one soul achieved God-realization. This does not happen because God-realization is a personal state of consciousness belonging to the soul that has transcended the domain of the mind. Other souls continue to remain in bondage, and they can only attain Realization by freeing their consciousness from the burden of the ego and the limitations of the individual mind. Hence the attainment of God-realization has direct significance only for the soul that has emerged out of the time process.

After the attainment of God-realization, the soul discovers that it has always been the infinite Reality that it now knows itself to be, and that its regarding itself as finite during the period of evolution and spiritual advancement was in fact an illusion. The soul also finds out that the infinite knowledge and bliss it now enjoys have also been latent in the infinite Reality from the very beginning of time, and that they merely became manifest at the moment of Realization. Thus the God-realized person does not actually become something different from what he was before Realization. He remains what he was; and the only difference Realization makes in him is that previously he did not consciously know his own true nature, and now he knows it. He knows that he has never been anything other than what he now knows himself to be, and that all he has been through was but the process of finding his Self.

What was latent in Infinite becomes manifest

The whole process of attaining God-realization is just a game in which the beginning and the end are identical. The attainment of Realization is nevertheless a distinct gain for the soul. In general there are two types of advantages: one consists in getting what one did not previously possess, the other in realizing fully what one really is. God-realization is of the second type. However, this creates an infinite difference between the soul that has attained God-realization and the soul that has not. Though the God-realized soul does not possess anything new, its explicit knowledge of all that it really is, has been, and will ever be, makes God-realization all-important. The soul that is not God-realized experiences itself as being finite and is constantly troubled by the opposites of fleeting joys and sorrows. But the soul that has Realization is lifted out of them and experiences the infinite knowledge and the unlimited bliss of being God-conscious.

Two types of advantages

In God-realization the soul drops its separate consciousness and transcends duality in the abiding knowledge of its identity with the infinite Reality. The shackles of limited individuality are broken; the world of shadows is at an end; the curtain of Illusion is forever drawn. The feverishness and the agonizing distress of the pursuits of limited consciousness are replaced by the tranquility and bliss of Truth-consciousness. The restlessness and fury of temporal existence are swallowed up in the peace and stillness of Eternity.

Value of God-realization

True Discipleship

When an aspirant becomes voluntarily affiliated with a Master, he is said to have become a disciple. But if this affiliation is merely formal, it does not constitute true discipleship. The relationship between disciple and Master is utterly different, for example, from the legal relations that create rights and liabilities through verbal transactions or formal agreements. Discipleship is one of the fundamental features that characterize the life of the advanced aspirant, and it does not come into existence through any artificial procedure. It arises out of the basic laws of spiritual life. It is therefore much more significant than the mundane relations that arise within the context of ordinary social life as a result of incidental associations or temporary contracts. Many of these mundane relations do not enter into the spiritual fabric of the life of the aspirant but remain superficially attached to his being.

Discipleship a vital bond

Thus it is not of any great consequence whether you purchase a thing from one shopkeeper or another as long as you pay the price for it; and it is immaterial whether you travel by one ship or another so long as you arrive at your destination. Even such transactions are no doubt inwardly determined by sanskaric ties and karmic laws, and therefore are not entirely devoid of spiritual significance. But these relations are in their very nature provisional and superficial, and are in no way comparable to the vital bond of discipleship, which gives substance and direction to the life of the aspirant.

The relationship between Perfect Master and disciple is an inevitable outcome of intrinsic conditions in the life of the aspirant. It is primarily a relationship between the lover and his divine Beloved.

Love constitutes core of discipleship

From the spiritual point of view it is the most important relationship into which a person can enter. The love that constitutes the core of discipleship stands by itself among the different types of love that prevail in ordinary social relations. Mundane love is an interplay between two centers of the God-unconscious; whereas the love implied in discipleship is the love of the God-unconscious for the God-conscious. Everyone is God; but some are unconscious of their divinity, some are partly conscious of their divinity, and a few are fully God-conscious. Those who are unconscious of their divinity can have no idea of the God state; they are only conscious of the body state. In order for them to inherit the God state, they have to love, worship, and be guided by the Master, who is constantly dwelling in the God state.

The love that the aspirant has for the Master is really the response evoked by the greater love the Master has for the aspirant. It is to be placed above all other loves. Love for the Master naturally

Supreme claim of Master

becomes a central power in the life of the aspirant because he knows the Master to be an embodiment and representation of infinite God. All his thoughts and aspirations therefore come to be woven around the personality of the Master. The Master thus has unquestioned supremacy among the claims recognized by the aspirant; and it is through this supremacy that the Master becomes the focal point for the radiation of spiritual forces — which dispel all darkness, pluck out the sins of the heart, and initiate the aspirant into a life of freedom and Truth-consciousness.

The fundamental requisite for the candidate who would be a true disciple is an unquestioning love for the Master. All the other streams

All love leads to Master, as in story of Majnun and Layla

of love ultimately join this great river of love for the Master and disappear in it; this is illustrated by the story of Majnun and Layla. Majnun loved Layla so intensely that every moment of his life he was filled with thoughts about her. He could not eat, drink, or sleep without thinking of her; and all he wanted was Layla's happiness. He would gladly have seen her married to some other person if he felt it to be in her interest, and he would even have died for her husband if he had thought she would thereby be happy. The utter self-denial and sincerity of his love ultimately led him to his Master. Every second of his life Majnun thought not of himself but of his beloved, and this lifted his love from the physical or intellectual level and made it spiritual. The spiritualization of his love led him to the divine Beloved.

Purification through love and surrender

The Master is the divine Beloved; and when the disciple meets his Master, all that he has to do is to love him. For if the disciple loves the Master out of the fullness of his heart, his final union with him is assured. He need not worry about the quality of his love. He should love in spite of his weaknesses and not tarry till he can purify his own heart. The Master is the very source of purity, and to set one's heart on the Master is the beginning of self-purification. When the disciple has wholehearted devotion for the Master, he opens himself to the reception of the divine love that the Master pours upon him. All his weaknesses are consumed in this fire of divine love of which he thus becomes the recipient. If the disciple is to be free from all weaknesses and attain incorruptible and infinite purity, he has to dedicate his life to the Master without any reservations or provisions. He must offer his weaknesses as well as his strengths, his vices as well as his virtues. There should be no ifs and buts about his offering. His self-surrender must be so complete as to allow no room in his mind for even a shadow of any secret self-desire.

Value of faith

Complete self-surrender and unquestioning love become possible when the disciple achieves unswerving faith in the Master. Faith in the Master is an indispensable part of true discipleship. Once God is realized there is no question of faith at all, just as there is no question of faith when a man knows himself to be a man. But till this state of Realization is attained, the faith that the disciple places in the Master is his most reliable guiding light and is comparable to the rudder of a ship. It is not correct to describe faith as being blind, for it is more like sight than like unrelieved ignorance; nonetheless faith is short of direct experience until the aspirant realizes God for himself.

It is not for nothing that all the religions are referred to as "faiths." One of the essentials of the aspirant's life is that he should have faith. Faith may express itself through diverse forms, but from the psychological point of view they are one and the same thing and cannot be diversely labeled. The only differences in faith are differences of degree. Faith may be strong and vital, or weak and lukewarm. A weak and lukewarm faith does not carry a person further than adherence to rituals and ceremonies; but a strong and vital faith is bound to take the aspirant beyond the external forms of religion, helping him to eschew the husk and get at the kernel of true spiritual life. Faith reaches its natural climax and goal when it comes to rest in one's own Master.

The faith of the disciple must always be securely grounded in his experience of the divinity of the Master. He must not be like a straw carried anywhere by the slightest breeze. He should be like a rock that remains unmoved in the severest of storms.

Story of Kalyan

The story of Kalyan brings out the meaning of a really sound faith in the Master. Kalyan was a disciple of Swami Ramdas Samarth, who was a Perfect Master at the time of Shivaji. A Master loves all disciples alike, but some might be particularly dear to him—just as an individual loves all parts of his body, though the eyes may be more dear to him than his fingers. Swami Ramdas Samarth had many disciples, but his favorite was Kalyan. The other disciples did not quite understand why Kalyan should be dearer to the Master than the others.

One day Swami Ramdas tested the devotion of his disciples. He asked all his disciples to come to him and pretended to be so sick as to be on the point of death. He had placed a mango on the joint of his knee and bound it in a bandage so that it looked like a huge swelling. Swami Ramdas pointed to this swelling and told the disciples that it was a malignant tumor and that there was no chance of his living unless someone sucked the poison from the joint of his knee. At the same time, he made it clear to all that whoever sucked out the poison would die instantaneously. Then he asked whether any disciple was prepared to suck out the poison from the swelling at the cost of his own life. All the disciples hesitated except Kalyan, who arose immediately and began to suck from the swelling. To his surprise Kalyan found sweet mango juice and not poison, and Swami Ramdas praised his unswerving faith and self-denying love. To be willing to die for the happiness of the Beloved is true love. Such implicit faith, unfaltering love, and undivided loyalty as that of Kalyan can come to the disciple only through the grace of the Master.

Undivided loyalty to the Master does not introduce any narrowness in the sphere of the disciple's life. To serve the Master is to serve one's own Self in every other self. The Master dwells in universal consciousness and wills universal spiritual well-being. To serve the Master is therefore to participate in his cause, which is to serve all life. While sharing in the work of the Master, the disciple may be required to be in touch with the world. But though moving in the world in accordance with the work allotted him, he is in inward contact with the Master as infinite Being. Therefore, by sharing in the work of the Master, the disciple comes closer to him and becomes an integral part of his consciousness. Serving the Master is the quickest means of realizing him.

Master realized by serving him

The service that the disciple can offer the Master is not only linked with the universal cause of humanity but is one of the most potent means of bringing the disciple nearer his spiritual goal. When the disciple's service is spontaneous, wholehearted, selfless, and unconditional, it brings him more spiritual benefit than can ever come by any other means. Serving the Master is a joy for the disciple, even when it means an ordeal that tries his body or mind. Service offered under conditions of discomfort or inconvenience is a test of the disciple's devotion. The more trying such service becomes, the more welcome it is for the disciple. And as he voluntarily accepts physical and mental suffering in his devoted service to the Master, he experiences the bliss of spiritual fulfillment.

Sharing work of Master

The sense of undivided and absolute loyalty to the Master is made possible by the right understanding of what the Master is and what he really stands for. If the disciple has an imperfect grasp of the true status and function of the Master, he is likely to set up a false antithesis between his own higher Self and the Master. As a consequence of this antithesis, he might create in his mind an artificial and imaginary conflict between the claims of the Master and other claims that seem legitimate. A disciple should be aware from the very beginning that the Master only requires the disciple to realize his own higher Self. In fact, the Master symbolizes this higher Self of the disciple and is none other than this higher Self, which is the same one

Allegiance to Master

Reality in all.

Thus allegiance to the Master is only another form of allegiance to one's higher Self. This does not mean, however, that merely formal allegiance to the higher Self is in any way an adequate substitute for allegiance to the Master. The disciple cannot have a clear perception of his own higher Self until he is God-realized; and often that which comes to him as his duty is really a prompting of some sanskaras interpolating themselves between the higher Self and his field of consciousness. The Master, on the contrary, is one with the higher Self and can make no mistake about right valuation.

The disciple therefore must always test his own promptings by means of the standards or orders given by the Master. In the event of any conflict between the two, he should thoroughly reexamine his own ideas to discover the points wherein they might be short of perfection. Almost always a little reflection is sufficient to perceive the basic harmony between the true dictates of his own higher Self and the requirements of the Master.

Cases of conflict

If, however, on some rare occasion the disciple is unable to reconcile the two, he may be sure that he has either not properly understood the dictates of his own higher Self or that he has not properly grasped the import of his Master's requirements. In such cases the Master gives latitude to the disciple to follow his own conscience. The Master may sometimes give instructions with the intent of preparing his disciple for a higher mode of life. It is under such circumstances that the disciple finds himself confronted by an apparent and temporary variance between his own inclinations and the Master's instructions. But usually the Master does not give any instructions for which the disciple has not had inward anticipatory preparation.

The Master is supremely impersonal, and always his only concern is to remove the veils between the consciousness of the disciple and his higher Self. Therefore there can never be any real conflict between the allegiance of the disciple to his Master and his allegiance to his own higher Self. Indeed, at the end of his search the disciple discovers that the Master is none other than his own higher Self in another form. The Master in his utter impersonality and unhampered divinity is so complete that he has no desire. In relation to the disciple all he requires is that the

Meaning of true discipleship

disciple reconstitute himself in the light of the highest Truth. To become a disciple is to begin to tread the path leading toward the spiritual goal. This is the meaning of true discipleship.

The Ways of the Masters

Masters ever ready to help

Masters are absolutely impersonal and universal in their consciousness, but for spiritual purposes they can limit the scope of their work and also allow their manifested personality to become the center of the aspirations of their disciples. They use personal relationships as well-defined channels to pass on their help to those aspirants who become connected with them. The Masters are always on the lookout for those who need and deserve their help, and the faintest gleams of spiritual yearnings are not overlooked by them. They foster and promote the advancement of all aspirants in multifarious ways that are unfailingly effective, although they might not necessarily be completely intelligible to others.

Nature of their help

The help of a Perfect Master consists in making the spiritual journey of the aspirant sure and safe, as well as in shortening the time he might otherwise take to arrive at the goal. The aspirant may go a long way through independent search, but he is unable to cross the sixth plane without the help of a Master. Even on the intermediate planes of involution of consciousness, the help of a Master is extremely valuable because he prevents the aspirant from getting stuck on the way and protects him from the pitfalls and dangers with which the spiritual path is beset. Kabir, the Perfect Master, has compared the three stages of the path to the three phases of fire. Just as first there is only smoke and no fire, then there is fire enveloped in smoke, and lastly there is only fire without smoke, so the beginnings of the path are enveloped in thick ignorance, midway there is confused perception of the goal, and finally there is realization of Truth without the slightest alloy of illusion. Since the path lies through illusions of many kinds, the aspirant is never safe without the guidance of a Master, who knows all the stages of the path and can take him through them.

Before the opening of the inner eye, the mind conceives of the goal as the Infinite; and this conception is based upon some symbolic image of infinity, such as the sky or the ocean, which suggests the idea of vastness. Although such a concept of the Infinite is clear and well defined, it has to be superseded by direct perception of the Infinite. The aspirant sees the Self directly when his inner eye of the spirit is opened. When this happens, the mind is dazed by what it sees and is no longer as clear as it was before the opening of this inner eye. Being dazed by the perception of the Self, the mind loses its capacity to think clearly and mistakes the seeing of the Self with its being actually realized. Hence comes the illusion of being at the end of the path when one is still traversing it. In Sufi terms this particular part of the path is known as *muqam-e-afsan*, or the abode of delusion. It is in such difficult phases of the path that the Master can, through his skillful intervention, give a push to the aspirant so that he keeps on going instead of getting caught up on the way.

Abode of delusion

In fact, there is danger of the aspirant being detained on each one of the inner planes, because each in its own way is very alluring and serves as a trap for the aspirant. The Master either takes the aspirant past these planes or through them without unnecessary delay. However, the aspirant has to walk his own way. The contribution of the Master consists in confirming and consolidating the previously acquired intuitions and perceptions of the aspirant, and in precipitating his consciousness into the next stage—which, though unavoidable, is by its nature impossible for the aspirant to anticipate.

Contribution of Master

The Master uses Maya to take the disciple out of Maya; and as he is himself beyond good and evil, he may often require things that are unacceptable and even shocking to the ordinary good sense of his disciples. The best thing for the disciple to do is to follow the instructions of the Master with implicit faith, without bringing them to the bar of his limited capacity of judgment. The following famous

Implicit faith

instances illustrate this point.

There is the Koranic story of Abraham* being called upon to sacrifice his beloved son Ishmael to the Lord. When Abraham, firm in his resolve and faith, was about to slaughter Ishmael, God intervened and accepted the sacrifice of a ram as ransom for the son.

When Shams-e-Tabriz ordered Maulana Jalaluddin Rumi, his disciple, to fetch wine for him, he unflinchingly complied in order to please and win the grace of his Master. At the time, the Maulana commanded a large following of Muslim divines because of his reputation as a great theologian in the Islamic world—and wine is religiously prohibited (*haram*) to the Muslims. Hence it was a crucial test for the Maulana to carry a jar of wine on his shoulders through the streets, but he did it.

Ghausali Shah was asked by one of his Masters, who lived in a hut by the side of the river Ganges, to fill a vessel with water for drinking—but only from midstream. It was about midnight, and the river Ganges was in heavy flood because of the monsoon. The disciple hesitated at first but finally gathered courage to attempt the impossible, believing in the omniscience of the Master. No sooner had he stepped into the angry waters of the Ganges than he witnessed a wonderful transformation of the scene. Instead of surging waves and floods, the river had turned into a thin stream; and the vessel to be filled almost touched the riverbed. The disciple nearly crossed the river to the opposite bank in search of midstream.

While thus occupied, the Master appeared on the scene and asked him the reason for his delay. When Ghausali Shah explained that the midcurrent could not be located, the Master allowed him to fill the vessel by handfuls and himself helped in the process. The Master then left the disciple on some pretext, asking him to follow immediately after filling the vessel. When Ghausali Shah returned to the hut with the vessel full of water, he was bewildered to learn from other disciples that the Master had never left the hut for a minute during his absence but was talking to them all the while about him.

Ordinary methods

These stories show how the Masters may use their powers on rare occasions to break down the ego of their disciples or help them further along the path. As a rule the Masters are very sparing in the use of their divine powers, and they never use them unless it is

*See Glossary.

absolutely necessary for spiritual purposes. Ordinarily they secure their purposes through normal, mundane ways. While doing so, they not only exhibit great understanding, a keen sense of humor, unending patience, and consummate tact, but they also take great trouble to help their disciples and adjust themselves in numberless ways to whatever might be entailed by the needs of the situation.

Some of these points are effectively brought out by the story of the great mystic Bahlul. Bahlul wanted to contact certain notables of Persia for reasons of his own. The only way to do this was to go to the prince's party that was attended by these notables. Unfortunately Bahlul was bald-headed, and in those days no one without hair was allowed to attend a party given by the prince. The prince had lost all his hair, and to see others without hair reminded him of it and prevented him from enjoying the party. Since the prince was very sensitive on this point, no one bald was allowed to come to the party. So when bald Bahlul went to the party in his shabby clothes, he was thrown out. The party lasted for three days, however; and on the second day Bahlul borrowed some fine clothes and a wig, disguised himself, and again went to the party.

Story of Bahlul

During the party no one recognized Bahlul, and in his fine clothes he made a great impression upon all the notables. He made himself so agreeable that even the prince offered him a warm welcome and invited him to sit near him. No sooner was Bahlul seated than he winked at the prince. The prince did not understand the meaning of his winking but vaguely felt that such a gesture from an illustrious man like him must mean something important. Thinking that it immediately required a suitable response, he also winked. Those who were nearby saw this exchange of winking and felt impelled to imitate them. They also winked at each other, and soon the winking spread throughout the crowd so that for five minutes the party saw nothing but winking.

Then Bahlul cried, "Stop! O you wise men. Why do you wink?" And the notables replied, "We are winking because you great men were winking. We only imitate you." Then immediately Bahlul took off his wig and said, "We two are both bald. Imitate us." The notables then went away, and on the third day they all came with shaved heads. Then Bahlul turned to the prince and said, "We two are permanently bald; these men will have to shave their heads daily in order to remain bald." Thus through his tactful handling and sense of humor, he secured access to those whom he wanted to help.

The Sadguru takes infinite pains to contact and win over the disciple for spiritual life. Since the progress of the disciple is secured only if his love for the Master is not allowed to dwindle, he takes every care to remove all obstacles that might be standing in the way of the wholehearted devotion of the disciple. If sometimes he is seen to humor the individual nature of the disciple, it is only to keep those obstacles from creating a serious impediment in his way. Sometimes he might even seem to feed the ego of the disciple, but all this is just allowing full scope to the ignorance of the disciple. It is only a preparation for the final extinguishing of his ego, just as animals to be offered in sacrifice are carefully nurtured before their annihilation. The Master is himself beyond good or evil and is not perturbed by the failings of the disciple. He tolerates them with unfailing patience and infinite capacity to wait, knowing full well that once the disciple gets established on the path these failings will be swiftly washed away.

Dealing with failings of disciple

Once the Master is satisfied that the disciple is firmly established on the path, he is keen to cleanse the mind of the disciple of all blemishes. Often he achieves this task even at the risk of appearing ruthless, just as when a surgeon, completely disregarding the protests of the patient, is active with his knife. Ultimately the disciple cannot fail to see that all such measures are really in his interest. Therefore he is never pushed away from his Master but is drawn closer to him in the very process of the cleansing that might have appeared irksome or painful.

The usual method of the Master, however, is as sweet and agreeable for the disciple as it is effective. The Master is very pleased when the disciple shows any real progress in the spiritual life. By conferring well-merited praise on the disciple, he confirms in him the spiritual qualities he is in the process of realizing and arouses in him the confidence that will enable him to cope with any situation. The glow of noble emotion, a gesture of self-denial, a heroic sacrifice, or an incident revealing extraordinary patience or love or faith—any one of these is sufficient to make the Master happy and evoke his approbation. The usual method of the Master to encourage the good qualities

Help through praise

in the disciple is plain and unconcealed appreciation of his attainments. The disciple soon begins to value the Master's approval and delights in it more than in anything else. He is ready to resist the greatest of temptations and undergo the most trying ordeals, which would otherwise have seemed impossible to him, if only he knows that this will make the Master happy.

Solution of all problems

Since the Master is, for the aspirant, a symbol of the supreme Self in all, the problem of true adjustment to the Master appears to him to be the same as realizing his own inner divinity and arriving at true adjustment with all other forms of the supreme Self. Through his allegiance to the Master, the aspirant achieves conscious appreciation of the fundamental unity of all these problems. From the psychological point of view, he is in a position to tackle them not as separate problems but as aspects of one problem. Thus he can arrive at true integration, which is different from a temporary compromise between conflicting claims. In order to help the disciple achieve this difficult task, the Master has to become the nucleus of all the spiritual idealism of the aspirant, because intensive concentration of mental energy is necessary if the aspirant is to break through the many barriers that lie between him and his goal.

Supreme claim of one's own Master

The supreme claim of the Master cannot be challenged or limited even by the spontaneous reverence that the disciple is bound to feel for Masters other than the one who has accepted him. All Perfect Masters are *one* in their consciousness, and it is absurd to imagine any grades between them. Though one Master is not greater than another, the disciple must, for his own purposes, place the claim of his own Master over and above the claims of other Masters—until he transcends the domain of duality and realizes the unity of all life. Mental energy would be dissipated unless there arose a supremely imperative claim among the many conflicting claims of life.

Exclusive concentration upon one Master is therefore usually indispensable for the gathering up of the dispersed mental energy of the disciple. In very rare cases, owing to special circumstances, the Masters themselves might decide to share the spiritual work in relation to a particular disciple. There are therefore exceptional cases of disciples who have had to affiliate themselves to two or more Masters.

This is an exception rather than the rule; and where there are more Masters than one, they arrange the distribution of their work so carefully that they do not set up any conflict of claims.

The Nature of the Ego and Its Termination

Part I
The Ego as the Center of Conflict

In the prehuman stage consciousness has experiences, but these experiences are not explicitly brought into relation with a central "I." For example, a dog may get angry, but it does not continue to feel "I am angry." Even in this case we find that the dog learns through some experiences and thus bases the action of one experience on another; but this action is a result of a semimechanical tension of connected imprints, or sanskaras. It is different from the intelligent synthesis of experiences that the development of "I"-consciousness makes possible. The first step in submitting the working of isolated impressions to intelligent regulation consists in bringing them all into relation with the center of consciousness, which appears as the explicit limited ego. The consolidation of ego-consciousness is most clear and defined from the beginning of human consciousness.

Origin of ego

Human consciousness would be nothing more than a repository for the accumulated imprints of varied experiences if it did not also contain the principle of ego-centered integration, which expresses itself in the attempt to organize and understand experience. The process of understanding experience implies the capacity to hold different bits of experiences together as parts of a unity and the

Formation of ego

the capacity to evaluate them by their being brought into mutual relationships. The integration of the opposites of experience is a condition of emancipating consciousness from the thralldom of diverse compulsions and repulsions, which tend to dominate consciousness irrespective of valuation. The early attempts to secure such integration are made through the formation of the ego as its base and center.

The ego emerges as an explicit and unfailing accompaniment to all the happenings of mental life in order to fulfill a certain need. The part played by the ego in human life may be compared to the function of ballast in a ship. The ballast in a ship keeps it from oscillating too much. Without it the ship is likely to be too light and unsteady and is in danger of being overturned by the lawless winds and waves. Thus mental energy would be caught up endlessly in the multitudinous mazes of dual experience and would all be wasted and dissipated if there were no provisional nucleus. The ego takes stock of all acquired experience and binds together the active tendencies born of the relatively independent and loose instincts inherited from animal consciousness. The formation of the ego serves the purpose of giving a certain amount of stability to conscious processes and also secures a working equilibrium, which makes for a planned and organized life.

Ego arises to fulfill need

It would be a mistake, therefore, to imagine that the arising of the ego is without any purpose. Though it arises only to vanish in the end, it does temporarily fulfill a need that could not have been ignored in the long journey of the soul. The ego is not meant to be a permanent handicap, since it can be transcended and outgrown through spiritual endeavor. But the phase of ego formation must nevertheless be looked upon as a necessary evil, which has to come into existence for the time being.

Necessary evil

The ego thus marks and fulfills a certain necessity in the further progress of consciousness. However, since the ego takes shelter in the false idea of being the body, it is a source of much illusion, which vitiates experience. It is of the essence of the ego that it should feel separate from the rest of life by contrasting itself with other forms of life. Thus, though inwardly trying to complete and integrate individual experience, the ego also creates an

Ego creates divisions and separation

artificial division between external and internal life in the very attempt to feel and secure its own existence. This division in the totality of life cannot but have its reverberations in the inner individual life over which the ego presides as a guiding genius.

While always striving to establish unity and integration in experience, the ego can never realize this objective. Though it establishes a certain kind of balance, this balance is only provisional and temporary.

Ego becomes source of conflicts

The incompleteness of its attainments is evident from the internal conflict that is never absent as long as experience is being faced from the point of view of the ego. From moment to moment the mind of man is passing through a series of conflicts. The minds of great and distinguished persons as well as the minds of common people are seen to be harassed by conflicting desires and tendencies. Sometimes the conflict the mind is faced with is so acute that the person concerned yields to the pressures, and there is either a partial or total derangement of the mind. There is really no vital difference between the normal and the so-called abnormal individual. Both have to face the same problems; but the one can more or less successfully solve his problems, and the other cannot solve them.

The ego attempts to solve its inner conflicts through false valuations and wrong choices. It is characteristic of the ego that it takes all that is unimportant as important and all that is important as unimportant.

False valuation

Thus, although power, fame, wealth, ability, and other worldly attainments and accomplishments are really unimportant, the ego takes delight in these possessions and clings to them as "mine." On the other hand, true spirituality is all-important for the soul, but the ego looks upon it as unimportant.

For example, if a person experiences some bodily or mental discomfort while doing work of spiritual importance, the ego steps in to secure the unimportant bodily or mental comfort, even at the cost of giving up the really important spiritual work. Bodily and mental comfort, as well as other worldly attainments and accomplishments, are often necessary; but they are not therefore important. There is a world of difference between necessity and importance. Many things come to the ego as being necessary, but they are not in themselves important. Spirituality, which comes to the ego as being unnecessary, is really important for the soul. The ego thus represents a deep and fundamental principle of ignorance, which is exhibited in always preferring the unimportant to the important.

The mind rarely functions harmoniously because it is mostly guided and governed by forces in the subconscious. Few persons take the trouble to attain mastery over these hidden forces that direct the course of mental life. The elimination of conflict is possible only through conscious control over the forces in the subconscious. This control can be permanently attained only through the repeated exercise of true valuation in all the cases of conflict presented to the mind.

Conflicts solved through true valuation

If the mind is to be freed from conflict, it must always make the right choice and must unfailingly prefer the truly important to the unimportant. The choice has to be both intelligent and firm in all cases of conflict—important as well as unimportant. It has to be intelligent because only through the pursuit of true and permanent values is it possible to attain a poise that is not detrimental to the dynamic and creative flow of mental life. An unintelligent choice, if it is firm, may temporarily overcome conflict; but it is bound in the long run to curtail the scope of life or to hamper the fulfillment of the whole personality. Moreover, the conflict will surely reappear in some other form if it has not been intelligently solved. An intelligent solution, on the other hand, requires an insight into true values, which have to be disentangled from false values. The problem of the conflict of desires thus turns out to be the problem of conflicting values, and the solution of mental conflict therefore requires a deep search for the real meaning of life. It is only through wisdom that the mind can be freed from conflict.

Need for intelligent and firm choices

Having once known what the right choice is, the next step is to stick to it firmly. Although the competing tendencies in the mind may be quieted by choosing one particular course in preference to other alternatives, they still continue to act as obstacles in making the choice fully effective and operative. At times there is a danger of a decision being subverted through the intensification of those competing forces in the subconscious. To avoid defeat, the mind must stick tenaciously to the right values it has perceived. Thus the solution of mental conflict requires not only perception of right values

Fidelity to right choice

but also an unswerving fidelity to them.

An intelligent and firm choice, however, has to be repeatedly exercised in *all* matters—small or great. For the ordinary worries of life are not in any way less important than the serious problems with which the mind is confronted in times of crisis. The roots of mental conflict cannot completely disappear as long as there is only intermittent exercise of intelligent and firm choice. The life of true values can be spontaneous only when the mind has developed the unbroken habit of choosing the right values. Three-quarters of our life is made up of ordinary things; and though conflict concerning ordinary things may not cause much mental agony, it still leaves in the mind a sense of uneasiness that something is wrong. The conflicts that turn upon ordinary things are rarely even brought to the surface of consciousness. Instead they cast a shadow on one's general feeling about life as if from behind a screen. Such conflicts have to be brought to the surface of consciousness and frankly faced before they can be adequately solved.

True values must govern all matters

The process of bringing conflict to the surface of consciousness should not degenerate, however, into a process of imagining conflict where there is none. The sure sign of a real hidden conflict is the sense that the whole of one's heart is not in the thought or action that happens to be dominant at the moment. There is a vague feeling of a narrowing down or a radical restriction of life. On such occasions an attempt should be made to analyze one's mental state through deep introspection, for such analysis brings to light the hidden conflicts concerning the matter.

Hidden conflicts

When the conflicts are thus brought to light it is possible to resolve them through intelligent and firm choices. The most important requirement for the satisfactory resolution of conflict is motive power or inspiration, which can only come from a burning longing for some comprehensive ideal. Analysis in itself may aid choice, but the choice will remain a barren and ineffective intellectual preference unless it is vitalized by zeal for some ideal appealing to the deepest and most significant strata of human personality. Modern psychology has done much to reveal the sources of conflict, but it has yet to discover methods of awakening

Longing for ideal as motive power

inspiration or supplying the mind with something that makes life worth living. This indeed is the creative task facing the saviors of humanity.

The establishment of a true ideal is the beginning of right valuation. Right valuation in turn is the undoing of the constructions of the ego, which thrives on false valuation. Any action that expresses the true values of life contributes toward the disintegration of the ego, which is a product of ages of ignorant action. Life cannot be permanently imprisoned within the cage of the ego. It must at some time strive toward the Truth. In the ripeness of evolution comes the momentous discovery that life cannot be understood and lived fully as long as it is made to move around the pivot of the ego. Man is then driven by the logic of his own experience to find the true center of experience and reorganize his life in the Truth. This entails the wearing out of the ego and its replacement by Truth-consciousness. The disintegration of the ego culminates in realizing the Truth. The false nucleus of consolidated sanskaras must disappear if there is to be a true integration and fulfillment of life.

Disintegration of ego ends in realizing Truth

The Nature of the Ego and Its Termination

Part II

The Ego as an Affirmation of Separateness

The ego is an affirmation of separateness. It takes many forms. It may take the form of a continued self-conscious memory expressing itself in recollections—like "I did this and I did that"; "I felt this and I felt that"; "I thought this and I thought that." It also takes the form of ego-centered hopes for the future expressing themselves through plans—like "I shall do this and I shall do that"; "I shall feel this and I shall feel that"; "I shall think this and I shall think that." Or again in the present, the ego manifests itself as a strong feeling of being someone in particular and asserts its distinctness and separateness from all other centers of consciousness. While provisionally serving a useful purpose as a center of consciousness, the ego, as an affirmation of separateness, constitutes the chief hindrance to spiritual emancipation and enlightenment of consciousness.

Ego a hindrance to spiritual emancipation

The ego affirms its separateness through craving, hate, anger, fear, or jealousy. When a person craves the company of others, he is keenly conscious of being separate from them and thus feels his own separate existence intensely. The feeling of separation from others is most acute where there is great and unrelieved craving. In hate and anger also, the other person is, so to speak, thrown out of one's own being and regarded not only as a foreigner but as definitely hostile to the thriving of one's ego. Fear also is a subtle form of affirming separateness and exists where the consciousness of duality is unabated. Fear acts as a thick curtain between the "I" and the "you." And it not only nourishes deep distrust of the other but inevitably brings about a shrinking and withdrawal of consciousness, so as to exclude the being of another from the context of one's own life. Therefore, not only other souls but God should be loved and not feared. To fear God or His manifestations is to strengthen duality; to love God and His manifestations is to weaken it.

Ego feeds upon exclusive feelings

The feeling of separateness finds most poignant expression in jealousy. There is a deep and imperative need in the human soul to love and identify itself with other souls. This is not fulfilled in any instance where there is craving or hate, anger or fear. In jealousy, in addition to the nonfulfillment of this deep and imperative need for identification with other persons, there is a belief that some other soul has successfully identified itself with the person whom one sought. This creates a standing and irreconcilable protest against *both* individuals for developing a relationship that one really wished to reserve for oneself. All exclusive feelings like craving, hate, fear, or jealousy bring about a narrowing down of life and contribute to the limitation and restriction of consciousness. They become directly instrumental in the affirmation of separateness of the ego.

Jealousy strengthens ego

Every thought, feeling, or action that springs from the idea of exclusive or separate existence binds. All experiences (small or great) and all aspirations (good or bad) create a load of impressions and nourish the sense of the "I." The only experience that makes for the slimming down of the ego is the experience of love, and the only aspiration that makes for the alleviation of separateness is the longing to become one with the Beloved. Craving, hatred, anger, fear, and jealousy are all exclusive attitudes that create a gulf between oneself and the rest of life. Love alone is an inclusive attitude, which helps bridge this artificial and self-created gulf and tends to break through the separative barrier of false imagination. In true love, the lover also longs, but he longs for union with the Beloved. When seeking or experiencing union with the Beloved, the

Slimming down of ego through love

sense of the "I" becomes feeble. In love the "I" does not think of self-preservation, just as the moth is unafraid of getting burned in the flame. The ego is the affirmation of being separate from the other, while love is the affirmation of being one with the other. Hence the ego can be dissolved only through real love.

Ego made of desires

The ego is implemented by desires of varied types. Failure to fulfill desires is a failure of the ego. Success in attaining desired objects is a success of the ego. Through fulfilled desires as well as through unfulfilled ones, the ego is accentuated. The ego can even feed upon a comparative lull in the surging of desires and assert its separative tendency through feeling that it is desireless. When there is a real cessation of all desires, however, there is a cessation of the desire to assert separativeness in any form. Therefore real freedom from all desires brings about the end of the ego. The ego is made of variegated desires, and the destroying of these desires amounts to the destruction of the ego.

Roots of ego in subconscious mind

The problem of erasing the ego from consciousness is very complicated, however, because the roots of the ego are all in the subconscious mind in the form of latent tendencies; and these latent tendencies are not always accessible to explicit consciousness. The limited ego of explicit consciousness is only a small fragment of the total ego. The ego is like an iceberg floating in the sea. About one-seventh of the iceberg remains above the surface of the water and is visible to the onlooker, but the major portion remains submerged and invisible. In the same way, only a small portion of the real ego becomes manifest in consciousness in the form of an explicit "I," and the major portion of the real ego remains submerged in the dark and inarticulate sanctuaries of the subconscious mind.

Ego heterogeneous in constitution

The explicit ego, which finds its manifestation in consciousness, is by no means a harmonious whole; it can and does become an arena for multitudinous conflicts between opposing tendencies. It has a limited capacity, however, for allowing simultaneous emergence of conflicting tendencies. Two persons have to be at least on speaking terms if they are to enter into articulate wrangling. If they are not on speaking terms, they cannot bring themselves to quarrel on common ground. In the same manner, two tendencies that can enter into conscious conflict must have some common ground. If they are too disparate, they cannot find admittance into the arena of consciousness—even as conflicting tendencies—but have to remain submerged in the subconscious mind until they are both modified through the tension exerted by the diverse activities connected with the conscious mind.

Explicit ego and implicit ego

Although the entire ego is essentially heterogeneous in its constitution, the explicit ego of consciousness is less heterogeneous than the implicit ego of the subconscious mind. The explicit ego operates as a formidable whole compared with the isolated subconscious tendencies that seek to emerge in consciousness. The organized ego of explicit consciousness thus becomes a repressive barrier that indefinitely prevents several constituents of the implicit ego from access to consciousness. All the problems of the ego can be tackled only through intelligent and conscious action. Therefore, complete annihilation of the ego is possible only when all the constituents of the ego pass through the fire of intelligent consciousness.

Intensified conflict ends in attaining poise and harmony

The action of intelligent consciousness on the components of the explicit ego is important, but in itself it is not sufficient for the desired results. The components of the implicit ego of the subconscious mind have to be brought to the surface of consciousness somehow and become parts of the explicit ego, and then be submitted to the action of intelligent consciousness. If this is to be achieved, there has to be a weakening of the explicit ego in such manner as to allow the emergence into consciousness of those desires and tendencies that could not hitherto find admittance into the arena of consciousness. This release of inhibited tendencies naturally brings about additional confusion and conflict in the explicit ego. Therefore the disappearance of the ego is often accompanied by intensified conflicts in the arena of the conscious mind rather than by any comfortable easing of them. However, at the end of the uncompromising and acute struggle lies the state of true poise and unassailable harmony that comes after the melting away of the entire iceberg of the ego.

The digging out of the buried roots of the ego from the deeper layers of the subconscious and bringing them to the light of consciousness is one important part of the process of wiping out the ego. The other important part consists in the intelligent handling of desires *after* they gain entrance to the arena of consciousness. The process of dealing with the components of explicit consciousness is by no means clear and simple, for the explicit ego has a tendency to live through *any* one of the opposites of experience. If it is ousted from one opposite by the intensive operation of intelligent consciousness, it has a tendency to move to the other extreme and live through it. Through repeated alternation between the opposites of experience, the ego eludes the attack of intelligent consciousness and seeks to perpetuate itself.

Ego lives through opposites of experience

The ego is hydra-headed and expresses itself in numberless ways. It lives upon any type of ignorance. Pride is the specific feeling through which egoism manifests. A person can be proud of the most unimportant and silly things. Instances are known, for example, of people developing their nails to an abnormal length and preserving them, despite much inconvenience to themselves, for no other reason than to assert separateness from others. The ego must magnify its attainments in grosteque ways if it is to live in them. Direct assertion of the ego through self-display in society is very common; but if such direct assertion is prohibited by the rules of conduct, the ego has a tendency to seek the same result through the slander of others. To portray others as evil is to glorify oneself by *suggesting* a comparison—a comparison the ego would willingly develop, though it often restrains itself from doing so.

Ego is hydra-headed

The ego is activated by the principle of self-perpetuation and has a tendency to live and grow by any and all means not closed to it. If the ego faces curtailment in one direction, it seeks compensating expansion in another. If it is overpowered by a flood of spiritual notions and actions, it even tends to fasten upon this very force, which was originally brought into play for the ousting of the ego. If a person attempts to cultivate humility in order to relieve himself of the monstrous weight of the ego and succeeds in doing so, the ego can, with surprising alacrity, transfer itself to this attribute of humility. It feeds itself through repeated assertions like "I am spiritual," just as in the

Tricks of ego

primary stages it achieved the same task by assertions like "I am not interested in spirituality." Thus arises what might be called a *spiritual* ego, or an ego that feels its separateness through the attainment of things considered to be good and highly spiritual. From the truly spiritual point of view, this type of ego is as binding as the primary and crude ego, which makes no such pretensions.

In fact, in the more advanced stages of the path, the ego does not seek to maintain itself through open methods but takes shelter in those very things that are pursued for the slimming down of the ego.

Guerrilla warfare

These tactics of the ego are very much like guerrilla warfare and are the most difficult to counteract. The ousting of the ego from consciousness is necessarily an intricate process and cannot be achieved by exercising a constantly uniform approach. Since the nature of the ego is very complicated, an equally complicated treatment is needed to get rid of it. As the ego has almost infinite possibilities for making its existence secure and creating self-delusion, the aspirant finds it impossible to cope with the endless cropping up of fresh forms of the ego. He can hope to deal successfully with the deceptive tricks of the ego only through the help and grace of a Perfect Master.

In most cases it is only when the aspirant is driven to realize the futility of all his efforts that he approaches a Master. By himself he can make no headway toward the goal that he dimly sights and seeks. The

Master as last resort

stubborn persistence of the ego exasperates him, and in this clear perception of helplessness he surrenders to the Master as his last and only resort. The self-surrender amounts to an open admission that the aspirant now has given up all hope of tackling the problems of the ego by himself and that he relies solely upon the Master. It is like saying, "I am unable to end the wretched existence of this ego. I therefore look to you to intervene and slay it." This step, however, turns out to be more fruitful than all other measures that might have been tried for the slimming down and subsequent annihilation of the ego. When through the grace of the Master the ignorance that constitutes the ego is dispelled, there is the dawn of Truth—which is the goal of all creation.

The Nature of the Ego and Its Termination

Part III
The Forms of the Ego and Their Dissolution

The ego subsists upon mundane possessions like power, fame, wealth, ability, attainments, and accomplishments. It creates and recognizes the "thine" in order to feel what is distinctively "mine."

Ego lives through idea of "mine"

However, in spite of all the worldly things that it claims as "mine," it constantly feels empty and incomplete. To make up for this deep restlessness in its own being, the ego seeks to fortify itself through further acquisitions. It brings the array of its entire varied possessions into relief by comparison with others who might be inferior in any one of the items stamped as "mine." And it often uses these possessions for wanton and uncalled-for self-display, even to the disadvantage of others. The ego is dissatisfied in spite if its mundane possessions; but instead of cultivating detachment from them, it seeks to derive satisfaction from a more intense sense of possession in contradistinction to others. The ego as an affirmation of separateness lives through the idea of "mine."

The ego wants to feel separate and unique, and it seeks self-expression either in the role of someone who is decidedly better than others or in the role of someone who is decidedly inferior. As long as there is ego, there is an implicit background of duality; and as long as

Forms of ego

there is the background of duality, the mental operations of comparison and contrast cannot be effectively stilled for long. Therefore, even when a person seems to feel a sense of equality with another, this feeling is not securely established. It marks a point of transition between the two attitudes of the ego rather than permanent freedom from the distinction between the "I" and the "you."

Idea of equality

This pseudo sense of equality, where it exists, may be stated in the formula "I am not in any way inferior or superior to the other." This will at once be seen to be a negative assertion of the ego. The balance between the "I " and the "you" is constantly disturbed by the predominance of a superiority or inferiority complex. The idea of equality arises to restore this lost balance. The negative assertion of the ego in the form of equality is, however, utterly different from the sense of unity that is characteristic of the life of spiritual freedom. Although the sense of equality is made the basis of many social and political ideals, the real conditions of rich cooperative life are fulfilled only when the bare idea of equality is replaced by the realization of the unity of all life.

Two complexes

The feelings of superiority and inferiority are reactions to each other, and the artificially induced feeling of equality might be regarded as a reaction to both. In all these three modes the ego succeeds in asserting its separateness. The superiority complex and the inferiority complex for the most part remain disconnected from each other. They both seek separate and alternate expression through suitable objects, as when a person dominates those whom he regards as his inferiors and submits to those whom he looks upon as his superiors. But such alternative expression through contrasting behavior only accentuates these opposite complexes instead of leading to their dissolution.

Superiority complex

The superiority complex is stirred when a person meets someone who is in some way remarkably inferior in mundane possessions. In spite of its many possessions, the ego is constantly confronted with the spectacle of its intrinsic emptiness. Therefore it clings to the comforting delusion of its worthwhileness by demonstrating the greatness of its possessions. This contrast is not confined to theoretical comparison but often exhibits itself in an actual clash with others. Thus, aggressiveness is a natural outcome of the need to compensate for the poverty of the ego-life.

Inferiority complex

The inferiority complex is stirred when a person meets someone who is in some way remarkably superior in respect to mundane possessions. But his submissiveness to the other is rooted either in fear or selfishness. It can never be whole-hearted or spontaneous because there is a lurking jealousy of and even hatred for the other for possessing something he would rather have for himself. All forced and outward submission is purely the effect of an inferiority complex and can only enhance the ego in one of its worst forms. The ego attributes its sense of emptiness to the apparently inferior possessions it can claim as "mine," rather than to its deep-rooted viciousness in seeking fulfillment through possessions. Awareness of its inferiority in possessions becomes only a further stimulus for making desperate efforts to add to its possessions through such means as are available to it. Thus while perpetuating the inward poverty of the soul, the inferiority complex, like the superiority complex, constitutes an agent for selfishness and social chaos, and for the accumulation of that type of ignorance which characterizes the ego.

Surrender different from inferiority complex

When a person comes into contact with a Perfect Master and recognizes him as having the state of egoless Perfection, he voluntarily surrenders himself to the Master. The disciple perceives the ego to be a source of perpetual ignorance, restlessness, and conflict; and he also recognizes his own inability to terminate it. But this self-surrender should be carefully distinguished from the inferiority complex because it is accompanied by awareness that the Master is the ideal and as such has a basic unity with the disciple. Such self-surrender is in no way an expression of loss of confidence. On the contrary, it is an expression of confidence in the final overcoming of all obstacles through the help of the Master. The appreciation of the divinity of the Master is the manner in which the higher Self of the disciple expresses its sense of dignity.

In order to bring about a rapid dissolution of these two chief forms of the ego, the Master may deliberately stir both of these complexes in alternation. If the disciple is on the point of losing heart and giving up the search, he might arouse in him deep self-confidence. If he is on the point of becoming egotistic, he might break through this new barrier by creating situations in which the disciple has to accept and recognize his own incapacity or futility. Thus the Master wields his influence over the disciple to expedite the stages that the melting ego passes through before its final disappearance.

Intervention of Master

The superiority and inferiority complexes have to be brought into intelligent relation with each other if they are to counteract each other. This requires a situation in which both would be allowed to have their play at the same time, without requiring the repression of one in order to express the other. When the soul enters into a dynamic and vital relation with the Master, the complexes concerned with the senses of inferiority and superiority are both brought into play; and they are so intelligently accommodated that they counteract each other. The disciple then feels that he is nothing in himself, but in and through the Master he is enlivened by the prospect of being Everything.

Adjustment to Master results in dissolution of complexes

Thus at one stroke the two complexes are brought into mutual tension and tend to annihilate each other in the attempt the disciple makes to adjust himself to the Master. With the dissolution of these opposite complexes, there comes a breaking down of the separative barriers of the ego in all its forms. With the breaking down of the barriers of separation, there arises divine love. With the arising of divine love, the separate feeling of "I," as distinguished from "you," is swallowed up in the sense of their unity.

For a car to move toward its destination, a driver is necessary. However, the driver may be susceptible to strong attractions for things that he encounters on the way; and he might not only halt at intervening places for an indefinite time but also get lost by the wayside in pursuit of things that have only temporary charm. Thus he might keep the car moving all the time but without coming nearer the goal, and he might even get further away from it. Something like this happens when the ego assumes control of human consciousness. The ego may be compared to a driver who has a certain amount of control over a car and a certain capacity to drive it, but who is in complete darkness about its ultimate destination.

Analogy of driver

For a car to reach its ultimate destination, it is not enough merely to have someone who can drive the car. It is equally necessary that this driver should be able to direct the car toward the destination. As long as the movement of consciousness is under the full and exclusive domination of the ego, the spiritual advancement of the person is jeopardized by the natural tendency of the ego to strengthen the separative barriers of false imagination. So, because of ego-centered activities, consciousness remains enclosed by the walls of its own creation and moves within the limits of this *mayavic* prison.

If consciousness is to be emancipated from its limitations and rendered adequate to serve the original purpose for which it came into existence, it must draw its directive momentum not from the ego but from some other principle. In other words, the driver who is ignorant of the ultimate destination must be exchanged for another driver who is free from all the allure of accidental things encountered on the way, and who centers his attention not on the rest stations or side attractions but on the ultimate goal of nonduality. The shifting of the center of interest from unimportant things to truly important values is comparable to the transference of power from the ignorant driver to the driver who knows the destination. Concurrent with this gradual shifting of the center of interest, there is progressive dissolution of the ego and motion toward the Truth.

Ego attempts integration around false idea

If the ego were nothing but a medium for the integration of human experience, it would be possible for one to get established in the final Truth merely by carrying further the activity of the ego. But while playing a specific part in the progress of consciousness, the ego also represents an active principle of ignorance that prevents further spiritual development. The ego attempts the integration of experience, but it does so around the false idea of separateness. Having taken an illusion as the foundation for the construction of its edifice, it never succeeds in anything but the building of illusions one upon another. Arriving at the Truth is actually hindered rather than helped by the function of the ego. The process of arriving at the Truth can be fruitful only if the integration presided over by the ego is carried further without bringing in the basic ignorance of separateness.

As long as human experience lies within the limitation of duality, integration of experience is an essential condition for a rational and significant life. But the ego as a nucleus for integration has to be renounced because of its inevitable alliance with the forces of ignorance. There arises, then, an imperative need for a new center of integration that will steer clear of the basic ignorance of separateness and will allow free scope for the incorporation of all values formerly inaccessible to the ego-center. Such a new center is provided by the Master, who expresses all that has real value and who represents the absolute Truth. The shifting of interest from unimportant things to important values is facilitated by allegiance and self-surrender to the Master, who becomes the new nucleus for integration.

Master becomes new nucleus of integration

The Master, when truly understood, is a standing affirmation of the unity of all life. Allegiance to the Master, therefore, brings about a gradual dissociation from the ego-nucleus, which affirms separateness. After this important crisis in the life of an individual, all mental activity has a new frame of reference. And its significance is to be gathered in the light of its relation to the Master as the manifestation of infinite Truth, not in the light of any relation to the ego-center as a limited "I." The person henceforth finds that all acts that flow from him are no longer initiated from the limited "I" but are all inspired by the Truth working through the Master. He is also no longer interested in the well-being of the limited self but is only interested in the Master as representing universal and undivided life. He offers all his experiences and desires to the Master, reserving neither the good nor the evil for the limited "I," stripping the ego of all content.

Union with Master and realization of Truth

This advancing bankruptcy of the ego does not interfere with the process of integration because the function is now performed around the new center of the Master as representing the Truth. When the ego-nucleus is completely bankrupt and devoid of any power or being, the Master, as Truth, is firmly established in consciousness as its guiding genius and animating principle. This constitutes both the attainment of union with the Master and the realization of the infinite Truth.

As the ego gradually adjusts itself to the spiritual requirements of life—through the cultivation of humanity, selflessness and love, wholehearted surrender and offering oneself to the Master, as

Truth—it suffers a drastic curtailment. It not only offers less and less resistance to spiritual unfoldment but also undergoes a radical transformation. This eventually turns out to be so great that in the end the ego, as an affirmation of separateness, completely disappears and is substituted by the Truth, which knows no separateness.

Knowledge of true Self

The intermediate steps of slimming down the ego and softening its nature are comparable to the trimming and pruning of the branches of a wild and mighty tree, while the final step of annihilation of the ego amounts to the complete uprooting of this tree. When the ego disappears entirely, there arises knowledge of the true Self. Thus, the long journey of the soul consists in developing from animal consciousness the explicit self-consciousness as a limited "I," then in transcending the state of the limited "I" of human consciousness, through the medium of the Master. At this stage the soul is initiated into the consciousness of the supreme and real Self as an everlasting and infinite "I am," in which there is no separateness and which includes all existence.

The Place of Occultism in Spiritual Life*

Part I
The Value of Occult Experiences

The spiritual path leading to the emancipation of consciousness brings with it an unfoldment of many psychic capacities, which are latent in the human soul. This unfoldment increases the scope and range of human consciousness. These new elements often play an important part in helping or hindering the spiritual emancipation of consciousness. Therefore, the aspirant not only has to understand the value of such experiences as unusual and significant dreams, visions, astral journeys, and glimpses of the subtle world, but he also has to learn to distinguish real occult experiences from hallucinations and delusions.

Psychic capacities help or hinder emancipation

Although it is customary to exaggerate the importance of occult experiences, it is not uncommon to doubt their validity and to treat them with the contempt usually accorded to all forms of mental aberrations and abnormalities. The attitude of unqualified contempt for occult experiences is of course

Contempt for occult born of ignorance

*In the following three Parts, *occult* and *occultism* are generally used in the broadest sense to mean hidden or beyond the range of ordinary experience; but in certain contexts they mean more specifically psychic or supernatural (see Glossary).—Ed.

most pronounced in those who are not even abecedarians in direct knowledge of the occult. It hurts the ego to admit and feel that there might be vast unexplored fields of the universe that are accessible just to a limited number of persons, and from which one happens to be excluded. The undeserved contempt that occultism at times receives is almost always the outcome of profound ignorance about its real meaning. This attitude of contempt is of course different from a cautious and critical attitude. Those who have a cautious and critical approach and who are endowed with humility and openness of mind are ever ready to recognize and admit occult phenomena when they occur.

Some dreams spiritually significant

An aspirant is usually helped by a Perfect Master through ordinary means, and the Master prefers to take him veiled along the spiritual path. But when there are specific indications, he may also use occult techniques to help the aspirant. Special types of dreams are among the common methods used for touching the deeper life of the aspirant. Masters have not infrequently first contacted aspirants by appearing in their dreams. Such dreams, however, have to be carefully distinguished from ordinary dreams. In ordinary dreams the subtle body is active in exercising its functions of seeing, tasting, smelling, touching, and hearing; but the soul is not using the subtle body with full consciousness. As these experiences in ordinary dreams are received subconsciously, they are in most cases purely subjective, relating to physical activities and concerning the gross world, and are the creations of nascent sanskaras stored in the mind. In some cases, however, a dream that is indistinguishable from ordinary dreams may be the reflection in the subconscious of some objective experience of the subtle body and not merely a product of fancy.

Rare types of dreams

Most dreams are purely subjective and subconscious experiences of the subtle body. They have no special spiritual significance, except that they can be occasions for forging new sanskaras or spending up old ones and that occasionally they shed light upon the hidden complexes and unfaced problems of one's personality. Such dreams can never include something that is not in some way a part of the past experience of the person. They allow scope for novelty only in respect to new combinations of items that have already appeared in past experience. The rare types of dreams are those about persons and things unknown in this life but known in some past life or lives. Still more rare are the dreams of persons and things that have never appeared in this life or former lives but are going to appear in the future. Ordinary dreams are thus utterly different from dreams that have occult significance.

Beginnings of occult experience

Very often, when the aspirant is undergoing psychic unfoldment, he has occasional mystic experiences of the subtle world in the form of significant visions, lights, colors, sounds, smells, or contacts. At first these experiences are fitful, and the aspirant is likely to treat them as hallucinations. But even when he treats them as hallucinations, he finds it impossible to resist their directive influence because of their intrinsic potency. The spiritual journey, however, becomes more smooth if the aspirant learns to cultivate the right attitude toward occult experiences, which consists in taking them for what they are worth. This balanced attitude is just what the aspirant in the initial stages finds difficult to maintain.

Balanced attitude difficult to maintain

The beginner is apt to exaggerate the importance of his glimpses into the inner worlds and to develop an ungovernable craving for repetition of these experiences, or he tries to treat them as abnormal phenomena and underrates their significance. Of these two alternatives, the attitude of exaggerating the importance of occult experiences is the most common, because the novelty and rarity of occult experiences are factors that contribute to charging them with overwhelming importance.

Craving for occult experiences

In fact, the ego of the aspirant tends to become attached to this new field revealed to him, which gives him the sense of being a rare person admitted to an exclusive privilege. The more experiences a person has, the greater scope he desires. He also develops the habit of depending upon occult goading for each step on the path, just as those who take drugs get addicted to them and require stimulation even for doing things they could formerly do without such stimulation. In order to avoid this pitfall for the aspirant, the Master takes good care not to cater to his new craving for occult experiences. Such experiences are vouchsafed to the aspirant if and when they are absolutely necessary for spiritual purposes and not when he wants or asks for them.

If the aspirant is found to attach undue importance to occult experiences or to develop an ungovernable craving for them, the Master might deal with this obstacle in his own way by actually weakening or annulling the occult experiences that have become the basis for such craving. This is like giving immediate relief to a patient by surgical removal of the cause of a physical disorder. It serves the purpose of protecting the aspirant from forging fresh chains for self-limitation. The aspirant must not be allowed under any circumstances to get caught up in false values and futile searching. These can only lead to sidetracking and cause unnecessary delay in achieving the real goal, which is to get initiated into the truly spiritual life. The introduction of the aspirant to occult phenomena is necessarily a very gradual and prolonged process. The Master is never anxious to expedite it, as few persons are really qualified to stand the expansion of their experience in this new dimension.

Dealing with craving for occult experiences

In the initial stages the appearance of occult phenomena is very fitful, and the aspirant sometimes doubts their validity, treating them with caution in order to rule out the possibility of his being deluded. But occult experiences often bear unmistakable credentials of their own validity. Even when any such credentials are not evident, they compel due respect and attention because of the unusual significance, bliss, peace, and directive value with which they are surcharged. Mainly because of these characteristics, the aspirant is able to distinguish real occult experiences from hallucinations and delusions.

Validity of occult experience

Hallucinations are erroneous perceptions and consist in actually seeing or hearing things that do not really exist. Though they are clearly different in this respect from merely imagining things, they remain objects of doubt in spite of their similarity to normal perceptions. Delusions are even more deceptive because they consist not only in actually seeing things that really do not exist but also in having complete conviction of their existence. However, hallucinations and delusions do not bring extraordinary bliss or peace to the person who

Occult distinguished from hallucination and delusion

experiences them. The bliss and peace that are attendant upon real occult experiences are fairly reliable criteria by which to distinguish them as genuine. Hallucinations and delusions are like the nightmares of wakeful consciousness.

Aspirant must develop self-confidence

Even when real occult experience can be clearly differentiated from illusion, it suffers in its power and efficacy if it becomes the object of doubt. This can happen when the person who has had the experience discusses the matter with others who, because of their incapacity to understand such things, throw out contrary thoughts and shake his conviction. For this reason, the Master usually requires a disciple to maintain strict secrecy about his experiences. Even a deep experience is likely to become weak through the contradiction and skepticism of others, unless the aspirant has learned to follow his own inner experience irrespective of what others might think or say. If the aspirant is to make quick progress and to profit most from the Master's help, he must develop immense and unshakable confidence in himself and the Master. He must not look to others for guidance, because those who will understand his problems or his experiences are very few. The aspirant must indeed be prepared to face the possibility of not being completely understood by any of his friends or relatives, for they may be in the dark about the grounds for his ideology and course of action.

Effect of doubt on occult experience

If at the time of its occurrence an occult experience has served the purpose of giving new momentum to spiritual endeavor, it often does not matter if the aspirant considers it in retrospective analysis and thought as being a form of delusion. However, there are some occult experiences that are deliberately vouchsafed to the aspirant in order that they should be standing sources of inspiration and guidance. With regard to these special experiences, it becomes necessary that the aspirant cease doubting their validity and importance.

The general attitude of seeking endless corroborations of occult experiences is definitely unhealthy, and the Master gives corroborative confirmation only when he considers it necessary. Further, he takes the initiative in the way he judges best in the situation. Whatever he does arises from his unfettered discretion and is in no way related to or dependent upon any expectation developed by the aspirant. But when it is spiritually necessary, the Master does increase the efficacy of occult experience by confirming its validity and authority through some direct or indirect corroboration from the aspirant's normal range of experience.

In the advancing stages leading to the beginning of the path, the aspirant becomes spiritually prepared for being entrusted with free use of the forces of the inner world of the astral bodies.* He may then undertake astral journeys in his astral body, leaving the physical body in sleep or wakefulness. The astral journeys that are taken unconsciously are much less important than those undertaken with full consciousness and as a result of deliberate volition. This implies conscious use of the astral body. Conscious separation of the astral body from the outer vehicle of the gross body has its own value in making the soul feel its distinction from the gross body and in arriving at fuller control of the gross body. One can, at will, put on and take off the external gross body as if it were a cloak, and use the astral body for experiencing the inner world of the astral and for undertaking journeys through it, if and when necessary.

Astral journeys

The sights, smells, tastes, contacts, and sounds that are experienced through conscious use of the astral body are clear and definite, like the experiences gained through conscious use of the gross body. They are not vague or subjective, as in ordinary dreams, but are as objective and effective as other experiences of wakeful consciousness. The ability to undertake astral journeys therefore involves considerable expansion of one's scope for experience. It brings opportunities for promoting one's own spiritual advancement, which begins with the involution of consciousness.

Expanded scope for advancement

The harnessing of occult forces is not to be regarded in any way as a substitute for the inner effort the aspirant must make to advance further. When occult experiences are gifts from a Perfect Master, they serve the purpose of unveiling much of the hitherto obscured intuition, removing some of the difficulties leading toward the spiritual path, and filling the aspirant with the great confidence and enthusiasm that

Occult experience no substitute for inner effort

*See Glossary.

are necessary to cope with the new requirements at each stage. But the aspirant makes real progress by putting into practice the best intuitions of his heart, not by being the merely passive recipient of occult experiences.

The Place of Occultism in Spiritual Life

Part II
The Relationship with the Master in Spiritual Life

Those who have even a preliminary acquaintance with the structure and laws of the inner spheres of existence know that complete isolation of human beings is a figment of the imagination. Whether they desire it or not, all persons are constantly acting and interacting upon each other by their very existence, even when they do not establish any contact on the physical plane. There are no limits to the spreading of the influence of the individual. The magnetic influence of the subtle spheres knows no barriers of national frontiers or any other conventional limitations.

People constantly interacting on inner spheres

Good thoughts as well as evil thoughts, cheerful moods as well as gloomy moods, noble and expansive feelings as well as petty and narrow emotions, unselfish aspirations as well as selfish ambitions —all these have a tendency to spread out and influence others, even when they are not expressed in words or deeds. The world of mental life is as much a unified system as the world of gross matter. The gross world as a vehicle of spiritual life has its own indubitable importance, but the links and connections existing between different persons can by no means be fully estimated if one merely considers the tangible transactions that take place in the gross world.

For an aspirant to see a Perfect Master does not yield its full significance except in the context of all the corresponding happenings of the inner planes of consciousness. The *rishis*, or sages, attach great importance to having the *darshan* (contact through sight) of Perfect Masters. For they are the source of the constant flow of love and light, which emanates from them and makes an irresistible appeal to the inner feelings of the aspirant, even when he receives no verbal instructions from them. The effect of darshan is dependent upon the receptivity and response of the aspirant, whose reaction is determined by his own sanskaras and past connections.

Value of darshan and sahavas

Often the aspirant is completely satisfied with the darshan of a Master, and he desires nothing further from him. To derive bliss and contentment from the mere darshan of the Master is a great thing because it indicates that the aspirant has desirelessness and love, which are the two essentials of spiritual life. Having had the darshan of the beloved Master, the aspirant naturally desires nothing except to have more of his darshan and is thus impelled by his inner spiritual urge to seek the *sahavas* (company) of the Master as often as possible. Further sahavas of the Master implements and strengthens the purifying effect of darshan, and also results in drawing the aspirant closer and closer to the Master on the inner planes.

Like darshan, falling at the feet of a Master also has special value of its own. The feet, which are physically the lowest part of the body, are the highest from the spiritual point of view. Physically, the feet go through everything—good and bad, beautiful and ugly, clean and dirty; yet they remain above everything. Spiritually, the feet of the Masters are above everything in the universe, which is like dust to them. When people come to a Perfect Master and touch his feet with their hands, they lay the burden of their sanskaras on him. He collects the sanskaras from all over the universe, just as an ordinary person, in walking, collects dust on his feet.

Feet of the Master

There is an ancient tradition that after the aspirant has the darshan of a Master and falls at his feet, he washes the Master's feet with milk and honey and places a coconut near them as his offering. Honey represents red (bad) sanskaras, milk represents white (good) sanskaras, and the coconut represents the mind. Thus this convention, which has become established in some areas in connection with greeting the Masters, really symbolizes throwing the burden of all sanskaras on the Master and surrendering the mind to him. Adoption of this inner attitude constitutes the most critical and important step that the aspirant must take in order to get initiated on the spiritual path.

Mental contact

Once the aspirant experiences the bliss of the darshan of a Master, that sight gets carved on his mind. And even when he is unable to establish frequent personal contact, his mind turns to the Master again and again in an effort to understand his significance. This process of establishing mental contact with the Master is essentially different from merely imaginative revival of past incidents. In the ordinary play of imagination, the recall of past incidents is not necessarily animated by a definite purpose; whereas in establishing mental contact there is a definite purpose. Owing to the directive power of purpose, imagination ceases to be a mere revolving of ideas and reaches out to the Master and establishes contact with him.

Such mental contact with the Master is often as fruitful and effective as his physical darshan. The inward repetition of such mental contacts is like constructing a channel between Master and aspirant—who becomes thereby the recipient of the grace, love, and light that are constantly flowing from the Master, in spite of the apparent distance between them. Thus, the help of the Master goes out not only to those who are in his physical presence but also to others who establish mental contact with him.

Special precautionary instructions

The Master devotes careful attention to the individual needs of the disciple, and the first thing he does is to protect the disciple from influences that will divert his attention from the path or interfere with his progress. Often the Master requires the disciple to accept some kind of temporary isolation so that his mind is guarded against impacts that might impede his spiritual progress. Thus some yogis, under instructions from their Masters, prepare their own food and do not allow anyone to remain present at the time of eating it. The reason is to avoid impressions of evil from the glance of bad persons. A disciple is also likely to catch the impressions of another's lust, just as a clean cloth may be readily soiled by dirt.

In the earlier stages the aspirant must guard against any complications that might arise through association with others who are not on the path. But the Master gives special instructions for the severance or avoidance of certain connections and contacts only when they are specifically indicated for a special case. In most cases, however, all that is necessary is secured merely by the constant company of the Master, and no need arises to submit the disciple to actual isolation. Although the disciple may be outwardly in touch with the world, he remains mentally detached from it because of his inner connection with the Master.

Helpful contacts and associations

Just as the Master may isolate a close disciple from undesirable contacts and connections, he may also actually encourage and bring about new and fresh contacts that he deems to be in the spiritual interest of the disciple. He has a consummate understanding of the sanskaras and karmic ties and their complications. Thus he can consciously help people to enter into such associations as will allow and call forth important responses and activities, and help the progress of all concerned along the line of least resistance or by the shortest possible route. He uses his knowledge of the past lives, sanskaras, and connections of people to help them economize their spiritual energy and use it for the best results.

Disciple used as instrument

The unity and solidarity of the inner planes make it possible for the Master to use his disciple as an instrument for his work even when the disciple is unaware of serving this larger purpose of the Master. This is possible because the disciple, through his love and understanding of the Master as well as his obedience and surrender, establishes a rapport with the Master and comes to be in tune with him. Those who come into direct contact with the Master receive his direct help, and those who are closely connected with his disciples receive the Master's indirect help.

Master as relay station

The sharing of spiritual work is by no means onesided. Even the disciples who merely think of the Master or meditate upon him have the privilege of sharing the spiritual and universal work in which the Master might be engaged at that moment. As he is one with Eternity, the Master is beyond time and all limitations of time. As he is also interested in the spiritual upliftment of humanity, he assumes many of the limitations of time; and his work can be helped by the voluntary cooperation of his disciples. The Master feeds upon the love of his disciples and utilizes the spiritual forces released by them for his universal work. In this way the Master is like the relay station that receives a song only in order to broadcast it to the world at large. To love the Master is to love all, not merely symbolically but actually; for what the Master receives on the inner planes of consciousness he spiritualizes and distributes. Thus he not only strengthens the personal links that the disciples may have with him but also gives them the privilege of sharing his divine work.

Internal eye

In infinite ways, the Sadguru tries to draw the aspirant into his own being so that the aspirant may get disentangled from the mazes of the universe and come to desire God. This longing for God is present in the aspirant from the very beginning, but the Master makes this primary longing more intense and articulate by opening the internal eye of the aspirant. When the internal eye is opened, God—who is the object of search and longing—is actually sighted. As the gaze of the soul is turned inward and fixed upon the supreme Reality, the desire to establish union with it becomes much more ardent than when the soul is groping for God through mere speculation or imagination. When the time is ripe, the Master can open this internal eye in an instant.

Om Point

Ultimately the aspirant has to realize that God is the only Reality and that he is really one with God. This implies that he should not be overpowered by the spectacle of the multiform universe. In fact, the whole universe is in the Self and springs into existence from the tiny point in the Self referred to as the *Om* Point. But the Self as the individualized soul has become habituated to gathering experiences through one medium or another, and therefore it comes to experience the universe as a formidable rival, other than itself. Those who have realized God constantly see the universe as springing from this Om Point, which is in everyone.

The process of perception runs parallel to the process of creation, and the reversing of the process of perception without obliterating consciousness amounts to realizing the nothingness of the universe as a separate entity. The Self as the individualized soul sees first through the mind, then through the subtle eye, and lastly through the physical eye; but it is vaster than all it can perceive. The big oceans and the vast spaces of the sky are tiny as compared with the Self. In fact, all that it can perceive is finite, but the Self itself is infinite. When the individualized Self retains full consciousness and yet sees nothing, it has crossed the universe of its own creation and has taken the first step to know itself as Everything.

Reversing process of perception

The entire process of withdrawing consciousness from the universe and becoming conscious of the Self is accompanied by an increasing control of all the vehicles of consciousness. Such control is made possible by the vivification and activation of unused centers of control, and the functioning of new centers brings in its train a number of hidden powers. These new powers are commonly known as *siddhis*, and they can come before the aspirant has become spiritually perfect. In fact, egotism can flourish through the acquisition of such powers. The aspirant may not only take delight in possessing them but might actually use them for mundane purposes from which he has not necessarily freed himself.

Siddhis

Siddhis are therefore rightly regarded as obstacles to the attainment of Realization. However, after God is realized all these powers dwindle in their importance. The siddhis have their scope in the nothingness that is the universe; whereas the person who realizes God is permanently and immovably established in the supreme Reality. Although the whole universe is like a zero to the God-realized person, he may voluntarily assume responsibility for those souls who are enmeshed in the tangles of the universe. In that case he can freely and legitimately make use of these powers for the spiritual good of others.

There is nothing that does not admit of direct or indirect control by the Masters of wisdom. Large social phenomena (such as wars, revolutions, and epidemics) as well as cosmic phenomena (such as earthquakes and floods) are equally amenable to their control and direction through the release of the forces of the exalted planes on which the Masters are consciously stationed. The Masters may also use occult forces to effect cooperative and coordinated spiritual work. They frequently hold meetings and conferences on the higher inner planes for securing the advancement of humanity. The Oversoul in all is only one, and it always functions

Furtherance of divine plan

as a unity. Those who have become conscious of this unity become fit to understand unlimited responsibility. Because they have shed the limitations of the human mind and have become so impersonal and universal in their interest, they are effective vehicles for the execution and furtherance of the divine plan on earth.

The Place of Occultism in Spiritual Life

Part III
Occultism and Spirituality

Occultism is a branch of knowledge concerned with the study of certain aspects and forces of the universe and the human personality. In this respect there is no difference in principle between occultism and other sciences concerned with the study of these subjects. The difference between occultism and other sciences arises because other sciences are concerned with aspects and forces directly or indirectly accessible to ordinary observation and manipulation; whereas occultism is concerned with those hidden aspects and forces that are essentially inaccessible to ordinary observation and manipulation. The development of occult knowledge is conditioned by the unfoldment of the latent powers of the human spirit. Many of the psychic research societies of modern times approach occult knowledge with the same attitude that characterizes the study of other fields of knowledge. In principle there seems to be no reason why it should be regarded as either less valuable or more valuable than other fields of theoretical knowledge. One finds these societies trying to pursue occult knowledge in an organized and cooperative manner.

Occultism as a science

The Perfect Masters have deemed it desirable at times to reveal to the generality of mankind some theoretical knowledge about certain important features of spiritual life—such as immortality and reincarnation, the existence of different bodies and planes, and the laws concerning evolution and the operation of karma. Such knowledge gives the right sort of background for spiritual aspiration and effort, and brings the perspective of the average person as near to the Truth as is possible under the circumstances. However, with the exception of such general knowledge about fundamentals, the Masters have consistently preferred to attach minimum importance to the spread of detailed knowledge about occult phenomena. They have even scrupulously withheld information concerning those points likely to have vital bearing upon occultism as an art.

Theoretical knowledge

In occultism, more than in any other science, there is a sharp and significant division between those who know and those who do not know. In other sciences, to a certain extent, indirect knowledge can take the place of direct knowledge. In occultism, indirect knowledge can in no way approximate direct knowledge in import and significance. Therefore, though occultism is an important science, the spread of purely theoretical information about the occult can have little importance. For those who have no firsthand experience of the occult, purely theoretical acquaintance with some occult facts can have no special value. These occult phenomena are bound to remain for them more or less in the same category as descriptions of unseen lands or works of imagination.

Those who know and those who do not know

However, even the spread of purely theoretical information about occult facts is accompanied at times with mischief, since it is likely to arouse idle curiosity and stimulate craving for acquiring control over unknown forces with a view to using them for selfish ends. There is nothing particularly spiritual about occult power as such. Like any other mundane power or scientific invention, it is capable of being used for good ends or bad. It gives immense scope for cooperative work on the higher planes, but this necessarily implies a spiritual preparedness to shoulder the special responsibility. Occultism as a science may be said to be more or less on the same footing as other sciences, but occultism as an art stands by itself.

Occultism as an art

The novice may seek some occult powers and, within certain limits, even succeed in acquiring them. But this new attainment will prove to be a curse rather than a blessing if he is not spiritually prepared for the adequate fulfillment of the new responsibility implied in the acquisition of the new powers. Even the slightest misuse of occult power causes a severe reaction and creates a binding for the soul. Sometimes it may retard the progress of the aspirant and may even lead to a considerable setback. Apart from the spiritual ruin the novice may invite upon himself through indiscreet use of occult power, he is bound to be a source of incalculable harm to others over whom he has succeeded in wielding a formidable advantage.

Misuse of occult power

In the hands of the Masters of spiritual wisdom, occult power is not only safe but has immense capacities that can be harnessed in the service of humanity; yet even they are very sparing and economical in its use. By its very nature, occultism as an art has its own natural limitations. It cannot be widely used for helping the material needs of humanity or helping it in its mundane purposes. The introduction of an uncertain and incalculable factor, which the free exercise of occult power would involve, is bound to create much confusion and disturbance in the ordinary pursuits of man, who must be left to his own limitations, resources, and possibilities for the equal and uninterrupted working out of the law of karma. The use of occult power, therefore, has to be strictly restricted to the furtherance of spiritual purposes.

Occult power must further spiritual purposes

Sometimes the Masters do fulfill some of the mundane desires of their devotees. However, this is not done because they are interested in mundane affairs but because they are interested in weaning their devotees away from their material cravings. When children are very young, they often cannot be induced to learn the alphabet. In order to attract their attention to the alphabet, their elders sometimes present them with letters specially constructed out of sweets. Then they attend to these lessons, not because they are interested in the letters as such, but because they are interested in the sweets. Yet this often proves to be the beginning of their interest in the letters themselves, and the sweets can soon be discarded after they have cultivated this interest. Worldly people are like such young children. Just as a parent may occasionally give a piece of chocolate to the baby in order to encourage it to be good, the Masters might give their worldly-minded devotees certain harmless objects

Material bait for spiritual purposes

they desire so that they may eventually be willing to part with them and become interested in true spirituality.

Worldly people are so immersed in material cravings that nothing interests them unless it has some direct bearing upon the fulfillment of these cravings. Thus they may come to a Perfect Master and serve or respect him in the expectation of being helped with their material problems. When a person approaches a Master with respect, it becomes the duty of the Master to help him spiritually, even when he has come with some other motive. The Master, with his perfect understanding of the human mind, may therefore decide to help the person materially in order to win him over to true spirituality. Such offering of material bait for spiritual purposes is an exception rather than the rule. Mostly the Masters discourage people from approaching them for any material advantage. From the spiritual point of view, it is infinitely better for a person to love a Master simply because he is lovable than to love him for some selfish ends. People should go to a Master because they are genuinely interested in true spirituality and for no other reason. It is only then that they derive the greatest benefit from their contact with the Master.

Masters not to be approached with material motives

Occultism as an art derives its justification solely from its capacity to subserve spiritual purposes; any diversion of occult power from this end may be looked upon as misuse. It must not be summoned merely for worldly purposes. Its true function is not to secure the fulfillment of human cravings but to secure the purification of the human heart. Occultism as an art is among the most effective and potent factors that can contribute to the purging of humanity by helping it to give up baser desires.

Purification of human heart

Occultism as an art becomes particularly relevant and necessary for those who are about to unfold their latent psychic powers and for those who already have considerably developed powers but sometimes are not fully alive to the gross world, owing to the withdrawal of their consciousness to the higher planes. Hence they have to be spoken to in a language they can understand. Many advanced aspirants develop a number of occult and mystic powers, but they are often as much in need of spiritual help as

Use of powers on higher planes

the ordinary run of humanity. As they are in possession of many powers, they can be readily and effectively helped by a Perfect Master irrespective of distance. When the Master's help can be consciously received in the higher planes, it becomes much more fruitful than the help he can give merely through the gross medium.

Apart from the difficulties existing in forward movement on the path, one of the characteristics of advanced aspirants is to get so deeply established in the happiness of their station that they are reluctant to "come down" for work in the gross sphere. This coming down of advanced aspirants must not be confused with the return to normal consciousness after the seventh plane experience, which is the state of God-realization of the Perfect Ones.

Coming down

A Perfect Master's return journey—as well as the consequent position in different planes after Realization—is actuated by altruistic motives and is the result of *prarabdha* (inevitable destiny), which he utilizes for the spiritual uplift of humanity in accordance with his vested authority. Although Perfect Masters are conscious of all the planes simultaneously, it is said that Khwaja Muinuddin Chishti of Ajmer, India, for instance, stationed himself in the fifth plane of involution of consciousness. It is also true that the Avatar functions from all the planes of consciousness simultaneously but sometimes for His universal work stations Himself in a particular plane. Therefore it is said, for example, that the Prophet Muhammad stationed Himself in the seventh plane, while Lord Buddha stationed Himself in the fifth.

The coming down of advanced aspirants, on the other hand, is induced in order to help accelerate their forward movement on the spiritual path when they find themselves hung up anywhere between the planes. Thus, if an aspirant gets hung up somewhere between the third and fourth planes, a Master usually brings him down to the third plane prior to pushing him up to the fourth. Coming down from a high station is also often necessary in the interest of those who are still in the wilderness of the world and have not yet entered the path. The Master may sometimes decide to get some spiritual work done through an advanced aspirant and may require him to postpone his efforts for individual advancement for the sake of others.

Such coming down eventually turns out to be a spiritual preparation for traversing the next stage of the path smoothly and quickly; but even so, the aspirant finds it difficult to renounce the advantages of his attainment for the purpose of helping others. Coming down is particularly difficult for a person intensely experiencing a state of enchantment. In Sufism, this enchantment is known as *hairat.* The aspirant finds it extremely difficult to get out of this state. However, it is necessary that he should resist getting lost in enchantment because sometimes he must come down for the sake of others in the world. A Master has ways of dealing with an advanced aspirant and can bring him around to any unpalatable move.

This is very well illustrated by the story of a famous *wali* named Baba Fariduddin, also known as Ganj-e-Shakkar. Much before he attained Illumination, this wali, or friend of God, was in hairat and completely absorbed in that state. He could not close his eyes, which were always open, dazed, and glassy; and he could not eat. His Master, Khwaja Muinuddin Chishti, wanted him to get out of this state of enchantment and to come down, but the wali found it difficult to obey his Master. Then the Master turned the key and brought him around in the following manner.

Story of Ganj-e-Shakkar

The Master inwardly inspired five thieves to come near the place of Ganj-e-Shakkar. They sat within five paces of the wali and began to divide the plunder they had stolen. Soon they began quarreling with each other, and two of them killed the other three. These two, who were successful in the quarrel, divided the loot between them and ran away. But while running away they passed by the place where the wali was sitting. As soon as they came near him, he regained normal consciousness. The proximity of the criminals was sufficient crude stimulus to bring him down to normal consciousness.

The first thing that the wali saw were some sparrows, and his first impulse was to try his nascent powers on them. He said, "O sparrows, die!" and the sparrows fell down dead. Then he said, "Sparrows, rise up!" and they rose. The two thieves who saw this were amazed, and they requested the wali to raise the three thieves whom they had killed in a moment of anger. On this, the wali addressed himself to the three dead thieves and said, "Rise up!" But they did *not* rise. He was aghast at the thought that he had lost his powers; and repenting for the frivolous use of his powers, he went crying to his Master. When he came near, he saw that those three thieves were massaging the feet of his Master.

The wali then went back to his original place, indifferent to food or drink. He became lean and remained in the same spot for ten years, until white ants began to eat his body. People used to come to the wali and place near him large quantities of sugar, which the ants ate instead. Since he was always surrounded by heaps of sugar, he came to be known as *Ganj-e-Shakkar*, or the "treasury of sugar." His story shows how even the most advanced aspirants need the help of a Master if they are to proceed further on the way to Realization.

Ganj-e-Shakkar's story illustrates the sort of occasion that calls forth the use of occult methods and occult powers; but it must be carefully noted that no occult phenomenon, regardless of magnitude, can have any intrinsic value in itself. The value that seems to belong to any phenomena—occult or nonoccult—is either purely illusory or entirely relative. Illusory values arise when anything acquires false importance, because it stimulates or promises to fulfill the passing cravings and the limited purposes born of ignorance. If the thing is taken out of the context of these passing cravings and limited purposes, it is immediately deprived of the entire meaning with which it seemed to be surcharged. Relative values arise when a thing acquires importance through serving the realization or expression of the Truth. The importance of such things is derived from their being the essential conditions for the game of divine life; and therefore, though it is relative, such value is real and not illusory.

Occult phenomena have no intrinsic value

Most persons consciously or unconsciously attach undue importance to occult phenomena and mistake them for spirituality. For them, miracles and the phenomena of the spirit world are the real topics of absorbing interest, and this is presumed to indicate an interest in a life of true spirituality. There is a very clear and definite distinction, however, between occultism and mysticism, spiritualism and spirituality; and any failure to grasp the full import of this difference can only lead to confusion.

Occultism distinct from spirituality

All miracles belong to the phenomenal world, which is the world of shadows. As phenomena, they are subject to change, and nothing that changes can have lasting value. Realization of the eternal Truth is an initiation into the unchangeable Being, which is the supreme Reality; and no acquaintance with the occult world or capacity to manipulate its forces can really amount to realization of the Truth.

Occult phenomena are as much within the domain of false imagination as are ordinary phenomena of the gross world. From the spiritual point of view, the only important thing is to realize Divine Life and to help others realize it by manifesting it in everyday happenings. To penetrate into the essence of all being and significance and to release the fragrance of that inner attainment for the guidance and benefit of others—by expressing, in the world of forms, truth, love, purity, and beauty—this is the sole game that has intrinsic and absolute worth. All other happenings, incidents, and attainments in themselves can have no lasting importance.

Only realization of Divine Life matters

The Types of Meditation

Part I
The Nature of Meditation and Its Conditions

Meditation a path cut through limitations of mind

Meditation may be described as a path that the individual cuts for himself while trying to get beyond the limitations of the mind. If a person caught in the tangles of a thick forest tries to get out into the open, his efforts to break through the encircling impediments will leave behind the marks of his journey. By the study of these marks an observer would be able to describe the path he traversed in his attempt to come out into the open. The movements of one who comes out of the forest are different in principle from those of a railway engine, for instance, which moves along rails already laid on the course it is to take. The individual is not following a ready-made path; the path becomes imprinted after he has traversed it. In the same way, the person who finds himself drawn into deep meditation is really grappling with the spiritual problems he faces and not merely trying to follow a rigid course that already exists in his mental makeup.

The development of meditation can nevertheless be anticipated in outline by those who have direct insight into the particular contours of the mind of an individual, in the same way that one who has a thorough acquaintance with the details of the constitution of the earth's solidified crust may, in general, expect the outburst of a volcano in one region rather than another. When the surging powers in the bowels of the earth are trying to burst out, they are bound to take the line of least resistance; and their actual passage will be dependent largely upon the nature of the surroundings with which they are confronted. The difference between volcanic forces and the spiritual urge is that the former are unconscious, while the latter is a conscious phenomenon. Intelligence plays an important part in the course of meditation; and it is this intelligence that is kindled by a Perfect Master, who gives the aspirant a few simple suggestions about what kinds of things he has to do or expect in his meditations.

General outline of meditation can be anticipated

Meditation has often been misunderstood as a mechanical process of *forcing* the mind upon some idea or object. Most people naturally have an aversion to meditation because they experience great difficulty in attempting to coerce the mind in a particular direction or to pin it down to one particular thing. Any purely mechanical handling of the mind is not only irksome but is bound ultimately to be unsuccessful. The first principle aspirants have to remember is that the mind can be controlled and directed in meditation only according to laws inherent in the makeup of the mind itself, and not by means of the application of any mechanical or semimechanical force.

Intelligent meditation sustained by interest

Many persons who do not technically meditate are oftentimes found to be deeply and intensely engrossed in systematic and clear thinking about some practical problem or theoretical subject. Their mental process is, in a sense, very much like meditation, inasmuch as the mind is engrossed in intense thinking about a particular subject to the exclusion of all other irrelevant things. Meditation is often easy and spontaneous in such mental processes because the mind is dwelling upon an object that it is interested in and that it increasingly understands.

The spiritual tragedy about ordinary trains of thought is that they are not directed toward things that really matter. On the other hand, the object of real meditation always has to be carefully selected and must be spiritually important; it has to be some divine form or object, or some spiritually significant theme or truth. In order to attain success in meditation, the mind must not only get interested in divine subjects or truths but must also begin trying to understand and appreciate them. Such intelligent meditation is a natural process of the mind; and since it avoids the monotonous rigidity and regularity of mechanical meditation, it becomes not only spontaneous and inspiring but easy and successful.

Meditation and concentration

Meditation should be distinguished from concentration. Meditation is the first stage of a process that gradually develops into concentration. In concentration the mind seeks to unite with its object by the process of fixing itself upon that object; whereas meditation consists in thorough thinking about a particular object to the exclusion of every other thing. In concentration there is practically no movement of the mind, but in meditation the mind moves from one relevant idea to another. In concentration the mind merely dwells upon some form or a pithy and concise formula, without amplifying it through a succession of ideas. In meditation the mind tries to understand and assimilate the object by dwelling upon diverse attributes of the form or various implications of the formula. In concentration as well as in meditation, there is a peaceful intermingling of love and longing for the divine object or principle on which the mind dwells; and both these activities are very different from the merely mechanical processes that have rigid regularity and unrelieved monotony.

Persons with no capacity for intense concentration have to begin with meditation; whereas for those who have a capacity for concentration, meditation is unnecessary. It is sufficient if they concentrate on the mere form of the God-Man or a Man-God or on some simple formula like "I am neither the gross body nor the subtle body nor the mental body: I am the *atma* (soul)."

Silence and seclusion

Meditation is essentially an individual matter in the sense that it is not for self-display in society but for one's own spiritual advancement. Utter isolation of the individual from social surroundings is almost always conducive to the unhampered practice of meditation. The ancient yogis took to mountain tops or caves in search of complete seclusion. Great quiet and undisturbed silence are essential for attaining success. However, it is not necessary for a person to go to the mountains or caves in search of these conditions.

Even in cities a little care and trouble can secure for the aspirant the quiet, silence, and seclusion necessary to facilitate and promote progress in the different forms of meditation.

Value of darkness

Darkness or closing one's eyes is not absolutely necessary for meditation. If the aspirant is face to face with the object of meditation, he may have a successful meditation even when his eyes are open. But in most cases, getting away from all gross sight and sound is more conducive to intensive meditation. To secure complete external silence involves careful selection of the spot for meditation, but one has only to close one's eyes in order to protect the mind from the disturbance of sights. Sometimes, when there is light, closing the eyes is not sufficient to ward off all visual stimulation. Then it is advisable to start meditation in complete darkness. Darkness normally promotes progress in meditation.

Posture for meditation

With regard to posture, there are no fixed rules. Any posture that is comfortable may be adopted, so long as it contributes to the alertness of the mind and does not induce sleep. The posture should not involve any physical tension or pain, because it would then draw attention to the body itself. The body should, therefore, be completely relaxed as when going to sleep, but the usual position taken in sleep should be avoided because of its tendency to induce sleep. When the body has assumed a convenient and suitable posture, it is helpful to think of the head as the center of the body. When the head is regarded as the center, it is easier to forget the body and to fix one's attention on the object of meditation.

Importance of fixing spot, posture, hour

It is desirable that the aspirant should maintain the same posture for each meditation. The previous associations the posture has with his meditations endow it with a special capacity to induce and facilitate similar meditations. When the body has assumed the chosen posture, it is constantly under the subconscious suggestion that it must no longer obtrude upon consciousness and that it has to serve the purpose of meditation. Choosing the same spot and a fixed hour also has a salutary effect. Hence the aspirant must be serious about resorting to an identical place, posture, and hour. The choice of the spot also involves consideration of the spiritual associations and possibilities of the spot. Special importance is attached to meditating in holy places where the Masters themselves have lived or meditated.

The place, posture, and hour of meditation all have their relative importance, which varies according to the peculiarities and history of the individual. A Master, therefore, often gives different instructions to each disciple to suit the individual case. However, when meditation has become habitual through constant practice, adherence to a fixed place, posture, or time can be dispensed with; and the aspirant can carry on his meditation at any time under any conditions. Even when he is walking, he may be inwardly absorbed in meditation.

Meditation should be joyous

Meditation should not be approached with a heavy heart, as if one were taking castor oil. One has to be serious about meditation but not grave or melancholy. Humor and cheerfulness not only do not interfere with the progress of meditation but actually contribute to it. Meditation should not be turned into a distasteful and tiresome thing. The aspirant should freely allow himself the natural joy that is attendant upon successful meditation, without getting addicted to it. Meditation should be something like a picnic on the higher planes. Like excursions into new and beautiful natural surroundings, meditation brings with it a sense of enthusiasm, adventure, peace, and exhilaration. All thoughts of depression, fear, or worry have to be cut out completely if there is to be really successful meditation.

Collective meditation

Though meditation is essentially an individual matter, collective meditation has its own advantages. If different aspirants who are in harmony with each other take to the same line of meditation together, their thoughts have a tendency to augment and strengthen each other. This is particularly noticeable when disciples of the same Master are collectively engaged in meditating upon their Master. If collective meditation of this type is to yield its full advantage, each aspirant who participates must be concerned with the course of his own meditation and not with what the others of the group are doing. Though he starts his meditation in the company of others, he has to lose himself in the object of his meditation. He has to be entirely oblivious of the whole world, including his body, and he has to be exclusively cognizant of the object agreed upon before the beginning of the meditation. When intelligently handled, collective meditation can be of immense help to beginners, while advanced aspirants can carry on by themselves.

Emergence of disturbing thoughts

In ordinary thinking, the uninterrupted flow of relevant trains of ideas is common; but when the mind sets itself to systematic meditation, there is inevitably a reactionary tendency for irrelevant and contrary thoughts to emerge and create disturbances. This is the law of the mind, and the aspirant should not be upset by the appearance in the consciousness of many contrary and unwholesome thoughts that had hitherto never made their appearance. Meditation involves bringing the subconscious contents of the mind to the forefront of consciousness. Like the conjurer who summons into existence many strange and unexpected things, the process of meditation invites many absurd and unwanted thoughts. The aspirant must expect and be prepared for all these disturbing thoughts and should exercise inexhaustible patience, with unshakable confidence that ultimately all these disturbances will be overcome.

Technique for dealing with disturbing thoughts

The last but not least important condition for attaining success in meditation is adoption of the right technique for handling disturbing thoughts and mental influences. It is useless to waste energy by trying to combat and repress disturbing thoughts *directly*. Any such attempt involves giving further attention to them; and they feed upon the very attention given for the purpose of repressing them, thereby being further strengthened and confirmed in the consciousness. It is best to ignore them and turn to the object of meditation as early as possible, without attaching any undue importance to the disturbing factors. By recognizing the irrelevance and worthlessness of disturbing thoughts and the relative value and importance of the object of meditation, it becomes possible to let the disturbing thoughts die through sheer neglect—thus making the mind permanently steady in the object of meditation.

The Types of Meditation

Part II
The Chief Types of Meditation
and Their Relative Value

Types of meditation classified by three principles

Meditation is of different types, which can be conveniently distinguished from each other on the basis of three distinct principles: (1) the function meditation performs in spiritual advancement, (2) the part of personality that is predominantly brought into play during the process of meditation, or (3) the items of experience it tries to understand. Any one of these three principles can be adopted for the classification of the different types of meditation. The last principle will be used while giving a detailed account of the different forms of meditation, as it is most suitable for enumerative purposes. This Part will make use of the first two principles, as they are helpful in different ways in explaining the relative value of the various forms of meditation.

Associative and dissociative meditation

With reference to the *first principle,* meditation has to serve the purpose of associating consciousness with the eternal Truth and of dissociating consciousness from the false and unimportant things of the phenomenal world. There thus arise two types of meditation. *Associative* meditation predominantly involves the synthetic activity of the mind (*anwaya*), and *dissociative* meditation predominantly involves the analytic activity of the mind (*vyatireka*). Associative meditation may be illustrated by the formula "I am infinite," and dissociative meditation may be illustrated by the formula "I am not my desires." Through associative meditation the aspirant tries to unite with the spiritual ideal as mentally constructed by him. Through dissociative meditation the aspirant tries to separate himself from the conditions that come to him as antispiritual. Associative meditation is a process of *assimilation* of the essentials of spiritual life; dissociative meditation is a process of *elimination* of those factors that prevent the life of the spirit.

Dissociative meditation paves way for associative

Associative meditation is concerned with objects that are, so to say, selected from the land of light, and dissociative meditation is concerned with objects that are parts of the land of shadows. The world of illusions, like the world of shadows, has a bewildering charm of its own. If a person is to succeed in getting out of the world of illusions and arrive at the Truth, he must develop resistance to the enticements of the world of illusions by repeated recognition of its real worthlessness—just as a person must develop discontent with the world of shadows if he is to come into the light. Therefore, dissociative meditation is a preliminary to associative meditation. It comes first and has its own value, but it is meant merely to pave the way for associative meditation.

Associative meditation most fruitful

Associative meditation and dissociative meditation are both necessary in their own way, but eventually associative meditation turns out to be far more fruitful and important than dissociative meditation. If a person is surrounded by shadows, it does not help very much to be continuously upset about them. If his only interest is being cross with the shadows, there will be no end to his worries. But if, instead of fretting and fuming about the engulfing shadows, he sets himself to the more important task of bringing himself under the full blaze of the sun, he will discover that all the shadows have disappeared.

What really matters is not aimless discontent with existing limitations but directive effort toward the established ideal. As long as the person is turned toward the sun and is trying to walk into the light, the shadows that encircle him cannot be serious handicaps to his emancipation. In the same way, the aspirant need not worry too much about his failings, as long as his heart is firmly set upon uniting with his spiritual ideal. His failings will all have vanished into nothingness when his pilgrimage ends.

Analogy of food

Associative meditation is to the spirit what the assimilation of food is to the body. The body can make up for its deficiencies by assimilating the right sort of food. Similarly the mind can secure its health by the assimilation of spiritual truths through meditation. It is necessary to strike a balance between the different forms of associative meditation, even though in their own way they are all good, just as it is necessary to balance one's diet, even when one is satisfied as to the nutritive value of the different components of the diet. Disproportionate development of mental life hampers advancement because of the internal fracturing that accompanies it; while happy combinations of the different forms of meditation facilitate rapid progress because they secure a harmonized and balanced mind. The right combinations are those that promote an advancing equilibrium by emphasizing just those aspects of the Truth that are relevant to removing the special obstacles the aspirant is faced with at the moment.

Extension of diet analogy

The analogy of diet can be extended even to the second type, dissociative meditation, which consists in avoiding and eliminating things that are antispiritual. As faulty diet can upset physical health, faulty types of meditation can throw the mind into disorder. As the wrong type of food can ruin health instead of nourishing it, instinctive meditation on the objects of craving creates further fetters for the mind instead of breaking those that already exist. Therefore it is as important to avoid the wrong type of meditation as it is to avoid the wrong type of food. Further, just as good health requires constant elimination of waste products and poisonous substances, spiritual health requires the expulsion of undesirable thoughts and emotions.

Second principle

Thus far, the explanations have differentiated the two types of meditation that may be observed from the standpoint of the first principle, the *function* meditation performs in spiritual advancement. It is equally illuminating to understand the principle by which the process of meditation is differentiated by considering the nature of the part of the personality that is predominantly brought into play during the process. The application of this *second principle* results in three distinct types of meditation.

Discriminative meditation and meditations of heart and action

In the first type of meditation, the intellect is predominantly brought into play; it might be called *discriminative* meditation. In the second type, the heart is predominantly brought into play; it might be called the meditation of the *heart*. In the third type, the active nature of man is predominantly brought into play; it might be called the meditation of *action*. Discriminative meditation is represented by intellectual assertion of a formula like "I am not my body but the Infinite." The meditation of the heart is represented by a steady and unhampered flow of love from the aspirant to the divine Beloved. The meditation of action is represented by an unreserved dedication of one's life to the selfless service of a Perfect Master or of humanity. Of these three types, the meditation of the heart is the highest and most important; but the other two types also have their own value and cannot be neglected without serious detriment to the spiritual progress of the aspirant.

Types of meditation supplement each other

The different types of meditation must not be looked upon as being entirely exclusive of each other. They can proceed in all sorts of combinations. Sometimes one type of meditation inevitably leads to another type, and progress in one of the meditations is often held up until there is corresponding progress in the others. All the different types of meditation are valuable for securing the spiritual advancement of the aspirant. They almost always make up for mutual deficiencies and supplement each other.

One type of meditation may interfere with another

One type of meditation may also interfere seriously with the progress of another type if it is resorted to at an inopportune moment. The different types of genuine meditation all dwell upon aspects of life that are equally true; but depending upon the mental state of the individual, the assimilation of a certain truth of life is often more urgently necessary than the assimilation of some other truths of life. Therefore, a Master never prescribes the same form of meditation to all but gives specific instructions according to the individual needs of the aspirant.

Need for instructions from Master

The type of meditation necessary in a particular situation often cannot be correctly ascertained by the aspirant for himself. The aspirant can get addicted to one type of meditation so exclusively that he finds it difficult to get out of the groove that has been cut into his mind by the type he has been practicing. He fails to see the importance of any other type of meditation and is not drawn to it. Of course the aspirant himself may come to feel his own deficiency along a particular line. But just as many medicines are disagreeable to the patient, the types of meditation that are really indicated in a specific situation often seem distasteful to the aspirant—and he is disinclined to take to them. The help and advice of a Master are indispensable on this point. The insight that the Master has into the deeper and real spiritual needs of the aspirant is infinitely greater than the insight the aspirant can hope to have into himself. Specific instructions from the Master supply the necessary corrective for the neglected aspects of personality.

True value of meditation perceived only in its practice

Although the aspirant may start with an initial aversion to the type of meditation he needs, he becomes interested in it when he sees its real value and purpose. He can come to appreciate the real value and purpose of a particular type of meditation only when he has tried it. It is not possible to discover the value and possibilities of any type of meditation by purely theoretical speculation about that mode of meditation. Such purely theoretical guesswork may have some superficial results, but it fails to fathom the real unity of meditation. Like many other things of spiritual importance, meditation yields its full significance after the person has gotten into it and not when he is trying to understand it by envisaging it from outside.

Determination necessary for success in meditation

In order to have real success in any mode of meditation, the aspirant must launch upon it with the determination to explore all its possibilities. He must not start with any limiting reservations and should be prepared to encounter unexpected states of consciousness. He should be willing to go where that line of meditation leads him without making any rigid demands based on preformed expectations. The very essence of meditation is one-pointedness and the exclusion of all other considerations, even when these considerations happen to be enticing.

Supervision of Master is indispensable

However, if the aspirant takes to any type of meditation on his own initiative and without having the benefit of the guidance and supervision of a Master, he may get into it so far that he loses perspective and is unable to recover himself. It may be impossible for him to change over to some other complementary mode of meditation, even when it is absolutely necessary. This risk is avoided if the aspirant has taken to a line of meditation on the orders of his Master. When he is under the guidance and supervision of a Master, the Master not only can ask the aspirant to halt at the right time but also can actually help him get out of the grooves cut by his previous meditation.

Illustrative story

In this connection there is an illustrative story of a man who was highly intelligent and who wanted to know from personal experience what it felt like to be suffocated by hanging. He was not content merely with imagining what it would be like but wanted to experience it himself. So he asked a friend to help him perform the experiment. He said that he would be hung by a rope and would signal to his friend when the feeling of suffocation reached the danger limit. He further asked his friend not to relieve him from the gallows before he received the intended signal.

His friend agreed to all this, and the man was hung by tying a rope around his own neck. But when he suffocated, he became unconscious and therefore could not give his friend the promised signal. The friend, however, was wise; finding that the suffocation of the man had really reached the danger point, he went beyond the limits of his agreement and relieved the man just in time to save his life. The man was saved not through his own thoughtfulness and precautions but through the wise discretion of his friend. In the same way, it is safer for the aspirant to rely upon the Master than upon any provisions of his own making.

The Types of Meditation

Part III
General Classification of the Forms of Meditation

The process of meditation aims at understanding and transcending the wide and varied range of experience. When meditation is interpreted in this manner, it is at once seen to be something that is not peculiar to a few aspirants. It turns out to be a process that every living creature in some way is engaged in. The tiger intent upon devouring a lamb that it has spied "meditates" upon the lamb. The lamb in its turn, having sighted the tiger, "meditates" upon the tiger. The passenger who waits on the platform for a train is "meditating" upon the train; and the driver of the train, expecting to be relieved at the next station, is "meditating" upon the station. The scientist who works upon an unsolved problem "meditates" upon that problem. The patient who is waiting with tense anxiety for a doctor is "meditating" upon the doctor; and the doctor who is awaiting payment of a bill is "meditating" upon the account. When a police officer tries to catch a thief, they both "meditate" upon each other.

Meditation is universal

The person who falls in love is "meditating" upon the beloved; and one who is jealously watchful of a rival is "meditating" upon the rival. The individual struck with grief at the death of a friend is "meditating" upon the friend. Someone who seeks revenge upon an enemy "meditates" upon the enemy. The woman lost in choosing attractive clothes to wear is "meditating" upon herself as the body; and the man who boasts of his intellectual or psychic attainments is "meditating" upon himself as the mind.

Spiritually important meditation

All these are, in a way, forms of meditation; but in spiritual discourses the term *meditation* is usually restricted to those forms of meditation that tackle the problem of understanding experience intensively and systematically. In the above examples, meditation is a result of a natural application of the mind to the objects with which it is presented. In this application of the mind, the individual is almost unconscious of the ultimate purpose of the process of meditation. In the realm of spirituality, however, meditation in the initial stages at least is deliberate.

During such meditation the subject is more specifically conscious of the ultimate objective. Nevertheless, the forms of meditation characteristic of the spiritual life are *continuous* with those found throughout the world of consciousness. The spiritual forms of meditation spring into existence only when the other more general forms of meditation have brought the person to a certain crisis or blind alley. Then he is forced to choose the object of meditation in the light of some spiritual ideal and must also revise the manner of meditation he may have become accustomed to.

General and specialized meditation

The spiritually important forms of meditation are of two kinds: general meditation, which consists in the assimilation of the divine Truths; and specialized meditation, in which the mind selects some definite item of experience and is exclusively concerned with it. General meditation is only a carrying further of the ordinary thought processes systematically and intensively. It is different from the many prespiritual meditations of a worldly person only in so far as the thought processes now come to be directed toward realities that have spiritual importance and the mind makes intelligent use of the expositions of the divine Truths given by those who *know*—without renouncing its critical powers and inherent zest for the Truth.

The specialized forms of meditation, on the other hand, imply and require something more than a purely intellectual approach to the

Truth. In the specialized forms of meditation, as in general meditation, the mind has an opportunity to have an intellectual understanding of the object of meditation. But in addition, they also help to cultivate mental discipline, develop capacities hitherto dormant, and unfold latent possibilities of personality. The problem in specialized forms of meditation is not theoretical but practical. Specialized forms of meditation are helpful for overcoming specific obstacles in the way of enlightenment and Realization; they aim at controlling the mind and going beyond it. Specialized forms of meditation are more like the desperate attempts of a person to break through the walls of a prison than like the idle speculative activity involved in forming opinions about the strength of the different parts of the prison walls or what may be visible after breaking into the open.

Specialized meditation is practical

In spiritual life, even a sincere mistake taken seriously may have more value than halfhearted allegiance to theoretical or formal truth. The practical purpose in the specialized forms of meditation must sometimes prevail, even at the cost of formal and theoretical truth. Thus in meditation, while concentrating on a particular form or formula, no other form or formula can be allowed access to the mind—although, intrinsically, this other form or formula may have the same or even greater spiritual importance. If an aspirant has been meditating upon the form of one Perfect Master, he has to exclude from his mind all ideas of any other Masters, though they are as perfect as the Master on whom he is meditating. The formula of intensive thinking on the Master can be as helpful in achieving the goal as the process of making the mind blank.

Practical purpose may prevail over formal truth

As a rule, mixing up the specialized forms of meditation is not desirable, though theoretically they may all be equally directed toward different aspects of the Truth. The task of bringing together the different facets of the Truth and building up a whole and complete view of life is attempted by general meditation, in which thought is free, comprehensive, and receptive to all aspects of the Truth. Such general meditation has its own value and justification. General meditation is helpful before special-

Function of general meditation

ized forms of meditation as well as after trying them, but it cannot take the place of specialized forms of meditation because these have a different purpose and function.

The different forms of specialized meditation are comparable to different forms of bodily exercise, each of which may have some specific purpose. Exercise of the muscles is meant only to strengthen the muscles, but this does not mean that the muscles are the only important part of the body. All types of exercise are important for securing the general health of the body, although it may not be possible to take all of them at the same time. The functions of the different specialized forms of exercise have, however, to be correlated and governed in the light of one's knowledge of true health or proportionate development of the body. In the same way, the functions of the specialized forms of meditation have to be correlated with and governed by the whole and complete ideal of life. This the aspirant constructs through the process of general meditation, or unrestrained thought, which knows no law except that of finding the Truth in all its aspects. Just as specialized forms of meditation cannot be replaced by general meditation, general meditation cannot be replaced by specialized forms of meditation. Both are necessary and have their own value.

Both forms of meditation necessary

For enumerative purposes, the different specialized forms of meditation can be conveniently classified (according to the *third principle*) on the basis of those items of experience the mind tries to understand. Human experience, in all its variety, is characterized throughout by the dual aspect of subject and object. Some forms of meditation are concerned with the *objects* of experience; some are concerned with the *subject* of experience; and some forms of meditation are concerned with the *mental operations* that are involved in the interaction of the subject and the object. Thus three kinds of meditation are defined.

Different specialized meditations

All the forms of meditation that the aspirant (*sadhak*) might adopt can ultimately culminate—through the grace of a Perfect Master—in the goal of the *Nirvikalpa* state. *Nirvikalpa Samadhi,* or divinity in expression, is the experience of the Nirvikalpa state of uninterrupted, spontaneous Self-knowledge of

Nirvana, Nirvikalpa and Sahaj Samadhi

a God-realized being (*Siddha*). It is preceded by *Nirvana,* or absorption in divinity. The Sadgurus experience *Sahaj Samadhi,* or divinity in action, which is preceded by the states of Nirvana and Nirvikalpa. Sahaj Samadhi is the effortless and continuous state of Perfection of the Sadgurus, while it is the very *life* of the Avatar.

Table of General Classification of the Types of Meditation

I	THE VARIED FORMS OF MEDITATION BEFORE A PERSON BECOMES AN ASPIRANT			
II	FORMS OF MEDITATION OF THE ASPIRANT (SADHAK)			
	A	General Meditation and the assimilation of divine Truths.	1	Philosophical thinking
			2	Hearing discourses from the Masters
			3	Reading the written expositions of the Masters
	B	Specialized Meditation, which selects some definite items of experience	1	Meditation concerned with the objects of experience
			2	Meditation concerned with the subject of experience
			3	Meditation concerned with mental operations
III	SAHAJ SAMADHI, OR DIVINITY IN ACTION, OF SADGURUS AND THE AVATAR			Nirvana, or absorption in divinity
				Nirvikalpa Samadhi, or divinity in expression

Table of General Classification

The general classification of the types of meditation has been given in the *Table of General Classification,* which serves to summarize this chapter (Part III). Among the different kinds of meditation mentioned in this Table, the varied forms of meditation that are encountered before becoming a sadhak have already been illustrated in the beginning of this Part. The different forms of General Meditation will be dealt with in Part IV. The different forms of Specialized Meditation, along with their subdivisions, will each be explained individually in Parts V and VI. Nirvikalpa Samadhi and Sahaj Samadhi will be explained in Parts VII and VIII.

The Types of Meditation

Part IV
Assimilation of the Divine Truths

Section A
Modes of General Meditation

The beginnings of spiritual life are marked and helped by general meditation, which is not concerned exclusively with selected specific items of experience but which, in its comprehensive scope, seeks to understand and assimilate the divine Truths of life and the universe. When the aspirant is interested in the wider problems of the ultimate nature of life and the universe and begins to think about them, he may be said to have launched himself upon such meditation. Much of what is included in philosophy is a result of trying to develop an intellectual grasp of the ultimate nature of life and the universe.

Limits of philosophical thinking

The purely intellectual grasp of divine Truths remains feeble, incomplete, and indecisive, owing to the limitations of the experiences that may be available as the foundation of the structures of speculation. The *philosophical* meditation that consists in free and unaided thinking does not lead to conclusive results. It often leads to diverse, conflicting systems or views; nevertheless, philosophical thinking is not without value. Besides leading the aspirant a certain extent into the realm of knowledge, it provides an intellectual discipline that enables him to receive and grasp divine Truths when he happens to come upon them through those who *know*.

The more fruitful mode of general meditation consists in studying the revealed Truths concerning life and the universe. This mode of understanding and assimilating the divine Truths can start by hearing or reading expositions of the divine Truth, which have their source in the Masters of wisdom. The discourses or the writings of the Avatar and the Perfect Masters, whether living or of the past, are suitable objects for this mode of general meditation, because the assimilation of divine Truths revealed through them enables the aspirant to bring his life into line with God's purpose in the universe.

Study of revealed Truths

The divine Truths are most easily grasped and assimilated when they are passed on directly to the aspirant by a living Master. Such personal communications of the Master have a power and efficacy that can never belong to information received by the aspirant through other sources. The word becomes alive and potent because of the life and personality of the Master. Hence many scriptures emphasize the need for *hearing* the divine Truths directly through the spoken word of a Master. The mode of general meditation that depends upon hearing expositions of the divine Truths is undoubtedly the best, when the aspirant has an opportunity to contact a living Master and listen to him.

Value of hearing

It is not always possible, however, for the aspirant to contact and listen to a living Master. In such cases meditation through *reading* has some advantages of its own. For the generality of aspirants, meditation through reading has hardly any suitable substitute because it starts from written expositions, which are available at any convenient time. Meditation that starts from reading about revealed Truths has this special advantage of being easily accessible to most aspirants.

Advantage of reading

Section B
Reading as Meditation

Meditation through reading has its handicaps because most written expositions of the divine Truths are meant for intellectual study rather than for assimilation through meditation. The difficulties aspirants experience in this connection are due either to the fact that the method of meditation is not adapted to the subject matter; or to some flaw in the method, which makes it mechanical and uninspiring; or to the unwieldiness or vagueness of the subject matter used for meditation.

Handicaps of reading

All these causes, which vitiate meditation and make it unsuccessful, have been avoided in the specific meditation recommended in this Part. It is intended not only to explain the manner of carrying on meditation through reading but also to provide an exposition of divine Truths in order to fulfill the requirements of this form of meditation. The usual difficulties existing in meditation through reading have been removed in this specific meditation: by ensuring that the process of meditation and the subject matter are adapted to each other and to the conditions of intelligent meditation; by elaborating the different phases of the meditation that starts from reading; and by providing a specially prepared brief exposition of the divine Truths that is suitable and valuable subject matter for meditation through reading.

Difficulties removed by specific meditation through reading

The form of meditation that starts from reading about the divine Truths has three stages:

Three stages of meditation through reading

1. In the first stage the aspirant will have to read the exposition daily and simultaneously think about it thoroughly.

2. In the second stage actual reading becomes unnecessary, but the subject matter of the exposition is mentally revived and thought over constantly.

3. In the third stage it is quite unnecessary for the mind to revive the words in the exposition separately and consecutively, and all discursive thinking about the subject matter comes to an end. At this stage of meditation, the mind is no longer occupied with any train of thought but has a clear, spontaneous, and intuitive perception of the sublime Truths expressed in the exposition.

Since intelligent meditation consists in thorough thinking about a particular subject, it follows that the best help for meditation would be a brief and clear exposition of the subject of meditation. The following concise exposition of the divine Truths comprises the whole story of creation, as well as a complete account of the spiritual path and the goal of Self-realization. The aspirant can intelligently read the exposition and assimilate the sublime Truths it embodies.

Subject for meditation

This special form of meditation is extremely easy and useful because reading the subject matter and thinking about it have to be done simultaneously. Further, by making the exposition of the subject clear and concise, the probability of any disturbance arising out of irrelevant thoughts is eliminated. It is extremely difficult to avoid the disturbance of irrelevant thoughts while meditating upon some lengthy essay or book, even if it is committed to memory. Spontaneous meditation about it therefore becomes impracticable. The appearance of irrelevant thoughts becomes very probable in lengthy meditation on abstract ideas or on some concrete object of experience. But irrelevant thoughts are extremely improbable if the subject matter used for meditation consists of a brief exposition of the supersensible Truth. If the aspirant meditates upon the following exposition of the divine Truths in the manner that has been indicated above, meditation will become not only spontaneous and easy, delightful and inspiring, but also helpful and successful. The aspirant will thus be taking a very important step toward the realization of the goal of life.

Brief exposition for meditation through reading

Section C
The Divine Truths
(for meditation through reading)
The Journey of the Soul to the Oversoul

Atma, or the soul, is in reality identical with *Paramatma,* or the Oversoul—which is one, infinite, and eternal. The soul is in fact beyond the gross, subtle, and mental worlds. But it experiences itself as being limited owing to its identification with the *sharir* (*sthul sharir,* or gross body); the *pran* (*sukshma sharir,* or subtle body, which is the vehicle of desires and vital forces); and the *manas* (*karan sharir,* or mental body, which is the seat of the mind). The soul in its transcendental state is *one*—formless, eternal, and infinite—and yet

Soul and its illusion

identifies itself with the phenomenal world of forms, which are many and finite and destructible. This is Maya, or cosmic Illusion.

States of phenomenal world

The phenomenal world of finite objects is utterly illusory and false. It has three states: the *gross,* the *subtle,* and the *mental.* Although all three of these states of the world are false, they represent different *degrees* of falseness. Thus the gross world is farthest from Truth (God), the subtle world is nearer Truth, and the mental world is nearest to Truth. All three states of the world owe their existence to cosmic Illusion, which the soul has to transcend before it realizes the Truth.

Purpose of creation

The sole purpose of creation is for the soul to enjoy the infinite state of the Oversoul *consciously*. Although the soul eternally exists in and with the Oversoul in an inviolable unity, it cannot be conscious of this unity independently of creation, which is within the limitations of time. It must therefore evolve consciousness before it can realize its true status and nature as being identical with the infinite Oversoul, which is one without a second. The evolution of consciousness requires the duality of subject and object—the center of consciousness and the environment (that is, the world of forms).

Cause of cosmic Illusion

How does the soul get caught up in Illusion? How did the formless, infinite, and eternal Soul come to experience itself as having form and as being finite and destructible? How did *Purusha*, or the supreme Spirit, come to think of itself as *prakriti,* or the world of nature? In other words, what is the cause of the cosmic Illusion in which the individualized soul finds itself? To realize the true status of the Oversoul—which is one, indivisible, real, and infinite—the soul needs consciousness. The soul does get consciousness; however this consciousness is not of God but of the universe, not of the Oversoul but of its shadow, not of the One but of many, not of the Infinite but of the finite, not of the Eternal but of the transitory. Thus the soul, instead of realizing the Oversoul, gets involved in cosmic Illusion; and hence, though really infinite, it comes to experience itself as finite. In other words, when the soul develops consciousness, it does not become conscious of its own true nature but of the phenomenal world, which is its own shadow.

In order to become conscious of the phenomenal world, the soul must assume some form as its medium for experiencing the world; and the degree and kind of consciousness are determined by the nature of the form used as the medium. The soul first becomes conscious of the gross world through a gross form. The consciousness of the gross world that it has in the beginning is of the most partial and rudimentary type. Correspondingly, the soul assumes the most undeveloped form, that of stone.*

Evolution and degrees of consciousness

The driving force of evolution consists in the momentum consciousness receives owing to the conservation of the impressions (sanskaras) left by diverse desires or conditions. Thus the sanskaras cultivated in a particular form have to be worked out and fulfilled through the medium of a higher form and a correspondingly more developed consciousness of the gross world. The soul, therefore, has to assume higher and higher forms (like metal, vegetable, worm, fish, bird, and animal) until as last it assumes a human form, in which it has fully developed consciousness —in all the aspects of knowing, feeling, and willing—of the gross world.

Driving force of evolution

The manner in which sanskaras result in the evolution of consciousness, and the corresponding forms, has a useful analogue in ordinary experience. If a man has the desire to act the part of a king on the stage, he can only experience it by actually putting on the garb of a king and going on the stage. This is true of aspirations and desires; they can only be worked out and fulfilled by bringing about an actual change in the entire situation, as well as the medium, through which the situation may be adequately experienced. The parallel is very helpful in understanding the driving force of evolution, which is not mechanical but purposive.

The sanskaras are not only responsible for the evolution of the form (body) and the kind of consciousness connected with it, but they are also responsible for the riveting of consciousness to the phenomenal world. They make emancipation of consciousness (that is, the withdrawal of consciousness from the phenomenal world to the soul itself) impossible at the subhuman stage and difficult at the human level. Since consciousness

Identification with forms

*For earlier identification of the soul with gaseous forms see *God Speaks* by Meher Baba.—ED.

clings to the previous sanskaras and experience of the phenomenal world is conditioned by the use of an adequate form (body) as a medium, the soul at every stage of evolution comes to identify itself with the form. Thus the soul, which in reality is infinite and formless, experiences itself as finite and thinks of itself as being stone, metal, vegetable, worm, fish, bird, or animal, according to the degree of the development of consciousness. Finally, while experiencing the gross world through the human form, the soul thinks that it is a human being.

The soul has fully developed and complete consciousness in the first human form, and therefore there is no need for any further evolution of the gross form (body). The evolution of forms thus comes to an end with the attainment of the human form. To experience the sanskaras cultivated in the human form, the soul has to reincarnate again and again in human forms. The innumerable human forms through which the soul has to pass are determined by the law of karma, or the nature of its previous sanskaras (whether of virtue or vice, happiness or misery). During these lives the soul, which is eternal, identifies itself with the gross body, which is destructible.

Reincarnation and law of karma

While developing full consciousness of the gross world, the soul simultaneously develops the subtle and mental bodies. But as long as its consciousness is confined to the gross world alone, it cannot use these bodies consciously in wakefulness. It becomes conscious of these bodies and the corresponding worlds only when its full consciousness turns *inward*, that is, toward itself. When the soul is conscious of the subtle world through the subtle body, it identifies itself with the subtle body; and when it is conscious of the mental world through the mental body, it identifies itself with the mental body; just as it identifies itself with the gross body when it is conscious of the gross world through the gross body.

Subtle and mental bodies

The homeward journey of the soul consists in freeing itself from the illusion of being identical with its bodies—gross, subtle, and mental. When the attention of the soul turns toward Self-knowledge and Self-realization, there is a gradual loosening and disappearance of the sanskaras that keep consciousness turned toward the

Spiritual path

phenomenal world. Disappearance of the sanskaras proceeds side by side with piercing through the veil of cosmic Illusion, and the soul not only begins to transcend the different states of the phenomenal world but also to know itself as different from its bodies. The spiritual path begins when the soul tries to find itself and turns its full consciousness toward Truth (God).

At the first stage the soul becomes totally unconscious of its gross body and of the gross world, and experiences the subtle world through the medium of its subtle body, with which it identifies itself. In the second stage the soul is totally unconscious of its gross and subtle bodies, and also of the gross and subtle worlds, and experiences the mental world through the medium of its mental body, with which it now identifies itself. At this stage the soul may be said to be face to face with God, or the Oversoul, which it recognizes as infinite. But though it recognizes the infinity of the Oversoul, which it objectifies, it looks upon itself as being finite because of its identification with the mental body, or mind.

Thus we have the paradox that the soul, which in reality is infinite, sees its infinite state but still continues to regard itself as finite; because while seeing its infinite state, it looks upon itself as the mind. It imagines itself to be the mind and looks upon the Oversoul as the object of the mind. Further, it not only longs to be one with the objectified Oversoul but also tries hard to fulfill that longing.

In the third stage the full consciousness of the soul is drawn still further inward toward itself, and it ceases to identify itself even with the mental body. Thus in the third and last stage, which is the goal, the soul ceases to identify itself with any of the three bodies that it had to develop for evolving full consciousness. Now it not only knows itself to be formless and beyond all the bodies and worlds but also realizes with full consciousness its own unity with the Oversoul, which is one, indivisible, real, and infinite. In this realization of the Truth it enjoys infinite bliss, peace, power, and knowledge, which are characteristics of the Oversoul.

The goal

In the beginning, because the soul has not yet evolved full consciousness, it is unconscious of its identity with the Oversoul. Hence, though intrinsically inseparable from the Oversoul, the soul cannot realize its own identity with it or experience infinite peace, bliss, power, and knowledge. Even after the evolution of full consciousness, it cannot realize the state of the Oversoul—although it is at all times in and with the Oversoul—because its consciousness is confined to the phenomenal world, owing to the sanskaras connected with the evolution of consciousness. Even on the path, the soul is not conscious of itself but is conscious only of the gross, subtle, and mental worlds, which are its own illusory shadows.

Summary of soul's journey to Oversoul

At the end of the path, however, the soul frees itself from all sanskaras and desires connected with the gross, subtle, and mental worlds. It then becomes possible for it to free itself from the illusion of being finite, which came into existence owing to its identification with the gross, subtle, and mental bodies. At this stage the soul completely transcends the phenomenal world and becomes Self-conscious and Self-realized. To attain this goal, the soul must retain its full consciousness and at the same time know itself to be different from the sharir (gross body); the pran (subtle body, which is the vehicle of desires and vital forces); and the manas (mental body, which is the seat of the mind)—and also know itself as being *beyond* the gross, subtle, and mental worlds.

The soul has to emancipate itself gradually from the illusion of being finite by liberating itself from the bondage of sanskaras and knowing itself to be different from its bodies—gross, subtle, and mental. It thus annihilates the *false ego* (that is, the illusion that "I am the gross body," "I am the subtle body," or "I am the mental body"). While the soul thus frees itself from its illusion, it still retains full consciousness, which now results in Self-knowledge and realization of the Truth. Escaping through the cosmic Illusion and realizing with full consciousness its identity with the infinite Oversoul is the goal of the long journey of the soul.

The Types of Meditation

Part V
Specialized Meditations That Are Personal

It was seen in Part III that specialized meditation is of three kinds: (1) meditation concerned with the *objects* of experience, (2) meditation concerned with the *subject* of experience, and (3) meditation concerned with *mental operations*. These three kinds of meditation are mostly intertwined with each other. The subject of experience, the objects of experience, and the different mental operations that arise as a result of their interaction are all inextricably interwoven. So these three kinds of meditation are not sharply defined or exclusive but often overlap each other.

Kinds of specialized meditation

Thus, meditation concerned with the objects of experience may often refer to the subject of experience, and also to the diverse mental operations involved in it. Meditation concerned with the subject of experience may often involve reference to the diverse mental operations and the objects to which these mental operations are directed. And meditation concerned with the diverse mental operations may often involve reference to both the subject and the objects of experience. Yet each kind of meditation, in a way, remains distinct because of some predominating factor. Hence the first kind of meditation remains predominantly concerned with the objects of experience, the second kind with the subject of experience, and the third kind with diverse mental operations.

Table of Enumerative Classification of the Forms of Specialized Meditation

A	Meditation concerned with the objects of experience	1	Meditation on the divine qualities of a Master	FORMS OF PERSONAL MEDITATION
		2	Concentration on the form of a Master	
		3	Meditation of the heart	
		4	Meditation of action	
		5	Meditation regarding the numerous forms of manifested life	FORMS OF IMPERSONAL MEDITATION
		6	Meditation regarding one's own body	
		7	Meditation on the formless and infinite aspect of God	
B	Meditation concerned with the subject of experience	8	Quest for the agent of action	
		9	Considering oneself as witness	
C	Meditation concerned with mental operations	10	Writing down thoughts	
		11	Watching mental operations	
		12	Making the mind blank	

These three kinds of meditation can each be further subdivided into numerous specific forms of meditation according to the content of the meditation and the manner in which it is conducted. Out of these numerous forms of specialized meditation only those that are representative or important need particular mention. Thus, twelve forms of specialized meditation are given in the *Table of Enumerative Classification*.

Table of Enumerative Classification

It should be noted that of these twelve forms of specialized meditation, the first four are forms of *personal* meditation and the remaining eight are forms of *impersonal* meditation. Meditation is personal when it is concerned with a person; and meditation is impersonal when it is concerned with aspects of human personality or something that falls outside the range of human personality as it is usually understood. The forms of specialized meditation that are personal will be explained individually in this Part, and the forms of specialized meditation that are impersonal will be explained individually in Part VI.

Personal and impersonal meditation

Personal meditation has some clear advantages over impersonal meditation. For beginners, personal meditation is easy and attended with joy, while impersonal meditation is often found dry and difficult unless one has a special aptitude for it. Moreover, forms of impersonal meditation are mostly disciplines for the mind or the intellect, whereas the forms of personal meditation are not only disciplines for the mind or the intellect but also draw out the heart. In spiritual Perfection the mind and the heart have to be fully developed and balanced. Therefore personal meditation, which helps the development and balancing of the mind and heart, has special importance. Impersonal meditation is especially fruitful and effective when the aspirant has been duly prepared through forms of personal meditation.

Special advantages of personal meditation

Personal meditation is directed toward those who are spiritually perfect. Just as a man who admires the character of Napoleon and constantly thinks about him has a tendency to become like him, an aspirant who admires one who is spiritually perfect and constantly thinks about him has a tendency to become spiritually perfect. A suitable object for personal meditation is a living or past Perfect

Master or the Avatar. It is important that the object of meditation be spiritually perfect. If the person selected for meditation happens to be spiritually imperfect, there is every chance of his frailties percolating into the mind of the aspirant who meditates upon him. If the person selected for meditation is spiritually perfect, however, the aspirant has taken to a safe and sure path.

Meditation on the spiritually perfect

Personal meditation often begins with the admiration an aspirant feels spontaneously for some divine quality that he sees in a Master. By allowing the mind to dwell upon the divine qualities expressed in the life of the Master, the aspirant imbibes them into his own being. Ultimately, the Master is beyond all qualities—good and bad. He is not bound by them. The qualities he exhibits, while interacting with life around him, are all different aspects of divinity in action; and the expression of divinity, through these qualities, becomes a medium for helping those who are appreciatively responsive to them.

Meditation on divine qualities of Master

Appreciation of the divinity perceived in the Master gives rise to forms of meditation in which the aspirant constantly and strenuously thinks of the Master as being an embodiment of qualities like universal love or complete detachment, egolessness or steadfastness, infinite knowledge or selfless action. Sometimes the mind may dwell upon such separate qualities or may dwell upon combined qualities that reveal their interrelatedness. This form of meditation is very valuable when it is spontaneous. It then leads to a greater understanding of the Master and gradually remolds the aspirant into a likeness of the Master, thus contributing toward his self-preparation for the realization of the Truth.

Dwelling upon the qualities of the Master often facilitates concentration on the form of the Master. In this type of meditation, the aspirant is aware of the spiritual Perfection of the Master; and he spontaneously fixes his attention upon the form of the Master, without analyzing his spiritual Perfection into any of its component qualities. However, though these qualities are not separately revived in the mind, all that the aspirant may have understood of them (through the preparatory meditation con-

Concentration on form of the Master

cerned with the diverse qualities of the Master) constitutes the implicit background of such one-pointed concentration and contributes toward its efficacy and value. This form of meditation involves complete identification of the Master with the spiritual ideal.

Meditation of the heart

Complete identification of the Master with the spiritual ideal is responsible for removing such barriers as might exist between the aspirant and the Master. This gives rise to the release of unrestrained love for the Master and leads to the meditation of the heart, which consists in constant thinking about the Master with an uninterrupted flow of limitless love. Such love annihilates the illusion of separateness, which seems to divide the aspirant from the Master; and it has in it a spontaneity that is virtually without parallel in other forms of meditation. In its final stages, meditation of the heart is accompanied by unbounded joy and utter forgetfulness of self.

Modes of meditation of action

Love for the Master leads to increasing identification with the Master, so that the aspirant desires to live in and for the Master and not for his own narrow self. This leads to the meditation of action. The initial modes of the meditation of action usually take the following forms: (1) The aspirant mentally offers the Master all that is in him, thus renouncing all that is good or evil in him. This frees him from the good as well as the bad ingredients of the ego and helps him not only in transcending these opposites but also in finding a lasting and true integration with the Master. (2) The aspirant volunteers himself in the service of the Master or his cause. Doing work for the Master in the spirit of selfless service is as good as meditation. (3) The aspirant does not allow the ego to feed upon any of his actions—small or great, good or bad. He does not think, "I do this," but on the contrary systematically develops the thought that through him the Master is really doing all that he does.

For example, when he looks, he thinks, "The Master is looking"; when he eats, he thinks, "The Master is eating"; when he sleeps, he thinks, "The Master is sleeping"; when he drives a car, he thinks, "The Master is driving the car." Even when he may happen to do something wrong, he thinks, "The Master is doing this." Thus he completely relinquishes all agency for his actions, and all that is done by him is brought into direct reference to the Master. This automatically and necessarily involves and entails determination of each action in the light of the spiritual ideal as seen in the Master.

Four forms of personal meditation represent ascending stages

The four forms of personal meditation on the Master represent four main ascending stages: (1) perceiving the spiritual ideal in the Master, (2) concentrating upon the Master as an embodiment of the spiritual ideal, (3) loving the Master as a manifestation of the spiritual ideal, and (4) expressing the spiritual ideal, perceived in the Master, in one's own life. Personal meditation on the Master, in its different forms, ultimately contributes toward the release of the creative life of spiritual fulfillment. Meditation on the Master is a meditation on the living ideal and not on the bare conception of Perfection. Therefore it generates that dynamic power that eventually enables the aspirant to bridge the gulf between theory and practice, and unify the spiritual ideal with everyday activity in his own life. To live a life inspired and illumined by the spiritual ideal, as embodied in the Master, is the culmination of all the forms of personal meditation.

The Types of Meditation

Part VI
Specialized Meditations That Are Impersonal

Part V was devoted to explanatory comments on those specialized meditations that are personal. This Part will be devoted to those specialized meditations that are impersonal. It might be recalled that meditation is personal when it is concerned with a person, and impersonal when it is concerned with aspects of personality or something that falls outside the range of human personality, as it is commonly understood. In the *Table of Enumerative Classification* given in Part V, the first four forms of meditation are personal and the remaining eight forms are impersonal. Like the forms of personal meditation, the forms of impersonal meditation also individually deserve separate explanatory comments.

Distinction between personal and impersonal meditation

Man's attention has a tendency to be riveted on his own body or on other forms independent of the spirit they manifest. This leads to illusions, entanglements, and other complications. Hence arises the need for a type of meditation that will enable the aspirant to develop a proper perspective concerning the real

Meditation on all forms of life

status and meaning of the numerous forms, and to cultivate a right attitude toward them. In this type of meditation the aspirant acquires the constant habit of regarding all forms as equally the manifestations of the same one all-pervading life and as nothing in themselves separately. This type of meditation aids disentanglement from the world of creation and furthers cultivation of the highest type of universal love, which regards the whole of humanity and all living creatures as members of an indivisible whole.

But the type of meditation concerned with the numerous forms of manifested life remains incomplete unless it is supplemented by another type of meditation that is concerned with one's own body.

Meditation regarding one's body

One's own body—gross, subtle, or mental—is, like the bodies of others, a form of the one all-pervading life. Nonetheless, consciousness is fixed on one's own bodies by an attachment so deep that it identifies itself with them. Continued thoughts of detachment concerning one's own body help emancipation of consciousness and the dawn of true Self-knowledge. Meditation of this type is very fruitful for the aspirant. The gross, subtle, and mental bodies are all then regarded as cloaks that one can put on or off.

The type of meditation concerned with the numerous forms of manifested life and the type of meditation concerned with one's own bodies are both preparations for the form of impersonal meditation in

Meditation on formless and infinite aspect of God

which an effort is made to withdraw consciousness from all the numerous forms of manifested life, including one's own bodies, and consciousness is centered on the formless and infinite aspect of God. In the initial phases, this form of impersonal meditation has to avail itself of some symbols of infinity. It is actually more helpful to start with some image that suggests and signifies infinity than the abstract idea of infinity. The mind may be made steady on an image of sky, ocean, or vast emptiness; but once a particular image is chosen, the aspirant should stick to it throughout the period of meditation and not allow it to be replaced by another image.

From these symbols of infinity, complete and unlimited emptiness is difficult to imagine; however, the best symbol is that which one can most successfully bring before one's mind. Even when unlimited emptiness is used to signify infinity, in this form of meditation the aspirant is not supposed to arrive at complete blankness of mind. Such blankness involves the cessation of all mental activity and having absolutely no thoughts or ideas; but in this form of meditation the mind tries to understand and realize the formless and infinite aspect of God by means of a significant symbol.

There is an important variation of this impersonal form of meditation. In it the infinity one imagines is not mentally externalized as if it were an unlimited stretch of something *outside* the aspirant. It is more helpful to picture infinity as *within* the aspirant. After picturing infinity within, the aspirant should give himself the strong suggestion of his identity with infinity by mentally repeating, "I am as infinite as the sky within" or "I am as infinite as the ocean within" or "I am as infinite as the emptiness within." It may be even more helpful to use the bare formula "I am the Infinite within" and, while mentally repeating this formula, to grasp and realize the significance of infinity through the image that has been chosen. It is not necessary to repeat the formula in so many words; it is enough to cling to the thought expressed in the formula.

Picturing infinity as being within

The "I am infinite" meditation may lead to a merging of the aspirant into the formless and infinite aspect of God. Some aspirants merge so completely that even if swarms of mosquitoes surround them, they do not hear them. Other aspirants might become restless or easily disturbed. They should not keep worrying about lack of success in meditation but should tenaciously persist whether they experience merging or not. A relaxed position is helpful for merging. The *final* merging, however, is impossible except through the help of a Perfect Master.

The forms of meditation thus far explained are predominantly concerned with the impersonal *objects* of experience, but some impersonal forms of meditation are concerned with the *subject* of experience. One such important form of meditation consists in ceaselessly pressing the query "Who is it that does all these things?" The aspirant finds himself thinking "I sleep, walk, eat, and talk"; "I see, hear, touch, taste, and smell"; "I think, feel, and desire"; and so forth. The searching question this form of meditation is concerned with is, Who is this "I"? The soul does not experience any of these things. The soul does not sleep, walk, eat, or

Quest for agent of action

talk; see, hear, touch, taste, or smell; think, feel, or desire. Who then is the agent? The *source* of all these activities has to be discovered, and the mystery of all life has to be explained.

There is a power that does all these things, and one must know oneself to be different from the power and be able to use it with detachment. The aspirant thinks that he walks; it is really his body that walks. The aspirant thinks that he sees, hears, thinks, feels, or desires; it is really his mind that does all these things through some convenient medium. As soul, the aspirant is everywhere and really does nothing. But it is not enough to think that, as soul, he is everywhere and really does nothing. He must *know* this.

Considering oneself a witness

Knowledge of the soul may also be approached through a form of meditation in which the aspirant tries to realize himself as merely a witness of all physical and mental happenings. After a person wakes from a dream, he realizes that he was not a real agent of the actions in the dream but that he was merely a witness of them. If the aspirant persistently practices considering himself a witness of all physical and mental happenings that he experiences in wakefulness as well as in dreams, he soon develops utter detachment, which brings freedom from all worries and sufferings connected with worldly events. This form of meditation is intended to lift the aspirant out of the bonds of time and to secure for him immediate relief from the fret and fever connected with the diverse expressions of limited energy. As a witness, the soul remains aloof from all events in time, and the results of actions do not bind it. All this has to be *experienced* and not merely thought about.

Importance of stilling mind

The forms of meditation concerned with the subject of experience, however, suffer from the handicap that the true subject of experience can never be the object of thought or meditation in the ordinary sense. Thus these forms of meditation can at best take the aspirant very close to Self-knowledge, which can only dawn in its full glory when the domain of the mind is completely traversed. Some impersonal forms of specialized meditation are therefore concerned with mental operations, and they ultimately aim at stilling the mind.

To acquire control over thoughts is to become fully conscious of what they are. They have to be attended to before they are controlled.

Writing down thoughts

In ordinary introspection it is seldom possible for the beginner to devote adequate attention to all the shadowy thoughts that pass through the mind. It is helpful, therefore, for the aspirant occasionally to write down all his thoughts as they come and then to inspect them carefully at leisure. This process is different from writing planned essays. Thoughts are allowed to arise without any direction or restraint so that even repressed elements from the subconscious mind have access to the conscious mind.

Observation of mental operations

In a more advanced stage, an intensive awareness of the mental processes can take place while thoughts appear in the consciousness; and writing them down becomes unnecessary. Observations of mental operations should be accompanied by critical evaluation of one's thoughts. Thoughts cannot be controlled except through an appreciation of their value or lack of value. When the diverse thoughts that assail the mind are critically evaluated and the internal stirrings of sanskaras are faced, understood, and taken for what they are worth, the mind is freed from all obsessions and compulsions in relation to them.

Making mind blank

A way is thus prepared for meditation that attempts to make the mind blank, which is one of the most difficult things to achieve. The mind is without any ideas during sleep, but consciousness is then in abeyance. If during wakefulness the mind has the idea of becoming blank, it is thinking about that idea and is far from being blank. However, this difficult trick of making the mind blank becomes possible by an alternation between two incompatible forms of meditation, so that the mind is caught between concentration and distraction.

Alternating between concentration and distraction

Thus the aspirant can concentrate on the Master for five minutes; and then as the mind is getting settled on the form of the Master, he can steady his mind for the next five minutes in the impersonal meditation in which the thought is "I am infinite." The disparity between the two forms of meditation can be emphasized by keeping the eyes open during meditation on the form of the Master and closing the eyes during impersonal meditation. Such alternation helps in making the mind blank; but to be successful, both forms of meditation have to be seriously pursued. Though after five minutes there is to be a changeover to another type of meditation, there should be no thought of it while the first type is going on. There is no distraction unless there is concentration. And when a changeover is effected, there should be no thought of the first type of meditation. The distraction has to be as complete as the previous concentration. When there is a quick alternation between concentration and distraction, mental operations are, as it were, cut through by a saw that goes backward and forward.

The disappearance of mental operations of all types contributes toward making the mind absolutely still without allowing consciousness to fall into abeyance. All thoughts that appear in the mind of the aspirant are forms of perturbation and have their origin in the momentum of stored sanskaras. The agitation of the mind can disappear only when the aspirant can so control his mind that all thoughts can be ruled out at will. Only in complete internal silence is Truth found. When the surface of the lake is still, it reflects the stars. When the mind is tranquil, it reflects the nature of the soul as it is.

Truth reflected in tranquil mind

The Types of Meditation

Part VII
Nirvikalpa Samadhi

The different forms of meditation practiced before consciously entering the spiritual path, as well as the different forms of general and special meditation adopted after becoming an aspirant, are preparatory to the attainment of the *Nirvikalpa* state (the "I am God" state). *Nirvikalpa Samadhi*, or divinity in expression, is the experience of the Nirvikalpa state in which the aspirant becomes permanently established after realizing the ultimate goal of life. The Nirvikalpa Samadhi of the *Siddha*, or God-realized being, is continuous with all the prior forms of meditation; and through the grace of a Perfect Master, it can be the culmination of them. However, it is unique and of an entirely different dimension.

Nirvikalpa Samadhi is unique

The spontaneity of Nirvikalpa Samadhi must be carefully distinguished from the pseudo sense of spontaneity present in the usual meditations of the worldly person who has not yet entered the path. The mind of the worldly individual is engrossed in sense objects, and he experiences no feeling of effort in meditating on these objects. His mind dwells upon them because of its natural interest in them and not because of any deliberate effort on his part. The sense of effort does not arise from allowing the mind to

Prespiritual meditation of the worldly

dwell upon these diverse worldly objects but from trying to dissuade it from them. So the prespiritual forms of meditation seem to have some similarity with the culminating Nirvikalpa Samadhi of the Siddha in having a sense of spontaneity. But this resemblance between the initial phase of meditation and its final phase is only superficial, since Nirvikalpa Samadhi and prespiritual meditations are divided from each other by vital differences of great spiritual importance.

Illusory spontaneity of prespiritual meditations

The sense of spontaneity experienced in prespiritual meditations concerned with worldly objects and pursuits is due to the interests created by sanskaras. Prespiritual meditations are the working out of the momentum of accumulated sanskaras of the past; and they are not only far from being the expression of true freedom but are actually symptoms of spiritual bondage. At the prespiritual level, man is engulfed in unrelieved ignorance concerning the goal of infinite freedom. Though he is far from being happy and contented, he identifies so deeply with sanskaric interests that he experiences gratification in their furtherance. But the pleasure of his pursuits is conditional and transitory; and the spontaneity he experiences in them is illusory because, throughout all his pursuits, his mind is working under limitations.

True freedom and spontaneity exist only in Nirvikalpa

The mind is capable of genuine freedom and spontaneity of action only when it is completely free from sanskaric ties and interests, and this is possible only when the mind is merged in the state of Nirvikalpa Samadhi of the Siddha. It is therefore important to note that though there may seem to be a superficial resemblance between the Nirvikalpa Samadhi of the Siddha and the prespiritual meditations of the worldly, this resemblance really hides the important difference between illusory spontaneity and true spontaneity, bondage and freedom, fleeting pleasure and abiding happiness. In the prespiritual meditations the movement of the mind is under unconscious compulsion, and in Nirvikalpa Samadhi mental activity is released under conscious and unfettered initiative.

The different forms of meditation that characterize the life of the spiritual aspirant stand midway between the prespiritual meditations of the worldly individual and the final Nirvikalpa Samadhi of the Siddha. They also constitute the link between them. When a person's primary acquiescence in sanskaric interests is profoundly disturbed by setback, defeat, and suffering, or is shaken by a spark of spiritual understanding, he becomes conscious of his bondage and the falseness of his perceptions. All the different forms of meditation that are then resorted to by the aspirant arise as parts of his struggle toward emancipation from the bondage of the deceptive desires of the worldly. The forms of meditation that are spiritually important begin when the person has become an aspirant, or sadhak.

Meditation a part of aspirant's struggle toward emancipation

The meditation of the aspirant in all its forms is *deliberate,* in the sense that it is experienced as counteracting instinctive or other tendencies inherent in the mind. The aspirant adopts different forms of meditation as means to an end, that is, because he looks upon them as avenues to the Truth. They are not working out of some given impulse but are parts of an intelligent and deliberate effort. Although these forms of meditation may be deliberate to start with, the mind gradually becomes habituated to them. The mind is also interested in the various aspects of Truth, which the different forms of meditation try to seize upon; and this increases spontaneity.

Meditation involves effort

In none of the meditations of a sadhak are the elements of spontaneity more pronounced than in those forms of personal meditation that give scope for and require the expression of love. But utter spontaneity and true freedom remain unattained until the goal of meditation is achieved. Till then there is usually a mixture of a sense of deliberateness and a sense of spontaneity. The reaching out toward spiritual freedom is accompanied throughout by a sense of effort, which persists in some degree until all obstacles of false perceptions are overcome. Though effort may vary in its intensity, it never disappears entirely until it is swallowed up in the tranquility of final attainment.

In Nirvikalpa Samadhi there is no effort because there are no obstacles to overcome or objectives to achieve. There is the infinite spontaneity of unfettered freedom and the unbroken peace and bliss of Truth-realization. Progression toward the Nirvikalpa state consists in a transition from a state of

Progression toward Nirvikalpa

unquestioned acquiescence in the momentum of sanskaras to a state of desperate struggle with sanskaric limitations and finally to a state of complete freedom, when consciousness is no longer determined by the deposits of the past but is active in the undimmed perception of the eternal Truth.

The Nirvikalpa Samadhi of the Siddha is different from the meditation of the aspirant, not only with respect to freedom and spontaneity of consciousness but also with respect to many other important points. All the different forms of meditation that the aspirant might be engaged in, directly or indirectly, aim at securing a complete merging of the mind in the infinite Truth. However, they only partially succeed in this merging and fall short of the annihilation of the individual mind. They represent varying degrees of approximation to the spiritual goal, but not its realization. On the other hand, in the Nirvikalpa state there is realization of the spiritual goal, since the limited mind is completely annihilated and has arrived at a total merging in the infinite Truth.

Individual mind annihilated in Nirvikalpa

The aspirant's meditation, in its higher flights, often brings a sense of expansion and freedom, as well as the joy and illumination of the higher planes. But none of these are abiding because in most cases, when the aspirant comes down from his exalted state of meditation, he is again what he was, namely, an ordinary person who is bound in the unyielding shackles of sanskaric limitations.

Temporary exaltation

The incompleteness of the different samadhis of the aspirant may be illustrated by the story of a yogi from Gwalior, India, who was very greedy. Through yoga he had mastered the art of going into samadhi. One day he sat opposite the palace of the raja and, before going into samadhi, thought, "I must have a thousand rupees from the raja." Then he went into samadhi and remained in that state for seven full days. During this period he took no food or drink but only sat in one place, completely absorbed in trance-meditation. People took him to be a saint; and when the raja came to know about him, he also went to have his darshan. The raja went near the yogi and happened to touch him on his back. That light touch was sufficient to bring him down from his samadhi; and as soon as he woke up from his trance-

Story of a yogi

meditation, he asked the raja for a thousand rupees.

Just as a prisoner who looks out of the window of his prison and gazes at the vast expanse of the sky may get lost in the vision of unlimited space, the aspirant who enters into trance-meditation may temporarily forget all his limitations while immersed in its light and bliss. But though the prisoner may have forgotten the prison, he has not escaped from it. In the same way, the aspirant who is absorbed in trance-meditation has lost sight of the chains that bind him to the world of Illusion, but he has not really broken through them. Just as the prisoner again becomes conscious of his bondage as soon as he gazes at his immediate surroundings, the aspirant becomes conscious of all his failings as soon as he regains normal consciousness. The ascending forms of trance-meditation may bring the aspirant increasing occult powers but not that unending state of knowledge and bliss that is continuously accessible in Nirvikalpa Samadhi to the Siddha, who has attained final Emancipation by breaking through the chains of Maya.

Analysis of trance-meditation

Another important difference is that in trance-meditation the aspirant is usually sustained by some object capable of exercising irresistible attraction. The lights, colors, smells, and sounds of the subtle sphere play a part in alluring the mind from the worldly things it may have been attached to. Thus trance-meditation is not self-sustained but is dependent upon the object to which the mind directs itself. The Nirvikalpa Samadhi of the Siddha is self-sustained and is in no way dependent upon any object of the mind. Trance-meditation is more like the stupor of intoxicating drugs. The intoxication lasts only as long as the effect of the drug lasts. So the trance continues to exist as long as the mind is under the sway of the object it is sustained by. Nirvikalpa, which is free from the domination of the object, is a state of full wakefulness in which there is no ebb and flow, waxing or waning, but only the steadiness of true perception.

Nirvikalpa Samadhi self-sustained

The different forms of general and specialized meditation resorted to by the aspirant are useful and valuable within their own limits. They must not be regarded as having the same value for all or as being equally necessary to all. They are among the ways that lead the aspirant toward his divine destination. For the few who are in an advanced spiritual state, most of the ordinary forms of meditation are unnecessary. For those who are in direct contact with a Perfect Master or the Avatar, many of the special forms of meditation are often unnecessary. It is enough for them to be under the guidance of the Master and to love him. And those rare beings who have attained Self-realization and have become Perfect Masters themselves are always in the state of *Sahaj Samadhi*, or divinity in action. They not only do not need any forms of meditation but they themselves become objects of meditation for the aspirants. For they are then able to give their best help to those who meditate upon them.

Those in Sahaj Samadhi as objects of meditation

The Types of Meditation

Part VIII
Sahaj Samadhi

When the mind totally merges in the Truth, it experiences the Nirvikalpa state of spontaneous bliss of uninterrupted Self-knowledge—in which the aspirant loses his limited individuality to discover that he is identical with God, who is in everything.

Culmination of meditation

By the grace of a Perfect Master, the Nirvikalpa state becomes the *culmination* of the earlier forms of personal and impersonal meditation and not their *product*. All forms of meditation followed by the aspirant as well as his other spiritual efforts, in spite of their differences, have only one aim, namely, to speed up the fruition of his longing to be united with the Infinite.

When this union is effected, the sadhak (aspirant) becomes a Siddha (one who has attained the Goal). The union with the Infinite that the Siddha achieves is referred to by the Sufis as *Vasl*. It is this state of Union with God that is described by Jesus Christ in the words "I and my Father are one." Many have written about this high state of consciousness, but it remains essentially indescribable. It cannot be expressed in words, and therefore it cannot be adequately explained. Though it can never be explained by one person to another, it can be

Nirvikalpa Samadhi experienced after Union

experienced by one for oneself. This Nirvikalpa state when experienced by the Siddha is Nirvikalpa Samadhi.

To dwell in Nirvikalpa Samadhi is to experience the *God state*, in which the soul knows itself to be God because it has shed all the limiting factors that had hitherto contributed toward false self-knowledge. The God state of the Siddha stands out in clear contrast with the *body state* of the worldly. The worldly individual takes himself to be the body and dwells in a state dominated by the body and its wants. His consciousness centers on the body. He is concerned with eating, drinking, sleeping, and the satisfaction of other bodily desires. It is for the body that he lives and seeks fulfillment. His consciousness cannot extend beyond the body; he thinks in terms of the body and cannot conceive of anything that has no body or form. The entire sphere of his existence is comprised of forms, and the theater in which he lives and moves and has his being consists of space.

Body state

The first step toward the God state of Nirvikalpa Samadhi is taken when the body state is transcended. Shedding the body state means entering the sphere of existence comprised of energy. The soul then dwells in a state that is no longer dominated by forms or bodies. It is lifted up to the domain of energy. Body or form is a solidification of energy, and to rise from the world of forms to the sphere of energy amounts to an advance toward a more primary and purer state of being. The *energy state* is free from many of the limitations that obtain in the world of forms. In this state, consciousness is linked with energy and continuously vibrates in and through energy.

Energy state

In the energy state, the eating and drinking of the body state are paralleled by the absorption and assimilation of energy. At this level the soul acquires full control over energy and seeks fulfillment through its use. But its actions are still within the domain of spiritual limitation. It can see, hear, and smell many things that are inaccessible in the body state, and can perform many feats (for example, producing light in the dark or living for innumerable years only on energy), which seem to be miracles for those who are in the body state. The entire sphere of the soul's existence is comprised of energy and is dominated by energy. All that it can conceive of or do is in terms of energy and is achieved by means of energy. The energy state is the state of spiritually advanced souls; but it is far from being the state of Perfection, which expresses itself through the Nirvikalpa Samadhi of the Siddha.

The second important step toward Nirvikalpa Samadhi is taken when the soul transcends the domain of energy and enters the domain of the mind. All energy is ultimately an expression of the mind; therefore the transition from the energy state to the *mind state* constitutes a still further advance toward the God state of Nirvikalpa Samadhi. In the mind state, consciousness is directly linked with the mind. It is in no way fettered by the domination of the body or energy, but it is mind-ridden. Advanced souls who are in the mind state can read and influence the minds of others. However, the mind-ridden state is still within the domain of duality and illusion, and it has to be transcended before the attainment of union with the Infinite.

Mind state

The entire advance, from the very beginning, consists in gradually curtailing and transcending the working of the individual mind. The mind is functioning even in the body state and in the energy state. In the body state the mind thinks in terms of the body, in the energy state it thinks in terms of energy, while in the mind state it thinks in its own terms. However, even when the mind thinks in its own terms, it does not attain knowledge and realization of the Infinite because it becomes its own veil between thought and Truth. Though the mind may be unencumbered by life in the body state or the energy state, it is still limited by separative consciousness. It might be compared to a mirror that is covered with dust. The mind has, therefore, to be completely merged and dissolved in the Infinite before it is possible to experience the God state of Nirvikalpa Samadhi. Form is solidified energy; energy is an expression of mind; mind is the covered mirror of Eternity; and Eternity is Truth that has thrown off the mask of mind.

Mind veils Truth

To discard the limiting mind is no easy thing. The chief difficulty is that the mind has to be annihilated through the mind itself. Intense longing for union with the infinite Reality as well as infinite patience are indispensable in the process of transcending the mind. One Master told his disciple that in order to attain the highest state he had to be thrown, bound hand and foot to a plank, into a river,

Transcending mind

where he must keep his garments dry. The disciple could not understand the inner meaning of this injunction. He wandered until he encountered another Master and asked him the meaning of the injunction.

This Master explained that in order to attain God he had to long intensely for union with Him—as if he could not live another moment without it—and yet to have the inexhaustible patience that could wait for billions of years. If there is lack of intense longing for union with God, the mind lapses into its usual sanskaric working; and if there is lack of infinite patience, the very longing that the mind entertains sustains the working of the limited mind. It is only when there is a balance between infinite longing and infinite patience that the aspirant can ever hope to pierce through the veil of the limited mind; and this combination of extremes can only come through the grace of a Perfect Master.

God state of Nirvikalpa Samadhi

To dwell in Nirvikalpa Samadhi is to dwell in Truth-consciousness. This God state cannot be grasped by anyone whose mind is still working. It is beyond the mind, for it dawns when the limited mind disappears in final union with the Infinite. The soul then knows itself through *itself* and not through the mind. The worldly individual knows that he is a human being and not a dog. In the same way, in Nirvikalpa Samadhi the soul just knows that it is God and not a finite thing. The worldly person does not have to keep repeating to himself that he is not a dog but a human being; he just knows, without having to make any special effort, that he is a human being. In the same way the soul, in Nirvikalpa Samadhi, does not need any artificial inducing of God-consciousness through repeated autosuggestions. It just knows itself to be God through effortless intuition.

Life in Eternity

One who experiences Nirvikalpa Samadhi is established in the knowledge of the Soul. This Self-knowledge does not come and go; it is permanent. In the state of ignorance the individual soul looks upon itself as a man or woman, as the agent of limited actions and the receiver of joys and pains. In the state of Self-knowledge it knows itself as the Soul, which is not in any way limited by these things and is untouched by them. Once it knows its own true nature, it has this knowledge forever and never again becomes involved in ignorance.

This state of God-consciousness is infinite and is characterized by unlimited understanding, purity, love, and happiness. To be in Nirvikalpa Samadhi—which for the rare few leads to Sahaj Samadhi—is the endlessness of life in Eternity.

Sahaj Samadhi, or divinity in action, is experienced by the Sadgurus and is preceded by two states: *Nirvana*, or absorption in divinity; and *Nirvikalpa Samadhi*, or divinity in expression. When consciousness is withdrawn entirely from all the bodies and the world of creation, it leads to Nirvana, or the beyond-mind state. But when consciousness again functions through the bodies without attachment or identification, it experiences the Nirvikalpa Samadhi of the Siddha. Here, though consciousness is attached to the bodies as instruments, it is detached from them inwardly by nonidentification.

Two states precede Sahaj Samadhi

The piercing of the mind amounts to the complete withdrawal of consciousness from the universe to its total absorption in God. This is the state where the universe becomes a zero: this is Nirvana. After Nirvana, those who become conscious of the universe experience it as nothing but God and remain constantly in Nirvikalpa Samadhi. Nirvikalpa Samadhi means a life where the mental activity of false imagination has come to an end, and the oscillations of the limited mind are all stilled in the realization of the unchangeable Truth.

Nirvana and Nirvikalpa are similar to the state of *Moksha* (Liberation), but only in representing the merging of the individual soul in God and in yielding eternal bliss. Moksha is experienced *after* the soul has dropped its bodies, while the states of Nirvana and Nirvikalpa can both be experienced *before* giving up the bodies. However, though the states of Nirvana and Nirvikalpa are similar as to retaining the bodies and though they are also fundamentally the same in essence, there *is* a difference between the two. When the soul comes out of the ego-shell and enters into the infinite life of God, its limited individuality is replaced by unlimited individuality. As the limitations of the individuality are entirely extinguished, the soul knows that it is God-conscious and thus preserves its unlimited individuality. Though the unlimited individuality of the soul is in a way retained in the union with the Infinite, it nevertheless remains quiescent and absorbed in the experience of *self-contained*

Moksha, Nirvana, and Nirvikalpa

divinity, that is, in the state of Nirvana. But when the soul, having entered the infinite life of God, establishes its unlimited individuality through the release of *dynamic* divinity, it is in Nirvikalpa Samadhi.

Sahaj Samadhi comes to the very few souls who descend from the seventh plane of consciousness as Sadgurus, while it is the very *life* of the Avatar. The poise and harmony of this state remain undisturbed even while giving energetic response to the changing circumstances of life. Those who are in this state live the life of God and experience God everywhere and in everything. Their God state is therefore in no way diminished when dealing with the things of this world. Whether drawing a bow or using a sword on the battlefield, whether flying in an airplane or talking to people, or whether engaged in other activities that may require the closest attention—they are continuously in the state of conscious enjoyment of the immutable Truth. Such is Sahaj Samadhi, the effortless and continuous life of Perfection and divinity in action.

State of Sadgurus and the Avatar

The Dynamics of Spiritual Advancement

Spiritual advancement begins when there is a radical change in the outlook of the worldly person. The worldly individual lives mostly for the body; and even in those pursuits that do not seem to have a direct reference to the body, in the last analysis the ultimate motive power is to be found in the desires connected with the body. For example, he lives to eat; he does not eat to live. He has not yet discovered any purpose clearly transcending the body, so the body and its comforts become the center of all his pursuits. But when he discovers values in which the soul is predominant, the body is at once relegated to the background. The maintenance of the body then becomes for him merely instrumental for the realization of a higher purpose. His body, which had formerly been a hindrance to true spiritual life, becomes an instrument for the release of higher life. At this stage the person attends to his bodily needs with no special feeling of self-identification, like the driver of a car who fills it with fuel and water so that it may be kept going.

Subjugation of body for higher life

The very beginning of spiritual advancement is conditioned by the quest of that goal for which man lives—the goal for which he unconsciously loves and hates, and for which he goes through variegated joys and sufferings. Though he may be stirred by the pull of this incomprehensible and irresistible divine destiny, it may take a long time before he arrives at the mountain top of Truth-

Quest for the goal

realization; and the path is constantly strewn with pitfalls and slippery precipices. Those who attempt to reach this mountain top have to climb higher and higher. And even if a person has succeeded in scaling great heights, the slightest mistake on his part might cast him down to the very beginning again. Therefore the aspirant is never safe unless he has the advantage of the help and guidance of a Perfect Master, who knows the ins and outs of the spiritual path, and who can not only safeguard the aspirant from a possible fall but lead him to the goal of Realization without unnecessary relapses.

Obstacles to advancement

The aspirant who attempts to reach the goal carries with him all the sanskaras he has accumulated in the past. But in the intensity of his spiritual longing, they remain suspended and ineffective for the time being. Time and again, however, when there is a slackening of spiritual effort, the sanskaras hitherto suspended from action gather fresh strength and, arraying themselves in a new formation, constitute formidable obstacles in the spiritual advancement of the aspirant.

Analogy of a river

This might be illustrated by the analogy of a river. The powerful current of a river carries with it great quantities of silt from the source and the banks. As long as these quantities are suspended in water they do not hinder the flow of the river, though they may slow it down. When the current becomes slower in the plains, and particularly toward the mouth, this bulk tends to deposit in the river bed and to form huge islands or deltas. These not only obstruct the current but often divert it or even split it into smaller streams and, on the whole, weaken the force of the mighty river. Or again, when the river is in flood, it sweeps away all obstacles of trees, bushes, and rubbish in its path; but when these accumulate to a certain degree, they can constitute a serious hindrance to the flow of the river. In the same way, the path of spiritual advancement is often blocked by the obstacles of its own creation, and these can be removed only through the help of the Master.

The help of the Master is most effective when the aspirant surrenders his ego-life in favor of the unlimited life that the Master represents. Complete self-surrender is most difficult to achieve, and yet the most essential condition of spiritual advancement is the decreasing of egoism to its minimum. The objective of spiritual advancement is not so much "works" but the quality of life free from ego-consciousness. If the aspirant has many great things to his credit that he has claimed as his, his ego fastens itself upon the achievements; and this constitutes a formidable hindrance to life unlimited. Hence comes the futility of rituals and ceremonies, acts of charity and good works, external renunciation and penances, when rooted in ego-consciousness.

Egoism must disappear

It is therefore most necessary for the aspirant to keep free from the idea "I do this, and I do that." This does not mean that the aspirant is to avoid all activity through fear of developing this form of the ego. He may have to take to the life of action to wear out the ego he has already developed. Thus he is caught up in a dilemma: if he stays inactive, he does nothing to break through the prison of his ego-life; and if he takes to a life of action, he is faced with the possibility of his ego being transferred to these new acts.

The dilemma

For spiritual advancement the aspirant has to avoid these two extremes and yet carry on a life of creative action. Treading the spiritual path is not like riding a saddled horse but like walking on the sharp edge of a sword. Once a rider is on horseback, he is practically at rest, sitting with more or less ease and requiring very little effort or attention to proceed. Treading the spiritual path, however, requires utmost attention and carefulness since the path affords no halting places or room for expansion of the ego-life. He who enters the path can neither remain where he is nor can he afford to lose his balance. He is thus like one who attempts to walk on the sharp edge of a sword.

Treading path like walking on edge of sword

To avoid inaction on the one hand and pride of action on the other, it is necessary for the aspirant to construct in the following manner a provisional and working ego that will be entirely subservient to the Master. Before beginning anything, the aspirant thinks that it is not he who is doing it but the Master who is getting it done through him. After doing the task he does not tarry to claim the results of action or enjoy them but becomes free of them by offering them to the Master. By training his mind in this spirit, he succeeds in creating a new ego—which, though only provi-

Constructing new ego subservient to Master

sional and working, is amply able to become a source of confidence, feeling, enthusiasm, and "go" that true action must express. This new ego is spiritually harmless, since it derives its life and being from the Master, who represents Infinity. And when the time comes, it can be thrown away like a garment.

There are thus two types of ego—one that can only add to the limitations of the soul, and the other that helps it toward emancipation. The passage from the limiting ego of the worldly to the egolessness of infinite life lies through the construction of a provisional ego generated by wholehearted allegiance to the Master. The construction of a new ego entirely subservient to the Master is indispensable to the dynamics of spiritual advancement.

Sudden transition to egoless life impossible

The aspirant has been accustomed to derive zest in life from his limited ego, and an immediate transition from the life of egoistic action to that of egoless action is impossible on one's own and also not advisable. If the aspirant were immediately required to avoid all forms of ego-consciousness, he would have to revert to a state of negative passivity, without any joy of expression. Or he would have to seek expression through activity that is merely automatic, like that of a lifeless machine, and therefore he could not derive any sense of fulfillment. The real problem is that the aspirant has to abandon his life of the limited ego and enter into the limitlessness of the egoless life without lapsing into a coma, where there would be an ebbing of all life. Such a coma might give temporary relief from the limitation of the ego-life, but it cannot initiate the aspirant into the infinity of egoless activity.

Spiritual advancement usually gradual

This is the reason why, in most cases, spiritual advancement has to be very gradual and often takes several lives. Where a person seems to have taken long strides in his spiritual advancement, he has merely recapitulated the advancement already secured in previous lives—or there has been special intervention by a Sadguru. In normal cases the advancement of the aspirant has to be gradual. The distance between the limited life of the ego and the limitlessness of the egoless life has to be covered by gradual stages of ego-transformation—so that egoism is replaced by humility, surging desires are replaced by steadily growing contentment, and selfishness is replaced by selfless love.

When the ego is entirely subservient to the Master, it is not only spiritually harmless but indispensable and directly contributory to the spiritual advancement of the aspirant, because it brings him closer and closer to the Master through the life of selfless service and love. The constant inward contact with the Master that it secures makes him particularly amenable to the special help the Master alone can give. The aspirant who renounces the life of an uncurbed and separative ego in favor of a life of self-surrender to the Master is operating, through this new subservient ego, as an instrument in the hands of the Master. In reality the Master is working through him. Just as an instrument has a tendency to get out of order while being put to use, the aspirant is also likely to go wrong during his working in the world. From time to time the instrument has to be cleansed, overhauled, repaired, and set right. In the same way the aspirant—who during his work has developed new problems, entanglements, and shelters for the personal ego—has to be put into working order so that he can move ahead.

Ego subservient to Master ensures his help

The aspirant who enlists in the service of the Master may be compared to a broom with which the Master sweeps the world clean of its impurities. The broom is bound to accumulate the dirt of the world; and unless cleansed again and again and given a new tone, it becomes less efficient in the course of time. Each time the aspirant goes to the Master, it is with fresh spiritual problems. He might have got caught in new entanglements connected with a craving for honor, riches, or other worldly things that allure man. If he pursues these, he might get them; but he might be far from the goal of experiencing God, on whom he had set his heart.

Need for recurring contact with Master

Only through the active intervention of the Master can such spiritual disorders be cured. This task of curing spiritual diseases is comparable to the performance of an operation by a surgeon, who promptly removes the very cause that had been sapping the vital energies of a patient. If a person develops physical ailments and complaints, he must go to the doctor; and if he develops spiritual troubles, he must go to the Master. Thus recurring contact with the Master is most necessary throughout the process of spiritual advancement.

The Master helps the aspirant in his own invincible ways, which have no parallel in the ways of the world. If the aspirant is to be the recipient of this help, he must make a real effort to surrender himself to the divine will of the Master. The personal ego, which the aspirant renounced in his first surrenderance to the Master, may reappear in a new aspect—even within the artificial ego meant to be completely subservient to the Master and create disorder in its smooth working. Hence this new resurrection of the limited personal ego of the aspirant needs to be counteracted through fresh surrender to the Master. The series of successive resurrections of the personal ego have to be accompanied by a series of fresh acts of surrenderance to the Master.

Each resurrection of ego needs fresh surrender

Progress from one surrender to greater surrender is a progression from a minor conquest to a major one. The more complete forms of surrenderance represent the higher states of consciousness, since they secure greater harmony between the aspirant and the Master. Thus the infinite life of the Perfect Master can flow through the aspirant in more abundant measure. Spiritual advancement is a succession of one surrender after another until the goal of the final surrenderance of the separate ego-life is completely achieved. The last surrender is the only complete surrenderance. It is the counterpart of the final union in which the aspirant becomes one with the Master. Therefore, in a sense, the most complete surrender to the Master is equivalent to the attainment of the Truth, which is the ultimate goal of all spiritual advancement.

Last surrenderance is that of separateness

The Deeper Aspects of Sadhana

For most persons, spiritual *sadhana*, or practice, consists in the external observance of rituals and ceremonies prescribed by their own religion. In the initial stages such observance has its own value as a factor contributing toward self-purification and mental discipline. But ultimately the aspirant has to transcend the phase of external conformity and become initiated into the deeper aspects of spiritual sadhana. When this happens, the external aspect of religion falls into the background; and the aspirant gets interested in the essentials revealed in all the great religions. True sadhana consists in a life that is based upon spiritual understanding, and it comes to a person who is truly keen about spiritual realities.

Transition to deeper aspects of sadhana

Sadhana must never be regarded as consisting in the application of rigid laws. Just as in life there cannot be and need not be strict and unrelieved uniformity, in spiritual life there is ample room for diversity of sadhanas. The sadhana that is useful for a particular aspirant is bound to be related to his sanskaras and temperament; and so, although the spiritual goal for all is the same, the sadhana of a given aspirant may be peculiar to himself. However, since the goal is the same for all, the differences with regard to sadhana are not of vital importance; and the deeper aspects of sadhana have importance for all aspirants in spite of their differences.

Diversity of sadhanas

Sadhana in the spiritual realm is bound to be essentially different from sadhana in the material field because the end is intrinsically different. The end sought in the material field is a product that has its beginning and end in time. The end sought in the spiritual realm is a completeness that transcends the limitations of time. Therefore in the material field, sadhana is directed toward the achievement of something that is yet to be; but in spiritual life it is directed toward the realization of that which always has been, will ever be, and now IS.

Sadhana in spiritual and material realms

The spiritual goal of life is to be sought in life itself and not outside life; thus sadhana in the spiritual realm has to be such that it brings one's life closer to the spiritual ideal. Sadhana in the spiritual realm does not aim at the achievement of a limited objective, which may have its day and then ingloriously disappear forever. It aims at bringing about a radical change in the quality of life, so that one's life permanently becomes an expression of the Truth in the eternal Now. Sadhana is spiritually fruitful if it succeeds in bringing the life of the individual in tune with the divine purpose, which is to enable everyone to enjoy consciously the bliss of the God state. Sadhana has to be completely adapted to this end.

Goal of spiritual sadhana

In the spiritual realm every part of sadhana must aim at the realization of the spiritual goal of securing godliness in all phases of life. Therefore the different aspects of spiritual sadhana will, from one point of view, represent different gradations of spiritual Perfection. Sadhana is perfect to the extent to which it expresses the spiritual ideal, that is, the degree to which it resembles the perfect life. Thus the greater the disparity that exists between the sadhana and the ideal at which it aims, the less perfect it is; the less disparity that exists between sadhana and the ideal at which it aims, the more perfect it is. When sadhana is perfect or complete, it merges into the goal—a spiritually perfect life—so that the division of means and end is swallowed up in an inviolable integrity of indivisible being.

Perfect sadhana merges into the goal

The relation between spiritual sadhana and the end sought through it may be contrasted with the relation that exists between them in the material field. In the material field the end usually falls more or less entirely outside the sadhana through which it is secured,

Sadhana as partial participation in goal

and there is a clear disparity of nature between the sadhana and the end achieved through it. Thus, pulling the trigger of a gun may become a means of killing a person, but killing someone is essentially different from the pulling of the trigger. In the spiritual realm, however, the sadhana and the end sought through it cannot be completely external to each other, and there is no clear disparity of nature between them. In the spiritual realm it is not possible to maintain an unbridgeable gulf between sadhana and the end sought through it. This gives rise to the fundamental paradox that in spiritual life, the practicing of a sadhana in itself amounts to a partial participation in the goal. Hence it becomes understandable why many of the spiritual sadhanas have to be taken seriously *as if* they were, in themselves, the goal.

Sadhanas of knowledge, action, and love

In its deeper aspects, spiritual sadhana consists in following (1) the yoga of knowledge (*dnyan*), (2) the yoga of action (*karma*), and (3) the yoga of devotion or love (*bhakti*). The sadhana of knowledge finds its expression through the exercise of detachment born of true understanding, the different forms of meditation, and the constant use of discrimination and intuition. Each of these modes through which spiritual knowledge is sought or expressed requires explanatory comments.

Detachment

The individual soul is entangled in the world of forms and does not know itself as one with the being of God. This ignorance constitutes the bondage of the soul, and spiritual sadhana must aim at securing emancipation from this bondage. External renunciation of the things of this world is therefore often counted among the sadhanas that lead to Liberation. Though such external renunciation may have its own value, it is not absolutely necessary. What is needed is *internal* renunciation of craving for the things of this world. When craving is given up, it matters little whether the soul has or has not externally renounced the things of this world, because the soul has internally disentangled itself from the illusory world of forms and has prepared itself for the state of *Mukti*, or Liberation. Detachment is an important part of the sadhana of knowledge.

Meditation is another means through which spiritual knowledge is sought. Meditation should not be regarded as some odd pursuit peculiar to dwellers in caves. Every person finds himself meditating on something or another. The difference between such natural meditation and the meditation of an aspirant is that the latter is systematic and organized thinking about things that have spiritual importance. Meditation, as sadhana, may be personal or impersonal.

Meditation

Meditation is personal when it is concerned with one who is spiritually perfect. A suitable object for personal meditation may be taken (according to the inclination of the aspirant) from among the living or past Perfect Masters or the Avatar. Through such personal meditation the aspirant imbibes all the divine qualities and the spiritual knowledge of the Master. Since it involves love and self-surrender, personal meditation invites the grace of the Master, which alone can give final Realization. So the sadhana of personal meditation not only makes the aspirant similar to the Master on whom he meditates but also prepares his way to be united with the Master in the Truth.

Impersonal meditation is concerned with the formless and infinite aspect of God. This may lead a person toward the realization of the impersonal aspect of God; but on the whole, this meditation becomes barren unless the aspirant has been duly prepared by the pursuit of personal meditation and a life of virtue. In the ultimate realization of Infinity there is neither the limitation of personality nor the distinction of the opposites of good and evil. In order to achieve Realization, one has to pass from the personal to the impersonal and from goodness to God, who is beyond the opposites of good and evil. Another condition of attaining Truth through impersonal meditation is that the aspirant should be able to make his mind absolutely still. This becomes possible only when all the diverse sanskaras (impressions) in the mind have vanished. As the final wiping out of the sanskaras is possible only through the grace of a Master, the Master is indispensable for success even along the path of impersonal meditation.

The sadhana of knowledge, or dnyan, remains incomplete unless the aspirant exercises constant discrimination and unveils his highest intuitions. Realization of God comes to the aspirant who uses discrimination as well as his intuitions about true and lasting values. Infinite knowledge is latent in everyone, but it has to be unveiled. The way to increase knowledge is to put into practice that bit of spiritual wisdom a person may already happen to

Use of discrimination and intuition

have. The teachings that have come to humanity through the Masters of wisdom and the inborn sense of values that the aspirant brings with him shed sufficient light upon the *next* step the aspirant has to take. The difficult thing is to act upon the knowledge he has. One of the best methods of adding to one's own spiritual wisdom is to make use of the knowledge one already has. If the sadhana of knowledge is to be fruitful, it must be implemented at every step by due emphasis on action. Everyday life must be guided by discrimination and inspired by the highest intuitions.

Karma-yoga, or the yoga of action, consists in acting according to the best intuitions of the heart without fear or hesitation. In sadhana, what counts is *practice* and not mere theory. Sound practice is far more important than sound theory. Practice based upon right knowledge will of course be more fruitful, but even a mistake in a practical direction may have its own valuable lessons to bring. Mere theoretical speculation, however, remains spiritually barren, even when it is flawless. Thus a person who is not very learned but who sincerely takes the name of God and does his humble duties wholeheartedly may actually be nearer to God than one who knows all the metaphysics of the world but does not allow any of his theories to modify his everyday life.

Importance of action

The difference between the comparative importance of theory and practice in the realm of sadhanas may be brought out by means of a well-known story of an ass. An ass, who was plodding along a road for a long time and was very hungry, happened to see two heaps of grass—one at some distance on the right side of the road and the other at some distance on the left side of the road. Now the ass thought that it was of utmost importance to be absolutely certain which of the two heaps was clearly the better before he could intelligently decide to go to one heap rather than the other. If he decided without thorough thinking and without having sufficient grounds for his preference, that would be impulsive action and not intelligent action.

Illustrative story

Therefore he first considered the distance at which the two heaps were respectively placed from the road he was treading. Unfortunately for him, after elaborate consideration, he concluded that the heaps were equally distant from the road. So he wondered if there were some other consideration that might enable him to make the "right" choice and speculated upon the respective sizes of the heaps. Even with this second attempt to be theoretically sure before acting, his efforts were not crowned with success because he concluded that both heaps were of equal size. Then, with the tenacity and patience of an ass, he considered other things, such as the quality of the grass. But as fate would have it, in all the points of comparison he could think of, the two heaps turned out to be equally desirable.

Ultimately it happened that since the ass could not discover any deciding factor that would make his preference appear theoretically sound, he did not go to either of the two heaps but went straight ahead—hungry and tired as before and not a whit better off for having come upon two heaps of grass. If the ass had gone to one heap, without insisting upon the theoretical certainty of having chosen wisely, he might perhaps have gone to the heap that was not as good as the other. And despite any mistakes in his intellectual judgment, he would have been infinitely better off from a practical point of view.

In the spiritual life it is not necessary to have a complete map of the path in order to begin traveling. On the contrary, insistence upon having such complete knowledge may actually hinder rather than help the onward march. The deeper secrets of spiritual life are unraveled to those who take risks and who make bold experiments with it. They are not meant for the idler who seeks guarantees for every step. Those who speculate from the shore about the ocean shall know only its surface, but those who would know the depths of the ocean must be willing to plunge into it.

Fulfillment of the sadhana of karma-yoga requires that action should spring from perception of the Truth. Enlightened action does not bind because it is not rooted in the ego and is selfless. Selfishness represents ignorance, while selflessness is a reflection of the Truth. The real justification for a life of selfless service is to be found in this intrinsic worth of such a life and not in any ulterior result or consequence. The paradox of selfless action is that it actually brings to the aspirant much more than could ever come within the purview of ignorant selfishness. Selfishness leads to a narrow life that revolves around the false idea of a limited and separate individual. Whereas selfless action contributes toward the dissipation of the illusion of separateness and turns out to be the gateway to the unlimited life

Selfless service

where there is realization of *All-selfness*. What a person has may be lost and what he desires to have may never come to him; but if he parts with something in the spirit of an offering to God, it has already come back to him. Such is the sadhana of karma-yoga.

Even more important than the sadhanas of knowledge (dnyan) and action (karma) is the sadhana of love (bhakti). Love is its own excuse for being. It is complete in itself and does not need to be supplemented by anything. The greatest saints have been content with their love for God, desiring nothing else. Love is not love if it is based upon any expectation. In the intensity of divine love, the lover becomes one with the divine Beloved. There is no sadhana greater than love, there is no law higher than love, and there is no goal that is beyond love—for love in its divine state becomes infinite. God and love are identical, and one who has divine love already has God.

Love

Love may be regarded as being equally a part of sadhana and a part of the goal. The intrinsic worth of love is so obvious that it is often considered a mistake to look upon it as a sadhana for some other end. In no sadhana is the merging in God so easy and complete as in love. When love is the presiding genius, the path to Truth is effortless and joyous. As a rule sadhana involves effort and sometimes even desperate effort, as in the case of an aspirant who may strive for detachment in the face of temptations. In love, though, there is no sense of effort because it is spontaneous. Spontaneity is the essence of true spirituality. The highest state of consciousness, in which the mind is completely merged in the Truth, is known as *Sahajawastha*, the state of unlimited spontaneity in which there is uninterrupted Self-knowledge. One of the paradoxes connected with spiritual sadhana is that all effort of the aspirant is intended for arriving at a state of effortlessness.

Through effort to effortlessness

There is a beautiful story of a *kasturi-mriga*, or musk deer, that brings out the nature of all spiritual sadhana. Once, while roaming about and frolicking among hills and dales, the kasturi-mriga was suddenly aware of an exquisitely beautiful scent, the like of which it had never known. The scent stirred the inner depths of its soul so profoundly that it determined to find the source. So keen was its longing that notwithstanding the severity of cold or the intensity of

Story of kasturi-mriga

scorching heat, by day as well as by night, the deer carried on its desperate search for the source of the sweet scent. It knew no fear or hesitation but undaunted went on its elusive search, until at last, happening to lose its foothold on a cliff, it had a precipitous fall resulting in a fatal injury. While breathing its last, the deer found that the scent that had ravished its heart and inspired all these efforts came from its own navel. This last moment of the deer's life was its happiest, and there was on its face inexpressible peace.

All spiritual sadhanas of the aspirant are like the efforts of the kasturi-mriga. The final fructification of sadhana involves the termination of the ego-life of the aspirant. At that moment there is the realization that he himself has, in a sense, been the object of all his search and endeavor. All that he suffered and enjoyed—all his risks and adventures, all his sacrifices and desperate strivings—were intended for achieving true Self-knowledge, in which he loses his limited individuality only to discover that he is really identical with God, who is in everything.

Goal of sadhana is Self-knowledge

The Avatar

Consciously or unconsciously, every living creature seeks one thing. In the lower forms of life and in less advanced human beings, the quest is unconscious; in advanced human beings, it is conscious. The object of the quest is called by many names—happiness, peace, freedom, truth, love, perfection, Self-realization, God-realization, union with God. Essentially, it is a search for all of these, but in a special way. Everyone has moments of happiness, glimpses of truth, fleeting experiences of union with God; what they want is to make them permanent. They want to establish an abiding reality in the midst of constant change.

This is a natural desire, based fundamentally on a memory—dim or clear as the evolution of the individual soul may be low or high—of its essential unity with God. For every living thing is a partial manifestation of God, conditioned only by its lack of knowledge of its own true nature. The whole of evolution, in fact, is an evolution from unconscious divinity to conscious divinity, in which God Himself, essentially eternal and unchangeable, assumes an infinite variety of forms, enjoys an infinite variety of experiences, and transcends an infinite variety of self-imposed limitations. Evolution from the standpoint of the Creator is a divine sport, in which the Unconditioned tests the infinitude of His absolute knowledge, power, and bliss in the midst of all conditions. But evolution from the standpoint of the creature, with its limited knowledge, limited power, limited capacity for enjoying bliss, is an epic of alternating rest and struggle, joy and sorrow, love and hate—until in the perfected person, God balances the pairs of opposites, and duality is transcended.

Then creature and Creator recognize themselves as one; changelessness is established in the midst of change; eternity is experienced in the midst of time. God knows Himself as God, unchangeable in essence, infinite in manifestation, ever experiencing the supreme bliss of Self-realization in continually fresh awareness of Himself by Himself. This Realization must and does take place only in the midst of life; for it is only in the midst of life that limitation can be experienced and transcended, and that subsequent freedom from limitation can be enjoyed. This freedom from limitation assumes three forms.

Most God-realized souls leave the body at once and forever, and remain eternally merged in the unmanifest aspect of God. They are conscious only of the bliss of Union. Creation no longer exists for them. Their constant round of births and deaths is ended. This is known as *Moksha* (ordinary Mukti), or Liberation.

Some God-realized souls retain the body for a time; but their consciousness is merged completely in the unmanifest aspect of God, and they are therefore not conscious either of their bodies or of creation. They experience constantly the infinite bliss, power, and knowledge of God; but they cannot consciously use them in creation or help others to attain Liberation. Nevertheless, their presence on earth is like a focal point for the concentration and radiation of the infinite power, knowledge, and bliss of God; and those who approach them, serve them, and worship them are spiritually benefited by contact with them. These souls are called *Majzoobs-e-Kamil*; and this particular type of Liberation is called *Videh Mukti*, or liberation with the body.

A few God-realized souls keep the body, yet are conscious of themselves as God in both His unmanifest and His manifest aspects. They know themselves both as the unchangeable divine Essence and as its infinitely varied manifestation. They experience themselves as God apart from creation; as God the Creator, Preserver, and Destroyer of the whole of creation; and as God, who has accepted and transcended the limitations of creation. These souls experience constantly the absolute peace, the infinite knowledge, power, and bliss of God. They enjoy to the full the divine sport of creation. They know themselves as God in everything; therefore they are able to help everything spiritually and thus help other souls realize God, either as *Majzoobs-e-Kamil, Paramhansas, Jivanmuktas*—or even *Sadgurus*, as they themselves are called.

There are fifty-six God-realized souls in the world at all times. They are always one in consciousness. They are always different in function. For the most part, they live and work apart from and unknown to the general public; but five, who act in a sense as a directing body, always work in public and attain public prominence and importance. These are known as Sadgurus, or Perfect Masters. In Avataric periods the *Avatar*, as the Supreme Sadguru, takes His place as the head of this body and of the spiritual hierarchy as a whole.*

Avataric periods are like the springtide of creation. They bring a new release of power, a new awakening of consciousness, a new experience of life—not merely for a few, but for all. Qualities of energy and awareness, which had been used and enjoyed by only a few advanced souls, are made available for all humanity. Life, as a whole, is stepped up to a higher level of consciousness, is geared to a new rate of energy. The transition from sensation to reason was one such step; the transition from reason to intuition will be another.

This new influx of the creative impulse manifests, through the medium of a divine personality, an incarnation of God in a special sense—the *Avatar*. The Avatar was the first individual soul to emerge from the evolutionary and involutionary process as a Sadguru, and He is the only Avatar who has ever manifested or will ever manifest. Through Him God first completed the journey from unconscious divinity to conscious divinity, first unconsciously became man in order consciously to become God. Through Him, periodically, God consciously becomes man for the liberation of mankind.

The Avatar appears in different forms, under different names, at different times, in different parts of the world. As His appearance always coincides with the spiritual regeneration of man, the period immediately preceding His manifestation is always one in which humanity suffers from the pangs of the approaching rebirth. Man seems more than ever enslaved by desire, more than ever driven by greed, held by fear, swept by anger. The strong dominate the weak; the rich oppress the poor; large masses of people are exploited for the benefit of the few who are in power. The individual, who finds no peace or rest, seeks to forget himself in excitement. Immorality in-

*Every advent of the Avatar (the God-Man, the Messiah, the Buddha, the Christ, the Rasool) is the direct descent of God on earth in human form—as the Eternal Living Perfect Master. The five Sadgurus of the age precipitate this advent once in a cyclic period of 700 to 1400 years. For details see *God Speaks* by Meher Baba.—ED.

creases, crime flourishes, religion is ridiculed. Corruption spreads throughout the social order. Class and national hatreds are aroused and fostered. Wars break out. Humanity grows desperate. There seems to be no possibility of stemming the tide of destruction.

At this moment the Avatar appears. Being the total manifestation of God in human form, He is like a gauge against which man can measure what he is and what he may become. He trues the standard of human values by interpreting them in terms of divinely human life.

He is interested in everything but not concerned about anything. The slightest mishap may command His sympathy; the greatest tragedy will not upset Him. He is beyond the alternations of pain and pleasure, desire and satisfaction, rest and struggle, life and death. To Him they are equally illusions that He has transcended, but by which others are bound, and from which He has come to free them. He uses every circumstance as a means to lead others toward Realization.

He knows that individuals do not cease to exist when they die and therefore is not concerned over death. He knows that destruction must precede construction, that out of suffering is born peace and bliss, that out of struggle comes liberation from the bonds of action. He is only concerned about concern.

In those who contact Him, He awakens a love that consumes all selfish desires in the flame of the one desire to serve Him. Those who consecrate their lives to Him gradually become identified with Him in consciousness. Little by little their humanity is absorbed into His divinity, and they become free. Those who are closest to Him are known as His Circle.

Every Sadguru has an intimate Circle of twelve disciples who, at the point of Realization, are made equal to the Sadguru himself, though they may differ from him in function and authority. In Avataric periods the Avatar has a Circle of ten concentric Circles with a total of 122 disciples, all of whom experience Realization and work for the Liberation of others.* The work of the Avatar and His disciples is not only for contemporary humanity but for posterity as well. The unfoldment of life and consciousness for the whole Avataric cycle, which had been mapped out in the creative world before the Avatar took form, is endorsed and fixed in the formative and material worlds during the Avatar's life on earth.

The Avatar awakens contemporary humanity to a realization of

*For details see "The Circles of the Avatar" discourse.—ED.

its true spiritual nature, gives Liberation to those who are ready, and quickens the life of the spirit in His time. For posterity is left the stimulating power of His divinely human example—of the nobility of a life supremely lived, of a love unmixed with desire, of a power unused except for others, of a peace untroubled by ambition, of a knowledge undimmed by illusion. He has demonstrated the possibility of a divine life for all humanity, of a heavenly life on earth. Those who have the necessary courage and integrity can follow when they will.

Those who are spiritually awake have been aware for some time that the world is at present in the midst of a period such as always precedes Avataric manifestations. Even unawakened men and women are becoming aware of it now. From their darkness they are reaching out for light; in their sorrow they are longing for comfort; from the midst of the strife into which they have found themselves plunged, they are praying for peace and deliverance.

For the moment they must be patient. The wave of destruction must rise still higher, must spread still further. But when, from the depths of his heart, man desires something more lasting than wealth and something more real than material power, the wave will recede. Then peace will come, joy will come, light will come.

The breaking of my silence—the signal for my public manifestation—is not far off. I bring the greatest treasure it is possible for man to receive—a treasure that includes all other treasures, that will endure forever, that increases when shared with others. Be ready to receive it.

The Man-God*

Part I
Aspirants and God-Realized Beings

Even before God-realization, advanced aspirants pass through states of consciousness that, in some ways, are akin to the state of God-realization. For example, the *masts* and advanced souls of the higher planes become desireless and immersed in the joy of God-intoxication. Since their only concern is God, they become the recipients of the unique happiness characteristic of the God state. They have no beloved except God, and they have no longing except for God. For them, God is not only the only Beloved but also the only Reality that counts. They are unattached to everything except God and remain unaffected by the pleasures and the pains to which worldly persons are subject. They are happy because they are always face to face with the divine Beloved, who is the very ocean of happiness.

Joy of God-intoxication

Advanced aspirants not only participate in some of the privileges of the Divine state, but also wield great occult and mystic powers (siddhis). Depending upon the powers they wield, the aspirants belong to different types. For example, even on the first plane the aspirant begins to see lights and colors, smell perfumes, and hear the music of the subtle world. Those who advance further can see and hear things at any distance. Some aspi-

Powers of advanced aspirants

*The Man-God is also called Perfect Master, Sadguru, Qutub, or Salik-e-Mukammil, and is most frequently referred to throughout the *Discourses* simply as "Master" (see Glossary).—Ed.

rants see the whole gross world as a mirage. Other advanced aspirants can take a new body immediately after their death. Some agents of Perfect Masters have such control over the gross world that they can change their bodies at will. In Sufi tradition they are called *abdal.* All these achievements of advanced aspirants pertain to the phenomenal world. The field of their powers is itself a domain of illusion, and the miracles they perform do not necessarily mean that they are in any way nearer to the God state.

Different states of aspirants

From the standpoint of consciousness also, aspirants belong to various types according to the line in which they have advanced and according to their nearness to the God state. Some get intoxicated with their extraordinary powers and, tempted to use them, have a long pause in their Godward march. They get stuck in the consciousness of the intermediate planes. Some become dazed, confused, and even self-deluded. Others are caught in a coma. There are some who, with difficulty, try to come down to gross consciousness by repeating a physical action or by repeating some utterance many times. There are those who, in their God-intoxication, are so indifferent to the life of the gross world that to all appearances their external behavior is like that of mad persons. And there are some who tread the spiritual path while performing their worldly duties.

State of the unmatta

Owing to their exalted states of consciousness, some advanced aspirants are worthy of adoration; but they are in no way comparable to God-realized beings, either in spiritual beauty and perfection of the inward state of consciousness or in their powers. All aspirants, right up to the sixth plane, are limited by finite consciousness; and they are all in the domain of duality and illusion. Aspirants are mostly happy: this is due to their contact and communion with God. For some the joy of inward companionship with the divine Beloved is so great that they become unbalanced in their behavior. As a result, in their unsubdued state of God-intoxication they may abuse people, throw stones at them, and behave as though possessed. Their state is often described as that of the *unmatta.* Owing to the exuberance of uncontrolled joy in their inward contact with the divine Beloved, they are utterly heedless of worldly standards or values. Because of the fearlessness that comes to them through complete detachment, they often manifest a self-expression that can easily be mistaken for idiosyncracy and unruliness.

Only when it attains God-realization on the seventh plane can the soul fully control its joy. The unlimited happiness that is eternally his does not in any way unbalance the person because he is now permanently established in the poise of nonduality. The extravagance of newly found love and joy is no longer for him. Occasional unsettlement due to increasing joy at the closer proximity of God is also finished because he is now inseparably united with Him. He is lost in the divine Beloved and merged in Him, who is the infinite ocean of unbounded happiness. The happiness of the God-realized person is unconditional and self-sustained. It is therefore eternally the same, without ebb and flow. He has arrived at unqualified finality and unassailable equanimity.

Poise and happiness of God-realized

The happiness of the aspirants is born of their increasing proximity and closer intimacy with the divine Beloved—who, however, remains externalized as the *Other*. Whereas the happiness of the God-realized is an inalienable aspect of the God state, in which there is no duality. The happiness of the aspirants is derivative, but the happiness of the God-realized is Self-grounded. The happiness of the aspirants comes from increasing bounty of divine grace, but the happiness of the God-realized merely IS.

When a person attains God-realization, he has infinite power, knowledge, and bliss. These intrinsic characteristics of inner Realization are always the same despite minor differences, which give rise to certain distinguishable types of God-realized beings. These differences between the God-realized are purely extrinsic and pertain only to their relation with the universe. They do not create any degrees of spiritual status between the God-realized, who are all perfect and one with all life and existence. From the point of view of the creation, however, these differences between the God-realized are not only definite but worth noting. After God-realization, most souls drop all their bodies and remain eternally immersed in God-consciousness. For them, God is the only Reality, and the entire universe is a zero. They are so completely identified with the impersonal aspect of the Truth that they have no direct link with the world of forms.

Differences in relation to universe

Some God-realized souls retain their gross, subtle, and mental bodies; but in their absorption in God-consciousness, they are totally unconscious of the existence of their bodies. Others in creation continue to see these bodies and treat them as persons incarnate, but the bodies exist only from the point of view of the observer. Such God-realized persons are called *Majzoobs-e-Kamil* in Sufi terminology. These Majzoobs do not use their bodies consciously, because their consciousness is wholly directed toward God and is not turned toward the bodies or the universe. For them their own bodies as well as the world of forms have no existence, so there can be no question of their using the bodies in relation to the world of forms. However, their bodies are necessarily the centers for radiation of the unpremeditated and constant overflow of the infinite bliss, knowledge, and love that they enjoy. Those who revere them derive great spiritual benefit from this spontaneous radiation of divinity.

Majzoobs-e-Kamil

In addition to consciousness of God, some God-realized beings have an awareness of the existence of other souls who are still in bondage. They know all these souls to be forms of the *Paramatma* (Oversoul), and that all are destined one day to achieve Emancipation—and some, God-realization. Being established in this knowledge, they remain indifferent to the provisional and changing lots of the souls who are in bondage. These God-realized souls know that, just as they themselves have realized God, others will also realize God at some time. They are uninterested, however, in speeding up the God-realization of those who are in bondage and take no active interest in the time process of creation.

Some God-realized souls indifferent to creation

A rare few God-realized souls not only possess God-consciousness but are also conscious of creation and their own bodies. They take active interest in the souls who are in bondage; and they use their own bodies consciously to work in creation, in order to help other souls in their Godward march. Such a God-realized soul is called *Man-God, Perfect Master, Sadguru, Qutub,* or *Salik-e-Mukammil.* The Man-God experiences himself as the center of the entire universe; and everyone—high or low, good or bad—is at the same distance from him. In the Sufi tradition this center is called the *Qutub*; the Qutub controls the whole universe through his agents.

Man-God (Sadguru)

When man becomes God and retains creation-consciousness, he is called a *Man-God*; but when God becomes man, He is called the *God-Man*, or the *Avatar*. The God-Man is the foremost Sadguru, who was the first to emerge through evolution and involution; and He helps all souls in bondage through His recurrent advents. However, from the point of view of the fundamental characteristics of consciousness and the nature of His work in creation, the God-Man is like any other Man-God. The God-Man and the Man-God never lose their God-consciousness even for an instant, although they may be engaged in all sorts of activities in relation to creation. Neither has a finite and limited mind; both work through the *universal mind* when they desire to help other souls.

God-Man (Avatar)

The Man-God

Part II
The State of the Man-God

Becoming God

Of all the subjects of human study, God is the most meaningful. But purely theoretical study of God does not take the aspirant very far toward the real purpose of human life, though it is always better to study God than to be completely ignorant of His existence. To seek God intellectually is infinitely better than to be merely a skeptic or an agnostic. And it is decidedly better to feel God than to study Him through the intellect, though even feeling for God is less important than the actual experience of God. However, even the experience of God does not yield the true nature of divinity because God, as the object of experience, remains different from and external to the aspirant. The true nature of God is known to the aspirant only when he attains unity with God, by losing himself in His Being. Thus, it is better to study God than to be ignorant of Him; it is better to feel God than to study Him; it is better to experience God than to feel God; and it is better to become God than to experience Him.

The state of God-realization is unmarred by the doubts that cloud the minds of those who are in bondage. Those in bondage are in a constant state of uncertainty about their "whence" and "whither." The God-realized, on the other hand, are at the very heart of creation where its source and end are known. The God-realized soul knows itself to be God as surely as an ordinary person knows himself to be a human being and not an animal. For the God-realized it is not a matter of doubt, belief, self-delusion, or guesswork. It is a matter of supreme and unshakable certainty, which needs no external corroborations and remains unaffected by the contradictions of others because it is based upon continuous Self-knowledge. This spiritual certainty cannot be challenged by anyone or anything. The realized soul cannot think of itself as anything but God, just as the ordinary person cannot think of himself as being anything except a human being. But the person thinks himself to be what he is not, in reality, and the God-realized soul knows itself to be what it is, in reality.

Supreme certainty

God-realization is the very goal of all creation. All earthly pleasure, however great, is but a fleeting shadow of the eternal bliss of God-realization. All worldly knowledge, however comprehensive, is but a distorted reflection of the absolute Truth of God-realization. All human might, however imposing, is but a fragment of the infinite power of God-realization. All that is noble, beautiful, and lovely, all that is great, good, and inspiring in the universe, is just an infinitesimal fraction of the unfading and unspeakable glory of God-realization.

Glory of God-realization

The eternal bliss, the infinite power, the unfading glory, and the absolute Truth of God-realization are not to be had for nothing. The individualized soul has to go through all the travail, the pain, and the struggle of evolution, reincarnation, and involution before it can inherit this treasure, which is hidden at the heart of creation. The price it has to pay for coming into possession of this treasure is its own existence as a separate ego. The limited individuality must disappear entirely if there is to be an entrance into the unlimited state of Godhood.

Price of God-realization

In the ordinary person of the world, the limited individuality, which is identified with a finite name and form, predominates and creates a veil of ignorance over the God within. If this ignorance is to disappear, the limited individual has to surrender his own limited existence. When he goes from the scene without leaving a vestige of his limited life, what remains is God. The surrenderance of limited existence is the surrender of the firmly rooted delusion of having a separate existence. It is not the surrender of anything real: it is the surrenderance of the false and the inheritance of the Truth.

When a person is crossing the inner planes toward God-realization, he becomes successively unconscious of the gross, subtle, and mental worlds as well as his own gross, subtle, and mental bodies. But after God-realization, a few souls again descend, or come down, and become conscious of the whole creation—as well as their gross, subtle, and mental bodies—without in any way jeopardizing their God-consciousness. Only five of them function as the Perfect Masters. God as God alone is not consciously man, and man as man alone is not consciously God; the Man-God is consciously God as well as man. Yet by again becoming conscious of creation, the Man-God does not suffer the slightest deterioration of spiritual status.

Two aspects of Man-God

What is spiritually disastrous for the soul still in bondage is not mere consciousness of creation but the fact that consciousness is *caught up* in creation because of sanskaras. Thus consciousness is covered with ignorance, and this prevents the realization of the Divinity within. In the same way, what is also spiritually disastrous is not mere consciousness of the bodies but *identification* with them due to sanskaras. These sanskaras prevent the realization of the infinite Soul, which is the ultimate Reality and the basis of all creation. In it alone is to be found the final meaning of the entire creation.

Man-God not caught up in creation

The soul in bondage is tied to the world of forms by the chain of sanskaras, which create the illusion of identification of the soul with the bodies. The disharmony within consciousness and the distortions in the expression of the divine will arise from sanskaric identification with the bodies and not merely through consciousness of the bodies. Since the Man-God is free from all sanskaras, he is constantly conscious of being different from the bodies and uses them harmoniously as mere instruments for the expression of the divine will in all its purity. The bodies are to the Man-God what a wig is to a bald man. The bald man puts on his wig when he goes to work during the day, and he takes it off when he retires at night. So the Man-God uses his bodies when he needs them for his work; but he is free of them when he does not need them and knows them to be utterly different from his true being as God.

The Man-God knows himself to be infinite and beyond all forms, and with complete detachment he can therefore remain conscious of creation without being caught up in it. The falseness of the phenomenal world consists in its not being understood properly, that is, as being an illusory expression of the infinite Spirit. Ignorance consists in taking the form as complete in itself, without any reference to the infinite Spirit of which it is the expression. The Man-God realizes the Truth. He is conscious of the true nature of God as well as the true nature of creation. And yet this does not involve him in any consciousness of duality because, for him, creation does not exist as anything but the changing shadow of God—who is the only eternal and real Existence, and who is at the heart of creation. The Man-God can therefore remain conscious of creation without lessening his God-consciousness; and he continues to work in the world of forms for the furtherance of the primary purpose of creation, which is to create full Self-knowledge, or God-realization, in every soul.

Changing shadow of God cannot affect God-consciousness

When the Sadguru descends into the world of forms from the impersonal aspect of God, he assumes universal mind; and he knows, feels, and works through this universal mind. No longer for him is the limited life of finite mind; no longer for him are the pains and the pleasures of duality; no longer for him are the emptiness and the vanity of separative ego. He is consciously one with all life. Through his universal mind he not only experiences the happiness of all minds but also their suffering. Since most minds have a great preponderance of suffering over happiness due to ignorance, the suffering that thus comes to the Man-God because of the condition of others is infinitely greater than the happiness. The suffering of the Man-God is great; but the infinite bliss of the God state, which he constantly and effortlessly enjoys, supports him in all the suffering that comes to him, leaving him unmoved and unaffected by it.

Man-God works through universal mind

The individualized soul has no access to the infinite bliss of the God state, and it is seriously moved and affected by its sanskaric happiness and suffering because of its ignorant identification with the limited mind. The Man-God does not identify himself even with the universal mind, which he assumes when he comes down for the world.

Man-God drops universal mind after his mission

He has taken the universal mind only for his mission in the world; and since he uses it solely for his work without identification with it, he remains unaffected by the suffering or happiness that comes to him through it. He drops the universal mind after his work is done. Even when he is working in the world through his universal mind, he knows himself to be the eternal and only God and not the universal mind.

The union that the Man-God has with God is perfect. Even when he comes down into duality for his universal work, he remains inseparable from God even for an instant. In his normal state as man, he has

Suffering of Man-God and the God-Man

to be on the level of all and eat, drink, and suffer like others. Yet as he retains his Godhood even while he does all these things, he constantly experiences peace, bliss, and power. But when God *becomes* man, He as the God-Man literally suffers as man. Jesus Christ, as the Avatar, *did* suffer on the Cross. However, with the continuous Knowledge that His conscious Godhood gave Him, He knew at the same time that everything in the world of duality is illusion; and He was sustained by this Knowledge of His God state.

The God-Man experiences all souls as His own. He experiences Himself in everything, and His universal mind includes all minds in its scope. The God-Man knows Himself to be one with all other souls in

Crucifixion

bondage. Although He knows Himself to be identical with God and is thus eternally free, He also knows Himself to be one with the other souls in bondage and is thus bound. Though He is conscious of the eternal bliss of His God state, He also experiences infinite suffering, owing to the bondage of others whom He knows to be His own forms. This is the meaning of Christ's Crucifixion. The God-Man is, as it were, continuously being crucified, and He is continuously taking birth. In the God-Man, the purpose of creation has been completely realized. He has nothing to attain for Himself by remaining in the world, yet He retains His body and continues to use it for emancipating other souls from bondage and helping them attain God-consciousness.

Even while working in the world of duality, the God-Man is in no way limited by duality. In His God state, the duality of "I" and "you" is swallowed up in the all-embracing divine love. The state of Perfection in which the God-Man dwells is beyond all forms of duality and opposites. It is a state of unlimited freedom and unimpaired completeness, immortal sweetness and undying happiness, untarnished divinity and unhampered creativity. The God-Man is inseparably united with God forever and dwells in a state of nonduality in the very midst of duality. He not only knows Himself to be one with all but also knows Himself to be the only One. He consciously descends from the state of being God to the state of experiencing God in everything. Therefore, His dealings in the world of duality not only do not bind Him but reflect the pristine glory of the sole Reality, which is God, and contribute toward freeing others from their state of bondage.

Nonduality in midst of duality

The Man-God

Part III
The Work of the Man-God

God-realization is the endless end of creation and the timeless consummation and fructification of intelligent and nonbinding karma. Souls who have not realized God are still in the domain of duality, and their dealings of mutual give-and-take in different fields create the chains of karmic debts and dues from which there is no escape. The Man-God, however, dwells in the consciousness of unity; and all that he does, not only does not bind him, but contributes toward the emancipation of others who are still in ignorance. For the Man-God there is no one who is excluded from his own being. He sees himself in everyone; and since all that he does springs from the consciousness of nonduality, he can freely give and freely take without creating bindings for himself or others.

Free and nonbinding give-and-take

If a person accepts without reserve from the bounty the Man-God showers, he creates a link that will stand by him until he attains Freedom and God-realization. If a person serves the Man-God, offering his life and all possessions in his service, he creates a link that will augment his spiritual progress by inviting upon himself the grace and help of the Man-God. In fact, even opposition to the work of the Man-God often turns out to be a begin-

Contact with Man-God beneficial to all

ning of development that imperceptibly leads a person Godward, because while opposing the work of the Man-God, the soul is establishing a link and a contact with him. Thus everyone who voluntarily or involuntarily comes into the orbit of his activities becomes, in some way, the recipient of a spiritual push.

The work of the Perfect Masters in the universe is fundamentally different from the kind of thing most priests or clergy of established religions aspire to. Most of them attach too much importance to external forms, rituals, and conformity. Since they themselves are not free from selfishness, narrowness, or ignorance, they exploit the weak and the credulous by holding before them the fear of hell or the hope of heaven. The Perfect Masters, on the other hand, have entered forever into the eternal life of love, purity, universality, and understanding. They are therefore concerned only with the things that really matter and that eventually bring about the inner unfoldment of spirit in all whom they help.

Perfect Masters inimitable and unlimited

Those who are themselves in ignorance may, out of self-delusion or deliberate selfishness, use the same language as that of the Masters; and they may try to imitate them in many of the external things associated with the life of the Masters. But they cannot, by the very nature of their spiritual limitations, really imitate the Man-God in possessing perfect understanding, experiencing infinite bliss, or wielding unlimited power. These attributes belong to the Man-God by virtue of his having attained unity with God.

Those who are in ignorance lack the fundamental traits of the Masters. And if out of self-delusion or hypocrisy they try to pose as a Man-God, their self-delusion or pretense is invariably exposed at some time. If a person becomes committed to a way of life out of self-delusion, it is an unfortunate situation. He believes himself to be what he is not and thinks that he knows when he actually does not know. But if he is sincere in all that he thinks or does, he is not to be blamed, though to a limited extent he can become a source of danger to others. The hypocrite, however, knows that he does not know and pretends to be what he is not for selfish reasons. In doing so he creates a serious karmic binding for himself. Though he is a source of considerable danger to the weak and the

Self-delusion and hypocrisy

credulous, he cannot go on indefinitely with his willful deceit; for in the course of time he is automatically exposed by some claim he is unable to substantiate.

In the performance of his universal work, the Man-God has infinite adaptability. He is not attached to any one method of helping others; he does not follow rules or precedents but is a law unto himself.

Man-God may play role of aspirant

He can rise to any occasion and play the role that is necessary under the circumstances without being bound by it. Once a devotee asked his Master the reason why he fasted. The Master replied, "I am not fasting to attain Perfection; for having already attained Perfection, I am not an aspirant. It is for the sake of others that I fast." A spiritual aspirant cannot act like one who has attained Perfection, since the Perfect One is inimitable; but the Perfect One can, for the guidance or benefit of others, act like an aspirant.

One who has passed the highest examinations of a university can write the alphabet without difficulty to teach children, but children cannot do what he can do. To show the way to divinity, the Man-God may often play the role of a *bhakta* (devotee) of God, although he has already attained complete unity with God. He plays this role, though God-realized, in order that others may know the way. He is not bound to any particular role, and he can adjust his technique of helping others to the needs of those who seek his guidance. Whatever he does is for the ultimate good of others. For him there is nothing worth attaining because he has become Everything.

Not only is the Man-God not necessarily bound to any particular technique in giving spiritual help to others, but also he is not bound to the conventional standard of good. He is beyond the distinction of good

Man-God uses Maya to annihilate Maya

and evil; although what he does may appear lawless in the eyes of the world, it is always meant for the ultimate good of others. He uses different methods for different persons. He has no self-interest or personal motive and is always inspired by compassion that seeks the true well-being of others. Therefore, in all that he does, he remains unbound.

He uses Maya to draw his disciples out of Maya and employs infinite ways and workings for his spiritual task. His methods are different with different persons, and they are not the same with the same person at all times. Occasionally he may even do something that shocks others because it runs counter to their usual expectations. However, this is always intended to serve some spiritual purpose. The intervention of a short shocking dream is often useful in awakening a person from a long beautiful dream. Like the shocking dream, the shocks the Man-God in his discretion deliberately administers are eventually wholesome, although they may be unpleasant at the time.

The Sadguru may even seem to be unduly harsh with certain individuals, but onlookers have no idea of the internal situation and cannot therefore understand properly the justification of his apparent cruelty. In fact his sternness is often demanded by the spiritual requirements of the situation and is necessary in the best interests of those to whom he seems to be harsh. A good and illustrative analogy for such apparently cruel action is when an expert swimmer tries to save a drowning person.

Saving a drowning person

It is well known that if someone is drowning, he has a tendency to cling to anything that comes to hand. In his desperation he is so blind to the consequences that his thoughtless grip on the one who has come to save him not only makes it impossible for him to be saved but is often instrumental in drowning the very person who tries to save him. In fact, an expert in this art of lifesaving must often hit the drowning person on the head and render him unconscious. Through his apparent cruelty he minimizes the danger the individual is likely to create, and so ensures success for his efforts. In the same way, the apparent sternness of the Man-God is intended to secure the ultimate spiritual well-being of others.

The soul in bondage is caught up in the universe, and the universe is nothing but imagination. Since there is no end to imagination, a person is likely to wander indefinitely in the mazes of false consciousness. The Man-God can help him cut short the different stages of false consciousness by revealing the Truth. When the mind does not perceive the Truth, it is likely to imagine all kinds of things—for example, the mind can imagine that it is a beggar or a king, a man or a woman, and so forth. The soul, through the mind, thus goes on gathering experiences of the opposites.

False consciousness

Wherever there is duality, there is a tendency to restore balance through the opposite. If a person has the experience of being a murderer, for instance, it has to be counterbalanced by the experience of being murdered. Or if one has the experience of being a king, this has to be counterbalanced by the experience of being a beggar. Thus the individual may wander ad infinitum from one opposite to the other without being able to put an end to false consciousness. The Man-God can help him arrive at Truth by giving him perception of the Truth and cutting short the working of his imagination, which would otherwise be endless. The Man-God helps the soul in bondage by sowing in it the seed of God-realization, but Realization always takes some time to attain. Every process of growth in the universe takes time.

Seed of God-realization

The help of the Man-God is, however, far more effective than the help some advanced aspirant may give. When an aspirant helps, he can take a person only up to the point he himself has reached. Even this limited help that he can give becomes effective very gradually; with the result that the person who ascends through such help has to stay in the first plane for a long time, then in the second, and so on. When the Man-God chooses to help, he may, through his grace, take the aspirant even to the seventh plane in one second—though in that one second the person has to traverse all the intermediate planes of involution of consciousness.

Help of Man-God

In taking an aspirant to the seventh plane, the Man-God is making him equal to himself; and the one who thus attains the highest spiritual status may also become a Perfect Master. This transmission of spiritual knowledge from the Man-God to his disciple is comparable to the lighting of one lamp from another. The lamp that has been lighted is as capable of giving light to others as the original lamp itself. There is no difference between them in importance or utility.

The Man-God is comparable to a banyan tree. The banyan tree grows huge and mighty, giving shade and shelter to travelers and protecting them from sun, rain, and storm. In the fullness of its growth, its descending rooting branches strike deep into the fallow ground below to create, in due time, another full-grown banyan tree. It too becomes equally huge and mighty—giving shade and shelter to travelers and protecting them from sun, rain, and storm—and has the same potential power to create similar full-grown banyan trees. The same is true of the Man-God, who arouses the

Analogy of banyan tree

Godhood latent in others. Thus the continued succession of the Perfect Masters on earth is a perpetual blessing to mankind, helping it onward in its struggle through darkness.

God-Man, the Lord and servant

The God-Man (Avatar), however, may be said to be both the Lord and servant of the universe at one and the same time. As the One who showers His spiritual bounty on all in measureless abundance, He is the Lord of the universe. As the One who continuously bears the burden of all and helps them through numberless spiritual difficulties, He is the servant of the universe. Just as He is Lord and servant in one, the God-Man is also the supreme Lover and the matchless Beloved. The love He gives or receives goes to free the soul from ignorance. In giving love He gives it to Himself in other forms; in receiving love He receives what has been awakened through His own grace, which is continuously showered on all without distinction. The grace of the God-Man is like the rain, which falls equally on all lands irrespective of whether they are barren or fertile; but it fructifies only in the lands that have been rendered fertile through arduous and patient toiling.

The Circle

After several lifetimes of search, purification, service, and self-sacrifice, some persons have the good fortune to meet and get connected with a God-realized Master. Through their several lifetimes of close connection with the one who has now become a Perfect Master, and through their love and service for this Master, they enter into his Circle. Those who have entered into the Circle of a Master are the souls who, through their efforts, have acquired the eligibility for God-realization. When the exact moment for Realization arrives, they attain it through the grace of the Master.

Entering Circle of Perfect Master

All actions in the world of duality are prompted by sanskaras of duality. Consciousness of duality implies the working of the impressions of duality. These impressions of duality first serve the purpose of evolving and limiting consciousness, and then they serve the purpose of liberating it so as to facilitate Self-knowledge, or God-realization. The soul cannot attain consciousness of its own unity unless it goes through the experiences of duality, which presuppose and require corresponding impressions of duality. From the very beginning till the very end, the soul is subject to the momentum of impressions, which constitute the destiny of the soul. These impressions are called *prarabdha sanskaras*. These prarabdha sanskaras always relate to the opposites of experience, for example, the sanskaras of greed and its opposite, the sanskaras of lust and its opposite, the sanskaras of anger and its opposite, the sanskaras of bad thoughts, words, and deeds and their opposites.

Prarabdha sanskaras

From the stage of the atom till the realization of God, the soul is bound by the impressions of duality; and all that happens to it is determined by these impressions. When the soul realizes God, all its sanskaras disappear. If it remains immersed in the experience of divinity without coming back to normal consciousness of the world of duality, it remains eternally beyond all types of sanskaras. It does not have any sanskaras and cannot have any.

Disappearance of sanskaras

If the God-realized soul returns to normal consciousness of the world of duality, it assumes universal mind. This universal mind has superfluous and nonbinding sanskaras, which are known as *yogayoga sanskaras*. In the Beyond state, the Perfect Master is eternally free from all sanskaras. Even when he is conscious of creation and is working in creation, he remains unbound by these yogayoga sanskaras, which sit loosely upon his universal mind. The yogayoga sanskaras merely serve as channels for his universal work. They do not form a restricting chain to his consciousness.

Yogayoga sanskaras of universal mind

The yogayoga sanskaras are automatic in their working. All the specific contacts and links to which the Man-God responds in his work are ultimately based upon these yogayoga sanskaras. They do not create a veil on the universal mind; they do not constitute a cloud of ignorance. They only serve as a necessary framework for the release of definitive action. Through these yogayoga sanskaras the universal will of God is particularized in its expressions. Any action released in the world of space and time must be in relation to a certain definite situation or set of circumstances. There must always be some reason why a response is given to one situation rather than another and why it is given in one way rather than another. The basis for the self-limitation of the actions of a soul in spiritual bondage is in its prarabdha sanskaras, which are binding. The basis for the self-limitation of the actions of a soul that is spiritually free is in its yogayoga sanskaras, which are not binding.

Function of yogayoga sanskaras

If the Man-God were not to get these yogayoga sanskaras while coming down to normal consciousness, he would not be able to do any work of a definite nature. Yogayoga sanskaras help the Man-God to particularize and materialize the divine will through him, and to fulfill his mission. The Master is and knows himself to be infinite in existence, consciousness, knowledge, bliss, love, and power; and he always remains infinite in the Beyond state. But the work he does in the world of creation is subject to the laws of creation and is therefore in one sense finite. Since his work is in relation to the unveiling of the hidden Infinity and Divinity in everyone, and since the realization of this Infinity and Divinity is the only purpose of the entire creation, his work is *infinitely* important. However, when it is measured by the standard of results, it can only be—like any work possible in the world—so much and no more.

Work of Man-God subject to laws of creation

Even when the work of the Man-God is measured by the magnitude of its results, the results achieved by the worldly-minded are mostly trivial in comparison. The greatest of souls who are still in spiritual bondage cannot approach the achievements of the Man-God. The Master has behind his work the infinite power of God, while the worldly person is working with the limited power available to him through his ego-mind. A Man-God may sometimes end his incarnation after achieving some limited task. This is not because he is limited in his power but because the work, which is determined by his yogayoga sanskaras, is so much and no more. He is in no way attached to work as such. Having finished the work given to him by his yogayoga sanskaras, he is ready to be reabsorbed in the impersonal aspect of the Infinite. He does not tarry in the world of unreality and duality a minute longer than is necessitated by his yogayoga sanskaras.

Master's work determined by yogayoga sanskaras

In the Beyond state, time, space, and the whole world of phenomena are nonexistent. Only in the phenomenal world of duality is there space, time, or operation of the law of cause and effect. When the Perfect Master works in the sphere of duality for the upliftment of humanity, his work becomes subject to the laws of time, space, and causality. From the point of view of external work, at times he appears to be limited; though in reality he is at all times experiencing the oneness and infinity of the Beyond state. Though he himself is beyond time, when he works for those who are in duality, time counts.

Beyond state

The Master's universal work for humanity, in general, goes on without break through the higher planes. When he works for the members of his Circle, his action follows a timing he himself fixes with utmost care; for it has to be a precise and definite intervention in the mechanical working out of their sanskaras. He works for the Circle at fixed times. Therefore those who, in following the instructions received from the Master, abide by the timing given by him have the benefit of his special work. From the standpoint of the special tasks the Master sets for himself, time becomes an extremely important factor. The special work that the Master undertakes in relation to the members of his Circle not only touches and affects these members themselves but also those who are closely connected with the members of his Circle.

Special work for Circle

Like the Perfect Masters, the Avatar also has His Circle (of ten concentric Circles). When the Avatar takes an incarnation, He has before Him a clear-cut mission that proceeds according to a plan; and this plan is always carefully adjusted to the flow of time. The process of the incarnation of the Avatar is unique. Before taking on a physical body and descending into the world of duality, He gives to Himself and members of His Circles special types of sanskaras, which are known as *vidnyani sanskaras*. The Circles of the Avatar always consist of a total of 122 members, and all of them have to take an incarnation when the Avatar takes an incarnation. The taking on of vidnyani sanskaras before incarnating in the physical body is like the drawing of a veil upon Himself and His Circles. After taking an incarnation, the Avatar remains under this veil of vidnyani sanskaras until the time that has been fixed by Himself. When the appointed time comes, He experiences His own original divinity and begins to work through the vidnyani sanskaras, which now have been transmuted into the yogayoga sanskaras of the universal mind.

Avatar and His Circles

For all intents and purposes, vidnyani sanskaras are like the ordinary sanskaras of duality, though they are essentially different in nature. Vidnyani sanskaras prompt activities and invite experiences that are similar to activities and experiences caused by ordinary sanskaras. But while the activities and experiences caused by ordinary sanskaras have a general tendency to strengthen the grip of illusory duality, the activities and

Nature of vidnyani sanskaras

experiences caused by vidnyani sanskaras systematically work toward the loosening of the grip of duality. The logic of the working out of vidnyani sanskaras necessarily invites the realization of the oneness of existence. They are therefore known as a threshold of Unity. The members of the Circles remain under the veil of vidnyani sanskaras until they attain realization of God at the time fixed by the Avatar. After they attain Realization through the Avatar, the vidnyani sanskaras they brought with them do not constitute a veil but for some, become yogayoga sanskaras—serving only as an instrument for the fulfillment of the divine plan on earth.

Differences between vidnyani and yogayoga sanskaras

There are important differences between vidnyani and yogayoga sanskaras. Though vidnyani sanskaras ultimately work toward the realization of Unity, they cause the experience of being limited until Realization. Yogayoga sanskaras come after Realization and do not in any way interfere with the experience of Infinity, which is above duality—although they serve as instruments for enabling and determining responses and activities in the dual world. The working out of vidnyani sanskaras contributes toward one's own Realization, while the working out of yogayoga sanskaras contributes toward the process of Realization in others who are still in bondage.

Avatar and Masters not circumscribed by Circles

The Circles of the Avatar, as well as the Perfect Masters, constitute the most important particular feature in relation to which and through which the Avatar and the Masters adjust their spiritual duty toward humanity. This particular feature has come into existence as a result of the close links and connections of several lifetimes. The Avatar and all Perfect Masters always have such Circles of very close disciples; but the Circles do not in any way create a limitation on their inner consciousness. In their God state, the Avatar and the Masters find themselves in the center of the universe as well as in the center of Everything; and there are no Circles to circumscribe their Being. In the infinity of nonduality, there are no preferences; the Circles exist only in relation to the duty and the work that the Avatar and the Perfect Masters have undertaken in the phenomenal world. But from the point of view of this spiritual work in the phenomenal world, the Circles are as much a reality as the Himalayas.

The Circles of the Avatar

Absolute Oneness prevails in Reality. Space and time are but illusory. They are merely the effect of the reflection of God's infinitude. When man realizes Reality, the reflection that has estranged him from Reality vanishes; and he experiences the absoluteness of the absolute Oneness of God. And when such a One continues to live his life in Illusion, he leads the life of a Man-God, or Perfect Master, on earth. With his abiding experience of the absolute Reality, he serves as the pivot around which rotates the entire cosmic universe. Every point in the cosmos is equidistant from the Perfect Master, who abides in Illusion as the nucleus of the cosmos.

Although the Perfect Master remains in Illusion as the center of the cosmic periphery and radiates his influence uniformly over the entire universe, in his lifetime he gathers around him twelve men who directly have their center of interest in his individuality. These men, through their constant and close association with him in the past —right from the earliest evolutionary stages of consciousness—reap the greatest benefit now when their past close associate has become a Perfect Master. Such a group of twelve men is called the Circle of a Perfect Master. However, besides this group of twelve men, there is an appendage of two women to complete the Circle of a Perfect Master in all its aspects. These two women also owe their position in regard to the Circle to their past connection with the Perfect Master.

One or more of these fourteen close ones associated with the Perfect Master realize the God state during or after the lifetime of the

Perfect Master, and in some instances, after one or a few more reincarnations. However, the Perfect Master fulfills his obligations by establishing his Circle during his lifetime; and the greatest good he bestows is God-realization, with all its perfection, to at least one from his Circle.

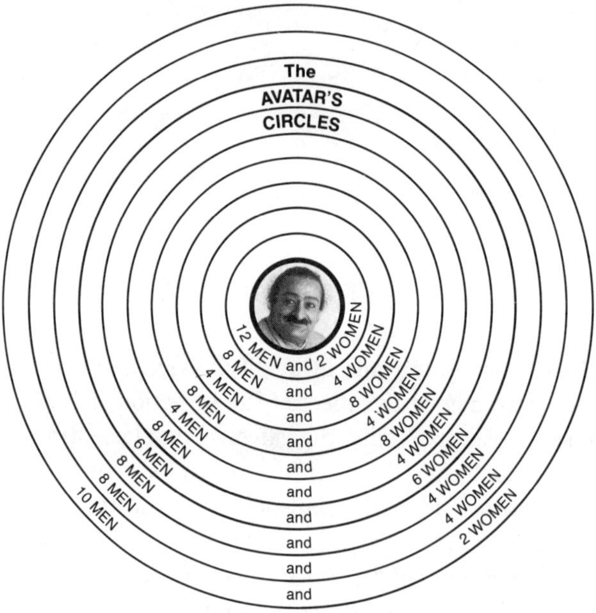

In the case of the Avatar it is different. He has ten Circles in all, as shown in the accompanying diagram. The first or inner Circle of the Avatar consists of twelve men with an appendage of two women; and each of the following nine outer Circles consists of twelve persons, both men and women. In all there are 120 persons in the ten Circles of the Avatar, plus the two women of the inner Circle who are but appendages to that particular Circle—122 in all. One or more of the 108 members of the nine outer Circles realize the God state during or after the life span of the Avatar, and some in the next incarnation or after a few more reincarnations.

As in the case of the Perfect Master's Circle, the inner Circle of the Avatar consists of only twelve men, with an appendage of two women. The difference between the Circle of the Perfect Master and the inner Circle of the Avatar is that the Perfect Master *establishes* his Circle from among those who were closely connected with him right from the earliest evolutionary stages of their consciousness. But the Avatar in

His recurrent advents does not pass through the process of evolution, reincarnation, and involution; therefore He does not have the same links of association to establish anew His inner Circle with every advent. In short, whereas the Perfect Master establishes his Circle, the Avatar is directly *allied* with His inner Circle, which is always the same in all His advents. With His descent on earth, the Avatar, as it were, brings along with Him the association of His inner Circle.

The connection of the inner Circle in relation to the Avatar may be compared to that of a person who associates himself with fourteen parts of his own body: two eyes, two ears, two nostrils, the mouth, two hands, two legs, the genitals, the anus, and the trunk of the body itself. As soon as an individual is born, he directly makes use of the these fourteen parts of his body; and these parts in turn respond to his dictates individually or collectively. Similarly, with the advent of the Avatar on earth, His inner Circle of the same twelve individualities and the appendage of the same two individualities directly begin to function, individually and collectively, according to the dictates of the Avatar Himself.

With every advent of the Avatar on earth, the twelve men of the inner Circle and its appendage of two women gather around the personality of the Avatar, as the selfsame fourteen types of individualities. These fourteen different individualities, in the shape of different *personalities*, always occupy their respective offices whenever the Avatar manifests on earth. And during and after the life span of the Avatar, they—individually and collectively—function in the same way as their predecessors, who had held and functioned in the same offices of the inner Circle during the past advents of the Avatar.

Therefore it would not be wrong to say that with the Christ's coming again, come Peter, Judas, and all His apostles. But this can never mean that the *very same* Peter or the selfsame Judas reincarnates again and again. These can never reincarnate, as all of the individual personalities of the Avatar's inner Circle attain God-realization in every Avataric period, either during or soon after the life span of the Avatar. Once God-realization is attained, reincarnation is impossible. The only exception to this rule is the Avatar Himself, who comes again and again to redeem humanity.

It is not the same individualized personalities of the inner Circle that reincarnate; it is the individualities of their particular *offices* that come with every advent of the Avatar. It is because in all the Avatar's advents each of the twelve men and two women of the inner Circle hold exactly the same office and function in exactly the same manner that it is said the Avatar always brings with Him the same Circle. As soon as the veil with which the Avatar descends on earth is rent—by the then-living Perfect Master or Masters—and the Avatar realizes His Avatarhood, the twelve men and two women automatically group around the personality of the Avatar to occupy their respective positions in the inner Circle and to function as usual, according to the dictates of the Avatar of the Age.

The position of the Avatar in regard to the inner Circle and its function may be compared to a person asleep. As soon as he is made to wake up through some external agency, the individual spontaneously finds that all the fourteen parts of his body (as mentioned before) are already there in their individual roles, ready to function at his slightest wish. Similarly, as soon as the Avatar is made to realize His Avatarhood through one or two or more of the five Perfect Masters of the time, He also realizes that the fourteen personalities in their characteristic roles of the inner Circle are ready at hand to discharge their duties.

To explain in detail why only these fourteen particular personalities hold such positions in every advent of the Avatar would take a volume of explanation. Who can become the fourteen members and how do they become attached to the inner Circle of the Avatar?—these questions would require yet more volumes of explanation. Suffice it to say that each of these fourteen particular personalities, when occupying the office and function of the inner Circle, not only must resemble the characteristic individuality of his or her predecessor in the previous advents of the Avatar but must be exactly similar in all respects. For example, one of the offices of the inner Circle of Jesus Christ was held by Peter. At the "second advent" of the Christ, this particular office must be held by another Peter, who may be named "A" but who has the same qualities of mind and heart and other characteristics as *the* Peter. The same applies to the offices held by Judas, John, James, and so forth, of the inner Circle in the time of Jesus Christ.

All fourteen members of the Avatar's inner Circle realize God by the grace of the Avatar, during the same Avataric period, which is of one hundred years duration after the manifestation of the Avatar on earth.

Regarding the outer Circles of the Avatar, none of the 108 persons in the nine Circles hold any office similar to that held by those of the inner Circle. All of these 108 persons attain God-realization by the grace of the Avatar, but not necessarily during the Avataric period. These 108 persons of the outer Circles have their respective places in the nine Circles in accordance with their past connections with the members of the Circle ahead of them. For example, the members of the second Circle of twelve persons, next to the inner Circle, are grouped around the Avatar in accordance with their past connections with the members of the inner Circle. Similarly, the twelve persons of the third Circle, next to the second Circle, are grouped around the Avatar in accordance with their past connections with the members of the second Circle—and so on, with all the remaining seven Circles.

The Travail of the New World Order*

The world storm that has been gathering momentum is now having its greatest outburst, and in reaching its climax it will work universal disaster. In the struggle for material well-being, all grievances have assumed fantastic proportions; and the various differences of human interests have been so accentuated that they have precipitated distinctive conflict. Humanity has failed to solve its individual and social problems, and the evidence for this failure is very clear. The incapacity of people to deal with their problems constructively and creatively reveals a tragic deficiency in the right understanding of the basic nature of man and the true purpose of life.

World storm

The world is witnessing an acute conflict between the forces of light and the forces of darkness. On the one hand, there are selfish persons who seek their happiness blindly through lust for power, unbridled greed, and unrelieved hatred. Ignorant of the real purpose of life, they have sunk to the lowest level of civilization. They bury their higher selves in the wreckage of crumbling forms that linger on from the dead past. Bound by material interests and limited conceptions, they are forgetful of their divine destiny. They have lost their way, and their hearts are torn by the ravages of hate and rancor. On the other hand, there are persons who unveil their inherent higher selves, through the endurance of pain and

Conflict between forces of light and darkness

*First printed in 1941.—ED.

deprivation and through noble acts of bravery and self-sacrifice. The present war is teaching man to be brave, to be able to suffer, to understand, and to sacrifice.

The disease of selfishness in mankind will need a cure that is not only universal in its application but drastic in nature. Selfishness is so deep-rooted that it can be eradicated only if it is attacked from all sides.

Cure for selfishness needed

Real peace and happiness will dawn spontaneously when there is a purging of selfishness. The peace and happiness that come from self-giving love are permanent. Even the worst sinners can become great saints if they have the courage and sincerity to invite a drastic and complete change of heart.

The present chaos and destruction will engulf the whole world, but in the future this will be followed by a very long period in which there shall be no war. The passing sufferings and miseries of our times will be worth enduring for the sake of the long period of happiness that is to follow eventually. What will the present chaos lead to? How will it all end? It can only end in one way: Mankind will become sick of it all. Man will be sick of wanting and sick of fighting out of hatred. Greed and hatred will reach such intensity that everyone will become weary of them. The way out of the deadlock will be found through selflessness. The only alternative that can bring a solution will be to stop hating and to love, to stop wanting and to give, to stop dominating and to serve.

Man will become sick of wanting, greed, hate

Great suffering awakens great understanding. Supreme suffering fulfills its purpose and yields its true significance when it awakens an exhausted humanity and stirs within it a genuine longing for real understanding. Unprecedented suffering leads to unprecedented spiritual growth. It contributes to the construction of life on the unshakable foundation of the Truth. It is now high time that universal suffering should hasten humanity to the turning point in its spiritual history. It is now high time that the very agonies of our times should become a medium for bringing a real understanding to human relationships. It is now high time for humanity to face squarely the true causes of the catastrophe that has overtaken it. It is now high time to seek a new experience of Reality. To know that life is real and eternal is to inherit unfading bliss. It is time

Suffering generates understanding

that man had this realization by being unified with his own Self.

Through unification with the higher Self, man perceives the infinite Self in all selves. He becomes free by outgrowing and discarding the limitations of the ego-life. The individual soul has to realize with full consciousness its identity with the universal Soul. Man shall reorient life in the light of this ancient Truth and will readjust his attitude toward his neighbors in everyday life. To perceive the spiritual value of *oneness* is to promote real unity and cooperation. Brotherhood then becomes a spontaneous outcome of true perception. The new life that is based upon spiritual understanding is an affirmation of the Truth. It is not something that belongs to utopia but is completely practical. Now that humanity is thrown into the fire of bloody conflicts, through immense anguish it is experiencing the utter instability and futility of a life based upon purely material conceptions. The hour is near when man in his eager longing for real happiness will seek its true source.

Affirmation of Truth

The time is also ripe when humanity will ardently seek to contact the embodiment of Truth in the form of the God-Man (Avatar), through whom it can be inspired and lifted into spiritual understanding. It will accept the guidance that comes from divine authority. Only the outpouring of divine love can bring about spiritual awakening. In this critical time of universal suffering, humanity is becoming ready to turn toward its higher Self and to fulfill the will of God. Divine love will perform the supreme miracle of bringing God into the hearts of man and of getting him established in lasting and true happiness. It will satisfy the greatest need and longing of mankind. Divine love will make people selfless and helpful in their mutual relationships, and it will bring about the ultimate solution of all problems. The new brotherhood on earth shall be a fulfilled fact, and nations will be united in the fraternity of Love and Truth.

Inherit divine love through the God-Man

My existence is for this Love and this Truth. To suffering humanity I say:

Have hope. I have come to help you in surrendering yourselves to the cause of God and in accepting His grace of Love and Truth. I have come to help you in winning the one victory of all victories—to win your Self.

Reincarnation and Karma

Part I
The Significance of Death

The worldly person completely identifies life with the manifestations and activities of the gross body. For him, therefore, the beginning and the end of bodily existence are also the beginning and the end of the individualized soul. All his experience seems to testify to the transitoriness of the physical body; and he has often witnessed the disintegration of physical bodies that were once vibrant with life. Hence he is naturally impelled to believe that life is coterminous with bodily existence.

Identification of soul with gross body

As the worldly individual considers death to be the cessation of life, he gives great importance to it. There are few, however, who contemplate death for prolonged periods. And in spite of the fact that most persons are completely engrossed in their worldly pursuits, they are impressed by the incident of death when confronted by it. For most people the earthly scene of life has, as its background, the inevitable and irresistible fact of death—which imperceptively enters into their greatest triumphs and achievements, their keenest pleasures and rejoicing.

Death as background of life

Apart from being the general background to the scene of life, death also assumes an accentuated and overwhelming importance among the variegated incidents of life. Death falls among those happenings that are most dreaded and lamented. People, in malice or anger, try to inflict death upon each other as the last penalty or the worst revenge, or they rely upon it as the surest way of removing aggression or interference by others. People also invite death upon themselves as the token of supreme self-sacrifice; and at times they seek it with the false hope of putting an end to all the worldly worries and problems they are unable to face or solve. Thus, in the minds of most persons, death assumes an accentuated and overwhelming importance.

The overwhelming importance of death is derived from man's attachment to particular forms. But death loses much of its sting and importance, even for the worldly, if one takes a broader view of the course of life. In spite of their transitoriness, there is an unbroken continuity of life through these forms—old ones being discarded and new ones being created for habitation and expression. The recurring incidence of death is matched by the recurring incidence of birth. Old generations are replaced by new ones; life is reborn in new forms, incessantly renewing and refreshing itself. The streams of life, with their ancient origin, are ever advancing onward through the forms that come and go like the waves of the ocean.

Continuity of life

So, even within the limits of experience of the worldly, there is much that should mitigate morbid thoughts of death as being an irreparable loss. A sane attitude toward death is possible only if life is considered impersonally and without any attachment to particular forms. This the worldly person finds difficult because of his entanglement with specific forms. For him, one form is not as good as another. The form he identifies himself with is by far the most important. The general preservation and advancement of the stream of life has for him no special interest. What the worldly individual craves is a continuation of his own form and other particular forms with which he is entangled. His heart cannot reconcile itself to his intellect. With the vanishing of the forms that have been dear to him, he becomes a victim of unending sorrow—though life as a whole may have replaced elsewhere the lost forms with new ones.

Attachment to specific forms

The sorrow of death, on closer analysis, turns out to be rooted in selfishness. The person who loses his beloved may know intellectually that life as a whole has elsewhere compensated for the loss; but his only feeling is, What is that to me? When one looks at it from one's own personal point of view, death becomes a cause of unending sorrow. From the point of view of life in general, it is an episode of minor importance.

Impersonal considerations go a long way to fortify the mind against the personal sorrow caused by death. But they do not by themselves solve the wider problems that confound even the impersonal intellect of man when he considers some of the implications of death within the limits of his ordinary experience. If death is regarded as the final annihilation of individual existence, there seems to be an irreparable loss to the universe. Each individual may be in a position to give to the universe something so unique that no one else can exactly replace it. Further, in most cases there is the cutting short of an earthly career long before the attainment of spiritual Perfection by the individual. All his struggles toward the ideal, all his endeavor and enthusiasm for the great, the good, and the beautiful, and all his aspirations for things divine and eternal seem to end in the vast nothingness created by death.

Problems of impersonal intellect

The implications in assuming death to be the termination of individual existence run counter to the ineradicable expectations based upon rationalized intuition. A conflict usually arises between the claims of intuition and the conclusions of impure intellect, which assumes death to be the termination of individual existence. Such conflict is often a beginning of pure thinking, which immediately seriously challenges the usually accepted belief that death is the real termination of individual existence. Death as an extinction of life can never be wholly acceptable to the spiritual aspirations of man. Therefore, belief in the immortality of the individualized soul is often accepted by the human mind without much resistance, even in the absence of direct supersensible knowledge about the existence of life after death.

Conflict between intellect and intuition

Those who know from personal experience the immortality of the soul to be true are few. Supersensible knowledge of the existence of life after death is inaccessible to the vast majority of persons. For them, immortality must remain an agreeable and acceptable *belief* but nothing more. It becomes a part of personal *knowledge* for those who, through their interest in the occult, have built up means of communication with "other worlds"; or those whose special circumstances have resulted in their personally experiencing the appearance or intervention of departed spirits; or those who, through their spiritual advancement, have automatically unfolded certain latent perceptual capacities of the inner vehicles of consciousness.

Immortality of the individualized soul is made possible by the fact that the individualized soul is *not* the same as the physical body. The individualized soul continues to exist with all its sanskaras in the inner worlds through its mental and subtle bodies, even after it has discarded its gross body at the time of death. Hence, life through the medium of the gross body is only a section of the continuous life of the individualized soul; the other sections of its life have their expression in other spheres.

Immortality of the soul

Nature is much greater than what a person can perceive through the ordinary senses of the physical body. The hidden aspects of nature consist of finer matter and forces. There is no unbridgeable gulf separating the finer aspects of nature from its gross aspect. They all interpenetrate one another and exist together. The finer aspects of nature are not perceptible to the ordinary individual, but they are nevertheless continuous with the gross aspect that is perceptible to him. They are not remote; and yet they are inaccessible to the consciousness that is functioning through the physical senses, which are not adapted for perceiving those finer aspects of nature. The ordinary person is unconscious of the inner planes, just as someone deaf is unconscious of sounds, and he cannot deal with them consciously. For all practical purposes, therefore, they are other "worlds" for him.

Three worlds

The finer and hidden part of nature has two important divisions, namely, the subtle and the mental, corresponding to the subtle and mental bodies of man. The whole of nature may therefore be conveniently divided into three parts—the gross world, the subtle world, and the mental world. When the individualized soul has incarnated in a physical body, it expresses its life in the gross world. When it drops the outer sheath, the physical body, it continues to have its expression of life either in the subtle world through the subtle body or in the mental world through the mental body.

Ordinarily, life in the physical body is terminated only when the sanskaras released for expression in that incarnation are all worked out. In some exceptional cases the soul gives up its gross body before the working out of these sanskaras is completed. For example, an individual who commits suicide cuts short the period of his life artificially and thereby prevents the working out of those sanskaras that were released for fructification.

Effects of untimely death

When, due to untimely death, the sanskaras released for fructification are withheld from expression, the discarnate soul remains subject to the propelling force of these sanskaras even after the physical body has been discarded. The momentum of the sanskaras that were prevented from being worked out is retained even in life after death, with the result that the departed spirit greatly desires the things of the gross world.

In such cases, the discarnate soul experiences an irresistible impulsion toward the gross world and craves gross objects so badly that it seeks gratification of its desires through the gross bodies of those souls still incarnate. Thus, for example, the discarnate soul may want so much to drink alcohol that it takes to unnatural methods of gratifying the craving. It awaits its opportunity. When it finds someone who is a suitable medium drinking alcohol in the gross world, the spirit satisfies its own desire through that person by possessing his physical body. In the same way, if it wants to experience the gross manifestations of crude anger, it does so through someone in the gross world who is feeling angry.

Irresistible impulsion

Such souls are constantly waiting to harass incarnate persons with similar sanskaras, and they try to maintain their contact with the gross world through others as long as possible. In life after death, any lingering entanglement with the gross world is a serious hindrance to the natural flow of the soul's onward life. Those who are subject to this precarious condition must be looked upon as particularly unfortunate, since they invite upon themselves and others much unnecessary suffering by seeking unnatural gratification of coarser desires through others who are still incarnate. Compared with these unfortunate souls, the posthumous life of other souls is much smoother.

In normal cases, death occurs when all the sanskaras seeking fructification are worked out. When the soul drops its physical body, it

Death begins interval between incarnations

is completely severed from all connections with the gross world, though the ego and the mind are retained with all the impressions accumulated in the earthly career. Unlike the exceptional cases of spirits still obsessed with the gross world, ordinary souls try to reconcile themselves to the severance from the gross world and conform to the limitations of changed conditions. They sink into a state of subjectivity in which a new process begins of mentally reviewing the experiences of the earthly career by reviving the sanskaras connected with them. Thus death inaugurates a period of comparative rest consisting in a temporary withdrawal from the gross sphere of action. It is the beginning of an interval between the last incarnation and the next.

Reincarnation and Karma

Part II
Hell and Heaven

After death there is no consciousness of the gross world for the ordinary soul, since such consciousness is directly dependent on the physical body. Though the consciousness of the gross world is thus lost, the impressions of the experiences of the gross world are retained in the mental body; and they continue to express themselves through the semisubtle world. During the interval between death and the next incarnation, the consciousness of the soul is turned toward these impressions resulting in a vivification of impressions and the revival of corresponding experiences. However, this soul does not become aware of the subtle environment; it is wrapped up in complete subjectivity and absorbed in living through the revived impressions.

Subjectivity of life after death

In life after death the experiences of pain and pleasure become much more intense than they were in earthly life. These subjective states of intensified suffering and joy are called hell and heaven. Hell and heaven are states of mind; they should not be looked upon as being places. And though subjectively they mean a great deal to the individualized soul, they are both illusions within the greater Illusion.

Hell and heaven states

In the hell state as well as in the heaven state, desires become much more intense since they no longer require expression through the gross medium. Like desires, the experiences incurred in their fulfillment or nonfulfillment also become greatly intensified. In the earthly career desires, as well as the pleasures and the sufferings they bring, are experienced through the medium of the gross body. The soul is of course actually using its higher bodies at the same time, but in the earthly career its consciousness is bound up with the gross body. Therefore the processes of consciousness have to pass through an additional veil that lessens their force, liveliness, and intensity—just as rays of light are dimmed when they are required to pass through a thick glass. During habitation in the body, desires and experiences suffer a deterioration in intensity; but when that habitation is given up, they undergo a relative increase of intensity.

Desires and experiences intensified after death

In the heaven state the fulfillment of desires is not, as in the gross sphere, dependent upon having the object of desire. Fulfillment of desire comes merely through thinking of the object desired. For example, if a person wishes to hear exquisite music, he experiences this pleasure merely by thinking about it. The imaginative idea of exquisite music becomes, in this state, a substitute for the physical sound vibrations in the gross sphere. The pleasure he derives from the thought of exquisite music is much greater than the pleasure he derived in his earthly career from the actual hearing of physical sounds. In the heaven state there are no obstacles between desires and their fulfillment; the pleasure of self-fulfillment through thought or feeling is always at hand.

Fulfillment of desires through thought

In fact, even in the earthly sphere of existence some individuals develop this capacity of making their pleasure independent of possession of a gross object. Beethoven, for example, was completely deaf; and yet through the exercise of imagination alone, he was able to enjoy intensely his own compositions of music. In a sense, even on earth he might figuratively be said to have been in the heaven state. In the same way, a person who meditates on the Beloved with love derives happiness merely through the thought of the Beloved, without requiring His physical presence. After death, in the heaven state, the

Heaven on earth

enjoyment of such imaginative fulfillment is infinitely greater since consciousness is then unburdened of the outermost veil of the gross body.

Some desires have a direct relation to the possession and assimilation of gross objects through the gross body. The coarser desires such as lust, gluttony, or the craving for alcohol or drugs are of this type.

Coarser desires contribute to hell state

These desires are specifically earthly because they are possessive and they involve an element of clinging to the physical object. In these desires there is not only a preponderance of sensations derived from contact with the object but also of those sensations that constitute the response of the body itself. These coarser desires contribute to the hell state.

In contrast with the finer desires, the coarser desires place an infinitely heavier premium on mere sensations, quite independently of any intellectual meaning or moral value. In the finer desires, such as

Difference between coarser and finer desires

the desire for music, there is of course an element of wanting sense contact with the physical sounds. But these sounds become important not so much in their own right as in their capacity to express beauty. In the same way, a desire to hear discourses has a hold upon the mind, not so much because of the sensations of sound, but because of the intellectual meaning and emotional appeal they convey.

Thus in the finer desires, the actual sensations play a subordinate role to the derivative aspects based upon the sensations. In the coarser desires the chief element is provided by the actual sensations con-

Bodily sensations of coarser desires

nected with the physical object and the sensations aroused by them through bodily response to their possession. The organic sensations of the physical body play the greatest part in experiences connected with the coarser desires. Through them the individualized soul feels its own existence as the gross body much more effectively and vividly than through experiences connected with finer desires.

Almost the entire significance of experiences brought about by the fulfillment or nonfulfillment of coarser desires is constituted by the *bodily* sensations themselves. Therefore they can rarely yield the full experience of fulfillment achieved through finer desires merely by the exercise of thought and imagination. It is characteristic of the coarser desires to insist on the possession and assimilation of the gross objects themselves. Any imaginative idea of the gross objects merely serves the purpose of accentuating the urge to reach out to them. Since the gross objects of the coarser desires are not available in the semisubtle world, these desires are mostly productive of an intensified experience of the suffering of nonfulfillment. Just as in the gross world the presence of coarser desires leads to the preponderance of suffering over pleasure, in the life after death the revived experiences connected with these coarser desires also lead to a preponderance of suffering over pleasure—thus bringing into existence the hell state. Similarly, in the life after death the revived experiences connected with the finer desires lead to a preponderance of pleasure over suffering, thus bringing into existence the heaven state.

Sufferings of hell and pleasures of heaven

Hell and heaven are both states of bondage, however, and subject to the limitations of the opposites of pleasure and pain. Both are states whose duration is determined by the nature, amount, and intensity of the accumulated impressions. Time in the semisubtle world is not the same as time in the gross world due to the increased subjectivity of the states of consciousness. Though time in the semisubtle world is thus incommensurable with time in the gross world, it is strictly determined by the impressions accumulated in the gross world. However, the important fact is that the hell state and the heaven state are far from being lasting; and after they have served their purpose in the life of the individualized soul, they both come to an end.

Time in semisubtle world

The coarser sensual desires, like lust and their emotional products like hate and anger, all contribute to the life of delusion and suffering prevalent in the hell state. The finer desires—like idealistic aspirations, aesthetic and scientific interests, goodwill toward neighbors and others, and their emotional products like personal love or fellow-feeling—contribute to the life of enlightenment and pleasure prevalent in the heaven state. These states for most souls consist in reliving the experiences of the earthly life by vivification of the impressions left by them. Their

Vivification of impressions

duration and nature are dependent upon the duration and nature of the experiences undergone by the soul while in the physical body.

Termination of hell and heaven

Just as a phonograph record is set aside after the needle has traveled through each groove, the hell state and the heaven state terminate after consciousness has traversed the imprints left by earthly life. Just as the song produced by the record is strictly determined by the original song recorded on it, the quality of intensified and magnified experiences the soul passes through after death is strictly determined by the kind of life that was led on earth in the physical body. From this point of view, heaven and hell are shadows cast by one's earthly life.

Retrospective survey of earthly experiences

Heaven and hell would, however, serve no specially useful purpose in the life of the individual soul if they were to consist merely of mental revival of the earthly past. That would mean bare repetition of what has already occurred. Consciousness in these after-death states is in a position to make a leisurely and effective survey of the animated record of earthly life. Through intensification of experiences, it can observe their nature with better facility and results. On earth, the consciousness of most persons is predominantly objective and forward-looking and under the pressure of unspent sanskaras. It is mostly concerned with the possible fulfillment of sanskaras through the present or the future. In life after death the consciousness of most persons is predominantly subjective and retrospective. With the absence of forward-goading sanskaras, it is, as in reminiscences, mostly preoccupied with reviewing and assessing the significance of the past.

Analogy of cinema

The fret and fury of immediate responses to the changing situations of earthly life is replaced in life after death by a more leisurely mood, freed from the urgency of immediately needed actions. All the experiences of the earthly career are now available for reflection in a form more vivid than is possible through memory in earthly life. The shots of earthly life have all been taken on the cinematic film of the mind, and it is now time to study the original earthly life through the magnified projections of the filmed record on the screen of subjectivized consciousness.

Thus the hell state and the heaven state become instrumental in the assimilation of experiences acquired in the earthly phase; and the individualized soul can start its next incarnation in a physical body with all the advantages of digested experience. The lessons learned by the soul through such stocktaking and reflection are confirmed in the mental body by the power of their magnified suffering or happiness. They become, for the next incarnation, an integral part of the intuitive makeup of active consciousness, without in any way involving detailed revival of the individual events of the previous incarnation. The truths absorbed by the mind in the life after death become in the next incarnation a part of inborn wisdom. Developed intuition is consolidated and compressed understanding, distilled through a multitude of diverse experiences gathered in previous lives.

Assimilation of earthly experiences

Different souls start with different degrees of intuitive wisdom as their initial capital for the experiments and adventures of their earthly careers. This intuition may seem to have been the product of past experiences, thus adding to the equipment of the psyche; but it is more truly an unfoldment of what was already latent in the individualized soul. From this deeper point of view, the experiences of earthly life—as well as the reflective and consolidating processes they are subjected to in life after death—are merely instrumental in gradually releasing to the surface the intuitive wisdom already latent in the soul from the very beginning of creation. As is true of the earthly career and its experiences, the states of hell and heaven in the life after death are also integral parts of and incidents in that journey of the individualized soul, which is ultimately meant to reach the Source of all things.

Heaven and hell and release of wisdom

Reincarnation and Karma

Part III
The Existence and the Memory of Past Lives

Those who have immediate access to the supersensible truths concerning the life of the soul and its reincarnation know, through their unclouded perception, that so-called birth is only an incarnation of the individualized soul in the gross sphere. The unbroken continuity of the life of the reincarnating soul is punctuated by birth and death, both of which are comparable to gateways in the stream of life as it advances from one type of existence to another. Both are equally necessary in the greater life of the soul, and the interval between death and birth is as necessary as the interval between birth and death.

Gateways of birth and death

As is true of those who consider death to be the termination of individual existence, those who consider the birth of body to be its beginning are also confronted with a conflict between their false assumptions and the claims of rationalized intuition. From the standpoint of individual justice, the uneven distribution of good and bad in relation to material happiness or prosperity seems seriously to impugn the rationality and justification of the entire scheme of the universe. To see the virtuous at times suffering deeply and the vicious

Demands of intuition

possessing the amenities of pleasure creates insurmountable difficulties for anyone who prefers to look upon life as being meant to fulfill an eternal and divine purpose.

Unless there is some deeper explanation forthcoming, the human mind is riddled with agonizing perplexities that tend to embitter a person's general outlook on life and foster a callous cynicism. This in many ways is even worse than the deepest personal sorrow that death may cause. But in spite of all appearances to the contrary, the human mind has in it an inborn tendency to try to restore to itself a deep and unshakable faith in the intrinsic sanity and value of life. Except where artificial resistances are created, it finds acceptable those explanations that are in conformity with this deeper law of the spirit.

Tendency to accept deeper explanations

Those who have direct access to the truth of reincarnation are even fewer than those who have direct access to the truth of the immortality of the individual soul. The memories of all past lives are stored and preserved in the mental body of the individual soul, but they are not accessible to the consciousness of ordinary persons because a veil is drawn over them. When the soul changes its physical body, it gets a new brain; and its normal waking consciousness functions in close association with the brain processes. Under ordinary circumstances, only the memories of the present life can appear in consciousness because the new brain acts as a hindrance to the release of the memories of those experiences that had been gathered through the medium of other brains in past lives.

Effect of getting a new brain

In rare cases, in spite of the resistance offered by the brain, some memories of past lives leak into the present life in the form of dreams that are completely unexplainable in terms of the present life. An individual may see persons in his dreams whom he has never seen in his present life. It often happens that those who appeared in the dreams were persons whom he had met in his past lives. But of course such dreams, when they are of the ordinary type, cannot be treated as a *memory* of past lives. They merely indicate that the imagination at work in the dreams was influenced by information taken from past lives. The real memory of past lives is clear, steady, and sure like the memory of the present life. When it comes to an individ-

Memory of past lives

ual, he no longer has any doubt about his having existed in several previous lives along with many other individuals. Just as he cannot doubt his own past life in the present incarnation, he cannot doubt his life in past incarnations.

The number of persons who can remember their past lives is very small compared with the vast majority, who are so completely bound to the gross sphere of existence that they do not even suspect super-sensible realities. The release of such memories is severely conditioned by the limitations of the brain, as long as consciousness is entangled with the physical body and its brain processes. When consciousness is emancipated from the limitations imposed by the brain, it can recover and reestablish the memories of past lives, which are all stored in the mental body. This involves a degree of detachment and understanding that only the spiritually advanced can have. The memory of past lives can come with full clarity and certainty, even to those who are still crossing the inner planes of consciousness but have not yet become spiritually perfect.

Release of memory of past lives

The memory of past lives does not come back to a person, except in abnormal and rare cases, unless he is sufficiently advanced from the spiritual point of view. This provision made by the laws of life secures unhampered spiritual evolution of the individualized soul. At first view it might seem that the loss of memory of previous lives is a total loss, but this is far from being so. For most purposes, knowledge about past lives is not at all necessary for the guidance of the onward course of spiritual evolution. Spiritual evolution consists in guiding life in the light of the highest values perceived through intuition, and not in allowing it to be determined by the past. In many cases, even the memory of the present life acts as an obstacle for certain adjustments demanded by the spiritual requirements of the changing situations of life. The problem of emancipation may in a sense be said to be a problem of securing freedom from the past—which, in the case of those who are bound to the wheel of birth and death, inexorably shapes the present life.

Loss of memory of past lives does not affect progress

Life would be infinitely more complicated if one who is not spiritually advanced were burdened by the conscious memory of numberless past lives. He would be dazed and unsettled by the diversity of settings in which persons would appear to him in the light of his memory. He is not called upon to face such confusion, however, because he is shielded from the resurrection of the memory of past lives. Things and persons come to him in a limited and definite context and setting, with the result that he finds it easy to determine his actions and responses in the light of what he knows from the present life.

Shielding from complications

This does not mean that his actions and responses are *entirely* determined by what he knows from his present life. All that has happened in past lives also has its own unconscious but effective share in determining his actions and responses. In spite of the actual influence of past lives, the fact remains that since he is shielded from the resurrection of conscious memory, his consciousness is not subject to the confusion that would result if the conscious memory of past lives were among the data he had to consider for the purpose of determining his actions and responses.

The resurrection of the memory of past lives can be faced without confusion or loss of balance only when the person has become desireless and has lost all feeling of "mine" and "thine." Those whom he once looked upon as belonging to him might be seen in the present life belonging to someone else. And if he were to continue his attachments and supposed claims, he would create untold complications, misery, and confusion for himself and others. Possessiveness of all types has to be purged from the mind if the aspirant is to be spiritually prepared to withstand the disturbing influence of memories from past lives.

Conditions for release of memory

When an individual is spiritually prepared, he is completely desireless and full of impersonal love. All entanglements of the personal ego have disappeared from his mind. He can look upon his old friends and enemies with the same equanimity. He is so lifted out of his limitations that he is the same to relations and nonrelations from his past and present lives. He is free from the idea of any pressing claims and counterclaims on his part against others, or of others against himself, because he has realized the deeper truth of the unity of all life and the illusoriness of mundane happenings.

Spiritual preparation

It is only when a person is thus spiritually prepared that he is unaffected by the revived memory of past lives. Only then is it worthwhile for him to have access to it. For he can then have that cool and unerring judgment and pure, incorruptible love that enable him to make right and wise use of the new knowledge gathered through the resurrected memory of past lives. This knowledge opens to him a great deal of information about his own incarnations and those of others connected with him in past lives. It not only enables him to advance further on the spiritual path by conscious karmic adjustments but also to help others on the path by directing them in the light of their past lives.

Wise use of resurrected memory

The speed of spiritual evolution is faster after the natural recovery of the memory of past incarnations. Disentanglement from mundane things is facilitated by conscious knowledge of the history of the development of such entanglements. Spiritual evolution, which was mostly unconscious of the limiting past, now becomes conscious of it. The obstacles as well as the facilities created by the past are now within the reach of consciousness and therefore are capable of being intelligently and carefully handled. Inarticulate intuition is supplemented by rationalized data. Therefore action has less possibility of error and becomes more potent in producing desirable results.

Advantages of recovered memory

The Masters of wisdom, having become spiritually perfect, have no special interest in past incarnations, which are among the many unimportant facts of mundane existence. If they make any use of their knowledge of the past lives of a person, it is only to help him on toward the eternal Truth. Their knowledge of the past places them in a special position to give an aspirant just the guidance he needs. The details of the aspirant's spiritual path are often determined by the incidents of the past, the manner in which he has sought the highest Truth in his past lives, and the obstacles or facilities he has created for himself through his past doings. All these things, which are hidden from the aspirant, are open to the unclouded perception of the Perfect Master, who uses his knowledge in order to accelerate the spiritual progress of the seeker of Truth. The Master leads the aspirant from the place in which he has landed himself

Knowledge of past lives

through the experimentation and search of several lives. In spiritual matters, as in mundane matters, greater and unerring knowledge means economy of energy and time.

Reincarnation and Karma

Part IV
Specific Conditions of an Incarnation

The individualized soul has its beginning and source in the infinite, formless, sexless, and indivisible being of God, who is beyond all forms of duality or evolution. With the beginning of the individualized soul, there is the beginning of duality and evolution, though the specific form of duality consisting in the distinction and attraction based upon sex makes its appearance at a later stage of evolution. Duality exists as soon as there is subject and object—a center of consciousness, however dim, and its environment. Sex, on the other hand, is a specific kind of bodily attraction that presupposes differentiation of forms, a specific kind of entanglement of the psyche with the forms, and specific expressions of life and energy.

Sex a specific form of duality

In the mineral kingdom there are no sexual distinctions. In the kingdom of plants and trees, the bodily differentiations of sex, with specialized biological functions, have come into existence. Plants and trees do not generate sexual consciousness, since the development of consciousness in plants and trees is rudimentary and its expressions are not influenced by these bodily differentiations. Contact between the male and the female in plants and trees is (due to their

Sex in subhuman forms

being fixed in the ground) not direct but only indirect, through the intermediate agency of winds, bees, and so forth. Therefore, from the standpoint of the evolution of *forms*, sexual differentiation may be said to have begun to emerge even at the level of plants and trees; but from the point of view of their own *consciousness*, they cannot be said to have any sexual distinctions because their consciousness of duality is not in any way colored by sex.

In the evolution of sexual duality, plants and trees stand midway between minerals, which have no sexual differentiation, and birds and animals, which have it in its complete form. Just before the soul incarnates in the first human form, it arrives at full consciousness and energy in its last animal form, which it then drops to take a human body. Reincarnation of the individualized soul through human forms is preceded by its successive incarnations in the subhuman forms.

In animals, sex not only expresses itself through the bodily differences and activities but is a deep-rooted factor that affects consciousness. Since humans inherit their bodies as well as consciousness from highly evolved animals, like apes, humans also find themselves subject to sexual duality. In humans, sex is so completely developed that it is no longer a matter merely of the body. It substantially modifies the psyche, which seeks its expression through the body in accordance with whether the form is male or female.

Psyche modified by sex

After attaining the human form, as a rule there is no reversion to animal forms; cases of retrogression to subhuman forms are special and rare exceptions. Once the soul has attained human status, the normal course is to go through countless reincarnations in the human form itself. The human form may sometimes be male and sometimes female, according to the sanskaras and the spiritual requirements of the soul. The female form has the special prerogative that even the Sadgurus and the Avatar have to be born through the female form. The male form has the prerogative that the majority of the Sadgurus appear in male form. Although women can become saints and Masters, the Avatar always appears in male form.

Male and female incarnations

The general advantages and handicaps of an incarnation are always determined by the specific sanskaras the individual soul has accumulated in the past. The needs involved in the further development of the soul are related to the nature of its accumulated sanskaras.

Specific incarnation determined by sanskaras

Therefore these accumulated sanskaras really determine whether the soul takes its incarnation on the earth in the East or in the West, in a male form or in a female form, in one cycle of existence or in another. The facilities afforded by a specific incarnation are dependent not only upon whether an incarnation is in the male form or female form but also upon whether it takes place in one cycle of existence or another cycle of existence, and whether it matches the tenor of earthly life in the Eastern Hemisphere or in the Western Hemisphere.

Generally speaking, today on the whole the East has developed more along spiritual lines than material lines, with the result that the Eastern mind has a more spontaneous aspiration for God. The West,

East and West

on the whole, has developed more along material lines than along spiritual lines, with the result that the Western mind has a more spontaneous urge toward intellectual and artistic things. An incarnation in the East usually brings with it a greater tendency toward spiritual life than in the West, and an incarnation in the West usually brings with it a greater tendency toward material life than one in the East. But the soul has to experience the material as well as the spiritual aspects of life before it is freed from the fetters of a divided life. Therefore the same soul has to incarnate in the East as well as in the West.

If a soul has had many successive incarnations in the East and then takes an incarnation in the West, it carries with it the impressions of its lives in the East; and though living in the West, it leads a

Change of sphere

life essentially in conformity with the Eastern pattern. If a soul has had many successive incarnations in the West and then takes an incarnation in the East, it carries with it the impressions of its lives in the West; and though living in the East, it leads a life that is in conformity with the Western pattern. Sometimes one may thus have, for example, a European soul in an Indian form or an Indian soul in European form. It must be borne in mind that this distinction is only relative to past incarnations and sanskaras, and that the soul as such is beyond such distinctions.

The facilities afforded by male and female incarnations are not rigidly invariable. They change according to the cycles of existence as well as whether the incarnation is in the East or in the West. In some ages men are more active, energetic, and materialistic than women. In other ages, the reverse is true. In the past the women of the East were brave and intellectual. They considered no sacrifice too great for the happiness and well-being of their husbands, and their spiritual humility extended to looking upon the husband as God Himself. Now in the Eastern Hemisphere, the average man has a greater spiritual inclination than the average woman, just as in the West the average woman of today has a greater spiritual inclination than the average man. A man living in the East is different from a man living in the West, and a woman living in the East is different from a woman living in the West.

Cycles of existence

The joke is that in comparison with members of the opposite sex, the *same* soul shows varying degrees of superiority, inferiority, or equality with regard to spiritual or material matters—depending upon the cycle of existence, the sex of its body, and the earthly sphere in which it takes an incarnation.

Reincarnation and Karma

Part V
The Need for Male and Female Incarnations

Though the facilities afforded by each sex vary according to the age and place in which the incarnation occurs, each sex affords special facilities for the development of experience along specific lines. The lessons readily learned in male incarnations may not be easily attainable through female incarnations, and the lessons readily learned in female incarnations may not be easily attainable in male incarnations. As a rule, men excel in qualities of the head and will. They are capable of sound judgment and steadfast purpose. As a rule, women excel in qualities of the heart. They are capable of intense love, which makes them welcome any sacrifice for the loved one. It is because of this capacity of women for love that, in devotional references to the Avatar, the name of a woman is often given precedence—as when bhaktas (devotees) of Rama or Krishna sing of "Sita-Ram" or "Radha-Krishna."

Facilities of male and female form

In qualities of the heart women are usually superior to men, and in qualities of the head and will men are usually superior to women. The interesting point is that the same soul excels in the qualities of the heart or in the qualities of the head and will, according to whether it takes an incarnation in a female or male form. The alternate development of specific spiritual qualities goes on through the alternation between the male and female forms, until the development is all-sided.

Since male and female incarnations are equally necessary for Self-knowledge, it is not right to look upon one as being more important than the other. Though there are differences between the nature of the respective facilities afforded by them, they are both indispensable. The soul must go through male incarnations as well as female incarnations if it is to have that richness of experience which is a condition of attaining the realization that the soul, in itself, is beyond all forms of duality—including the accentuated duality based on sex.

Male and female incarnations equally indispensable

Before the soul is set free from all sanskaras, it assumes numerous male forms and numerous female forms. If the soul were to incarnate only in male forms or only in female forms, its experience would remain one-sided and incomplete. The duality of experience can be overcome only through understanding, and the understanding of experience is only partial as long as it moves within the limits of only one of the two opposites. Unity of the subject and object of experience is unattainable as long as there is in the object any aspect or element not fully covered by one's own experience; and this applies particularly to sexual duality.

Unity of subject and object

The mind retains the gathered experience of male and female incarnations. Since the soul identifies itself with the body, the psychological tendencies that harmonize with the sex of the body find a suitable medium for expression. The tendencies that are characteristic of the opposite sex are ordinarily suppressed into the unconscious part of the mind because they do not harmonize with the sex of the body and find the medium of expression obstructive. When the soul takes a female body, the male tendencies are, so to speak, held in abeyance; and only the female tendencies are released for expression. In the same way, when the soul takes a male body, the female tendencies are held in abeyance; and the male tendencies are released for expression.

Mind retains experience of incarnations

Identification with the body involves identification with the sex of the body. It therefore implies a free play only for that limited part of the mind which is in tune with the sex of the body. Since the other part of the mind is repressed and latent in the unconscious, there arises in the conscious part a feeling of incompleteness as well as a tendency to restore completeness through attachment to persons of the opposite sex. By getting entangled with the opposite sex, the buried part of the mind that is not in tune with the body seeks some kind of expression through another. From this point of view sexual attraction might be said to be a result of the effort the mind makes to unite with its own unconscious part.

Genesis of sexual entanglement

Sex is a manifestation of the ignorant attempt the conscious mind makes to compensate for the fragmentation entailed in identification with the sex of the body. This attempt to compensate for fragmentation is doomed to be futile, however, because it is not only based upon identification with the body but actually accentuates it by setting into opposition the body of the opposite sex and getting entangled with it through attachment and possessiveness.

When the soul is trying to overcome sexual duality through detachment from the opposite sex, it is paving a way for understanding the experience associated with the opposite sex from *within*. Then a man tries to understand a woman, not through the eyes of the male, but through the imaginative reaching out toward what the woman feels herself to be, in her own personal experience. In the same way, a woman then tries to understand a man, not through the eyes of the female, but through the imaginative reaching out toward what a man feels himself to be, in his own personal experience. So, paradoxical though it may seem, the form of the opposite sex prevents the true understanding of experience associated with the opposite sex. Detachment from the form of the opposite sex facilitates true understanding of the experience associated with the opposite sex because it removes the barrier created by sex-obsessed imagination.

Understanding through detachment

If one is transcending sexual duality and trying to understand the experience associated with the opposite sex, sometimes one actually exhibits the traits usually associated with the opposite sex. Thus, for example, some aspirants in the male body at one phase or another actually put on the clothes of women, talk like them, feel like them, and take on their habits. But this is

Freedom from sex-ridden imagination

only a passing phase. When inner understanding of the relevant experiences is complete, they neither experience themselves as male alone nor as female alone but as being *beyond* the distinction of sex. The experiences connected with the male and female forms are both accessible and intelligible to the aspirants who have transcended sexual distinctions. They remain unaffected by the limitations of either, because through understanding they have freed themselves from the limiting obsessions characteristic of sex-ridden imagination.

Reconciliation of conscious and unconscious mind

The completeness that the mind seeks is not attainable through attachment to other forms and their accession. It is to be sought *within* by recapturing the lost unity of the mind. Reconciliation of the conscious and the unconscious mind is possible, not through sexual attraction or through other forms of possessiveness, but through nonidentification with the body and its sex. Nonidentification with the body removes the barrier that prevents the amalgamation and integration of the total of experience deposited in the mind. Completeness within is to be sought by overcoming sexual duality and distinction, which accentuate identification with the body.

Divine love

To be free from attachment to the opposite sex is to be free from domination of the sex of the body in which the soul has incarnated itself, thereby annihilating the majority of those sanskaras that compel the soul to identify itself with the body. The transcending of sexual duality does not in itself amount to the overcoming of all duality, but it certainly goes a long way toward facilitating the complete transcendence of duality in all its forms. On the other hand, it is equally true that the problem of sexual duality is a part of the problem of duality as such. Its complete solution comes when the wider problem of all duality is solved through divine love, in which there is neither "I" nor "you," neither man nor woman. The purpose of male and female incarnations is the same as the purpose of evolution itself: it is to enable the soul to arrive at its own undivided and indivisible existence.

Reincarnation and Karma

Part VI
The Operation of Karma Through Successive Lives

In the successive incarnations of an individual soul, there is not only a thread of continuity and identity—manifested in personal memory and revived in the case of advanced souls—but there is also an uninterrupted reign of the law of cause and effect through the persistence and operation of karma. The successive incarnations with all their particulars are closely and unfailingly determined by rational law, so that it becomes possible for the individual soul to mold its future through wise and intelligent action. The actions of past lives determine the conditions and circumstances of the present life, and the actions of the present life have their share in determining the conditions and circumstances of future lives. Successive incarnations of the individual soul yield their full significance only in the light of the operation of the law of karma.

Incarnations governed by law of karma

The intermittent incarnations in the gross world are only apparently disconnected. Karma persists as a connecting link and determining factor through the mental body, which remains a permanent and constant factor through all the lives of the soul. The law of karma and its manner of operation cannot be fully intelligible as long as the gross body and the gross world are considered to be the only facts of existence. Karmic determination is

Karma persists through mental body

made possible by the existence of the subtle and mental bodies and worlds.

The plane on which one can possess physical consciousness is the gross world. The planes on which one can possess consciousness of desires are in the subtle world, and the planes on which the soul can have mental consciousness are in the mental world. The source of desire is to be found in the mind, which is on the mental planes. Here the seed of desire is attached to the mind; the desire exists here in a latent form, in the same way as the tree is latent in the seed. The mental body, which is the seat of the mind, is often called *karan sharir,* or the causal body, because it stores within itself the seeds or the causes of all desires. The mind retains all impressions and dispositions in a latent form. The limited "I," or ego, is composed of these sanskaras. However, the actual manifestation of sanskaras in consciousness, as expressed through different mental processes, takes place in the subtle body.

Mental and subtle bodies

The soul, which in reality is one and undifferentiated, is apparently individualized through the limitations of the mental body, which is the seat of the ego-mind. The ego-mind is formed by the accumulated impressions of past experiences and actions. And it is this ego-mind that constitutes the kernel of the existence of the reincarnating individual. The ego-mind, as a reservoir of latent impressions, is the state of the mental body. The ego-mind, becoming spirit and experiencing activated and manifested impressions, is the state of the subtle body. The ego-mind, as descended in the gross sphere for creative action, is the state of a physical incarnation. Thus the ego-mind, which is seated in the mental body, is the entity that contains all the phases of continued existence as a separate individual.

Formation and continuation of ego-mind

The ego-mind, seated in the mental body, takes lower bodies according to the impressions stored in it. These impressions determine whether individuals will die young or old; whether they will experience health or illness or both; whether they will be beautiful or ugly; whether they will suffer from physical handicaps, like blindness, or will enjoy general efficiency of the body; whether they will have a

Stored impressions determine conditions of incarnation

sharp or a dull intellect; whether they will be pure or impure of heart, fickle or steadfast in will; and whether they will be immersed in the pursuit of material gains or will seek the inner light of the spirit.

Game of duality

The ego-mind, in its turn, becomes modified through the deposited impressions of karma, which include not only gross and physical action but thought and feeling. And the circumstances of each incarnation are adjusted to the composition and needs of the ego-mind. Thus, if a person has developed certain special capacities or tendencies in one incarnation, he takes them on to the succeeding incarnations. Similarly, things that have been left incomplete in one incarnation can be completed in the incarnations that follow. Through the persistence of impressions, the karmic links that have been forged in one incarnation are carried on and developed in succeeding incarnations. Those who have been closely associated with each other through good or bad dealings therefore tend to have recurring contacts. Thus the game of duality is carried on long enough to gather so much experience of the opposites that the soul, out of the fullness of its experience, eventually becomes ripe for dropping the ego-mind and turning inward to know itself as the Oversoul.

Claims and counterclaims created by give-and-take

If there has been a give-and-take between certain persons that forges karmic and sanskaric ties between them and creates claims and counterclaims, they have to come together and carry on fresh dealings in order to meet these claims and counterclaims. That which a person gives with a selfish motive binds him in the same way as that which he takes with a sense of separateness. The transaction of give or take, which thus binds, need not be purely on a material plane in the form of exchange of goods or money, nor in the performing of some physical tasks. It could consist of the exchange of views or feelings.

Karma of interference

If a person pays respect to a saint on the higher planes of consciousness, he creates a claim against him. The saint, who is still crossing the inner planes and treading the spiritual path, must then tarry and give such help as will bring the person paying respect to that point on the path which he himself has reached. Paying respect to an advanced soul thus amounts to karma of *interference*. Though respect, as such, is a good thing to receive, in receiving it the advanced soul may have to halt on the spiritual path until he has helped the person who came to him and paid respect.

The quick and unfailing responsiveness of souls is expressed in the law that hate begets hate, lust begets lust, and love begets love. This law operates not only during a single lifetime but across several lives. An individual feels impelled to hate or fear an enemy from past lives, although the present life may not have provided him with any apparent reason for this attitude. In the same way, without any apparent reason from the present life, he is impelled to love and help a friend from past lives. In most cases the person may not be aware of the reason for his unaccountable attitude, but that does not mean there is no reason for it. Many things that seem inexplicable on the surface become intelligible when considered in the light of karmic links brought forward from past lives.

Responsiveness of souls

The law of karma is law exhibiting itself through continuously changing mutual adjustments, which must go on when there are individual souls who seek self-expression in a common world. It is an outcome of the responsiveness of ego-minds. The rhythm in which two souls start their relationship tends to perpetuate itself unless the souls, through fresh intelligent karma, change the rhythm and raise it to a higher quality.

As a rule, accumulated karma has a certain inertia of its own. It does not change the nature of its momentum unless there is a special reason for it. Before karma is created, the individual has a sort of freedom to choose what it shall be. But after it has been delineated, it becomes a factor that cannot be ignored and that either has to be expended through the results it invites or counteracted by fresh and appropriate karma. The pleasure and pain experienced in life on earth, the successes or failures that attend it, the attainments and obstacles with which it is strewn, the friends and foes who appear in it—all are determined by the karma of past lives. Karmic determination is popularly designated as fate. Fate, however, is not some foreign and oppressive principle. Fate is man's own creation pursuing him from past lives; and just as it has been shaped by past karma, it can also be modified, remolded, and even undone through karma in the present life.

Freedom to choose and fate

Just as the nature of karma in earthly life is determined by impressions stored in the ego-mind, the impressions in turn are determined by the nature of karma in earthly life. The impressions in the ego-mind and the nature of karma are interdependent. Karma on earth plays an important part in shaping and reshaping the impressions in the ego-mind, and giving it a momentum that decides the further destiny of the individual. It is in the arena of earthly existence that creative and effective karma can be expressed, through the medium of the gross body. Proper understanding and use of the law of karma enables man to become master of his own destiny through intelligent and wise action. Each person has become what he is through his own accumulated actions. And it is through his own actions that he can mold himself according to the pattern of his heart or finally emancipate himself from the reign of karmic determination, which governs him through life and death.

Becoming master of own destiny

Broadly speaking, karma is of two kinds: that which binds and that which helps toward Emancipation and Self-realization. Good as well as bad karma binds as long as it feeds the ego-mind through wrong understanding. But karma becomes a power for Emancipation when it springs from right understanding and wears out the ego-mind. Right understanding in this respect is best imparted by the Perfect Masters, who know the soul in its true nature and destiny, along with the complications created by karmic laws.

Two kinds of karma

The karma that truly counts comes into existence after a person has developed a sense of distinction between good and bad. During the first seven years of childhood, the impressions that are released for expression are very faint. They also entail a consciousness of the world correspondingly less responsive to the distinctions of the world. Therefore the actions of children under seven years do not leave any strong or effective impressions on the ego-mind, and they do not play any important part in shaping their future. True and effective karma, which molds the ego-mind and its future, begins after the individual develops a sense of responsibility. This sense of responsibility is dependent upon a sense of distinction between good and bad, which usually dawns fully after one has passed the first few years of childhood.

True karma begins with distinction between good and bad

The law of karma, in the world of values, can be compared to the law of cause and effect that operates in the physical world. If there were no law of cause and effect in the physical world, there would be chaos; and people would not know what to expect. In the same way, if there were no law of karma in the world of values, there would be an utter uncertainty of the results that people cherish; and they would not know whether to expect good or bad from their actions. In the world of physical events there is a law of conservation of energy, according to which no energy is ever lost. In the world of values there is a law that once karma comes into existence, it does not mysteriously flitter away without leading to its natural results but persists until it bears its own fruit or is undone through counteracting karma. Good actions lead to good results, and bad actions lead to bad results.

Comparison with law of cause and effect

The moral order of the universe is sustained through the systematic connection between cause and effect in the world of values. If the law of karma were subject to any relaxation, reversals, or exceptions, and if it were not strictly applicable in the domain of values, there would be no moral order in the universe. Human existence would be precarious from the standpoint of the attainment of values. In a universe without moral order, human endeavor would be perpetually fraught with doubt and uncertainty. There cannot be any serious pursuit of values if there is no assured connection between means and ends, or if the law of karma can be set aside. The inflexibility of the law of karma is a condition for significant human action, which would be utterly impossible if the law of karma could be safely ignored or flouted.

Law of karma maintains moral order of universe

In its inviolability, the law of karma is like the other laws of nature. However, the rigorousness of the operation of karmic laws does not come to the soul as the oppressiveness of some external and blind power but as something involved in the rationality of the scheme of life. Karmic determination is the condition of true responsibility. It means that an individual will reap as he sows. What a person gathers by way of experience is invariably connected with what he does. If a person has done an evil turn to someone, he must accept the penalty for it and welcome the

Law of karma an expression of justice

evil rebounding upon himself. If he has done a good turn to someone, he must also receive the reward for it and enjoy the good rebounding upon himself. What he does for another he has also done for himself, although it may take time for him to realize that this is exactly so. The law of karma is an expression of justice and a reflection of the unity of life in the world of duality.

Reincarnation and Karma

Part VII
The Destiny of the Reincarnating Individual

The series of incarnations, which the soul is impelled to take through karmic determination, has a tendency to become endless. Through innumerable lives an individual has come into contact with countless persons, and he has had all kinds of dealings of give-and-take with them. He is entangled in a web consisting of all sorts of debts to pay and dues to recover. According to karmic law, he can avoid neither the debts nor the dues, since both are the outcome of karma inspired by desire. He keeps incarnating in order to pay off his debts and to recover his dues; but even when he means to clear up the account, he is often unable to do so.

Karmic debts and dues

All persons with whom an individual has karmic links of debts or dues may not be incarnate when he has taken a body. Or owing to the limitations imposed by his own capacities and circumstances, he may be unable to meet all the complex requirements of a situation. While he is trying to clear up accounts with those with whom he has past links, in this very attempt he cannot help creating fresh claims and counterclaims concerning them. Even with new persons he cannot help but create debts and dues of

Difficulty of clearing up debts and dues

diverse kinds and magnitudes, and get involved with them. An individual thus goes on adding to his debts and dues, with the result that there is no getting out of his endlessly increasing and complex karmic entanglements.

Master can clear debts and dues

The spinning of the yarn of karmic debts and dues would be endless if there were no provision for getting out of the karmic entanglements through the help of a Perfect Master. He can not only initiate an aspirant into the supreme art of nonbinding karma, but can become directly instrumental in freeing him from his karmic entanglements. The Master has attained unity with God, whose cosmic and universal life includes all persons. Being one with all life and in his representative capacity, he can become, for the sake of the aspirant, the medium for the clearing up of all debts and dues that have come into existence through the aspirant's dealings with countless individuals contacted in his incarnations. If a person must get bound to someone, it is best for him to get bound to God or a Master, because this tie ultimately facilitates emancipation from all other karmic ties.

Relationship with Master carried on through lifetimes

When the good karma of past lives has secured for the aspirant the benefit of having a Master, the best thing that he can do is to surrender himself to the Master and to serve him. Through surrenderance the aspirant throws the burden of his karma on the Master, who has to find ways and means of freeing him from it. Through serving the Master he wins an opportunity to get clear of his karmic entanglements. The relationship between the Master and the disciple is often carried on from one life to another for several reincarnations. Those who have been connected with a Master in past lives are drawn to him by an unconscious magnetism, not knowing why they are thus drawn. There is usually a long history to the apparently unaccountable devotion that the disciple feels for his Master. The disciple is often beginning where he had left off in the last incarnation.

When the disciple invites the attention and the grace of a Master, it is not without reason. Sometimes the Master seems to impart spirituality to a disciple without there being any apparent effort or sacrifice on the part of the disciple. But these are always cases in which the disciple has earned the right to this favor by his associations and endeavors in past lives. The love and devotion the disciple may have felt for the Master in his past lives have formed a deep connection between him and the Master, so that the awakening of spiritual longing in the disciple has its counterpart in the grace and help that flow to him from the Master. It is through his own past nonbinding karma that a person invites the grace of the Master; just as it is through his own binding karma that he invites upon himself the pleasure and pain, as well as the good and evil, of which he is the recipient in this life.

Inviting grace of Master

As a rule, the person who has entered the spiritual path gradually advances until he attains the goal; this does not apply to those who have not definitely entered the path or have no Master to guide them. Through their chaotic pursuits of several lifetimes, most persons are likely to go further away from the goal by the heaping up of binding sanskaras. Hence spiritual progress cannot be said to be automatic, in the sense that it will come about without the active effort of the person concerned.

Spiritual progress requires active effort

Sooner or later, however, the logic of experience gathered through several lives drives everyone to enter the path and seek the highest goal. Once the aspirant enters the path, he usually goes forward with steady progress. As he advances on the path, he often develops certain latent capacities that enable him not only to experience consciously the inner subtle and mental worlds but also to manipulate the forces and powers available on the higher planes of consciousness. Yet, the crossing of the first few planes does not necessarily ensure safe and steady progress. There are many pitfalls on the path itself, and unless there is the assured guidance of a Master, the aspirant is in danger of falling back.

Danger of falling back

From any of the first few planes the aspirant, instead of going forward toward the goal, may have such a setback. In exceptional cases an aspirant of the fourth plane may, through abuse of his powers, invite upon himself such a fall that it takes ages for him to return to his earlier point of progress. The aspirant who has such a fall is known as a *yoga-bhrashta*. Even the yogis are subject to the unyielding law of karma, which knows no exceptions, concessions,

Yoga-bhrashta

or preferences. It is only when the aspirant has the advantage of the guidance by a Perfect Master that the spiritual journey is rendered safe and steady, and it is only then that there is no possibility of a fall or retrogression. The Master steers the aspirant from negative karma in which he might otherwise become involved.

Treading the spiritual path continues for several incarnations before the aspirant attains the goal. Centuries of continued sacrifices, service, self-purification, suffering, and determined search have to roll on if the aspirant is to be spiritually prepared for the final realization of God. God-realization, which is the goal of the reincarnating individual, is never an attainment of a single life. It is always the culmination of his continued endeavor through many lives. Unintelligent karma of many lives has created the bindings of the individual soul, and it has to be undone by the persistent creation of intelligent and nonbinding karma carried on for many more lives.

Power behind incarnations is craving

The power that keeps the individual soul bound to the wheel of life and death is its thirst for separate existence, which is a condition for a host of cravings connected with objects and experiences of the world of duality. It is for the fulfillment of cravings that the ego-mind keeps on incarnating itself. When all forms of craving disappear, the impressions that create and enliven the ego-mind disappear. With the disappearance of these impressions, the ego-mind itself is shed, with the result that there is only the realization of the one eternal, unchanging Oversoul, who is the only Reality. God-realization is the end of the incarnations of the ego-mind because it is the end of its very existence. As long as the ego-mind exists in some form, there is an inevitable and irresistible urge for incarnations. When there is cessation of the ego-mind, there is cessation of incarnations in the final fulfillment of Self-realization.

Culmination of reincarnations

The life of the reincarnating individual has many events and phases. The wheel of life makes its ceaseless rounds, lifting the individual to the heights or bringing him down from high positions. It thus contributes to the enrichment of his experience. Ideals left unattained in one life are pursued further in the next life; things left undone are finished; rough edges left by incomplete endeavor are rounded off; wrongs are eventually set right. The accounts of give-and-take between persons receive renewed adjustment by the repayment of karmic debts and the recovery of karmic dues. At last, out of the ripeness of experience and through the dissolution of the ego-mind, the soul enters into the sole unity of divine life. In this divine life there is neither the binding of giving nor the binding of taking, because the soul has completely transcended the consciousness of separateness or duality.

The drama of the continued life of the individual soul has many acts. From the standpoint of the worldly existence of the soul, a curtain may be said to be drawn over its life after the closing of each act. But no act yields its real significance if it is regarded as complete in itself. It has to be viewed from its wider context as being a link between the acts already performed and the acts still to come. Its meaning is entwined with the theme of the whole drama of which it is a part. The end of the act is not the end of the progressive theme. The actors disappear from the stage of earth only to reappear again in new capacities and new contexts.

Analogy of drama

The actors are so engrossed in their respective roles that they treat them as the be-all and end-all of all existence. For the major part of their continued lives (running into innumerable incarnations), they are unconscious of the closely guarded truth—that the *Author* of the drama, in His imaginative production, Himself became all the actors and played the game of hide and seek in order to come into full and conscious possession of His own creative infinity. Infinity has to go through the illusion of finitehood to know itself as Infinity; and the Author has to play the parts of all of the actors to know Himself as the Author of this greatest detective story, worked out through the cycles of creation.

Game of hide and seek

Live for God and Die for God

This war* is a necessary evil; it is in God's plan, which is to awaken humanity to higher values. If humanity fails to profit by the lessons of the war, it will have suffered in vain. This war is teaching that even an ordinary person can rise to the greatest heights of sacrifice for the sake of a selfless cause. It is also teaching that all the mundane things of the world—wealth, possessions, power, fame, family, and even the very tenor of life on earth—are transitory and devoid of lasting value. Through the lessons they bring, the incidents of war shall win man over for God, who is the Truth; and they will initiate him into a new life that is inspired by true and lasting values.

People are making unlimited sacrifices and enduring untold sufferings for the sake of their country or political ideology. They are therefore capable of the same sacrifices and endurance for the sake of God, or the Truth. All religions have unequivocally claimed man for a life in the Truth; thus it is sheer folly to fight in the name of religion. It is time humanity had a fresh vision of the truth that all life is one and God is the only thing that is real and that matters. God is worth living for, and He is also worth dying for. All else is a vain and empty pursuit of illusory values.

*World War II.—Ed.

Work for the Spiritual Freedom of Humanity

All over the world the spirit of man is crying out for freedom. Love of freedom and the search for freedom are the principal characteristics of humanity. In all races and in all climes, in all countries and at all times, the watchword for groping and struggling humanity has always been *freedom*! There are very few persons, however, who really understand the full implications of true and unqualified freedom. And there are many who, in their partial understanding of the real conditions of freedom, strive only for the attainment of that kind of existence which gives them a sense of relative freedom. Thus different persons long for different kinds of freedom according to the different things they have come to value.

Cry for freedom

Freedom to live as one wishes is sought in all spheres of life. This imperative demand for freedom usually expresses itself by fastening upon some external conditions of the kind of existence people wish to lead. Hence those who identify their being with their country seek national or political freedom. Those who are animated by economic purposes seek economic freedom. Those who are inspired by religious aspirations seek freedom of religion. Those who are enthusiastic about sociological or cultural ideology seek freedom of movement and freedom to express the ideals that they cherish and wish to propagate. But there are few who realize that the basic freedom, which alone gives the stamp of true value to any of these different kinds of

Kinds of freedom

relative freedom, is spiritual freedom. Even if all the external conditions of a free life were completely fulfilled and guaranteed, the soul of man would still remain in woeful bondage if it failed to realize spiritual freedom.

Limits of freedom

All the different types of freedom that fasten upon some external conditions must, in their very nature, exist within certain limits. For the freedom that an individual or community or state seeks must be consistent with a similar freedom for other individuals, communities, or states. National, economic, religious, or cultural freedom expresses itself in and by means of the duality of existence. It lives on duality and is sustained by duality; therefore it has to be relative and limited and cannot be infinite. It exists in varying degrees. Even when it is won through persistent effort, it cannot be a permanent attainment, since the external conditions having once been secured are not secured forever but are capable of deteriorating in the course of time.

Spiritual freedom alone is unlimited

Only spiritual freedom is absolute and unlimited. When it is won through persistent effort, it is secured forever. Though spiritual freedom can and does express itself in and through the duality of existence, it is grounded in the realization of the inviolable unity of all life and is sustained by it. One important condition of spiritual freedom is freedom from all wanting. It is want that fetters life through attachment to conditions that would fulfill that want; if there is no want, there is no dependence or limitation. The soul is enslaved through wanting. When the soul breaks asunder the shackles of wanting, it emancipates itself from its bondage to the bodies—gross, subtle, and mental. This is the spiritual freedom that brings with it the final realization of the unity of all life and puts an end to all doubts and worries.

Importance of spiritual freedom

It is only in spiritual freedom that one can have abiding happiness and unimpaired Self-knowledge. It is only in spiritual freedom that there arises the supreme certainty of Truth. It is only in spiritual freedom that there is the final ending of sorrow and limitation. It is only in spiritual freedom that one can live for all, and yet be detached in the midst of all activities. Any lesser type of freedom is comparable to a house built on sand, and any lesser type of attainment is frought with the fear of decay. Therefore there is no gift greater than the gift of spiritual freedom, and there is no task more important than the task of helping others to achieve spiritual freedom. Those who have understood the supreme importance of spiritual freedom have not only to strive for it for themselves but also to share the God-given duty of helping others win it.

True service

Those who are inspired by a spirit of selfless service are quick to render unto humanity all possible help through provision of the necessities of life—like clothes and shelter, food and medicine, education and other amenities of civilization. In pursuing the path of duty they are not only prepared to fight for the weak against aggression and oppression but also to lay down their very lives for the sake of others. All these types of service are great and good; but from the ultimate point of view, the help that secures spiritual freedom for humanity surpasses them all. It is insuperable in importance.

Way to help others attain spiritual freedom

The way to help others attain spiritual freedom is far different from the way of rendering other types of help. For the hungry you can provide food, and they have only to eat it. For the naked you can provide clothes, and they have only to wear them. For the homeless you can provide houses, and they have only to dwell in them. For those who are in the agonies of spiritual bondage, however, there is no ready-made provision that can give them immediate relief. Spiritual freedom has to be won by oneself for oneself through watchful and unfailing war against the lower self and the lower desires. Those who would be soldiers in the cause of Truth have to help all, not only in launching upon the thrilling enterprise of attaining victory over themselves, but also in every step they take toward that attainment. There is no other way of sharing their burden.

The call

I have full confidence that you, my devotees, will share this burden. Many of you, for years together, have obeyed my orders and carried out my instructions, through faith in me and love for me. You have stuck to me and my spiritual cause through storm and stress and thick and thin. Now the time has come for you to offer all your services in my mission of helping humanity tread the spiritual path and realize God. The eternal truth that God alone is real has to be clearly understood and unreservedly accepted, and it has to be unequivocably expressed through words and deeds. In the full realization of the Truth, humanity shall attain spiritual freedom.

No sacrifice is too big to set man free from spiritual bondage and help him to inherit the Truth, which alone shall bring abiding peace to all and which alone will sustain an unassailable sense of universal fellowhood—cemented by the ungrudging love of all, for all, as expressions of the same Reality. In this God-willed, divinely planned, and predestined task of bringing spiritual freedom to humanity, you, my devotees, have to help me—even at the cost of your lives. In your duty of helping others to find God, you have to welcome every type of suffering and sacrifice.

The Task for Spiritual Workers

I am very happy that, in response to my call, you have gathered to receive my message to you. On the path, the most important condition of discipleship is readiness to work for the spiritual cause of bringing humanity closer and closer to the realization of God. I am glad to note that through faith and love for me you have wholeheartedly offered yourselves to share in my universal work of spiritualizing the world. I have full confidence that you will not only inherit for yourselves the Truth that I bring but also become enthusiastic and valiant torchbearers for humanity, which is enveloped in deep ignorance.

Be torchbearers for humanity

Because of its supreme importance for the true and final well-being of humanity, spiritual work has a natural and imperative claim on all who love humanity. It is therefore very necessary to be quite clear about its nature. The whole world is firmly established in the false idea of separateness; and being caught up in the illusion of duality, it is subject to all the complexities of duality. Spiritual workers have to redeem the world from the throes of imagined duality by bringing home to it the truth of the unity of all life.

Nature of spiritual work

The cause of the illusion of manyness is that the soul, in its ignorance, identifies itself with its bodies. The gross, subtle, and mental bodies are all mediums for experiencing, through the ego-mind, the different states of the world of duality. But they cannot be the mediums for knowing the true nature of the soul, which is above them all. By identifying with the bodies, the soul gets caught up in the ignorance of manyness. The soul in all the bodies, with the ego-mind, is really one undivided existence. However, as it gets mixed up with these bodies and the ego-mind, which are only its vehicles, it considers itself as limited; and it looks upon itself as being only one among the many of creation, instead of looking upon itself as the only one Reality without a second.

Origin of manyness

Every soul is eternally and inviolably one with the one undivided and indivisible universal Soul, which is the sole Reality. Yet false identification with the bodies and the ego-mind creates the illusion of manyness and of differentiation within the whole. The bodies, with the ego-mind, are only the mediums or the vehicles of consciousness; and as the soul experiences the different inner planes through its different mediums or vehicles, it goes through different states of consciousness.

States of consciousness

Most souls are unconscious of their true nature as God, who is the Unity and the Reality of all souls. God-realization is latent in them, since it has not yet come to be experienced consciously. Those who have cast off the veil of duality experience the soul through itself independently of any mediums or vehicles. In this experience the soul consciously knows itself as being identical with God. Life in the Truth of the unity of all brings with it freedom from all limitations and sufferings. It is the self-affirmation of the Infinite as infinite. In this state of spiritual Freedom and Perfection, the ego-life is finally and completely surrendered in order to experience and release the divine life in the Truth; and God is known and affirmed as the only Reality worth living for.

God-realization

To realize God is to dwell in eternity; it is a timeless experience. But spiritual work must be done for the souls who are caught up in the mazes of creation, which is bound by time. Spiritual workers cannot afford to ignore the element of time in creation. To ignore time would be to ignore the spiritual work itself. It is imperative to be discriminatingly aware of the flow of time in creation and to appre-

Importance of time

ciate fully the supreme importance of the moment in the future that shall witness the universal dispensation of the Truth of spiritual wisdom.

Task for spiritual workers

The task for spiritual workers is to help me in this universal dispensation of the Truth to suffering humanity. You have not only to prepare humanity to receive this Truth but also to get established in it yourself. It is extremely important to remember that you can help others to gain spiritual freedom and to come out of the illusion of duality only if you yourself do not forget this idea of unity while working for others—who are inclined to create divisions where they do not exist and who thus allow no respite to spiritual workers. The minds of people have to be completely purged of all forms of selfishness and narrowness if they are to inherit the life in eternity that I bring. It is by no means an easy task to persuade people to give up their selfishness and narrowness.

It is not by accident that people are divided into the rich and the poor, the pampered and the neglected, the rulers and the ruled, the leaders and the masses, the oppressors and the oppressed, the high and the low, the winners of laurels and the recipients of ignominy. These differences have been created and sustained by those who, through their spiritual ignorance, are attached to them and who are so settled in perverse thinking and feeling that they are not even conscious of their perversity. They are accustomed to look upon life as divided into inviolable compartments, and they are unwilling to give up their separative attitude. When you launch upon your spiritual work, you will be entering into a field of divisions that people desperately cling to, and that they accentuate and strive to perpetuate consciously or unconsciously.

Win people to life of Truth

Mere condemnation of these divisions will not enable you to destroy them. The divisions are being nourished by separative thinking and feeling, which can yield only to the touch of love and understanding. You have to win people to the life of Truth; you cannot coerce them into spirituality. It is not enough that you should have unimpaired friendliness and untarnished goodwill in your own hearts. If you are to succeed in your work, you have to bring home to them the faith and the conviction that you are helping them to redeem themselves from bondage and suffering, and to realize the Highest—to which they are rightful heirs. There is no other way to help them attain spiritual freedom and enlightenment.

For rendering spiritual help you should have a clear understanding of the following four points:

1. *Apparent descent to a lower level.*

It may often be necessary for you to *apparently* descend to the lower level of those whom you are trying to help. Though your purpose is to raise people to higher levels of consciousness, they might fail to profit by what you say if you do not talk in terms they understand. What you convey to them through your thoughts and feelings should not go over their heads. They are bound to miss the point unless you adapt it to their capacity and experience. However, it is equally important to remember that while doing this, you should not *actually* lose your own high level of understanding. You will change your approach and technique as they gradually arrive at deeper and deeper understanding, and your apparent descent to the lower level will be only temporary.

Hints for spiritual workers

2. *Spiritual understanding ensures all-sided progress.*

You must not divide life into departments and then begin to deal with each department separately and exclusively. Departmentalized thinking is often an obstacle to integral vision. Thus if you divide life into politics, education, morality, material advancement, science, art, religion, mysticism, and culture—and then think exclusively of only one of these aspects—the solutions that you bring to life can neither be satisfactory nor final. But if you succeed in awakening spiritual inspiration and understanding, progress in all these spheres of life is bound to follow automatically. You will have to aim at providing, as spiritual workers, a complete and real solution for all the individual and social problems of life.

3. *Spiritual progress consists in the spontaneous growth of understanding from within.*

As spiritual workers, you have also to remember that the spiritual wisdom you desire to convey to others is already latent in them, and that you have only to be instrumental in unveiling that spiritual wisdom. Spiritual progress is not a process of accumulating from without; it is a process of unfoldment from within. A Perfect Master is absolutely necessary for anyone to arrive at Self-knowledge, but the true significance of the help given by the Master consists in the fact that he enables others to come into the full possession of their own latent possibilities.

4. *Some questions are more important than answers.* You, as spiritual workers, must not lose sight of the real work the Master desires to get done through you. When it is clearly understood that spiritual wisdom is latent in all, you will no longer be anxious to provide others with ready-made answers and solutions. In many cases you will be content to set up for others a new problem or to clarify for others the nature of the problems they face. You may have done your duty if you ask them a question that they would not ask of themselves, when placed in some practical situation. In some cases you will have done your duty if you succeed in putting them in a searching and questioning attitude, so that they themselves begin to understand and tackle their problems along more fruitful and creative lines. To give them a deeper point of view or to suggest to them a fruitful line of thought and action may itself mean much more than thrusting upon them the results of your judgment. The questions that you may help them formulate for themselves should neither be merely theoretical nor unnecessarily complicated. If they are simple, straight, and fundamental, these questions will answer themselves; and people will find their own solutions. You will have rendered indispensable and valuable service to them because, without your tactful intervention, they would not have arrived at the solution of their multifarious problems from the *spiritual* point of view.

Overcoming obstacles

It has been seen that spiritual workers must necessarily be confronted with many obstacles, but obstacles are meant to be overcome. Even if some of them seem to be insuperable, you have to do your best to help others irrespective of results or consequences. Obstacles and their overcoming, success and failure, are all illusions within the infinite domain of Unity. Your task is already done when it is performed wholeheartedly. If you are steadfast and one-pointed in your desire to help my cause of awakening humanity to the sole reality and the ultimate worthwhileness of God and God alone, you will get many opportunities for spiritual work. There is ample scope for work in this field.

You must do your work without worrying about consequences, irrespective of success or failure; but be confident that the result of work done in this spirit and with this understanding is assured.

Results of spiritual work

Through the untiring activities of spiritual workers, humanity shall be initiated into a new life of abiding peace and dynamic harmony, unconquerable faith and unfading bliss, immortal sweetness and incorruptible purity, creative love and infinite understanding.

Qualifications of the Aspirant

Part I
Entering into the Realities of Inner Life

Though realization of the Truth is the ultimate destiny of all persons, there are very few who have the necessary preparation for the early fulfillment of this glorious destiny. The mind of the worldly individual is darkened by a thick layer of accumulated sanskaras, which must be considerably weakened for the aspirant even to enter the spiritual path. The usual method for gradually dissipating the load of sanskaras is to follow as strictly as possible the external code of religious rituals and ceremonies.

Value and limitations of external conformity

This stage of external conformity to religious injunctions or traditions is known as the pursuit of *shariat*, or *karma-kanda*. It covers actions like offering daily prayers, visiting holy places, performing duties prescribed by the scriptures, and observing well established rules of the ethical codes generally accepted by the moral consciousness of the times. The stage of external conformity is useful in its own way as a spiritual discipline, though it is by no means free from evil effects. For it not only tends to make one dry, rigid, and mechanical but it often nourishes some kind of subtle egoism. However, most persons are attached to the life of external conformity because they find it the easiest way of placating their uneasy consciences.

The soul often spends several lives in gathering the lessons of external conformity; but there always comes a time when it tires of external conformity and becomes more interested in the realities of the inner life. When a worldly person takes to this higher kind of search, he might be said to have become an aspirant. Like the insect that passes on through metamorphosis to the next stage of existence, the aspirant transcends the phase of external conformity (shariat, or karma-kanda) and enters upon the path of spiritual emancipation, known as *tariqat*, or *adhyatma-marga*. In this higher phase the aspirant is no longer satisfied by external conformity with certain rules but wants to acquire those qualifications that would make his inner life spiritually beautiful.

Realities of inner life

From the standpoint of the realities of inner life, the life of external conformity may often be spiritually barren; and a life that deviates from such rigid conformity may often be spiritually rich. In seeking conformity with established conventions and formality, one is almost always prone to slip into a life of false or illusory values rather than a life based upon true and lasting values. What is conventionally recognized need not always be spiritually sound. On the contrary, many conventions express and embody illusory values since they have come into existence as a result of the working of average minds that are spiritually ignorant. Illusory values are mostly conventional because they grow into that matrix of mentality which is most common. This does not mean that conventions necessarily embody nothing but illusory values.

Limitations of conventions

Sometimes people stick to unconventional things for no other reason than that they are out of the ordinary. The unusual nature of their pursuits or interests enables them to feel their separateness and difference from others, and to take delight in it. Unconventional things also often generate interest merely through their novelty in contrast with those that are conventional. The illusory values of the usual become insipid through familiarity; and the mind then has a tendency to transfer the illusion of value to those things that are not usual, instead of trying to discover true and lasting values.

Freedom from convention due to critical thought

Transcending the stage of external conformity does not imply a merely mechanical and thoughtless change from conventionality to unconventionality. Such change would be essentially in the nature of reaction and could in no way contribute toward a life of freedom and truth. The freedom from conventionality that appears in the life of the aspirant is not due to any uncritical reaction but is due to the exercise of critical thought. Those who would transcend the stage of external conformity and enter into the high life of inner realities must develop the capacity to distinguish between false and true values, irrespective of conventionality or unconventionality.

The rise from shariat (karma-kanda) to tariqat (adhyatma-marga) is not to be interpreted, therefore, as being merely a departure from external conformity. It is not a change from conventionality to idiosyncracy, from the usual to the unusual. It is a change from a life of thoughtless acceptance of established traditions to a mode of being that is based upon thoughtful appreciation of the difference between the important and the unimportant. It is a change from a state of implicit ignorance to a state of critical thoughtfulness. At the stage of mere external conformity, the spiritual ignorance of an individual is often so complete that he does not even realize that he is ignorant. But when the person is being awakened and enters the path, he begins by realizing the need for true light. In the initial stages the effort to attain this light takes the form of intellectual discrimination between the lasting and the transitory, the true and the false, the real and the unreal, the important and the unimportant.

Discrimination between true and false

For the spiritual aspirant, however, it is not enough to exercise merely intellectual discrimination between the false and the true. Though intellectual discrimination is undoubtedly the basis for all further preparation, it yields its fruit only when newly perceived values are brought into relation with practical life. From the spiritual viewpoint, what matters is not theory but *practice*. The ideas, beliefs, opinions, views, or doctrines that a person might hold intellectually constitute a superficial layer of human personality. Very often someone believes in one thing and does exactly the opposite. The bankruptcy of barren beliefs is all the more pitiable because the person who feeds upon them often suffers from the delusion that he is spiritually advanced, when in truth he has not even begun spiritual life.

Bankruptcy of barren beliefs

Sometimes even a wrong view, which is held with fervor, may indirectly invite an experience that opens the gates to spiritual life. Even at the stage of shariat, or karma-kanda, allegiance to religions is not infrequently a source of inspiration for many selfless and noble acts. For while the dogmas or creeds are blindly accepted, they are often held with a fervor and enthusiasm that supply a dynamic element to the ideology that has been accepted by the person for the moment. Dogmas and creeds, as compared with barren views and doctrines, have the distinct advantage of being embraced not only by the intellect but also by the heart. They cover and affect a wider part of personality than purely theoretical opinions.

Dogmas and creeds

Dogmas and creeds generally, however, are as much a source of evil as of good, because in them the guiding vision is clouded owing to degeneration or suspension of critical thinking. If allegiance to creeds and dogmas has sometimes been good for the individual or the community to which he belongs, it has more often done harm. Though the mind and the heart are involved in allegiance to dogmas and creeds, *both* function in such cases under the serious handicap of suspension of critical thought. Hence dogmas and creeds do not contribute to unmixed good.

Dogmas and creeds often harmful

When a person gives up uncritically accepted dogmas and creeds in favor of views and doctrines to which he has devoted thought, there is a certain amount of advance—insofar as his mind has now begun to think and critically examine its beliefs. Very often, however, the newly held beliefs are seen to lack the fervor and enthusiasm that characterized allegiance to dogmas and creeds. If these newly held beliefs lack motive power, they belong only to the superficial aspects of life; and they hang loosely upon the person like an overcoat. The mind has been emancipated from the domination of uncultured emotion, but this is often achieved by sacrificing the cooperation of the heart. If the results of critical thought are to be spiritually fruitful, these results must again invade and recapture the heart so as to enlist its cooperative functioning.

Need for putting theory into practice

In other words, the ideas that have been accepted after critical examination must again be released into active life if they are to yield their full benefit. In the process of practical living, they often undergo a healthy transformation and become more soundly interwoven with the very fabric of life.

The transition from external conformity (shariat, or karmakanda) to the life of inner realities (tariqat, or adhyatma-marga) involves two steps: (1) freeing the mind from the inertia of uncritical acceptance based upon blind imitation and stirring it to critical thinking; and (2) bringing the results of critical and discriminative thinking into practical life. In order to be spiritually fruitful, thinking must be not only critical but creative. Critical and creative thinking leads to spiritual preparation by cultivating those qualities that contribute toward the perfection and balancing of the mind and the heart—and the release of unfettered Divine Life.

Critical and creative thinking balances mind and heart

Qualifications of the Aspirant

Part II
Some Divine Qualities

Qualities necessary for spiritual life interconnected

If the inner life of an aspirant is to be harmonious and enlightened, he has to develop and express many divine qualities while he is engaged in his daily duties. Each quality by itself may not seem to be extremely important, but to consider it apart from its necessary relationship with other important qualities is not correct. In spiritual life all these qualities implement and support each other, and their interconnection is so vital that not one of them can be completely ignored without detriment to many other essential qualities. So, considered in its true function, each of these divine qualities turns out to be absolutely indispensable for a complete life.

Patience and persistence

Every person is a rightful heir to the Truth. But he who would inherit it must be spiritually prepared for it, and this spiritual preparation sometimes takes several lives of patient and persistent effort. Therefore, one of the first requirements of the aspirant is that he should combine unfailing enthusiasm with unyielding patience. Once an individual is determined to realize the Truth, he finds that his path is beset with many difficulties, and there are very few who persist with steady courage till the very end. It is easy to give up the effort when one is confronted with obstacles.

This might be illustrated by a story of a man from Poona, India. He once read a spiritual book that impressed him so deeply that he felt like renouncing everything. He left Poona and went to a forest near the city; and sitting under a tree with prayer beads in his hand, he began to repeat God's name. He kept doing this all day in spite of much inconvenience and dwindling enthusiasm. After sunset he heard from all sides the cries of animals; and though these cries grew louder and louder in the gathering darkness of the night, he persisted in his determination. However, when he saw through the darkness a huge bear coming toward him, he fled for his life and ran at top speed until he fell unconscious in a shop back in Poona. As he regained consciousness, he related his adventure to those who had gathered around him, much to their amusement—and that finished his mood for renunciation.

Spiritual effort demands not only physical endurance and courage but also unshrinking forbearance and unassailable moral courage. The world is caught up in Maya and is addicted to false values.

Accepting world as it is

Therefore the ways of the world run counter to the standards the aspirant has set for himself. If he runs away from the world, that does not help him. He will again have to come back to the world to develop that quality which would enable him to face and accept the world as it is. Very often his path lies through the world that he has to serve in spite of not liking its ways. If the aspirant is to love and serve the world that does not understand him or even is intolerant toward him, he must develop infinite forbearance.

As the aspirant advances on the spiritual path, he acquires, through his contact with a Perfect Master, an increasingly deeper understanding of true love. This makes him painfully sensitive to the

Forbearance

impact from outside actions that not only do not taste of love but actually bring him into contact with cold contempt, cynical callousness, agonizing antipathy, and unabating hatred. All these encounters try his forbearance to the utmost. Even the worldly person suffers in a world he occasionally finds indifferent or hostile, but he is more thick-skinned and his suffering is less acute. He does not expect anything much better from human nature and thinks that these things are inevitable and incurable. The aspirant, who has tasted a deeper love, knows the hidden possibilities in every soul. Thus his suffering is more acute because he feels the gulf between that which is and that which might have been, if only the world had even faintly appreciated the love he has begun to understand and cherish.

Moral courage and confidence

The task of forbearance would be easy if the aspirant could become reconciled to the ways of the world and accept them without challenge. Having seen the higher truths, however, it becomes his imperative duty to stand by them, even if the whole world opposes him. Loyalty to the higher truths of his own perception demands unshakable moral courage and readiness to face the criticism, the scorn, and even the hatred of those who have not yet begun to open up to these truths. Although in this uneven struggle he does get unfailing help from the Master and other aspirants, he has to develop the capacity to fight for these truths single-handedly, without relying upon external help all the time. This supreme moral courage can only come with supreme confidence in oneself and in the Master. To love the world and serve it in the ways of the Masters is no game for the weak and fainthearted.

Freedom from worry

Moral courage and self-confidence should be accompanied by freedom from worry. There are very few things in the mind that eat up as much energy as worry. It is one of the most difficult things not to worry about anything. Worry is experienced when things go wrong, and in relation to past happenings it is idle merely to wish that they might have been otherwise. The frozen past is what it is, and no amount of worrying is going to make it other than what it has been. Nonetheless, the limited ego-mind identifies itself with its past, gets entangled with it, and keeps alive the pangs of frustrated desires. Thus worry continues to grow into the mental life of a person until the ego-mind is burdened by the past.

Worry is also experienced in relation to the future, when this future is expected to be disagreeable in some way. In this case worry seeks to justify itself as a necessary part of the attempt to prepare for coping with the anticipated situations. But things can never be helped merely by worrying. Besides, many of the things that are anticipated never happen; or if they do occur, they turn out to be much more acceptable than they were expected to be. Worry is the product of feverish imagination working under the stimulus of desires. It is the living through of sufferings that are mostly of one's own creation. Worry has never done anyone any good; and it is very much worse than mere dissipation of energy, for it substantially curtails the joy and fullness of life.

Cheerfulness, enthusiasm, equipoise

Among the many things the aspirant needs to cultivate, there are few that are as important as cheerfulness, enthusiasm, and equipoise. When the mind is gloomy, depressed, or disturbed, its actions are chaotic and binding. Hence arises the supreme need to maintain cheerfulness, enthusiasm, and equipoise under all circumstances. All these are rendered impossible unless the aspirant succeeds in eliminating worry from his life. Worry is a necessary result of attachment to the past or to the anticipated future, and it always persists in some form or other until the mind is completely detached from everything.

One-pointedness

The difficulties on the spiritual path can be overcome only if the aspirant has one-pointedness. If his energies are dissipated in worldly pursuits, the progress he makes is very slow. One-pointedness implies dispassion concerning all the allurements of the phenomenal world. The mind must turn away from all temptations, and complete control must be established over the senses. Thus control and dispassion are both necessary to attain one-pointedness in the search for true understanding.

Guidance from Master

The supreme condition for sure and steady progress on the path is the benefit of guidance from a Perfect Master. The Master gives just that guidance and help which is necessary according to the immediate needs of the aspirant. All the Master expects is that the aspirant will try his best for spiritual advancement. He does not expect immediate transformation of consciousness except where the ground has been previously made ready. Time is an important factor in spiritual advancement, as it is in all material endeavors. When the Master has given a spiritual push to the aspirant, he waits till the help thus given is completely assimilated by him. An overdose of spirituality always has an unhealthy reaction, particularly when it is inopportune. The Master therefore carefully selects the moment when his intervention is assured of maximum results; and having intervened, he waits with infinite patience till the aspirant really needs further help.

Qualifications of the Aspirant

Part III
Readiness to Serve

The aspirant always has to be in readiness to serve the cause of humanity. He need not apply himself to any type of work irrespective of his capacities. He has to select that type of work which he is qualified to do by virtue of his individual aptitude and abilities. But whatever service he can render by virtue of his capacities, he renders it even when the circumstances are most trying. The ordeals through which he may have to pass are many, but his determination to serve whenever possible must remain unshaken.

Aptitude and abilities

The aspirant is not in any way attached to the idea of service, however, in the sense of maximum results being secured through himself alone. If any service needs to be rendered, he is willing to render it with any amount of sacrifice; but he is never bound by the false idea "I alone should have the credit for doing this." If the privilege of rendering the service falls to the lot of someone else, he is not envious. If he were to seek opportunities for himself to render service, it would be a form of selfishness. In service that really counts in spiritual life, there can be no thought of the self at all. There should be no feeling of having something for oneself or of being the one who

No claims of limited "I"

can give something to others. The self in all its forms has to be left entirely out of the picture. Service should spring out of the spontaneity of freedom, if and when it is necessary; and it has to come in the cooperative spirit in which there is no insistence upon the claims of the limited "I."

If the aspirant is completely detached from all works and their results, he becomes free from the vitiating opposites of great and small. The worldly-minded feel their separative existence through achievements. Therefore they have a natural tendency to judge their achievements in terms of tangible quantities. They grasp at the great things and avoid the little things. From the spiritual point of view, the so-called little things are often seen to be as important as the so-called great. Hence the aspirant has no reason to eschew the one and seek the other; he attends to little things with as much zest as to great things. Although in spiritual life even little things matter as much as great things, the conventions of the world usually fail to recognize this simple truth. By following conventionally accepted ideas, the scope of possible service to fellow beings gets artificially restricted to those activities that are conventionally regarded as important. Much that really is of vital importance to life is neglected, with the result that life is spiritually impoverished.

Freedom from opposites of great and small

Thus, in a society dominated by merely material conceptions of life, service is interpreted in terms of providing for bread or clothes or other physical amenities of existence. In a society responsive to the value of intellectual culture, service is interpreted in terms of spreading learning in different forms. In a society that has developed a taste for beauty, service is interpreted in terms of organizing the production and distribution of works of art. In a society responsive to the ineffable values of the heart, service is interpreted in terms of constructing those channels that will facilitate culture and expression of the heart. In a society alive to the supreme importance of the spirit, service is interpreted in terms of imparting spiritual understanding. Of these different types of service, the service that is concerned with spiritual understanding is the highest, because spiritual understanding includes the right perspective to all human problems and promotes their solution.

Accepted values determine types of service

If there is no spiritual understanding, the desire for rendering service to others is harnessed by limited conceptions. Service is of two kinds: it consists in adding to the lives of others those things that are really worthwhile; or it consists in removing from the lives of others those handicaps that prevent them from having things that are worthwhile. If one's ideas of things that are worthwhile are narrow, the scope of possible service also becomes correspondingly narrow.

Two kinds of service

The scope of service is not limited to great gestures like giving big donations to public institutions. They also serve who express their love in little things. A word that gives courage to a drooping heart or a smile that brings hope and cheer in the midst of gloom has as much claim to be regarded as service as onerous sacrifices and heroic self-denials. A glance that wipes out bitterness from the heart and sets it throbbing with a new love is also service, although there may be no thought of service in it. When taken by themselves, all these things seem to be small; but life is made up of many such small things. If these small things were ignored, life would be not only unbeautiful but unspiritual.

Little things that matter

Just as the worldly-minded have a tendency to judge positive contributions in terms of magnitudes, they also make a similar mistake in judging obstacles, handicaps, and adversities. Thus, for most persons, the adversity of another must assume colossal proportions if it is to deserve notice. It is characteristic of the worldly to give more importance to things that take shape in external and tangible ways than to things that are silent elements of inner life. Devastating war, for example, is considered to be a greater calamity than lingering lives filled with bitter hatred; though from the purely spiritual point of view, lives filled with bitter hatred are not in any way less evil than devastating wars. War assumes so much importance because of the many visual instances of cruelty, but hatred is equally unbeautiful even when it does not materialize itself into outward action. In the same way, epidemics, injuries, and the sufferings of the deathbed invite more attention from the worldly-minded than the agonies of the heart that is heavy with the burden of unquenchable desire.

Mistakes in worldly judgment

For the aspirant who is eager to serve without any desire for recognition and credit, everything that thwarts or perverts the release of a full life is worthy of attention, irrespective of whether it is great or small in the opinion of the world. Just as the building up or the collapse of empires has a place in the flow of universal life, the fleeting moments of sadness also have their own place in it. The importance of the one should not be measured in terms of the other, and the claims of the one should not be ignored for the claims of the other. The aspirant looks at life as an integral whole, without allowing any part to monopolize his attention at the cost of others.

Life as integral whole

Even when the aspirant is rendering service that is selfless, he keeps constant guard upon his mind. The aspirant must be humble, honest, and sincere. The service he renders must not be for the sake of mere show; it should be an outcome of true love. If the aspirant is inspired by love, his love will enable him to be in complete harmony with other aspirants without being jealous. If there is not complete harmony among fellow workers, the service that is rendered falls short of the spiritual ideal. Further, if the aspirant renders the outward service without a spirit of love, he is acting from a sense of duty, as in worldly institutions where there are paid workers. In the institutions of the world people work for pay. At best it is a cold sense of duty that prompts them to be efficient. Their work cannot have the inward beauty of work spontaneously done out of love.

Service inspired by love ensures harmony

The aspirant can best assimilate the lessons of true service if he has the good fortune to be in contact with a Perfect Master. The Master teaches not through preaching but through example. When the Master is seen in his capacity of rendering service to humanity, the aspirant is quick to catch that spirit because of his love for the Master. Contact with the Master is also helpful in imbibing the spirit of cooperation, which the aspirants can cultivate easily because of their common love for the Master. They serve because the Master wants it. They do the Master's work, not their own; and they do it not of their own accord but because they have been entrusted with that work by the Master. Therefore they are all free from any ideas of individualistic claims, rights, or privileges.

Importance of contact with a Master

They are keen only about the Master's work, ready to serve his cause to the best of their ability when they are called upon to do so, and equally ready to hand over that work to another aspirant if he can do it better.

In cooperation of this type the aspirants are in a way serving each other because the Master's work is accepted by them all as their own. And in being useful to a fellow aspirant in doing the Master's work, the aspirant is rendering a service to him as much as to the Master. In such service there can be no bossing because the aspirant is always conscious that it is the Master's work, which he has accepted as his own, that he is doing. He further knows that, as aspirants, they are all equal; and it is easy for him to cultivate the habit of serving in the spirit of utter humility. If service makes him proud, he might as well not have served. One of the most difficult things to learn is to render service without bossing, without making a fuss about it, and without any consciousness of high and low. In the world of spirituality, humility counts at least as much as utility.

Service without fuss

When the Master serves others, he does so not because he is attached to the work but in order to help, and also to set his disciples an example of selfless service. While serving others, he sees himself in them and thus experiences having served himself. In his unwaning blissful feeling of oneness, the Perfect Master knows himself to be at once the master of all and the servant of all. He therefore exemplifies the ideal of service in which there is no enslavement, either of the one who receives service or of the one who renders it. The aspirant can speedily realize the ideal of true service if he has before him the example of a Master. However, the spiritual preparation of the aspirant can never be termed complete unless he has learned the art of rendering service that gives not boredom but joy, that brings not enslavement but freedom, that does not set claims and counterclaims but springs from the spontaneity of free give-and-take, that is free from the burden of personal want, and that is sustained by the sense of ever-renewed fulfillment.

Ideal of service

Qualifications of the Aspirant

Part IV
Faith

One of the most important qualifications for the aspirant is faith. There are three kinds of faith: faith in oneself, faith in a Perfect Master, and faith in life. Faith is so indispensable to life that unless it is present in some degree, life itself would be impossible. It is because of faith that cooperative and social life becomes possible. It is faith in each other that facilitates a free give-and-take of love, a free sharing of work and its results. When life is burdened with unjustified fear of one another, it becomes cramped and restricted.

Faith and its forms

Children have a natural faith in their elders. They instinctively look to them for protection and help without requiring any letters of introduction. This quality of trusting others persists in later life unless a person is rudely shocked by others who, through self-interest, deceive and exploit him. So, though faith is natural to man, it grows and flourishes in a society where people are reliable, honest, and worthy of faith; and it fades in a hostile environment. Faith in one another becomes complete and steady when it finds its counterpart in those qualities that invite and confirm faith. Being worthy of the faith others place in one and having faith in others are two complementary virtues. They are the conditions for an unhampered flow and development of individual and

Faith and its counterpart

collective life.

Unqualified and implicit faith in each other belongs to the world of ideals. In actual practice it exists only in special cases. Though it is very much to be desired, it cannot come unless the world is populated by persons who deserve unlimited faith. This condition requires a perfect development of the qualities of being reliable, steadfast, and invariably helpful. But these qualities that foster mutual faith remain undeveloped unless one has supreme faith in oneself. If an individual has no faith in himself, he cannot develop those qualities that invite and foster faith from others. The confidence that you can remain loyal under all sorts of trying circumstances to your own perception of what is right is the very foundation of the superstructure of a reliable character.

Importance of faith in oneself

Unshakable faith in oneself is as rare as implicit faith in some other person. Few have developed it to the degree that ensures effective and constructive control of oneself. In most persons faith in oneself is always being challenged and undone by the constant experience of one's own frailties and failings, which often prove to be unyielding, even when one knows what is right. Self-confidence, which is thus in perpetual danger of being shattered, can be securely established only when the individual has before him the vision of a living example of Perfection, and has faith in it.

Secure basis of self-confidence

Faith in a Perfect Master becomes all-important because it nourishes and sustains faith in oneself and faith in life—in the very teeth of setbacks and failures, handicaps and difficulties, limitations and failings. Life, as a person knows it in himself, or in most of his fellow beings, may be narrow, twisted, and perverse; but life as he sees it in the Master is unlimited, pure, and untainted. In the Master, the aspirant sees his own ideal realized; the Master is what his own deeper self would rather be. He sees in the Master the reflection of the best in himself, which is yet to be but which he will surely one day attain. Faith in the Master therefore becomes the chief motive power for realizing the divinity that is latent in man.

Faith in a Master

True faith is grounded in the deeper experiences of the spirit and the unerring deliverances of purified intuition. It is not to be regarded as the antithesis of critical reason but as the unfailing guide of critical reason. When critical reason is implemented by a deep and living faith based on pure intuition, its functioning becomes creative, fruitful, and significant instead of barren, ineffective, and meaningless. On the other hand, many forms of naive credulity cannot be broken through except by the fearless and free working of critical reason.

Faith and critical reasoning

However, it remains true that critical reason can touch and inform only those kinds of faith that are not based upon pure intuition. True faith grounded in pure intuition always remains an imperative that cannot be ultimately reduced to the conclusions of rational intellect. It is not derived from the limited intellect but is more fundamental and primary, with the result that it cannot be silenced by any intellectual acrobatics. This does not mean, however, that faith need at any stage be blind, in the sense that it is not allowed to be examined by critical intellect. True faith is a form of sight and not of blindness. It need not be afraid of the free functioning of critical reason.

The right of testing the Master through critical reasoning has always been conceded to the disciples. But if, after testing and being satisfied about the Perfection of the Master, a disciple shows any wavering of faith, it is a result of a deplorable deficiency in his sincerity of approach and integrity of purpose. As there is much uncritical and undeserved credulity given to claimants of spiritual wisdom, so there is much unjustified wavering of faith in spite of a convincing basis for it in one's own experience. Just as uncritical credulity is ultimately the result of the unconscious operation of many worldly wants, unjustified wavering of faith is also due to the unconscious operation of desires that run contrary to the effective manifestation of a rationalized faith. In the first case desire is the source of unwarranted belief, and in the second case desire is the source of unwarranted doubt. Cravings have a tendency to pervert the functioning of critical reason. An unwavering faith grounded in pure intuition can come only to a mind that is free from the pressure of diverse wants. True faith is therefore a matter of gradual growth. It grows in proportion to the success that the disciple attains in freeing his consciousness from diverse cravings.

Credulity and doubt

Faith must be carefully distinguished from mere intellectual belief or opinion. When a person has a good opinion about someone, he is said to have a certain kind of faith in him. But this kind of opinion does not have that spiritual potency which belongs to a living faith in a Perfect Master.

Beliefs and opinions

The beliefs and opinions of a person often constitute a very superficial layer of the human psyche. They do not have any integral relationship with the deeper forces of the psyche. They remain in one region of the mind without bringing about any radical changes in the core of personality, which determines the attitude toward life. People hold such beliefs just as they wear clothes, and in times of emergency they tend to change their clothes to suit their immediate purposes. In such cases, beliefs are unconsciously determined by other purposes; the purposes are not consciously determined by beliefs.

Living faith creatively dynamic

Living faith, on the other hand, has the most vital and integral relation with all the deeper forces and purposes of the psyche. It is not held superficially; nor does it hang, like mere intellectual beliefs, in the periphery of consciousness. On the contrary, living faith becomes a powerful factor that reconstructs the entire psyche; it is creatively dynamic. There is no thought unenlivened by it, no feeling unillumined by it, no purpose not recast by it. For the disciple such living faith in the Master becomes a supreme source of inspiration and unassailable self-confidence. It expresses itself primarily through the spirit of active reliance upon the Master and not merely through some opinion about him. Living faith is not a sort of certificate given by the disciple to the Master. It is an active attitude of confidence in the Master, expressing itself not only through implicit and trustful expectation of help from him but also through the spirit of self-surrender and dedication.

Living faith born of experience

Such fruitful and living faith in the Master is always born of some deep experience that the Master imparts to the deserving disciple. It is fundamentally different from the beliefs people hold either through uncritical acceptance or superficial thinking. Mere intellectual beliefs for the most part have very little spiritual importance. The Master, therefore, is utterly unconcerned with whether the disciple believes in him or in someone else; and he is equally unconcerned with whether the disciple, at any moment, does or does not believe in him. If in some fortunate case the Master, through his benign intervention, wins for himself the living faith of the disciple (as distinguished from mere belief), it is because he knows that the disciple will be helped through it.

Just as the disciple is testing the Master's capacity to guide him, the Master in turn is testing the disciple's integrity of purpose. The Master is unconcerned whether the disciple doubts him or has faith in him. What he tests is whether the disciple is or is not sincere and wholehearted in his spiritual search and pursuit. The Perfect Master is not at all interested in giving proof of his own divinity to the disciple, except when he feels that such proof is likely to be unfailingly useful and unavoidably necessary for the spiritual benefit of one who has surrendered himself to him.

Testing the disciple

Maya

Part I
False Values

Everyone wants to know and realize the Truth, but Truth cannot be known and realized as Truth unless ignorance is known and realized as being ignorance. Hence arises the importance of understanding Maya, or the principle of Ignorance. People read and hear much about Maya, but few understand what it really is. It is not enough to have a superficial understanding of Maya; it is necessary that Maya should be understood as it is, in its reality. To understand Maya, or the principle of Ignorance, is to know half of the Truth of the universe. Ignorance in all its forms must disappear if the soul is to be established in the state of Self-knowledge.

Importance of understanding Maya

Therefore it is imperatively necessary for humanity to know what is false, to know it to be false, and to get rid of the false by knowing it to be false. What is the essential nature of falsehood? If the true is known as being true or if the false is known as being false, there is no falsehood but only a form of knowledge. Falsehood consists in taking the true as being false or the false as being true, that is, in considering something to be other than what in itself it really is.

Essence of falsehood

Falsehood is an error in judging the nature of things.

Broadly speaking there are two kinds of knowledge: purely intellectual judgments about the facts of existence; and judgments of valuation, which imply the appreciation of the worth or importance of things. Purely intellectual judgments or beliefs derive their importance from being related to values in some way. Divorced from values, they have very meager importance in themselves. For example, no one takes much interest in counting exactly the number of leaves on a particular tree, although from the purely theoretical point of view such information would be a form of knowledge. Such information or knowledge is treated as unimportant because it is not vitally connected with other values. Intellectual knowledge becomes important when it enables man to realize certain values by giving him control over the means to their realization or when it enters into valuation itself as an important factor, modifying or in some other way affecting the accepted values.

Two kinds of knowledge

Just as there are two kinds of judgment, there are two kinds of falsehood: mistakes in accepting as facts those things that are not facts and mistakes in valuation. Mistakes in valuation can be committed in the following ways: (1) in taking as important that which is unimportant, (2) in taking as unimportant that which is important, or (3) in giving to a thing an importance other than the importance it really has. All these falsehoods are creations of Maya. Although Maya includes all falsehoods from the spiritual point of view, there are some falsehoods that count and some falsehoods that do not count very much. If a person takes a throne to be higher than it is, it would be a falsehood, but one that does not matter very much. On the other hand, if a person regards the throne as the be-all and the end-all of his life, that would be a falsehood which substantially affects the course and significance of his life. On the whole, mistakes in valuation are far more effective in misguiding, perverting, and limiting life than mistakes in purely intellectual judgments about certain objective facts.

Mistakes in valuation

Mistakes in valuation arise owing to the influence of subjective desires or wants. True values are values that belong to things in their own right. They are intrinsic; and because they are intrinsic, they are absolute and permanent and are not liable to change from time to time or from person to person. False values are derived from desires or wants. They are dependent upon subjective factors; and being dependent upon subjective factors, they are relative and impermanent, and are liable to change from time to time and from person to person.

Examples of relative values

For example, an individual who is very thirsty and is in a desert like the Sahara thinks that nothing is more precious than water; while someone who has at hand an abundance of water and who is not very thirsty does not attach the same importance to it. In the same way, a person who is hungry considers food very important, but the individual who has had a full dinner does not even think of food until he is hungry again. The same thing applies to other lusts and longings, which project imaginary and relative values onto those objects that will fulfill those lusts and longings.

False values derivative and relative

The value of sense objects is great or small according to the intensity or urgency with which they are desired. If these lusts and longings increase, the corresponding objects assume greater importance. If they subside in their intensity or urgency, the objects also lose much of their importance. If the lusts and longings appear intermittently, those objects retain possible value when the lusts and longings are latent and actual value when they are manifested. These are all false values because they are not inherent in the objects themselves. When in the light of true knowledge all the lusts and longings disappear completely, objects vested with importance through the working of these lusts and longings immediately lose all their borrowed importance and appear meaningless.

Emptiness of sense objects

Just as a coin that is not in current use is treated as false, though it has a kind of existence, the objects of lusts and longings when seen in their emptiness are treated as false, though these objects might continue to have some kind of recognition. They all exist, and they may be known and seen; but they no longer mean the same thing. They hold false promise of fulfillment to an imagination perverted by lusts and longings; yet to tranquil and steady perception, they are seen to have no importance when they are considered as separate from the soul.

When a loved one dies, there is sorrow and loneliness; but this sense of loss is rooted in attachment to the form independently of the soul. It is the form that has vanished, not the soul. The soul is not dead; in its true nature it has not even gone away, for it is everywhere. Nonetheless, through attachment to the body, the form was considered important. All longings, desires, emotions, and thoughts were centered upon the form; and when through death the form disappears, there is a vacuum, which expresses itself through missing the departed one.

Taking as important the unimportant

If the form as such had not come to be surcharged with false importance, there would be no sorrow in missing the one who has passed away. The feeling of loneliness, the lingering memory of the beloved, the longing that he or she should still be present, the tears of bereavement, and the sighs of separation—they are all due to false valuation, the working of Maya. When an unimportant thing is regarded as important, we have one principal manifestation of the working of Maya. From the spiritual point of view it is a form of ignorance.

On the other hand, the working of Maya also expresses itself by making an important thing look unimportant. In reality, the only thing that has importance is God; but very few persons are really interested in God for His own sake. If the worldly-minded turn to God at all, it is mostly for their own selfish and mundane purposes. They seek the gratification of their own desires, hopes, and even revenges through the intervention of the God of their imagination. They do not seek God as Truth. They long for all things except the only Truth, which they regard as unimportant. This again is the blinding of vision caused by the working of Maya. People pursue their happiness through everything except God, who is the only unfailing source of abiding joy.

Taking as unimportant the important

The working of Maya also expresses itself by making the mind give to a thing an importance other than the importance it really has. This happens when rituals, ceremonies, and other external religious practices are considered to be ends in themselves. They have their own value as means to an end, as vehicles of life, as mediums of expression; but as soon as they assume claims in their own right, they

Wrong importance

are being given an importance other than that which belongs to them. When they are considered important in themselves, they bind life instead of serving the purpose of expressing it. When the inessential is allowed to predominate over the essential by giving it wrong importance, one has the third principal form of ignorance concerning valuation. This again is the working of Maya.

Maya

Part II
False Beliefs

The shackles that hold the soul in spiritual bondage consist chiefly of wrong values or falsehoods concerning valuation. Some falsehoods, in the nature of wrong beliefs, also play an important part in holding the soul in spiritual bondage. False beliefs implement false values, and they in turn gather strength from the false values in which the soul has been hung up. All false beliefs are as much creations of Maya as are false values, and they are used by Maya to keep the soul still in ignorance in its clutches.

Shackles of Maya

Maya becomes irresistible by taking possession of the very seat of knowledge, which is human intellect. Surmounting Maya is difficult because, with the intellect under its sway, Maya creates barriers and upholds false beliefs and illusions. It creates barriers to the realization of the Truth by persistent attempts to sustain and justify erroneous beliefs. The intellect that functions in freedom prepares the way to the Truth, but the intellect that plays into the hands of Maya creates obstacles to true understanding.

Intellect plays into hands of Maya

The false beliefs created by Maya are so deep-rooted and strong that they seem to be self-evident. They take on the garb of veritable truths and are accepted without question. For example, a person believes that he is his physical body. Ordinarily it never occurs to him that he may be something other than his body. Identification with the physical body is assumed by him instinctively without requiring proof, and he holds the belief all the more strongly because it is independent of rational proof.

False beliefs may seem self-evident

An individual's life is centered around the physical body and its desires. To give up the belief that he is the physical body involves the giving up of all the desires pertaining to the physical body and the false values they imply. The belief that he is his physical body is conducive to the physical desires and attachments; but the belief that he is other than his physical body runs counter to accepted desires and attachments. Therefore the belief that the individual is his physical body becomes natural. It is a belief easy to hold and difficult to uproot. On the other hand, the belief that he is something other than his physical body seems to call for convincing proof. It is difficult to hold and easy to resist. All the same, when the mind is unburdened of all physical desires and attachments, the belief that he is his physical body is seen to be false, and the belief that he is something other than his body is seen to be true.

Identification with physical body

Even when a person succeeds in shedding the false belief that he is the physical body, he remains a victim of the false belief that he is his subtle body. His life is then centered around the subtle body and *its* desires. To give up the belief that he is the subtle body involves the giving up of all desires pertaining to the subtle body and the false values they imply. Therefore the belief that he is his subtle body now becomes natural for him, and the belief that he is something other than his subtle body seems to call for convincing proof. But when the mind is unburdened of all desires and attachments pertaining to the subtle body, the person gives up the false belief that he is his subtle body as readily as he gave up the false belief that he was his physical body.

Identification with subtle body

This is not the end of false beliefs, however. Even when a person abandons the false belief that he is his subtle body, he cherishes the illusory belief that he is his mental body. The person cherishes this false belief because he relishes it. Throughout his long life as an individual soul, he has clung fondly to the false idea of his separate existence. All his thoughts and emotions and activities have repeatedly assumed and confirmed but one affirmation, namely, the existence of the separate "I." To surrender the false belief that he is the ego-mind of the mental body is to surrender all that has seemed to constitute his very existence.

Identification with mental body

In surrendering the false belief that he is his physical or subtle body, it is necessary to surrender various desires and attachments. It is a giving up of something one has had for a long time. In surrendering the false belief that he is his ego-mind, the individual is called upon to surrender the very core of what he has thought himself to be. To shed this last vestige of falsehood is therefore the most difficult thing. But this last falsehood is no more lasting than the earlier falsehoods that had seemed to be unchallenge-able certainties. It also has its ending, and it is shed when the soul renounces its craving for separate existence.

Shedding last falsehood

When the soul knows itself to be different from the gross, subtle, and mental bodies, it knows itself to be infinite. As infinite Soul, it does nothing; it merely IS. When the mind is added onto the individualized soul, it appears to think. When the subtle body is added onto the soul with the mind, it appears to desire. When the gross body is added onto these, the soul appears to be engaged in actions. The belief that the soul is doing anything is a false belief. For example, an individual believes that *he* is sitting in the chair, but in fact it is the body that is sitting in the chair. The belief that the soul is sitting in the chair is due to identification with the physical body. In the same way a person believes that *he* is thinking, but in fact it is the mind that is thinking. The belief that the soul is thinking is due to identification with the mind. It is the mind that thinks and the body that sits. The soul is neither engaged in thinking nor in any other physical actions.

Soul is beyond thinking, desiring, and doing

Of course it is not mere mind or mere body that does the thinking or other physical actions, for mere mind and mere body do not exist. They exist as illusions of the individualized soul, and it is when the soul falsely identifies itself with them that the thinking or the doing of things occurs. The soul, and mental, subtle, and gross bodies taken together constitute the agent of actions, or the limited "I"; but the soul in its true nature is neither responsible for thinking, for desiring, nor for actions. The illusion that the soul is the mind or the bodies and the illusion that the soul is the agent of thinking, desiring, or actions are created by Maya—which is Illusion and the principle of Ignorance.

Illusion that soul is the agent

In the same way, the belief that the soul experiences the pleasures and the pains of life or is going through the opposites of experience is also false. The soul is beyond the opposites of experience, but it does not know itself as such. And so it takes on the experiences that are characteristic of the opposites because of identification with the mind and the subtle and gross bodies. The soul that is mixed up with the mind and the bodies becomes the recipient of pains and pleasures. Thus all the pleasures and the pains that one is subject to are rooted in ignorance.

Belief that soul subject to dual experience

When an individual thinks that he is the most miserable person in the world, he is embracing an illusion that comes into existence through Ignorance, or Maya. He is really not unhappy but imagines that he is unhappy because he identifies himself with the mind and the bodies. Of course it is not the mind by itself or the bodies by themselves that can have any experiences of the opposites. It is the soul and the mind and the bodies taken together that become the subject of dual experience; but the soul, in its true nature, is beyond the opposites of experience.

Thus it is the mind and the bodies together that constitute the agent of activities and the subject of dual experiences. However, they do not assume this double role in their own right but only when they are taken along with the soul. It is the mind and the bodies, which are ensouled, that together become the agent of activities or the subject of dual experience. The process of ensoulment is based upon ignorance, for the soul in its true nature is eternally unqualified, unmodified, and unlimited. It appears to be qualified, modified, and limited through Ignorance, or the working of Maya.

Nature of ensoulment of mind and bodies

Maya

Part III
Transcending the Falsehoods of Maya

Countless are the falsehoods that a Maya-ridden person embraces in the stupor of ignorance; and from the very beginning, falsehoods carry within themselves their own insufficiency and bankruptcy. Sooner or later they are known to be falsehoods. This brings one to the question, How does one discern the falsehood as falsehood? There is no way out of falsehood except by knowing it as falsehood, but this knowledge of falsehood as falsehood would never come unless it was in some way latent in falsehood itself from the very beginning.

Discerning falsehood

The acceptance of falsehood is always a forced compromise. Even in the very depths of ignorance, the soul gives some kind of challenge to falsehood. However feeble and inarticulate it might seem to be in its initial stages, it is the beginning of that search for the Truth which ultimately annihilates all falsehood and all ignorance. In the acceptance of a falsehood there is an ever-growing restlessness, a deep suspicion, and a vague fear. For example, when an individual considers himself and others to be identical with the gross body, he cannot completely reconcile himself to this belief. In embracing this false belief there is fear of death and fear of losing others. If a person depends for his happiness only upon the possession of forms, he knows in his heart that he is building his

In falsehood there is suspicion and fear

castles on shifting sands, that this surely is not the way to abiding happiness, that the support he so desperately clings to may give way any day. Hence, he is deeply suspicious of his grounds.

The individual is restlessly aware of his own insecurity. He knows that something is wrong somewhere and that he is counting upon *false* hopes. Falsehood is treacherously unreliable. He simply cannot afford to embrace it forever. He might as well garland himself with a poisonous snake or go to sleep on the top of a volcano that is only temporarily inactive. Falsehood bears the hallmark of being incomplete and unsatisfactory, temporary and provisional. It points to something else. It appears to the person to be hiding something greater and truer than what it seems to be. Falsehood betrays itself, and in doing so leads one on to know the truth.

Falsehood betrays itself

Falsehoods are of two types: those that arise due to irregular and loose thinking, and those that arise due to vitiated thinking. Falsehoods that arise due to irregular thinking are less harmful than those that arise from vitiated thinking. The untruths of a purely intellectual nature arise because of some mistake in the application of the intellect. Whereas falsehoods that are important from the spiritual point of view arise because of the vitiation of the intellect through the operation of blinding and unreasoning desires.

Two types of falsehood

The difference between these two types of falsehood may be brought out by a physiological analogy. Some disorders of the vital organs of the body are *functional* and some are *structural*. Functional diseases arise because of some irregularity in the functioning of a vital organ. In these cases there is nothing seriously wrong with the structure of the vital organ. It has merely become sluggish or irregular, and needs only slight stimulation or correction in order to function properly. In structural disorders the disease comes into existence because of the development of some deformity in the structure or constitution of the vital organ. In these cases the disorder of the vital organ is of a much graver nature. It has become damaged or rendered inefficient due to some tangible factor that has affected the very constitution of the organ. Both types of diseases can be corrected, but it is far easier to correct merely func-

Analogy of functional and structural diseases

tional disorders than to correct structural ones.

Falsehoods that arise due to some irregularity in the application of the intellect are like functional disorders, and falsehoods that arise due to the vitiation of the intellect are like structural ones. Just as the functional disorders are easier to correct than the structural, falsehoods arising out of irregularity in the application of the intellect are easier to correct than those that arise due to the vitiation of intellect. In order to correct a functional disease of a vital organ, all that is necessary is to give it a better tone and strength. If there is a structural disease, it is often necessary to perform an operation. In the same way, if falsehoods arise due to some mistakes in the application of the intellect, all that is necessary is more carefulness in the application of the intellect. But if falsehoods arise due to vitiation of the intellect, it is necessary to purify the intellect. This requires the painful process of removing those desires and attachments that are responsible for vitiating the intellect.

Importance of purifying intellect

The falsehoods of vitiated thinking spring from initial mistakes in valuation. They arise as a by-product of intellectual activity, which consists in the pursuit of certain accepted values. They come into existence as a part of the rationalization and the justification of accepted values, and they owe their hold upon the human mind to their apparent support of those accepted values. If they did not affect human values or their realization, they would immediately dwindle into insignificance and lose their grip upon the mind. When false beliefs derive their being and vitality from deep-rooted desires, they are nourished by false seeking. If the error in false beliefs is purely intellectual, it is easy to set right. But false beliefs that are nourished by false seeking are the citadels of Maya. They involve much more than intellectual error and are not diminished by mere counterassertions of a purely intellectual nature.

Citadels of Maya

Elimination of desires and attachments that vitiate thinking is not accomplished purely by sheer intellect. This requires right effort and right action. Not by armchair speculation but by the doing of right things shall spiritual truths be discovered. Honest action is a preliminary to the elimination of spiritual falsehoods. The perception of spiritual truths requires not

Clarity of perception from inner purity

merely strenuous and furious thinking but clear thinking, and true clarity of thought is the fruit of a pure and tranquil mind.

Not until the shedding of the last vestige of Maya-created falsehood is God known as *the* Truth. Only when Maya is completely overcome does there arise the supreme knowledge that God is the *only* Truth. God alone is real. All that is not God, all that is impermanent and finite, all that seems to exist within the domain of duality, is false. God is one infinite Reality. All divisions that are conceived within this Reality are falsely conceived; they do not actually exist.

God as only Truth

When God is considered as divisible, it is due to Maya. The variegated world of multiplicity does not effect the partitioning of God into several different portions. There are different ego-minds, different bodies, different forms, but only one Soul. When the one Soul (God) takes different ego-minds and bodies, there are different individualized souls; however, this does not introduce any multiplicity within the one Soul itself. The Soul is and always remains indivisible. The one indivisible Soul is the base of the different ego-minds and bodies, which do the thinking and acting of various types and which go through innumerable types of dual experiences. But the one indivisible Soul is and always remains beyond all thinking and doing and beyond all dual experience.

God is indivisible

Different opinions or different ways of thinking do not introduce multiplicity within the one indivisible Soul, for the simple reason that there are no opinions or any ways of thinking within the Soul. All the activity of thinking and conclusions drawn therefrom are within the ego-mind, which is finite. The individualized soul as Soul does not think; it is only the ego-mind that thinks. Thinking and the knowledge that comes through thinking are both possible in the state of imperfect and incomplete knowledge that belongs to finite ego-minds. In the individual soul itself there is neither thinking nor the knowledge that comes through thinking.

No opinions or ways of thinking within Soul

The individualized soul as Soul is infinite thought and infinite intelligence; there is no division between the thinker and the thinking and the conclusions of thinking, nor the duality of the subject and object. Only the ego-mind with the background of the soul can become the thinker. The individual soul as Soul, which is infinite thought and infinite intelligence, does not think or have any activity of the intellect.

Soul is infinite thought and intelligence

Intellect with its limited thinking comes into existence only with the finite ego-mind. In the completeness and the sufficiency of the infinite intelligence, which is the one Soul, there is no need for the intellect or its activities.

With the shedding of the last vestige of falsehoods created by Maya, the individualized soul not only knows its reality to be different from the gross, the subtle, or the mental body but it knows itself to be God, who is the *only* Reality. In this state the soul knows that the mind, the subtle body, and the physical body were all equally the creations of its own imagination, and that in reality they never existed. It knows that through Ignorance it conceived itself as the mind or the subtle body or the physical body. The individual soul knows also that, in a sense, it became the mind, the subtle body, and the gross body, and then identified itself with all these self-created illusions.

God the only Reality

Part IV
God and Maya

God is infinite because He is above the limiting opposites of duality. He is above the limited aspects of good and bad, small and great, right and wrong, virtue and vice, happiness and misery; therefore He is infinite. If God were good rather than bad or bad rather than good, or if He were small rather than great or great rather than small, or if He were right rather than wrong or wrong rather than right, or if He were virtuous rather than evil or evil rather than virtuous, or if He were happy rather than miserable or miserable rather than happy—He would be finite and not infinite. Only by being above duality is God infinite.

God above duality

Whatever is infinite transcends duality; it cannot be a part of duality. That which is truly infinite cannot be the dual part of the finite. If the Infinite is regarded as existing side by side with the finite, it is no longer infinite; for it then becomes the second part of duality. God, who is infinite, cannot descend into duality. So the apparent existence of duality, as infinite God and the finite world, is illusory. God alone is real; He is infinite, one without a second. The existence of the finite is only apparent; it is false; it is not real.

Infinite cannot be dual part of finite

How does the false world of finite things come into existence?

Why does it exist? It is created by Maya, or the principle of Ignorance.

World of finite things created by Maya

Maya is not illusion; it is the creator of Illusion. Maya is not false; it is that which gives false impressions. Maya is not unreal; it is that which makes the real appear unreal and the unreal appear real. Maya is not duality; it is that which causes duality.

For the purposes of intellectual explanation, however, Maya must be looked upon as being infinite. It creates the illusion of finitehood, yet it is not in itself finite. All the illusions created by Maya are finite; and

Illusion of finitehood

the entire universe of duality, which appears to exist due to Maya, is also finite. The universe may seem to contain innumerable things, but that does not make it infinite. Stars may be countless; there are a huge number, but the total collection of stars is nevertheless finite. Space and time might seem to be infinitely divisible, but they are nevertheless finite. Everything that is finite and limited belongs to the world of Illusion, though the principle that causes this illusion of finite things must, in a sense, be regarded as *not* being an illusion.

Maya cannot be considered as being finite. A thing becomes finite by being limited by space and time. Maya does not exist in space and cannot be limited by it. Maya cannot be limited in space because space

Maya not limited by space and time

is itself the creation of Maya. Space, with all that it contains, is an illusion and is dependent upon Maya. Maya, however, is in no way dependent upon space. Hence it cannot be finite through any limitations of space. Nor can Maya be finite because of any limitations of time. Though Maya comes to an end in the state of Superconsciousness, it need not be considered finite for that reason. Maya cannot have a beginning or end in time because time itself is a creation of Maya. Any view that makes Maya a happening that takes place at some time and disappears after some time puts Maya in time and not time in Maya. Time is in Maya; Maya is not in time. Time, as well as all happenings in time, is the creation of Maya. Maya is in no way limited by time. Time comes into existence because of Maya and disappears when Maya disappears. God is timeless Reality; thus the realization of God, and the disappearance of Maya, is a timeless act.

Nor can Maya be considered finite for any other reasons. If it were finite, it would be an illusion; and being an illusion, it would not have any potency to create other illusions. Thus Maya is best regarded as being both real and infinite, in the same way that God is usually regarded as being both real and infinite. Among all possible intellectual explanations, the explanation that Maya, like God, is both real and infinite is most acceptable to the intellect of man. Nevertheless, Maya cannot be *ultimately* true. Wherever there is duality, there is finitehood on both sides. The one thing limits the other. There cannot be two real Infinites. There can be two huge entities, but there cannot be two *infinite* entities. If we have the duality of God and Maya and if both are regarded as coordinate existences, then the infinite reality of God would be considered as the second part of a duality. Therefore the intellectual explanation that Maya is real does not have the stamp of final knowledge, though it is the most plausible explanation.

Maya as infinite ultimately untrue

There are difficulties in regarding Maya as illusory and also as ultimately real. Thus all attempts of the limited intellect to understand Maya lead to an impasse. On the one hand, if Maya is regarded as finite, it itself becomes illusory; and then it cannot account for the illusory world of finite things. Therefore Maya has to be regarded as being both real and infinite. On the other hand, if Maya is regarded as being ultimately real, Maya itself becomes a second part of the duality of another infinite Reality, namely God. Hence from this point of view, Maya actually seems to become finite and therefore unreal. So Maya cannot be ultimately real, though it has to be regarded as such in order to account for the illusory world of finite objects.

Intellectual difficulty in understanding Maya

In whatever manner the limited intellect tries to understand Maya, it falls short of true understanding. It is not possible to understand Maya through the limited intellect; it is as unfathomable as God. God is unfathomable, ununderstandable; so is Maya unfathomable, ununderstandable. Thus it is said that Maya is God's shadow. Where a person is, there is his shadow also. Where God is, there is this inscrutable Maya. Though God and Maya are inscrutable for the limited intellect working in the domain of duality, they can be

Maya as God's shadow

thoroughly understood in their true nature in the final knowledge of Realization. The enigma of the existence of Maya can never be finally solved until after Realization, when it is known that Maya does not exist in Reality.

Two states in which Maya does not exist

There are two states in which Maya does not exist: in the original unconscious state of Reality there is no Maya and in the Self-conscious, or Superconscious, state of God there is no Maya. It exists only in God's consciousness of the phenomenal world of duality, that is, when there is consciousness of the gross world or of the subtle world or of the mental world. Maya exists when there is no Self-consciousness but only consciousness of the imagined other, and when consciousness is helplessly dominated by the false categories of duality. Maya exists only from the point of view of the finite. It is only as illusion that Maya exists as a real and infinite creator of unreal and finite things.

Knowledge of Realization

In the last and the only Truth of Realization, nothing exists except infinite and eternal God. There the illusion of finite things as separate from God has vanished, and with it also has vanished Maya, the creator of this illusion. Self-knowledge comes to the soul by looking within, and by overcoming Maya. In this Self-knowledge it not only knows that the different ego-minds and bodies never existed but also that the entire universe and Maya itself never existed as a *separate* principle. Whatever reality Maya ever had is now swallowed up in the indivisible being of the one Soul. The individualized soul now knows itself to be what it has always been—eternally Self-realized, eternally infinite in knowledge, bliss, power, and existence, and eternally free from duality. But this highest form of Self-knowledge is inaccessible to the intellect, and it is incomprehensible except to those who have attained the heights of final Realization.

The Conditions of Happiness

Part I
The Overcoming of Suffering Through Detachment

Everyone seeks happiness

Every creature in the world is seeking happiness, and man is no exception. Seemingly man sets his heart on many kinds of things, but ultimately all that he desires or undertakes is for the sake of happiness. If he is keen to have power, it is because he expects to derive happiness from its use. If he strives for money, it is because he thinks it will secure the conditions and means for his happiness. If he seeks knowledge, health, or beauty, science, art, or literature, it is because he feels that his pursuit of happiness is directly dependent upon them. If he struggles for worldly success and fame, it is because he hopes to find happiness in their attainment. Through all his endeavors and pursuits, man wants to be happy. Happiness is the ultimate motive power, which drives him in all that he does.

Intertwining of pleasure and pain

Everyone seeks to be happy, yet most persons are immersed in some kind of suffering. If at times they do get small installments of happiness in their lives, it is neither unadulterated nor abiding. Their lives are never a series of unmixed pleasures. It moves between the opposites of pain and pleasure, which are entwined like darkened clouds and shining rainbows. The moments of pleasure occasionally appearing in their lives soon vanish—like rainbows, which shine in their splendor only to disappear from the sky. If these moments of pleasure leave any trace, it is of a memory that only augments the pain of having lost them. Such memory is an invariable legacy of most pleasures.

Desire bears two kinds of fruit

Man does not seek suffering, but it comes to him as an inevitable outcome of the very manner in which he seeks happiness. He seeks happiness through the fulfillment of his desires, but such fulfillment is never an assured thing. Hence in the pursuit of desires, man is also unavoidably preparing for the suffering from their nonfulfillment. The same tree of desire bears two kinds of fruit: one sweet, which is pleasure, and one bitter, which is suffering. If this tree is allowed to flourish it cannot be made to yield just one kind of fruit. Those who have bid for one kind of fruit must be ready to have the other also. Man pursues pleasure furiously and clings to it fondly when it comes. He tries to avoid the impending suffering desperately, and smarts under it with resentment. His fury and fondness are not of much avail, for his pleasure is doomed to fade and disappear one day. And his desperation and resentment are equally of no avail, for he cannot escape the suffering that results.

Changing moods

Goaded by multifarious desires, man seeks the pleasures of the world with unabating hope. His zest for pleasures does not remain unalloyed, however, because even while he is reaching for the cup of pleasure, he often has to gulp down doses of suffering. His enthusiasm for pleasure is abated by suffering, which often follows in pleasure's wake. He is subject to sudden moods and impulses. Sometimes he is happy and elated, at other times he is very unhappy and downhearted. His moods change as his desires are fulfilled or frustrated. Satisfaction of some desires yields momentary happiness; but this happiness does not last, and it soon leads to the reaction of depression. His moods subject him to ups and downs and to constant change.

Suffering caused by desires

Fulfillment of desires does not lead to their termination; they are submerged for awhile only to reappear with added intensity. When a person is hungry, he eats to satisfy the desire, but soon feels hungry again. If he eats too much, even in the fulfillment of his desire he experiences pain and discomfort. It is the same with all the desires of the world; they can only yield a happiness that is fleeting. Even in the very moment of their fulfillment, the happiness they yield has already begun to fade and vanish. Worldly desires can therefore never lead to abiding happiness. On the contrary, they invariably invite unending suffering of many kinds. When an individual is full of worldly desires, a plentiful crop of suffering is unavoidably in store for him. Desire is inevitably the cause of much suffering: this is the law.

Mitigation of desires through suffering

If a person experiences or visualizes the suffering that waits upon desires, his desires become mitigated. Sometimes intense suffering makes him detached from worldly life, but this detachment is often again set aside because of a fresh flood of desires. Many persons temporarily lose their interest in worldly objects due to the impact of acute suffering brought on by desires, but detachment must be lasting if it is to pave the way for freedom from desires. There are varying degrees of detachment, and not all of them are lasting.

Temporary detachment

Sometimes a person is greatly moved by an unusually strong experience, such as seeing someone die or witnessing a burial or a cremation. Such experiences are thought-provoking, and they initiate long trains of ideas about the futility and emptiness of worldly existence. Under the pressure of such experiences the person realizes that one day he must die and take leave of all the worldly objects so dear to him. But these thoughts, as well as the detachment born thereof, are short-lived. They are soon forgotten, and the person resumes his attachment to the world and its alluring objects. This temporary and passing mood of detachment is known as *shmashan vairagya*, cremation- or burial-ground detachment, because it usually arises when witnessing a cremation or a burial and stays in the mind only while in the presence of the dead body. Such a mood of detachment is as temporary as it is sudden. It seems to be strong and effective while it lasts, but it is only sustained by the vividness of some experience. When the experience vanishes, the mood of detachment also quickly passes, without seriously affecting one's general attitude toward life.

The passing mood of detachment might be illustrated by the story of a person who once saw at the theater a spiritual drama about

Gopichanda, the great Indian king who renounced everything in pursuit of Truth. The drama impressed him so deeply that, disregarding all his duties to his family, he joined a band of *bairagis* (wandering ascetics) belonging to the cult of Gopichanda. Renouncing all his former modes of life, he dressed as a bairagi, shaved his head, and sat under a tree, as advised by the other members of the group. At first he plunged into deep meditation, but as the heat of the sun grew stronger his enthusiasm for meditation began to cool down. As the day went on he began to feel hungry and thirsty and became very restless and miserable.

Illustrative story

When the members of his family noticed his absence from home, they became worried about him. After some searching they found him sitting under the tree in this miserable plight. He had grown haggard and was plainly unhappy. His wife seeing him in this strange condition was furious and rushed to upbraid him. His mood of detachment had flitted away; and as he was thoroughly tired of his new life, he took her reproach as a boon from heaven. So, silencing her quickly, he put on his turban and ordinary clothes and meekly followed her home.

Sometimes the mood of detachment is more lasting and not only endures for a considerable time but also seriously modifies one's general attitude toward life. This is called *tivra vairagya*, or intense dispassion. Such intense dispassion usually arises from some great misfortune—such as the loss of one's own dear ones or the loss of property or reputation. Under the influence of this wave of detachment, the person renounces all worldly things. Tivra vairagya of this type has its own spiritual value, but it is also likely to disappear in the course of time or be disturbed by the onset of a recurring flood of worldly desires. The disgust for the world that a person feels in such cases is due to a powerful impression left by a misfortune, and it does not endure because it is not born of understanding. It is only a severe reaction to life.

Intense dispassion

The kind of detachment that really lasts is due to the understanding of suffering and its cause. It is securely based upon the unshakable knowledge that all things of this world are momentary and passing, and that any clinging to them is bound eventually to be a source of pain. Man seeks worldly objects of pleasure and tries to avoid

Complete detachment

things that bring pain, without realizing that he cannot have the one and eschew the other. As long as there is attachment to worldly objects of pleasure, he must perpetually invite upon himself the suffering of not having them—and the suffering of losing them after having got them. Lasting detachment, which brings freedom from all desires and attachments, is called *purna vairagya*, or complete dispassion. Complete detachment is one of the essential conditions of lasting and true happiness. For the person who has complete detachment no longer creates for himself the suffering that is due to the unending thralldom produced by desires.

Desirelessness makes an individual firm like a rock. He is neither moved by pleasure nor by sorrow; he is not upset by the onslaughts of opposites. One who is affected by agreeable things is bound to be affected by disagreeable things. If a person is encouraged in his endeavors by an omen considered auspicious, he is bound to be discouraged by one considered to be inauspicious. He cannot resist the discouraging effect of an inauspicious omen as long as he derives strength from an auspicious one. The only way not to be upset by omens is to be indifferent to auspicious as well as inauspicious omens.

Opposites

The same is true of the opposites of praise and blame. If a person is pleased by receiving praise, he is bound to be miserable when he receives blame. He cannot keep himself steady under a shower of blame as long as he is inwardly delighted by receiving praise. The only way not to be upset by blame is to be detached from praise also. Only then can a person remain unmoved by the opposites of praise and blame. Then he does not lose his equanimity. The steadiness and equanimity that remain unaffected by any opposites is possible only through complete detachment, which is an essential condition of lasting and true happiness. The individual who has complete detachment is not at the mercy of the opposites of experience; and being free from the thralldom of all desires, he no longer creates his own suffering.

Praise and blame

Humanity is subject to much suffering, physical and mental. Of these two, mental suffering is the more acute. Those with limited vision think that suffering can only be physical. Their idea of suffering is of some kind of illness or torture of the body. Mental suffering is worse than physical suffering. Physical

Physical and mental suffering

suffering sometimes comes as a blessing because it serves the purpose of easing mental suffering by weaning away one's attention from the mental suffering.

Abiding happiness through desirelessness

It is not right to make much of purely physical suffering. It can be borne through the exercise of willpower and endurance. The true suffering that counts is mental. Even yogis who can endure great physical suffering find it difficult to keep free from mental suffering, which is rooted in the frustration of desires. If a person does not want anything, he is not unhappy under any adverse circumstances, not even in the jaws of a lion. The state of complete desirelessness is latent in everyone. And when through complete detachment one reaches the state of wanting nothing, one taps the unfailing inner source of eternal and unfading happiness—which is not based upon the objects of the world but is sustained by Self-knowledge and Self-realization.

The Conditions of Happiness

Part II
Contentment, Love, and God-Realization

Most of man's suffering is self-created through his ungoverned desires and impossible demands. All this is unnecessary for self-fulfillment. If man becomes desireless and contented, he will be free from his self-inflicted suffering. His imagination will not be constantly harassed by feverish reaching out toward things that really do not matter, and he will be established in unassailable peace. When an individual is thus contented, he does not require any solutions to problems, because the problems that confront worldly persons have disappeared. He has no problems, therefore he does not have to worry about their solution. For him the complexities of life do not exist because his life becomes utterly simple in the state of desirelessness.

Contentment free from self-created problems

When a person understands desires as being merely the bondage of the spirit, he decides to give them up; but even when voluntary, this is often a painful process. The suffering that comes from purging the mind of its many desires exists—even when the soul may be ready to renounce them—because this decision of the soul goes counter to the inclination of the ego-mind to persist through its habitual desires. Renunciation of desires curtails the very life of the ego-mind. Therefore it is a process invariably accom-

Suffering of renunciation

panied by acute suffering. But such suffering is wholesome for the soul because it liberates the soul from bondage.

Analogies

Not all suffering is bad. When suffering leads to the eternal happiness of desirelessness, it should be regarded as a blessing in disguise. Just as a patient may have to suffer an operation at the hands of a surgeon in order to free himself of persistent and malignant pain, the soul has to welcome the suffering of renouncing desires in order to be free from the recurrent and unending suffering caused by them. The suffering the soul has in renouncing desires may be very acute, but it is endured because of a sense of greater freedom that comes when desires gradually disappear from the mind. If an infected swelling on the body is opened and allowed to drain, it gives much pain, but also much relief. Similarly, the suffering from renunciation of desires is accompanied by the compensating relief of progressive initiation into the limitless life of freedom and happiness.

True nature of suffering

The simple life of freedom and happiness is one of the most difficult things to achieve. Man has complicated his life by the growth of artificial and imaginary desires, and returning to simplicity amounts to the renunciation of desires. Desires have become an essential part of the limited self of man, with the result that he is reluctant to abandon them unless the lesson that desires are born of ignorance is impressed upon his mind through acute mental suffering. When an individual is confronted with great suffering through his desires, he understands their true nature. When such suffering comes, it should be welcomed. Suffering may come in order to eliminate further suffering. A thorn may be taken out by another thorn, and suffering by suffering. Suffering has to come when it is of use in purging the soul of its desires; it is then as necessary as medicine to a sick person.

Suffering caused by dissatisfaction

However, ninety-nine percent of human suffering is not necessary. Through obstinate ignorance people inflict suffering upon themselves and their fellow beings; and then, strangely enough, they ask, "Why should we suffer?" Suffering is often symbolized by scenes of war: devastated houses, broken and bleeding limbs, the agonies of torture and death. But war does not embody any *special* suffering; people really suffer all the time. They suffer because they are not satisfied—they want more and more. War is more an outcome of the universal suffering of dissatisfaction than an embodiment of representative suffering. Through their greed, vanity, and cruelty, people bring untold suffering upon themselves and others.

People are not content to create suffering only for themselves but are relentlessly zealous in creating suffering for their fellow beings. Everyone seeks his own happiness even at the cost of the happiness of others, thus giving rise to cruelty and unending wars. As long as he thinks only of his own happiness, he does not find it. In the pursuit of his own individual happiness, the limited self becomes accentuated and burdensome. When someone is merely selfish he can, in the false pursuit of separate and exclusive happiness, become utterly callous and cruel to others; but this recoils upon him by poisoning the very spring of his life. Loveless life is most unlovely; only a life of love is worth living.

Selfish pursuit of happiness

If an individual is desireless, he will not only eliminate much suffering that he causes others but also much of his own self-created suffering. Mere desirelessness, however, cannot yield positive happiness, though it protects one from self-created suffering and goes a long way toward making true happiness possible. True happiness begins when one learns the art of right adjustment to other persons, and right adjustment involves self-forgetfulness and love. Hence arises the spiritual importance of transforming a life of the limited self into a life of love.

Happiness through self-forgetful love

Pure love is rare because in most cases love becomes adulterated with selfish motives, which are surreptitiously introduced into the consciousness by the operation of accumulated bad sanskaras. It is extremely difficult to purge the consciousness of the deep-rooted ignorance that expresses itself through the idea of "I" and "mine." For example, even when a person says that he *loves* his beloved, he often only means that he possessively *wants* the beloved to be with him. The feeling of "I" and "mine" is notably present even in the expression of love.

Selfless love is rare

If a man sees his own son wearing tattered clothes, he does all that he can to give him good clothes and is anxious to see him happy. Under these circumstances he would consider his own feeling toward his son as that of pure love. But in his quick response to the distress of his son, the part played by the idea of "mine" is by no means inconsiderable. If he happened to see the son of some stranger on the street wearing tattered clothes, he would not respond as he had in the case of his own son. This shows that though he may not be fully conscious of it, his behavior toward his own son was in fact largely selfish. The feeling of "mine" is there in the background of the mind, though it can be brought to the surface only through searching analysis. If his response to the son of a stranger is the same as to his own son, then only can he be said to have pure and selfless love.

Domain of pure love

Pure love is not a thing that can be forced upon someone, nor can it be snatched away from another by force. It has to manifest from within, with unfettered spontaneity. What *can* be achieved through bold decision is the removal of those factors that prevent the manifestation of pure love. The achievement of selflessness may be said to be both difficult and easy. It is difficult for those who have not decided to step out of the limited self, and it is easy for those who have so decided. In the absence of firm determination, attachments connected with the limited self are too strong to break through. But if a person resolves to set aside selfishness at any cost, he finds an easy entry into the domain of pure love.

Need for bold decision

The limited self is like an external coat worn by the soul. Just as an individual may take off his coat by the exercise of will, through a bold, decisive step he can make up his mind to shed the limited self and get rid of it once and for all. The task that otherwise would be difficult becomes easy through the exercise of a bold and unyielding decision. Such a decision can be born in his mind only when he feels an intense longing for pure love. Just as someone who is hungry longs for food, an aspirant who wants to experience pure love must have an intense longing for it.

True love awakened only by Master

When the aspirant has developed this intense longing for pure love, he may be said to have been prepared for the intervention of a Perfect Master—who through proper direction and necessary help ushers him into the state of divine love. Only the Master can awaken pure love through the divine love that he imparts; there is no other way. Those who want to be consumed in love should go to the eternal flame of love. Love is the most significant thing in life. It cannot be awakened except by coming into contact with the Incarnation of love. Theoretical brooding on love will result in weaving a theory about love, but the heart will remain as empty as before. Love begets love; it cannot be awakened by any mechanical means.

Love leads to God-realization

When true love is awakened in the aspirant, it leads him to the realization of God and opens up the unlimited field of lasting and unfading happiness. The happiness of God-realization is the goal of all creation. It is not possible for a person to have the slightest idea of that inexpressible happiness without actually having the experience of Godhood. The idea that the worldly have of suffering or happiness is entirely limited. The real happiness that comes through realizing God is worth all the physical and mental suffering in the universe. Then all suffering is as if it had never been.

Happiness of God-realization

Those who are not God-realized can control their minds through yoga to such an extent that nothing makes them feel pain or suffering, even if they are buried alive or thrown into boiling oil. But though the advanced yogis can brave and annul any suffering, they do not experience the happiness of realizing God. When one becomes God, everything else is zero. The happiness of God-realization, therefore, cannot suffer curtailment by anything. The happiness of God-realization is self-sustained, eternally fresh and unfading, boundless, and indescribable. It is for this happiness that the world has sprung into existence.

God as Infinite Love

Those who try to understand God through the intellect alone arrive at some cold and dry concept that misses the very essence of the nature of God. It is true that God is infinite Knowledge, infinite Existence, infinite Power, and infinite Bliss; but God is not understood in His essence until He is also understood as infinite Love. In the Beyond state, from which the entire universe springs and into which it ultimately merges, God is *eternally* infinite Love. It is only when God's love is viewed in the limited context of forms (which arise in the interim period between the appearance of the illusory universe of duality and its merging) that its infinity *seems* to have been impaired.

Essence of God is Love

When God's love experiences itself *in* and *through* the manifested forms of the universe, it goes through the following phases: (1) experiencing itself as extremely limited; (2) experiencing itself as becoming less and less limited and becoming more and more like infinite love; and (3) experiencing itself to be what it really is—infinite in essence and existence. The experience of limitation in love arises due to the ignorance caused by sanskaras, which are the by-products of the evolution of consciousness. And the process of love becoming infinite is characterized by the shedding of these limiting sanskaras.

Phases of manifest love

As love, latent in the universe, goes through the early, almost unconscious stages of the various kingdoms, it gradually makes its appearance as lust in the animal kingdom. Its appearance in human consciousness is initially also in the form of lust. Lust is the most

Love as lust

limited form of love in human consciousness. In spite of the clear reference lust has to other persons, it is indistinguishable from undiluted selfishness, because all the objects lust clings to are desired for the sake of and from the viewpoint of the limited and separate self. At the same time, it is a form of love because it has in it some kind of appreciation for others, though this appreciation is completely vitiated by thick ignorance about the true Self.

Love in gross sphere

When human consciousness is completely caught up in the duality of the gross sphere of existence, love cannot express itself as anything other than lust of some type. One may like curry because it tickles one's palate. There are no higher considerations, so it is a form of lust. It is only a craving for the sensations of taste. Mind also has cravings for the bodily sensations of sight, smell, sound, and touch; and it nourishes its crude ego-life through the excitement derived from these sensations. Lust of every type is an entanglement with gross forms, independent of the spirit behind them. It is an expression of mere attachment to sensual objects.

Since in all forms of lust the heart remains unfed and unexpressed, it becomes a perpetual vacuum and is in a state of unending suffering and nonfulfillment. Love that expresses itself as undiluted or one hundred percent lust is in a state of extreme limitation because it is helplessly caught up in ceaseless craving. When the heart is in the clutches of lust, the spirit remains, as it were, in a state of delusion or stupor. Its functioning is severely curtailed and perverted by the limiting ignorance it is subject to. Its higher potentialities are denied expression and fulfillment, and this thwarting and suppression of the life of the spirit entails a state of utter bondage.

In lust Infinity asserts itself indirectly

Lust is the most limited form of love functioning under the thralldom of ignorance. The unambiguous stamp of insufficiency that lust invariably bears is in itself a sign that it is an incomplete and inadequate expression of something deeper that is vast and unlimited. Through the manifold and unending sufferings that are attendant upon undiluted lust and the continued experiences of the frustration it brings, the spirit is ceaselessly registering its unyielding protest against the utter superficiality of a life of unqualified lust. In this manner the irrepressible voice of the infinity of God's love indirectly asserts the imperative claims of its unexpressed but unimpaired reality.

Stages of love

Even in the lowest lustful life of the gross sphere, God is experiencing Himself as a lover; but it is the state of a lover who is completely ignorant about the true nature of himself or of God the Beloved. It is the state of a lover who is inexorably separated from the divine Beloved by an opaque curtain of ununderstood duality. It is nevertheless the beginning of a long process by which the lover breaks through the enveloping curtain of ignorance and comes into his own truth as unbounded and unhampered Love. But in order to get initiated into infinite love, the lover has to go through two other stages that are characteristic of the subtle and mental spheres.

Love in subtle sphere

The lover in the subtle sphere is not free from lust, but the lust he experiences is not undiluted as in the gross sphere. The intensity of lust in the subtle sphere is about half that in the gross sphere. Besides, there is no gross expression of lust as in the gross sphere. The lover in the gross sphere is inextricably entangled with gross objects; hence lust finds gross expression. However, the lover in the subtle sphere has gotten free from attachment to gross objects; hence in this case lust remains unexpressed in its gross form. This lust has subtle expressions, but it cannot have gross expressions. Moreover, since about half of the original lust of the gross sphere gets sublimated in the subtle sphere, the lover in the subtle sphere experiences love not as undiluted lust but in a higher form—as longing to be united with the Beloved.

Love as longing

In the gross sphere, then, love expresses itself as lust, and in the subtle sphere it expresses itself as longing. Lust is a craving for sensations and as such is completely selfish in motive. It has utter disregard for the well-being of the worldly beloved. In longing there is less selfishness; and though it continues to be possessive in a way, the object of love is recognized as having infinite worth and importance. Longing is a less limited form of love than lust. In longing the curtain of duality has become more transparent and less obstructive, since the lover now consciously seeks to overcome duality between the lover and the Beloved by yearning for His presence. In lust the emphasis is solely on the limited self, and the worldly beloved is completely subsidiary to the gross needs of the self. In longing the emphasis is equally distributed on the self and on the divine Beloved; and the lover realizes that he exists for the Beloved, just in the same way as the Beloved exists for him.

Love in mental sphere

The lover in the mental sphere has an even higher and freer expression of love. In this case, though lust has not completely disappeared, it is mostly sublimated. Only about one-fourth of the original lust of the gross sphere remains, but it remains in a latent form without any expression. In the mental sphere, lust does not have even subtle expression. The lover in the mental sphere is detached from subtle objects; and he is free from possessive longing for the object of love, which is characteristic of the lover in the subtle sphere.

Love as resignation

In the mental sphere love expresses itself as complete resignation to the will of God, the Beloved. All selfish desire, including longing for the presence of the Beloved, has disappeared, as now the emphasis is solely on the worth and will of the Beloved and to be united with Him. Selfishness is utterly wiped out, and there is a far more abundant release of love in its pure form. However, even in the mental sphere love has not become infinite, since there is still present the thin curtain of duality that separates the lover from the Beloved. Love is no longer in the clutches of selfishness; but it is still short of being infinite because it is experienced through the medium of the finite mind—just as in the lower spheres it is experienced through the medium of the lower bodies.

Divine love is infinite

Love becomes consciously infinite in being as well as in expression when the individual mind is transcended. Such love is rightly called divine, because it is characteristic of the God state in which all duality is finally overcome. In divine love, lust has completely disappeared. It does not exist even in latent form. Divine love is unlimited in essence and expression because it is experienced by the soul through the Soul itself. In the gross, subtle, and mental spheres, the lover is conscious of being separated from God, the Beloved; but when all these spheres are transcended, the lover is conscious of his unity with the Beloved. The lover loses himself in the being of the

Beloved and knows that he is one with the Beloved. Divine love is entirely free from the thralldom of desires or the limiting self. In this state of Infinity the lover has no being apart from the Beloved: he is the Beloved Himself.

Divine romance

One thus has God, as infinite Love, first limiting Himself in the forms of creation and then recovering His infinity through the different stages of creation. All the stages of God's experience of being a finite lover ultimately culminate in His experiencing Himself as the sole Beloved. The sojourn of the soul is a thrilling divine romance in which the lover—who in the beginning is conscious of nothing but emptiness, frustration, superficiality, and the gnawing chains of bondage—gradually attains an increasingly fuller and freer expression of love. And ultimately the lover disappears and merges in the divine Beloved to realize the unity of the lover and the Beloved in the supreme and eternal fact of God as infinite Love.

Epilogue

Twelve Ways of Realizing Me

1. **Longing**
If you experience that same longing and thirst for union with Me as one who has been lying for days in the hot sun of the Sahara experiences the longing for water, then you will realize Me.

2. **Peace of mind**
If you have the peace of a frozen lake, then too you will realize Me.

3. **Humility**
If you have the humility of earth, which can be molded into any shape, then you will know Me.

4. **Desperation**
If you experience the desperation that causes a person to commit suicide and you feel that you cannot live without seeing Me, then you will see Me.

5. **Faith**
If you have the complete faith that Kalyan had in his Master—in believing it was night although it was day because his Master said so—then you will know Me.

6. **Fidelity**
If you have the fidelity that your breath has in keeping you company till the end of your life—even without your constantly feeling it, both in happiness and suffering, never turning against you—then you will know Me.

7. **Control through love**

When your love for Me drives away your lust for the things of the senses, then you will realize Me.

8. **Selfless service**

If you have the quality of selfless service unaffected by results similar to that of the sun, which serves the world by shining on all creation—on the grass in the field, on the birds in the air, on the beasts in the forest, on all of mankind with its sinners and saints, its rich and poor—unmindful of the attitude toward it, then you will win Me.

9. **Renunciation**

If you renounce for Me everything physical, mental, and spiritual, then you will have Me.

10. **Obedience**

If your obedience is as spontaneous, complete, and natural as light is to the eye or smell to the nose, then you will come to Me.

11. **Surrenderance**

If your surrenderance to Me is as wholehearted as that of one who, suffering from insomnia, surrenders to sudden sleep without fear of being lost, then you will have Me.

12. **Love**

If you have that love for Me that Saint Francis had for Jesus, then not only will you realize Me but you will please Me.

—Meher Baba

Glossary

The Glossary is divided into two parts. Part I lists terms used in the text of the *Discourses* and includes all non-English words, names, and selected English terms that call for clarification of their usage. Part II is a brief list of non-English terms and names that commonly appear in other Meher Baba literature.

Most of the non-English terms in the Glossary are from either the Sufi or Vedanta traditions (*Sufism* and *Vedanta* are defined in Part I) and are labeled accordingly by the abbreviation "S." or "V." respectively. The Sufi terms have their origins in the Arabic and Persian languages. The terms drawn from the Vedanta tradition are derived from Sanskrit. Corresponding forms are given for both traditions when appropriate. Words that come from outside these two traditions are labeled by the language of their origin.

Definitions. The terms are defined according to the sense and meaning used by Meher Baba, which may differ occasionally from commonly accepted or traditional usage.

Spelling. The spelling of non-English terms is generally the form used in *God Speaks;* this decision necessitated some changes in the spellings used in earlier editions of the *Discourses* for the sake of consistency. Since the spellings are not phonetic nor based on a scientific scheme of romanization, the pronunciation guide and the phonetic transcriptions should be consulted. Words are entered in the singular or plural depending on the predominant form found in the text; the opposite form is given when appropriate. Plurals of non-

English terms have usually been made by adding the English plural suffix "–s."

Cross-references. There are numerous cross-references in the Glossary, indicated by *see, see also, see under, cf.,* and *q.v.* These will lead the reader either *from* variant or corresponding terms or *to* related ones, under which full or additional information is given.

Bold type. When a term is printed in **bold** type within a definition, it indicates that the reader should also refer to that term for its own full definition.

Abbreviations and symbols used in the Glossary: *adj.,* adjective; *Ar.,* Arabic; *ca.,* circa; *cf.,* compare, confer; *d.,* died; *fem.,* feminine; *lit.,* literally; *Mar.,* Marathi; *Pers.,* Persian; *pl.,* plural; *pron.,* pronounced; *q.v.,* which see; *S.,* Sufi; *sing.,* singular; *Skt.,* Sanskrit; *V.,* Vedanta; *var.,* variant spelling or form. The slant or slash (/) between two words denotes "and/or," indicating variant usage or forms found in the text; a word enclosed within two slants is the phonetic transcription of the preceding term.

Pronunciation. The following guidelines are based on English pronunciation as far as possible. Complete accuracy in phonetic transcription has been sacrificed for greater simplicity. Many of the more subtle sound distinctions between and within the various languages often had to be disregarded. The principle aim of the guide is to provide the reader with an approximation of correct pronunciation and stress of terms drawn from a variety of linguistic origins. The vowels and consonants listed below describe only those sounds that actually occur in the Glossary and do not represent all the possibilities in any of the languages concerned.

Pronunciation Guide

Consonants that are pronounced as in English:

b, d, f, j, k, l, m, n, p, t, v, w, y, z

Consonants needing special comment:

bh	b-h in *rob him,* said quickly.
ch	ch in *church.*
dh	dh in *adhere.*
g	always as g in go.
gh	gutteral g, pron. far back in the throat, similar to r in Parisian French.

h	as in English but also sounded when occurring at the end of a syllable.
kh	gutteral k, as ch in Scottish *loch* or German *ach.*
q	k pron. as far back in the throat as possible, but not gutteral.
r	lightly rolled.
s, ss	always as s in *see, cross.*
sh	sh in *show.*
th (t'h)	t-h in *but he,* said quickly (never as in *the* or *thin*); the apostrophe is added in phonetic transcriptions.

Doubled consonants should be sounded nearly twice as long as single consonants, e.g., *Shakkar* is pron. more as shák-kar than shá-kar.

Vowels used in phonetic transcriptions:

a	a in *about, tuna;* final a in Vedantic/Indic terms is often silent, resulting in the variant spellings where the final a is dropped.
aa	a in *father, star.*
ai	ai in *aisle.*
ar	closer to a in *around* than in *far.*
au	ow in *how.*
ay	a in *fate, say,* but without a diphthong glide into ee.
e	e in *net.*
ee	ee in *sweet.*
i	i in *sit;* final i as y in *fancy.*
ir	as in *ear.*
o	o in *old*
oo	oo in *pool.*
u	u in *full.*

Stress. Primary stress is indicated by an acute accent (′) above the stressed vowel or diphthong, e.g., dáaman. Secondary stress in compounds spelled as one word is indicated by a grave accent (‵), e.g., Maháabhàarata.

The Glossary has been compiled by the Editors and designed and formatted by the Publisher.

Part I
Terms Used in the Text of the Discourses

abdal (S.) (*sing./pl.*):spiritually advanced souls who can take different physical forms at will.
Pron.: abdáal.

Abraham: the Prophet; the Patriarch. In the Koranic story, Abraham (Ibrahim) is called upon to sacrifice his son Ishmael (Ismail); in the Bible he is called upon to sacrifice his son Isaac.

abrar. See **wali.**

Absolute Vacuum state. See **Nirvana.**

adhyatma-marga (V.): the inner **path** of spiritual advancement.
Pron.: adhyáatma máarga. *Var.:* adhyatmic marga. Also V.: moksha-marga /móksha máarga/.S.: **tariqat.**

ahadiyat. See under **vidnyani sanskaras.**

Aham Brahmasmi (V.): "I am the Reality"; the affirmation of the God-realized state.
Pron.: ahám brahmáasmi. S.: **Anal Haqq.** See also **"I am God"; Realization.**

Aikya. See **Union; Vasl.**

alam-e-jabrut. See **mental sphere.**

alam-e-malakut. See **subtle sphere.**

alam-e-nasut. See **gross sphere.**

amavasya (Skt.): the darkest night of the lunar month.
Pron.: amaaváasya.

Anal Haqq (S.): "I am the Reality"; the affirmation of the God-realized state.
Pron.: anáal haq (sounds like "hock"). V.: **Aham Brahmasmi.** See also **"I am God"; Realization.**

anna bhuvan. See **gross sphere.**

anwaya (V.): synthetic activity of the mind; connective process.
Pron.: ánwaiya.

Arjuna. See under **Krishna.**

aspirant. See **sadhak; yogi.**

astral body: the form that experiences the astral world, which serves as a link between the **gross** and **subtle** worlds.
See also **semisubtle world.** (For further information see *God Speaks.*)

atma (V.): the soul.
Pron.: áatma. *Var.:* atman. S.: jan /jaan/; ruh /rooh/.

Atmapratisthapana. See **Sahaj Samadhi.**

Aum. See under **Om Point.**

Avatar, the (*also* Avatarhood, Avataric) (V.): the total manifestation of God in human form on earth, as the Eternal Living **Perfect Master;** the direct descent of Reality into Illusion; the Savior, the Highest of the High, the Ancient One. Also called the **God-Man,** the **Messiah,** the **Buddha,** the **Christ,** the **Rasool.**
Pron.: avatáar *or* ávataar. *Var.:* Avatara. S.: Saheb-e-Zaman /sáaheb ay zamáan/.

Azad-e-Mutlaq. See **Jivanmuktas.**

Baba Farid/Fariduddin. See **Ganj-e-Shakkar.**

Bahlul: a Persian king who left all and became a great mystic.
Pron.: báahlool.

bairagi (Hindi) (*pl.*–s): wandering ascetics or renunciates.
Pron.: báiraagi (–z).

Baqah-Billah. See **Sahaj Samadhi.**

Beyond state: a state of God beyond time and space; also the highest state, in which God in manifested form is infinitely conscious of both Reality and Illusion. (See *God Speaks* for further information).

Bhagavad Gita. See under **Krishna.**

bhakta (V.) (*pl.*-s): a devotee.
Pron.: bhákta (-z).

bhakti (V.): devotion or love.
Pron.: bhákti. See also **para-bhakti.**

bhas (V.) (*sing.*): illusion.
Pron.: bhaass. *Var.:* bhasa. Cf. **Maya.**

Bible. See under **Abraham; Jesus Christ.**

Brahmi Bhoots. See **Majzoobs-e-Kamil.**

Buddha: Gautama Buddha, the Enlightened One; the **Avatar** (q.v.) whose teachings come to us through Buddhism.
Pron.: búddha; gáutama búddha. *Var.:* Siddhartha Gautama.

Buddha, the: the Enlightened One, the **Avatar** (q.v. for full definition).
Pron.: búddha.

causal body. See **karan sharir; manas; mental body.**

Chishti, Muinuddin, Khwaja: 12th century **Sufi Perfect Master** of Ajmer, India.
Pron.: chíshti, muéenuddìn, khwáaja. *Var.:* Khwaja Saheb; Moenuddin Chisti.

Christ, the: the **Messiah,** the **Savior,** the **Avatar** (q.v. for full definition). See also **Jesus Christ.**

Christianity. See under **Jesus Christ.**

consciousness, planes of. See **planes of consciousness.**

Creation Point. See **Om Point.**

darshan (V.): the act of seeing; folding of hands in adoration or bowing at the feet to express devotion to the one worshipped; silent audience with **saints** and **Masters;** public veneration.
Pron.: dárshan. *Var.:* darshana.

dharma shastra. See under **karma-kanda.**

divine powers. See **occult experiences/powers; siddhis.**

dnyan (V.): knowledge; knowledge of spiritual truths; gnosis.
Pron.: dnyaan (soft d). *Var.:* dnyana; jnana. S.: irfan /irfáan/. See also under **vidnyani sanskaras.**

ego-mind: the seat of individuality (i.e., the individualized soul) that experiences the impressions through the **gross, subtle,** and **mental** bodies.

Emancipation. See under **Freedom.**

enchantment. See **hairat.**

enlightenment. See **Illumination.**

Everything, the: God, the Infinite; the Everything, being infinite, includes the **Nothing.**

fana (S.) (*pl.*-s): annihilation, dissolution; the annihilation of some aspect of the false self (ego), which precedes entering each **plane of consciousness.**
Pron.: fanáa (-z).

fana-e-batili (S.): annihilation of the false; the merging into the second **plane of consciousness.**
Pron.: fanáa ay báatili.

fana-e-jabruti (S.): annihilation of all desires; the merging into the fifth **plane of consciousness.**
Pron.: fanáa ay jabróoti. *Var.:* fana-e-jabaruti.

fana-e-mahabubi (S.): annihilation of the self (lover) in the Beloved (God); the merging into the sixth **plane of consciousness.**
Pron.: fanáa ay mahabóobi.

fana-e-malakuti (S.): annihilation leading toward freedom; the merging into the fourth **plane of consciousness.**
Pron.: fanáa ay malakóoti.

fana-e-zahiri (S.): annihilation of the apparent; the merging into the third **plane of consciousness,**

where one experiences **videh samadhi,** or the state of divine coma.

Pron.: fanáa ay záahiri. *Var.:* fana-e-zaheri.

Fana-Fillah (S.): the **"I am God"** state of the **Perfect Ones;** final annihilation of the false self in God; the final merging into the seventh **plane of consciousness.**

Pron.: fanáa filláah. V.: **Nirvikalpa state.** See also **Realization.**

Fana, final. See under **Nirvana.**

Francis, Saint (1181 or 2–1226): of Assisi /aasséezi/, Italy.

Freedom: the release from the bondage of births and deaths (reincarnation); Emancipation. See also **Liberation; Mukti.**

Ganj-e-Shakkar (*also* Baba Fariduddin): the well-known **wali** who was trapped in the state of enchantment (**hairat**) but was finally led on to become a **Perfect Master** by his Master, Khwaja Muinuddin **Chishti.**

Pron.: ganj ay shákkar; báabaa faréeduddìn. *Var.:* Baba Farid Ganje-Shakar.

Ghausali Shah: a Muslim saint of northern India.

Pron.: ghausáali shaah. *Var.:* Ghousali Shah.

God-intoxicated, the. See **masts; unmatta.**

God-Man: the direct descent of God on earth in human form; God-become-man; the **Avatar** (q.v. for full definition). See also **Man-God.**

God-realization. See **Realization.**

God state: a state of God; the state in which the soul experiences itself as God.

Gopichanda: the great Indian king who renounced everything in pursuit of Truth.

Pron.: gópichanda.

gross body/form: the physical body or form, which functions in the **gross sphere.**

S.: jism-e-kasif /jism ay kaséef/. V.: **sharir; sthul sharir.**

gross sphere/world: the world of matter; the visible and invisible worlds in creation, which can be experienced by the **gross body** through one's dense, gross impressions.

S.: alam-e-nasut /áalam ay naasóot/. V.: anna bhuvan /ánna bhúvan/; sthul bhuvan /st'hul bhúvan/.

hairat (S.): enchantment.

Pron.: háirat.

haram (S.): forbidden or prohibited, in Islam.

Pron.: haráam.

Hinduism. See under **Krishna; Rama; Vedanta.**

"I am God": the affirmation of the God-realized state.

S.: **Anal Haqq.** V.: **Aham Brahmasmi.** See also **Realization.**

Ignorance. See **Maya.**

Illumination: the state of spiritual enlightenment in which the mind sees the Soul (God) but has not realized God. Cf. **Realization.**

Illusion. See **bhas; Maya.**

impressions. See **sanskaras.**

Insan-e-Kamil. See **Perfect One.**

involution of consciousness, planes of. See **planes of consciousness.**

irfan. See **dnyan.**

Ishmael and Isaac. See under **Abraham.**

Islam. See under **Muhammad, the Prophet; Sufism.**

Jalaluddin Rumi. See **Rumi, Jalaluddin, Maulana.**

Jami (1414–1492): Persian poet and mystic.

Pron.: jáami.

jan. See **atma.**

Jesus Christ: the Son of God; the **Avatar** (q.v.) whose teachings come to us through Christianity and the New Testament of the Bible. See also **Christ, the.**

jism-e-altaf. See **karan sharir; manas; mental body.**

jism-e-kasif. See **gross body; sharir; sthul sharir.**

jism-e-latif. See **pran; subtle body; sukshma sharir.**

Jivanmuktas (V.) (*sing.* Jivanmukta): those who have attained the **"I am God"** state with creation-consciousness but are free of spiritual duties; liberated incarnate souls.

Pron.: jèevanmúktaz. S.: Azad-e-Mutlaq (*sing.*) /áazaad ay mútlaq/; Salik-e-Kamil (*sing.*) /sáalik ay káamil/.

Jivanmukti. See under **Mukti.**

jnana. See **dnyan.**

Kabir (1440–1518): **Perfect Master** and poet of northern India.

Pron.: kabéer.

Kalyan: (1) favorite disciple of the Perfect Master Swami **Ramdas Samarth,** mentioned in the discourse "True Discipleship"; (2) Kalyan (mentioned in the "Epilogue: Twelve Ways of Realizing Me"), also known as Kamal, favorite disciple of **Kabir**, the Perfect Master.

Pron.: kalyáan; kamáal.

Kamal. See under **Kalyan.**

karan sharir (V.): the causal or **mental body;** the seat of the mind.

Pron.: káaran sharéer. *Var.:* karana sharira. S.: jism-e-altaf /jism ay altáaf/. See also **manas.**

karma (V.) (*adj.* karmic): action, work; effect; fate. The natural and necessary happenings in one's life, preconditioned by one's past lives.

Pron.: káarma *or* kárma.

karma-kanda (V.): external conformity and adherence to dharma shastra (religious injunctions and traditions); orthodoxy.

Pron.: kárma káanda; dhárma sháastra. S.: **shariat.**

karma-yoga (V.): the **yoga** of selfless action; yoga through the selfless performance of duties.

Pron.: kárma yóga.

karma-yogi (V.): one who practices the **yoga** of selfless action.

Pron.: kárma yógi. *Var.:* karmayogin.

kasturi-mriga (Skt.): musk deer; a deer whose navel yields musk.

Pron.: kastóori mréega.

Kauravas. See under **Krishna.**

Khwaja Saheb. See **Chishti, Muinuddin, Khwaja.**

Koran. See under **Abraham; Muhammad, the Prophet.**

Krishna: the **Avatar** (q.v.) whose history is narrated in the Hindu epic the Mahabharata and whose teachings come to us through Hinduism. His discourse to the warrior Arjuna just before battle against the Kauravas is known as the Bhagavad Gita.

Pron.: kríshna; maháabhàarata; arjóona; káuravaz (*pl.*); bhagavád géetaa. See also **Radha-Krishna.**

Kutub. See **Qutub.**

lahar (V.): impulse; wave, ripple; the whim of God that caused creation.

Pron.: lahár. *Var.:* lahari.

Layla. See **Majnun and Layla.**

Liberation: release from the cycle of births and deaths (reincarnation).

S.: Najat /najáat/. V.: **Moksha; Mukti.** See also **Freedom.**

Mahabharata. See under **Krishna.**

Mahapralaya (V.): the great dissolution of creation at the end of a cosmic cycle.

Pron.: maháapràlaiya. S.: Qiamat /qiyáamat/.

mahapurush. See **wali.**

Majnun and Layla: the Islamic tale of Majnun's one-pointed love for Layla has its origins in Arabia and is thought to be based on a true story.

Pron.: majnóon; láyla. *Var.:* Majnu; Laila; Leila.

Majzoobiyat. See **Videh Mukti.**

Majzoob-Saliks. See **Paramhansas.**

Majzoobs-e-Kamil (S.) (*sing.* Majzoob-e-Kamil): God-merged souls of the seventh **plane of consciousness** who are divinely absorbed and overpowered but who retain the **gross body** for a time.

Pron.: majzóobz ay káamil. *Var.:* Majzubs. V.: Brahmi Bhoots /bráhmi bhoots/; Videh Muktas /vidáyh múktaz/.

manas (V.) (*sing.*): *lit.* mind; the causal or **mental body**; the seat of the mind.

Pron.: mánass. *Var.:* mana. S.: jism-e-altaf /jism ay altáaf/. See also **karan sharir.**

Man-God: man-become-God; a **Perfect Master** (q.v. for full definition).

S.: **Qutub; Salik-e-Mukammil.** V.: Param Mukta /páram múkta/; **Sadguru.** See also **God-Man.**

mano bhuvan. See **mental sphere.**

Manonash. See **Nirvana.**

Master: the term most frequently used throughout the text for **Perfect Master** (q.v. for full definition), **Man-God,** or **Sadguru.**

Var.: Masters of wisdom.

Masters of wisdom. See **Master; Perfect Master.**

masts (S.) (*sing.* mast; *fem. sing.* mastani): souls on the spiritual **path** experiencing the state of God-intoxication (masti).

Pron.: masts (rhymes with "trusts"); mastáani; másti. See also **unmatta.**

Maya (V.) (*adj.* mayavic): Illusion, Ignorance; the shadow of God.

Pron.: máiyaa; maiyáavik. S.: Mejaz /mejáaz/. Cf. **bhas.**

Mejaz. See **Maya.**

mental body/form: the causal body, which functions in the **mental sphere;** the seat of the mind.

S.: jism-e-altaf /jism ay altáaf/. V.: **karan sharir; manas.** See also **ego-mind.**

mental sphere/world: the sphere consisting of the fifth and sixth **planes of consciousness** as experienced by the **mental body** through one's mental impressions, which are finer and more feeble (i.e., much less dense) than the subtle impressions.

S.: alam-e-jabrut /áalam ay jabróot/. V.: mano bhuvan /máno bhúvan/.

Messiah, the: the expected Savior; the **Avatar** (q.v. for full definition).

Moksha (V.): ordinary **Mukti,** or the **Liberation** achieved by most souls, i.e., the release from the cycle of births and deaths (reincarnation).

Pron.: móksha. S.: Najat /najáat/.

moksha-marga. See **adhyatma-marga.**

Muhammad, the Prophet: the **Rasool;** the **Avatar** (q.v.) whose teachings come to us through Islam and the Koran.

Pron.: muháammad. *Var.:* Mohammed.

Muinuddin Chishti. See **Chishti, Muinuddin, Khwaja.**

mujahida. See **sadhana.**

mukam-e-afasan. See **muqam-e-afsan.**

Mukta. See under **Mukti.**

Mukti (V.): **Liberation;** the release from the cycle of births and deaths (reincarnation). There are four types of Mukti: (1) ordinary Mukti, or **Moksha;** (2) **Videh Mukti;** (3) Jivanmukti, of the **Jivanmuktas;** (4) Param Mukti, of the **Perfect Masters.**

Pron.: múkti; jèevanmúkti; páram múkti. S.: Najat /najáat/.

muqaddar. See **prarabdha.**

muqam. See under **muqam-e-afsan.**

muqam-e-afsan (S.): abode of delusion; the illusion of being at the end of the spiritual **path** when one is still traversing it.

Pron.: muqáam ay afsáan. *Var.:* mukam-e-afasan. (muqam: a station or place. V.: sthan /st'haan/.)

mystic powers. See **occult experiences/powers; siddhis.**

Najat. See **Liberation; Moksha; Mukti.**

neti neti (V.): *lit.* not-this, not-this; the principle of negation.

Pron.: náyti náyti

Nirvana (V.): total and final absorption in divinity (God); annihilation of the mind (self); the Absolute Vacuum state; the first stage of the final **Fana.**

Pron.: nirváana. Also V.: Manonash /manonáash/.

Nirvikalpa Samadhi (V.): divinity in expression; the experience of the **"I am God"** state of the **Perfect Ones.**

Pron.: nirvikálpa samáadhi.

Nirvikalpa state (V.): the **"I am God"** state of the **Perfect Ones.**

Pron.: nirvikálpa. S.: **Fana-Fillah.** See also **Realization.**

Nothing, the: the infinite shadow of the **Everything** (God).

nuqush-e-amal. See **sanskaras.**

occult: beyond the range of ordinary experience; hidden, concealed, not revealed; psychic, supernatural.

occult experiences/powers: experiences and powers that occur in the **gross** and **semisubtle** spheres, including the **astral world.** On the first three **planes of consciousness** (q.v.), the occult powers are known as mystic powers. The powers of the fourth plane are the divine, almighty powers of God.

See also **siddhis.** (For further information see *God Speaks.*)

occultism: occult theory or practice; belief in or study of the action or influence of occult or supernatural powers and forces.

occultism as an art: applied occultism; the use of occult powers, especially for spiritual purposes.

occultism as a science: the study of occult phenomena.

Om Point (V.): Creation Point; the point from which all creation springs.

(Om: the primal, oceanic sound at the beginning of creation; the sacred syllable. *Pron.:* om. *Var.:* Aum.)

Oversoul: the supreme, universal Soul; Almighty God.

Var.: Over-Soul. V.: **Paramatma.** See also Glossary Part II under **Ahuramazda; Allah; Yezdan.**

para-bhakti (V.): divine love.

Pron.: paráa bhákti.

Paramatma (V.): the **Oversoul** (q.v.); the supreme, universal Soul; Almighty God.

Pron.: pàramáatma. *Var.:* Paramatman.

Paramhansas (V.) (*sing.* Paramhansa): **Perfect Ones** who are sometimes totally absorbed in God (called Majzoob-Saliks) and at other times conscious of creation (called Salik-Majzoobs).

Pron.: pàramhánsaz (nasalized n). *Var.:* Paramahansas. S.: Majzoob-Saliks /majzóob sáaliks/; Salik-Majzoobs /sáalik majzóobz/.

Param Mukta. See **Perfect Master.**

Param Mukti. See under **Mukti.**

path, the: the inner path of spiritual advancement that the aspirant traverses through the **planes of consciousness** (q.v.).

S.: **tariqat.** V.: **adhyatma-marga.**

Perfect Master: a **Man-God.** A God-realized soul who retains God-consciousness and creation-consciousness simultaneously, and who works in creation to help other souls toward the **Realization** of God. Referred to most frequently throughout the text simply as **"Master."**

Var.: Masters of wisdom. S.: **Qutub; Salik-e-Mukammil.** V.: Param Mukta /páram múkta/; **Sadguru.**

Perfect One: one who has realized God and attained **Perfection** in human form.

S.: Insan-e-Kamil /insáan ay káamil/. V.: Shiv-Atma /shiv áatma/.

Perfection: a state of God-realization.

See also **Realization.**

planes of consciousness (*also* planes of involution of consciousness): the states of consciousness experienced by the soul while traversing the spiritual **path**. During the first six planes, the soul gradually withdraws the focus of its consciousness from the **gross sphere** to the **subtle sphere** and then to the **mental sphere:** this is involution. At the seventh plane the soul experiences **Realization** and knows itself to be God.

(See *God Speaks* for further information.)

prakriti (V.): the phenomenal world; creation. Also, the unmanifest cosmic energy that in conjunction with **Purusha** generates phenomenal existence.

Pron.: prakríti.

pran (V.): vital energy; the **subtle body** (the seat of desires and vital forces).

Pron.: praan. *Var.:* prana. S.: jism-e-latif /jism ay latéef/. See also **sukshma sharir.**

pran bhuvan. See **subtle sphere**.

prarabdha (*also* prarabdha sanskaras) (V.): the inevitable destiny of each lifetime; the impressions (**sanskaras**) that predetermine the destiny of a person.

Pron.: práarabdha (sanskáaraz). S.: muqaddar /muqáddar/.

psychic. See under **occult.**

purna vairagya (V.): complete dispassion or detachment; total renunciation.

Pron.: póorna vairáagya.

Purusha (V.): the supreme Spirit, which in conjunction with **prakriti** causes phenomenal existence.

Pron.: purúsha. *Var.:* Purush.

Qiamat. See **Mahapralaya.**

Qutub (S.): *lit.* hub or axis; the spiritual center of the universe; a **Perfect Master** (q.v. for full definition).

Pron.: qútub. *Var.:* Kutub; Qutb. Also S.: **Salik-e-Mukammil.** V.: Param Mukta /páram múkta/; **Sadguru.**

Radha-Krishna: Radha was the milkmaid whose unsurpassed love for the Lord **Krishna** (q.v.) earned her the status of being His beloved.

Pron.: ráadhaa kríshna.

rah-e-tariqat. See **tariqat.**

rahrav. See **sadhak; yogi.**

Rama: the **Avatar** (q.v.) whose life is the subject of the Hindu epic the Ramayana and whose teachings come to us through Hinduism.

Pron.: ráama; raamáayana. *Var.:* Ram. See also **Sita-Ram.**

Ramdas Samarth, Swami: 17th century **Perfect Master.**

Pron.: ráamdaass samárt'h, swáami. *Var.:* Swami Ramdas.

Rasool (S.): the Messenger of

God; the **Avatar** (q.v. for full definition).

Pron.: rasóol. See also **Muhammad, the Prophet.**

Realization (*also* God-realization, Self-realization): when the soul experiences itself as God; the **"I am God"** state.

S.: **Fana-Fillah.** V.: **Nirvikalpa state.**

rishis (V.) (*sing.* rishi): sages; seers.

Pron.: ríshiz.

ruh. See **atma.**

Rumi, Jalaluddin, Maulana (*ca.* 1207–1273): **Sufi Perfect Master** and Persian poet; originator of dervish dancing and disciple of **Shams-e-Tabriz.**

Pron.: róomi, jaláaluddin, mauláana. *Var.:* Jalal ad-Din ar-Rumi; Maulana Rumi.

Sadguru (V.) (*pl.* -s): Guide to the Truth; a **Perfect Master** (q.v. for full definition).

Pron.: sádguru (-z). S.: **Qutub; Salik-e-Mukammil.** Also V.: Param Mukta /páram múkta/.

sadhak (V.): an aspirant; one who traverses the spiritual **path.**

Pron.: sáadhak. *Var.:* sadhaka. S.: rah-rav /ráahrav (soft v)/. See also **yogi.**

sadhana (V.) (*pl.* -s): practice, striving, endeavor; directing toward the goal.

Pron.: sáadhana (-z). S.: mujahida /mujáahida/.

Sahaj Samadhi (V.): the spontaneous experience of the **Perfect Masters** and the **Avatar** of their effortless and continuous life of **Perfection;** divinity in action.

Pron.: saháj samáadhi. S.: Baqa-Billah /baqáa billáah/. Also V.: Atmapratisthapana /àatmapratistʹháapana/.

Sahajawastha (V.): the effortless state of infinite consciousness with unlimited spontaneity and uninterrupted Self-knowledge.

Pron.: sahajáawastʹhàa.

sahavas (V.) (*sing./pl.*): dwelling together; in the company of.

Pron.: sahaváass (soft h). *Var.:* sahavasa.

Saheb-e-Zaman. See **Avatar, the.**

saint: one eminent for piety or virtue; a spiritually advancing soul on the inner **planes of consciousness.** (See *God Speaks* for further information.)

Salik-e-Kamil. See **Jivanmuktas.**

Salik-e-Mukammil (S.): a supremely **Perfect One; a Perfect Master** (q.v. for full definition).

Pron.: sáalik ay mukámmil. Also S.: **Qutub.** V.: Param Mukta /páram múkta/; **Sadguru.**

Salik-Majzoobs. See **Paramhansas.**

samadhi (V.) (*pl.* -s): meditative trance; absorption, union.

Pron.: samáadhi (-z). See also **Nirvikalpa Samadhi; Sahaj Samadhi; videh samadhi.** Cf. **samadhi** (tomb), Glossary Part II.

Samarth, Swami Ramdas. See **Ramdas Samarth, Swami.**

sanskaras (V.) (*sing.* sanskara; *adj.* sanskaric): impressions; accumulated imprints of past experiences, which determine one's desires and actions.

Pron.: sanskáaraz. *Var.:* samskara. S.: nuqush-e-amal (*pl.*) /nuqóosh ay aamáal. See also **prarabdha sanskaras; vidnyani sanskaras; yogayoga sanskaras.**

sant. See **saint; wali.**

Self-realization. See **Realization.**

semisubtle world: a stage between the **gross** and **subtle** spheres in which the disembodied soul experiences the heaven and hell states through the **astral body** (q.v.).

Shams-e-Tabriz (*d.* 1247): **Sufi Perfect Master** and Master of Jalaluddin **Rumi.**

Pron.: shamss ay tabréez. *Var.:* Shams ad-Din; Shamsi Tabriz.

shariat (S.): external conformity to religious injunctions and traditions; orthodoxy.

Pron.: sharéeyat. *Var.:* sharia. V.: **karma-kanda.**

sharir (V.): *lit.* body; the physical form or **gross body.**

Pron.: sharéer. *Var.:* sharira. S.: jism-e-kasif /jism ay kaséef/. Also V.: **sthul sharir.** See also **karan sharir; sukshma sharir.**

Shivaji (1630–1680): founder of the Maratha kingdom in India; social reformer, military leader, and champion of religious tolerance.

Pron.: shiváaji. *Var.:* Sivaji.

Shiv-Atma. See **Perfect One.**

shmashan vairagya (V.): *lit.* burial- or cremation-ground detachment; sudden but temporary detachment.

Pron.: shmasháan vairáagya. *Var.:* smashan vairagya.

Siddha (V.): one who has realized God and attained **Perfection.**

Pron.: síddha. See also **Realization.**

siddhis (V.) (*sing.* siddhi): divine or mystic powers; also occult powers.

Pron.: síddhiz. S.: tajalliyat (*sing.* tajalli) /tajalliyáat; tajálli/. See also **occult experiences/powers.**

Sita-Ram: Sita was the consort and beloved of Lord **Rama** (q.v.).

Pron.: séetaa raam.

sthan. See under **muqam-e-afsan.**

sthul bhuvan. See **gross sphere.**

sthul sharir (V.): the physical form or **gross body.**

Pron.: st'hul sharéer. *Var.:* sthula sharira. S.: jism-e-kasif /jism ay kaséef/. Also V.: **sharir.**

subtle body/form: the vital energy force (**pran**), which functions in the **subtle sphere;** the vehicle of desires and vital forces.

S.: jism-e-latif /jism ay latéef/. V.: **pran; sukshma sharir.**

subtle sphere/world: the sphere consisting of the first four **planes of consciousness** as experienced by the **subtle body** through one's subtle impressions, which are less dense than the gross impressions. The fourth plane serves as the threshold to the **mental sphere** but is neither fully subtle nor mental.

S.: alam-e-malakut /áalam ay malakóot/. V.: pran bhuvan /praan bhúvan/. See also **semisubtle world.**

Sufism (*also* Sufi, *pl.* Sufis): mysticism in which the goal is to purge the heart of everything but God, through spiritual contemplation and ecstacy, and to eventually achieve total absorption in God. Such mysticism, whose beginnings are lost in antiquity, is an expression of the way of life recurring after every advent of the **Avatar** (q.v.) by those who adhere to the very kernel of His teachings. Adherents of the esoteric teachings of **Muhammad, the Prophet,** came to be known as Sufis.

Pron.: sóofism; sóofi (–z).

sukshma sharir (V.): the **subtle body,** which is the vehicle of desires and vital forces.

Pron.: sóokshma sharéer. S.: jism-e-latif /jism ay latéef/. See also **pran.**

tajalliyat. See **siddhis.**

tariqat (S.): the way; the inner **path** of spiritual advancement.

Pron.: taréeqat. *Var.:* tarikat; tariqa. Also S.: rah-e-tariqat /raah ay taréeqat/. V.: **adhyatma-marga.**

tivra vairagya (V.): intense dispassion, detachment, or renunciation.

Pron.: téevra vairáagya.

Union: the state of being united with God, the Infinite.

S.: **Vasl.** V.: Aikya /áikya/.

unmatta (V.): one who is in the state of unsubdued God-intoxication, heedless of worldly standards and values; frantic.

Pron: óonmatta. See also **masts.**

vairagya. See **bairagi; purna**

vairagya; shmashan vairagya; tivra vairagya.

vali. See **wali.**

Vasl (S.): **Union;** the state of being united with God, the Infinite.

Pron.: vasl. V.: Aikya /áikya/.

Vedanta (*also* Vedantic, -ist, -ists): the system of Hindu philosophy (derived from and dependent upon the thoughts expressed in the Vedas) that is concerned with the ultimate Reality, the **Liberation** of the soul, and the soul's identity with the **Oversoul.**

Pron.: vedáanta; váydaz. *Var.:* Vedantism.

Videh Muktas. See **Majzoobs-e-Kamil.**

Videh Mukti (V.): a state of **Liberation**, or **Mukti** (q.v.), in which the **gross body** is retained for a time.

Pron.: vidáyh múkti. *Var.:* Videha Mukti. S.: Majzoobiyat /majzoobéeyat/.

videh samadhi (V.): the state of divine coma, where one is totally unconscious of one's body or the world.

Pron.: vidáyh samáadhi. *Var.:* videha samadhi. See also **fana-e-zahiri.**

vidnyan. See under **vidnyani sanskaras.**

vidnyani sanskaras (V.): the special type of **sanskaras** (impressions) the **Avatar** has before His unveiling, and the type of sanskaras He gives to those in His Circles.

Pron.: vidnyáani sanskáaraz. *Var.:* vijnani samskaras. (vidnyani conscious unity; oneness; the highest consciousness. *Pron.:* vidnyáan. S.: ahadiyat /ahadéeyat/.) See also **dnyan.**

vyatireka (V.): the analytic activity of the mind.

Pron.: vyatiráyka.

wali (S.): *lit.* friend; friend of God; one who is on the fifth **plane of consciousness.**

Pron.: wáli. *Var.:* vali. Also S.: abrar /abráar/; wali Allah /wáli alláah/. V.: mahapurush /maháapurùsh/; sant /sant/.

yoga (V.): yoking, union; disciplined activity or way of life.

Pron.: yóga. See also **bhakti-yoga; dnyan-yoga; karma-yoga.**

yoga-bhrashta (V.): an aspirant who has a setback or downfall on the spiritual **path.**

Pron.: yóga bhráshta.

yogayoga sanskaras (V.): the nonbinding **sanskaras** (impressions) of the **Perfect Ones** who return to normal consciousness; the impressions of the impressionless Ones.

Pron.: yogáayoga sanskáaraz.

yogi (V.) (*pl.* -s): one who practices or has attained **yoga;** an aspirant.

Pron.: yógi (-z). *Var.:* yogin. S.: rahrav /ráahrav (soft v)/. See also **karma-yogi; sadhak.**

Part II
Terms Commonly Used in Other Meher Baba Literature

Ahuramazda (Avestan): Almighty God; the supreme Being in Zoroastrianism.

Pron.: ahòoramázda. *Var.:* Ahura Mazda. Cf. **Oversoul,** Glossary Part I.

Allah (S.): Almighty God; the supreme Being in Islam.

Pron.: alláah. Cf. **Oversoul,** Glossary Part I.

Amartithi (Hindi/Mar.): *lit.* amar, deathless; tithi, day. The anniversary of the day (31 January) that Meher Baba, the deathless One, dropped His body.

Pron.: ámartit'hèe.

arti (V.) (*pl.* -s): a devotional song or prayer with a refrain or theme expressing the yearning for and the offering of oneself to the one worshipped; an act of devotion; the performance of devotional songs and prayers.

Pron.: áarti (-z). *Var.:* arati.

Avesta. See under **Zoroaster.**

daaman (Urdu): hem of a garment; as used by Meher Baba, holding on to His daaman implies holding on to Him, the **Avatar** (q.v., Glossary Part I).

Pron.: dáaman. *Var.:* daman.

dhuni (Hindi): purifying fire that symbolizes divine light.

Pron.: dhóoni.

Elahi (Ar./Pers.): the one God; related to the Hebrew *Elohim* (God).

Pron.: eláahi; elohéem.

Ezad (Avestan): the one God, the only One worthy of worship.

Pron.: éezad.

jai (*also* -ki jai) (Skt./Hindi): hail, victory, glory; -ki is a suffix meaning *to* or *belonging to.* Most frequently used in "Jai Meher Baba" and "Avatar Meher Baba-ki jai."

Pron.: jay (-kee jáy); avatáar máyhayr báabaa-kee jáy.

mandali (Skt./Mar.): a circle of intimate disciples.

Pron.: mándali.

Parabrahma (V.): supreme Spirit; God in the Beyond Beyond state (q.v. in *God Speaks*).

Pron.: pàrabráhma.

Parameshwar (V.): Almighty God.

Pron.: pàramáyshwar.

Parvardigar (S.): God as the Preserver and Sustainer.

Pron.: parvardigáar. V.: Vishnu /víshnoo/.

Prabhu (V.): the Lord (God).

Pron.: prabhóo.

prasad (V.): a precious gift from God; a small gift, often edible, given by or in the name of a **saint, Perfect Master,** or the **Avatar** (q.v., Glossary Part I).

Pron.: prasáad.

samadhi (Hindi/Mar.): tomb; tomb-shrine, e.g., the Tomb-Shrine of Meher Baba.

Pron.: samáadhi. Cf. **samadhi** (meditative trance), Glossary Part I.

Vedanta. See **Vedanta,** Glossary Part I.

Vishnu. See **Parvardigar.**

Yezdan (Avestan): Almighty God.

Pron.: yezdáan. See also **Ahuramazda.** Cf. **Oversoul,** Glossary Part I.

Zoroaster: the **Avatar** (q.v., Glossary Part I) whose teachings come to us through Zoroastrianism and the Avesta.

Pron.: zoroáaster; avésta. *Var.:* Zarathushtra.

Bibliography

Books by Meher Baba

Beams from Meher Baba on the Spiritual Panorama. Walnut Creek, CA: Sufism Reoriented, 1958.

The Everything and The Nothing. Berkeley, CA: Beguine Library, Meher Baba Information, 1971.

God Speaks. 2nd edition, New York: Dodd, Mead, 1973.

God to Man and Man to God: the Discourses of Meher Baba. Myrtle Beach, SC: Sheriar Press, 1984.

Life at Its Best. New York: Harper and Row, 1972.

Selected List of Books about Meher Baba

The Ancient One edited by Naosherwan Anzar. Englishtown, NJ: Beloved Books, 1985.

Avatar by Jean Adriel. Berkeley, CA: John F. Kennedy University Press, 1971.

Avatar of the Age: Meher Baba Manifesting by Bhau Kalchuri. North Myrtle Beach, SC: Manifestation, Inc., 1985.

Because of Love: My Life and Art with Meher Baba by Rano Gayley. Myrtle Beach, SC: Sheriar Press, 1983.

The Beloved by Naosherwan Anzar. Myrtle Beach, SC: Sheriar Press, 1974.

The Dance of Love by Margaret Craske. Myrtle Beach, SC: Sheriar Press, 1980.

Darshan Hours edited by Eruch Jessawala and Rick Chapman. Berkeley, CA: Beguine Library, Meher Baba Information, 1973.

Eighty-Two Family Letters by Manija S. Irani. Myrtle Beach, SC: Sheriar Press, 1976.

Glimpses of the God-Man, Meher Baba, Vol. I (January 1943-1948) by Bal Natu. Walnut Creek, CA: Sufism Reoriented, 1977.

Glimpses of the God-Man, Meher Baba, Vol. II (January 1949-January 1952) by Bal Natu. Bombay: Meher House Publications, 1979.

Glimpses of the God-Man, Meher Baba, Vol. III (February 1952-February 1953) by Bal Natu. Myrtle Beach, SC: Sheriar Press, 1982.

Glimpses of the God-Man, Meher Baba, Vol. IV (February-December 1953) by Bal Natu. Myrtle Beach, SC: Sheriar Press, 1985.

The God-Man by Charles B. Purdom. Myrtle Beach, SC: Sheriar Press, 1971.

Is That So? compiled by Bill LePage (stories by Eruch Jessawala). Ahmednagar, India: Meher Nazar Books, 1985.

Just to Love Him by Adi K. Irani. Myrtle Beach, SC: Sheriar Press, 1985.

Letters from the Mandali, Vol. I edited by Jim Mistry. Myrtle Beach, SC: Sheriar Press, 1981.

Letters from the Mandali, Vol. II edited by Jim Mistry. Myrtle Beach, SC: Sheriar Press, 1983.

Listen, Humanity narrated and edited by D.E. Stevens. Monaco: Companion Books, 1985.

Love Alone Prevails by Kitty Davy. Myrtle Beach, SC: Sheriar Press, 1981.

Love Personified: Photographs of Avatar Meher Baba compiled by Lawrence Reiter. North Myrtle Beach, SC: Manifestation, Inc., 1982.

A Love So Amazing by Bili Eaton. Myrtle Beach, SC: Sheriar Press, 1985.

Meher Baba Is Love compiled by Adah Shifrin. 2nd edition. Santa Monica, CA: Shifrin, 1986.

Merwan: Stories of Meher Baba for Children by Anne E. Giles. Myrtle Beach, SC: Sheriar Press, 1980.

Much Silence by Tom and Dorothy Hopkinson. New York: Dodd, Mead, 1975; 2nd revised Indian edition, Bombay: Meher House Publications, 1981.

Our Constant Companion compiled by Bal Natu. Ahmednagar, India: Meher Nazar Books, 1983.

Path of Love edited by Filis Frederick. Hermosa Beach, CA: Awakener Press, 1986.

The Perfect Master: the Early Life of Meher Baba by Charles B. Purdom. Myrtle Beach, SC: Sheriar Press, 1975.

Practical Spirituality with Meher Baba by John Grant. Milsons Point, Australia: Merwan Publications, 1987.

Ramjoo's Diaries, 1922-1929 by Ramjoo Adulla. Walnut Creek, CA: Sufism Reoriented. 1979.

Showers of Grace compiled by Bal Natu. Ahmednagar, India: Meher Nazar Books, 1984.

Sparks of the Truth from the Dissertations of Meher Baba edited by C. D. Deshmukh. Myrtle Beach, SC: Sheriar Press, 1971.

Tales from the New Life with Meher Baba narrated by Eruch, Mehera, Mani, and Meheru. Berkeley, CA: Beguine Library, Meher Baba Information, 1976.

Three Incredible Weeks with Meher Baba, September 11-September 30, 1954 by Malcolm Schloss and Charles B. Purdom. Myrtle Beach, SC: Sheriar Press, 1979.

Treasures from the Meher Baba Journals edited by Jane Haynes. Myrtle Beach, SC: Sheriar Press, 1980.

While the World Slept by Bhau Kalchuri. North Myrtle Beach, SC: Manifestation, Inc., 1984.

There are many books by and about Meher Baba. For a free booklist or further information contact: Sheriar Press, 3005 Highway 17 N. ByPass, Myrtle Beach, SC 29577, U.S.A.

This bibliography has been compiled by the Publisher.

Index

This book is addressed to those who long for God and His love, and since its themes throughout are God-realization and love of God, only the most important references to these subjects are given.

The Publisher

Centers of Information about Meher Baba

For additional information about Meher Baba as well as publications by and about Meher Baba, the following centers may be contacted:

Avatar Meher Baba Trust
King's Road
Ahmednagar (MS) 414 001
India

Meher Spiritual Center
10200 Highway 17 North
Myrtle Beach, SC 29577
U.S.A.

Avatar's Abode Trust
P.O. Box 779
Nambour, 4560 Qld.
Australia

Meher Baba Information
Box 1101
Berkeley, CA 94701
U.S.A.

Avatar Meher Baba Center of Southern California
10808 Santa Monica Boulevard
Los Angeles, CA 90025
U.S.A.

Meher Baba Association
1/228 Hammersmith Grove
London W67FH
England